C000090435

University of Wisconsin Studies in Language and Literature

by University of Wisconsin

Address:
HardPress
8345 NW 66TH ST #2561
MIAMI FL 33166-2626
USA
Email: info@hardpress.net

UC-NRLF
B 4 017 081

UNIVERSITY OF WISCONSIN STUDIES

IN LANGUAGE AND LITERATURE

NUMBER 10

THE DRAMATIC ASSOCIATIONS OF THE EASTER SEPULCHRE

BY

KARL YOUNG

PROFESSOR OF ENGLISH

MADISON

1920

UNIVERSITY OF WISCONSIN STUDIES

NUMBER 13
SEPTEMBER, 1920

LANGUAGE AND LITERATURE, NO. 10
PRICE, FIFTY CENTS

Published bi-monthly by the University of Wisconsin at Madison, Wisconsin

Entered as second class matter August 31, 1919 at the postoffice at Madison, Wisconsin, under the Act of August 24, 1912. Accepted for mailing at special rate of postage provided for in section 1103, Act of October 3, 1917. Authorized September 17, 1918.

No. 1. British criticisms of American writings, 1783–1815, by William B. Cairns. 98p. Fifty cents.

No. 2. Studies by members of the department of English. 394p. One dollar.

No. 3. Classical studies in honor of Charles Forster Smith. 190p. One dollar.

No. 4. Ordo Rachelis, by Karl Young. 66p. Fifty cents.

No. 5 The position of the *Roode en Witte Roos* in the saga of King Richard III, by Oscar James Campbell. 170p. Fifty cents.

No. 6. Goethe's lyric poems in English translation prior to 1860, by Lucretia Van Tuyl Simmons. 202p. Fifty cents.

No. 7. Lucilius and Horace—a study in the classical theory of imitation, by George Converse Fiske. 524p. Two dollars and fifty cents.

No. 8. The first quarto edition of Shakespeare's *Hamlet*, by Frank G. Hubbard. 120p. Fifty cents.

No. 9. Traces of matriarchy in Germanic hero-lore, by Albert William Aron. 76p. Fifty cents.

No. 10. The dramatic associations of the Easter sepulchre, by Karl Young. 130p. Fifty cents.

UNIVERSITY OF WISCONSIN STUDIES

IN LANGUAGE AND LITERATURE

NUMBER 10

THE DRAMATIC ASSOCIATIONS OF THE EASTER SEPULCHRE

BY

KARL YOUNG
PROFESSOR OF ENGLISH

MADISON
1920

CONTENTS

THE DRAMATIC ASSOCIATIONS OF THE EASTER SEPULCHRE

To the student of the drama of the mediaeval church nothing is more familiar than the fact that the liturgical structure, or *locus*, known as the Easter *sepulchrum* was the center of three separate dramatic observances: the *Depositio*, the *Elevatio*, and the *Visitatio Sepulchri*.[1] The *Depositio* took place on Good Friday, at some point in the liturgy after the Adoration of the Cross; the *Elevatio* occurred on Easter morning, usually before Matins; and the normal position of the *Visitatio Sepulchri* was at the end of Easter Matins, immediately before the *Te Deum*. The nature of these dramatic offices may be conveniently shown in the following versions of the fourteenth century from the monastery of St. Blaise, in the Black Forest:[2]

<DEPOSITIO HOSTIÆ>[3]

COMMUNICATIS[4] OMNIBUS SONENTUR TABULÆ OMNES. POST HÆC FIET ORATIO ANTE VESPERAM. INTERIM SACERDOS SUMAT VIATICUM, EATQUE AD SEPULCHRUM CUM INCENSO & CANDELIS CANTANDO *responsorium:*

> Agnus Dei Christus <immolatus est pro salute mundi. Nam de parentis protoplasti fraude factor condolens, quando pomi noxialis morte morsu corruit; ipse lignum tunc notavit, damna ligni est solveret. VERSUS: Christus factus est pro nobis obediens usque ad mortem, mortem autem crucis. Ipse lignum.[5]

---

[1] For a survey of these observances see E. K. Chambers, *The Mediaeval Stage*, Vol. II, Oxford, 1903, pp. 11–36.

[2] M. Gerbert, *Monumenta Veteris Liturgiae Alemannicae*, St. Blasien, 1777–1779, Part II, pp. 234–235, 236. The *Depositio* is incompletely reprinted in *Decreta Authentica Congregationis Sacrorum Rituum*, Vol. IV, Rome, 1900, 432. The *Visitatio* is reprinted from Gerbert by C. Lange, *Die lateinischen Osterfeiern*, Munich, 1887, pp. 30–31. For a bibliography of other reprints of this version of the *Visitatio* see Lange, p. 6.

[3] Gerbert, *Monumenta*, Part II, p. 234.

[4] Communion of the *Missa Præsanctificatorum* of Good Friday. See below, pp. 19–20.

[5] Responsory from Matins of Holy Saturday. See Migne, *Patrologia Latina*, Vol. LXXVIII, col. 768.

<RESPONSORIUM:>

Ecce quomodo moritur<justus, et nemo percipit corde; et viri justi tolluntur, et nemo considerat; a facie iniquitatis oblatus est justus, et erit in pace memoria ejus. VERSUS: In pace factus est locus ejus, et in Sion habitatio ejus. Et erit.>,[6]

CUM VERSIBUS & REPETITIONIBUS; PONENSQUE ILLUD IN SEPULCHRUM INCENSET, & CLAUDENS ILLUS CANTET *Responsorium:*

Sepulto Domino,<signatum est monumentum; volventes lapidem ad ostium monumenti, ponentes milites qui custodirent illud. VERSUS: Ne forte veniant discipuli ejus et furentur eum, et dicant plebi: Surrexit a mortuis. Ponentes.>,[7]

CUM VERSU & REPETITIONE; PONATURQUE CEREUS ARDENS ANTE SEPULCHRUM. DEINDE LEGATUR VESPERA.

<ELEVATIO HOSTIÆ>[8]

NOCTE SACRATISSIMA RESURRECTIONIS DOMINI CUM TEMPUS FUERIT PULSANDI MATUTINUM, SECRETARIUS SURGAT, SUMENS LATERNAM CUM LUMINE DOMNUM ABBATEM EXCITABIT, ATQUE PRIOREM, DEINDE ALIOS DE FRATRIBUS AD COMPULSANDAS CAMPANAS, QUI SIBI PLACUERINT. SURGENS AUTEM DOMNUS ABBAS AD ECCLESIAM EAT, & INDUIT SE ALBA, STOLA, ET CAPPA, PRIOR AUTEM ALBA ET CAETERI FRATRES. SUMENTESQUE DUO THURIBULA CUM INCENSO, PRAECEDENTIBUS CANDELABRIS, EANT AD SEPULCHRUM CUM *Responsorio:*

Maria Magdalena<et altera Maria ibant diluculo ad monumentum. Jesum quem quæritis non est hic; surrexit sicut locutus est, præcedet vos in Galilæam, ibi eum videbitis, alleluia, alleluia. VERSUS: Cito euntes dicite discipulis ejus et Petro quia surrexit Dominus. Præcedet.>,[9]

CUM VERSU. & EANT AD SEPULCHRUM, AC ILLUD INCENSENT EXTERIUS; DEINDE LEVATO TEGIMENTO ITERUM INCENSENT INTERIUS. POSTEA SUMENS CORPUS DOMINI SUPER ALTARE PONIT CANTANS *Responsorium:*

Surrexit pastor bonus<qui animam suam posuit pro ovibus suis, et pro suo grege mori dignatus est, alleluia, alleluia, alleluia. VERSUS: Surrexit Dominus de sepulcro, qui pro nobis pependit in ligno. Et pro suo.>,[10]

CUM VERSU. INTERIM LEVET CORPUS DOMINICUM, INCENSISQUE CANDELIS SONETUR CLASSIS. POST TERNAS ORATIONES INCIPIAT DOMNUS ABBAS *XV* GRADUS. OMNES QUI IN HAC NOCTE ALIQUID CANTARE VEL LEGERE VOLUNT, DEBENT ESSE REVESTITI ALBIS PRAETER PUERUM QUI DICIT VERSUM. INFRA *XV* GRADUS SONENTUR DUO MAXIMA SIGNA IN ANGULARI; DEINDE DUO MAIORA SIGNA IN CHORO. POSTEA FIAT COMPULSATIO AB OMNIBUS CAMPANIS. TUNC

---

[6] Responsory from Matins of Holy Saturday. See Migne, *Pat. Lat.*, LXXVIII, 768.

[7] See *ibid*.

[8] Gerbert, *Monumenta*, Part II, p. 236.

[9] First responsory of Matins of Easter Monday. See Migne, *Pat. Lat.*, LXXVIII, 771.

[10] The third responsory of Matins of Thursday after Easter. See Migne, *Pat. Lat.*, LXXVIII, 773.

VENIENS DOMNUS ABBAS ANTE ALTARE INDUTUS CAPPA INCIPIAT: Domine, labia mea aperies.[11]

<VISITATIO SEPULCHRI>[12]

TERTIUM VERO RESPONSORIUM CANTENT TRES CANTORES IN CAPPIS, QUORUM DUO INCENSENT ALTARE, UT SUPRA SCRIPTUM EST. *Responsorium:* Dum transissent, QUOD POST Gloria patri REINCIPIENDUM EST.

INTERIM DUO SACERDOTES SE CAPPIS INDUUNT SUMMENTES DUO THURIBULA, & HUMERARIA IN CAPITA PONENT, INTRANTES CHORUM, PAULATIM EUNTES VERSUS SEPULCHRUM, VOCE MEDIOCRI CANTANTES:

Quis revolvet nobis lapidem?

QUOS DIACONUS QUI DEBET ESSE RETRO SEPULCHRUM INTERROGET PSALLENDO:

Quem quaeritis?

DEINDE ILLI:

Iesum nazarenum.

QUIBUS DIACONUS RESPONDET:

Non est hic.

MOX INCENSENT SEPULCHRUM, & DICENTE DIACONO: Ite, nuntiate, VERTENT SE AD CHORUM REMANENTES SUPER GRADUM, & CANTENT:

Surrexit Dominus de sepulchro,

USQUE IN FINEM. FINITA ANTIPHONA, DOMNUS ABBAS INCIPIAT:

Te Deum laudamus,

IN MEDIO ANTE ALTARE, MOXQUE CAMPANAE SONENTUR IN ANGULARIBUS. CUM CANTATUR: Per singulos dies, SONENTUR OMNIA SIGNA IN CHORO.

It will be observed that the *mise en scène* for all three of these dramatic offices is some kind of *sepulchrum*. This particular version of the *Depositio* occurs between Mass and Vespers on Good Friday, and consists essentially in the burial in the *sepulchrum* of the Host (*Viaticum*, *Corpus Domini*), in commemoration of the burial of Christ. The essence of the *Elevatio* is the raising of the Host from the *sepulchrum*, before Matins on Easter morning, in commemoration of the Resurrection. The *Visitatio Sepulchri*, at the end of Easter Matins, has as its central representation the visit of two Maries[13] to the empty *sepulchrum*. A notable fact concerning all three observances is that they are extra-liturgical: that is to say, they are not

---

[11] This versicle opens Matins.

[12] Gerbert, *Monumenta*, Part II, p. 236.

[13] It will be noted that, whereas impersonation is entirely absent from the *Depositio* and *Elevatio* before us, the *Visitatio* contains at least hints of *mimesis* in the rubric *duo Sacerdotes . . . summentes duo thuribula & humeraria in in capita ponent*. See below, pp. 128–129.

authorized and essential parts of the traditional liturgy of the Roman church, but pious *additions*.

The third of these dramatic offices, the *Visitatio Sepulchri*, has been assiduously studied in isolation, and a large number of versions have been published.[14] It has been discerned, indeed, that the *Visitatio* had a double development within the liturgy of Easter,—at the Introit of Mass and at the end of Matins,—and this phenomenon has been sufficiently expounded.[15] Of the *Depositio* and *Elevatio*, however, no thorough study has ever been made. Only a relatively small number of texts of these ceremonials are available in print, and such versions as are already published have never been brought together for critical examination.[16] In view of the obvious interrelations of the three ceremonials, this neglect is unfortunate; for it is clear that no consideration of the *Visitatio* can

---

[14] For bibliography see *Publications of the Modern Language Association*, Vol. XXIX (1914), p. 3.

[15] See *id.*, pp. 1–49.

[16] For actual texts of the *Depositio* and *Elevatio* previously published see especially E. Martène, *Tractatus de Antiqua Ecclesiæ Disciplina*, Lyons, 1706, pp. 367, 477–479, 503–505; K. Young, *The Harrowing of Hell in Liturgical Drama*, in *Transactions of the Wisconsin Academy of Sciences, Arts, and Letters*, Vol. XVI, Part II (1909), pp. 897–934. Isolated printed texts are referred to below, *passim*. In regard to the bearing of the *Depositio* and *Elevatio* upon *modern* liturgical usage the most important study is found in *Decreta Authentica Congregationis Sacrorum Rituum*, Vol. IV, Rome, 1900, pp. 419–441 (referred to below as *Decreta Authentica*). As a treatise upon *mediaeval* observances this study is far from complete. For discussions of some aspects of the *Depositio* and *Elevatio* see A. Heales, in *Archæologia*, Vol. XLII (1869), pp. 264–277; H. P. Feasey, in *Ecclesiastical Review*, Vol. XXXII (1905), pp. 491–499 *pass.*; H. J. Feasey, *Ancient English Holy Week Ceremonial*, London, 1897, pp. 132–137, 169–177; J. B. Thiers, *Traité de l'Exposition du S. Sacrement de l'Autel*, Vol. II, Avignon, 1777, pp. 193–202; C. Davidson, *Studies in the English Mystery Plays*, New Haven, 1892, pp. 16–20; [A. De Santi], in *La Civiltà Cattolica*, 1910, Vol. I, pp. 709-711; A. De Santi, *Il Mattino di Pasqua nella Storia Liturgica*, Rome, 1917, pp. 6–20; H. Thurston, *Lent and Holy Week*, London, 1904, pp. 299–468; Chambers, II, 16–26; V. Thalhofer, *Handbuch der katholischen Liturgik*, Vol. I, Freiburg, 1912, pp. 636–637; *De Processionibus Ecclesiasticis Liber*, Paris, 1641, pp. 171–197; H. Alt, *Theater und Kirche*, Berlin, 1846, pp. 348–349; E. G. C. F. Atchley, *A History of the Use of Incense in Divine Worship* (*Alcuin Club Collections*, No. XIII), London, 1909, pp. 296–300; J. D. Chambers, *Divine Worship in England in the Thirteenth and Fourteenth Centuries*, London, 1877, Appendix, pp. xxvi–xl.

be definitive without reference to the content and associations of the *Depositio* and *Elevatio*. I therefore venture to undertake a special study of these two offices.[17] For my texts I draw chiefly upon unpublished manuscripts and incunabula; but I have been glad to avail myself also of such versions as are found in modern print.[18]

I

Since the *Depositio* and *Elevatio* are extra-liturgical developments within the authorized liturgy of Holy Week and Easter morning, we may appropriately examine their liturgical associations for suggestions concerning their origins.[1]

---

[17] It should be remembered that in the present study I do not undertake an orderly and detailed consideration of the *sepulchrum* itself. I concern myself, not with this material structure, but with the dramatic ceremonials surrounding it. My observations concerning the *sepulchrum* itself are merely incidental. Bibliography upon this special subject is given by the present writer in *Transactions of the Wisconsin Academy of Sciences, Arts, and Letters*, XVI, Part II, pp. 895–896, and by J. K. Bonnell, in *Publications of the Modern Language Association*, Vol. XXXI (1916), pp. 664–712.

[18] It is inevitable that some published versions escape me; and I do not, of course, pretend to have exhausted the possibilities of the thousands of liturgical manuscripts in European libraries. I have not been able to include the versions published by F. Arens, *Der Liber Ordinarius der Essener Stiftskirche*, Paderborn, 1908, as reported by A. De Santi in *La Civiltà Cattolica*, 1910, Vol. I, pp. 709–711. Unpublished examples of the *Depositio* and *Elevatio* in manuscripts are referred to by N. C. Brooks in *Journal of English and Germanic Philology*, Vol. VIII (1909), 469, 481, and in *Zeitschrift für deutsches Altertum*, LV (1914), pp. 55, 56, 58. I take this occasion for acknowledging the invaluable assistance given me by my friend Dom G. M. Beyssac, of Quarr Abbey, Isle of Wight.

[1] In my discussion of origins I venture to ignore certain vague or obviously inadequate suggestions made by other writers. In speaking of the "sepulchre rite" as a whole, H. J. Feasey (*Ancient English Holy Week Ceremonial*, p. 129) speaks of "some [persons] inclining to the suggestion that its source lay in the old Mystery Plays which were of old performed in the churches." Cf. H. P. Feasey, in *Ecclesiastical Review*, XXXII, 337. We are, of course, seeking the source *behind* "the old Mystery Plays." Feasey, again, speaks (*Ancient English Holy Week Ceremonial*, p. 130) of others who "think the ceremony arose as occasion or devotion required, as did the Christmas Crib and other like devotions." This view simply evades the investigation of what "occasion or devotion required." The rise of the "devotions" surrounding the Christmas Crib is

Such suggestions appear, for example, in connection with the reservation of a Host from the Mass of Holy Thursday for the mass of the Presanctified (*Missa Præsanctificatorum*) on Good Friday.[2] This reservation was necessary through the fact that from about the fifth century to the present time the Roman rite has not permitted the consecration of the sacred elements on Good Friday itself.[3] The result of this prohibition is the supplying of the mass of Good Friday with a Host consecrated upon the previous day,—a *presanctified* Host. Hence the term *Missa Præsanctificatorum*. The absence of the consecration of the Host from the mass of Friday automatically eliminates a large part of the usual *Ordo Missae*, including such central elements as the consecratory prayer of the Canon and the words of the Institution. This reduced form of Mass is, in fact, primarily a mere communion service, for which the Host is reserved from the day before.[4]

Our immediate interest in the *Missa Præsanctificatorum*, however, lies not so much in the liturgical content itself as in the implications of the reserving of the Host from Thursday to Friday. The laying away of the *Corpus Domini* from one day to another naturally surrounded itself with a special ceremonial and was inevitably interpreted by a special symbolism.

---

investigated by the present writer in *Transactions of the Wisconsin Academy of Sciences, Arts, and Letters*, Vol. XVII, Part I (1912), pp. 299–395. Feasey makes also the following suggestion (*Ecclesiastical Review*, XXXII, 337–338): "Others again with much more show of reason think the necessity of providing a suitable place and receptacle for the Sacred Host, which the rubric directed to be reserved from Maunday Thursday till Holy Saturday [sic], gave rise to the ceremony." I infer that the "rubric" referred to is that (see below, pp. 40, 45, 114) requiring the consecration on Holy Thursday of a *third* Host to be deposited in the *sepulchrum* on *Friday* and to be left until *Sunday* morning. But the question before us is, What is the origin of this practice of reserving a third Host and of laying it in a *sepulchrum* from Good Friday until Easter?

[2] This reservation is considered at length by Raible, *Ueber Ursprung, Alter und Entwickelung der Missa Præsanctificatorum*, in *Der Katholik* (Mainz), Dritte Folge, XXIII (1901), pp. 143–156, 250–266, 363–374.

[3] See Raible, pp. 152, 250, 261, 266. The reasons for this prohibition do not concern us here. See Raible, p. 144; Mabillon, *Museum Italicum*, Vol. II, Paris, 1724, pp. lxxv–lxxvi; Belethus, *Rationale Divinorum Officiorum*, cap. xcvii, in Migne, *Pat. Lat.*, CCII, 99–100.

[4] The liturgical content of the *Missa Præsanctificatorum* is more definitely outlined below, pp. 19–20.

For an understanding of this ceremonial we can scarcely do better than to examine the prescriptions of the *Ordines Romani.* Thus *Ordo I,* in passages that probably represent the traditions of the sixth century,[5] speaks of the Thursday reservation in the laconic words *et servat de sancta usque in crastinum,*[6] and of the bringing forth of the presanctified Host during the Mass of Friday, as follows:[7]

Presbyteri vero duo priores . . . intrant secretarium, vel ubi positum fuerat Corpus Domini quod pridie remansit, ponentes eum in patena; & subdiaconus teneat ante ipsos calicem cum vino non consecrato, & alter subdiaconus patenam cum Corpore Domini; quibus tenentibus accipit unus presbyter patenam et alter calicem, & deferunt super altare nudatum.

However uncommunicative these rubrics may seem,[8] they establish the fact that the reserved Host was not left upon the altar upon which it was consecrated on Thursday,[9] but was kept over night in a special place,—for example, a *secretarium.* Had we no other information we should safely infer that the surroundings of the Host in this special *locus* must have been reverential, and that the carrying of the *Corpus Christi* to and from this place must have assumed a processional character. As a matter of fact, however, information of this sort is at hand. In the tenth Roman *Ordo,* for example, the ceremonial of the reservation in connection with the papal mass at the Church of St. John Lateran is described as follows:[10]

Postquam autem communicavit,[11] ponit calicem super altare, & patenam juxta eum cum Corpore Domini reservato, quia sexta feria de ipso sacrificio resumit; & cooperitur utrumque sindone munda. . . . Reserventur tamen oblatæ integræ de Corpore Domini in die Parasceve; sanguis vero Domini penitus assumatur. . . . Sed antequam Pontifex revertatur ad altare ad

---

[5] See Raible, pp. 253–259; Thalhofer, I, 78.

[6] Mabillon, II, 21.

[7] Mabillon, II, 23.

[8] Similar brief rubrics from the *ordines* of St. Amand and Einsiedeln may be seen in L. Duchesne, *Christian Worship,* London, 1904, pp. 467, 482, 483.

[9] Such a removal was necessitated by the washing of the altar on Thursday evening. See J. Corblet, *Histoire dogmatique, liturgique et archéologique du Sacrement de l'Eucharistie,* Vol. I, Paris, 1886, p. 538.

[10] Mabillon, II, 100–101. The date of the formulation of *Ordo Romanus X* is uncertain. The ceremonials that it presents probably date back at least to the eleventh or twelfth century. See Thalhofer, I, 80.

[11] This refers to the Communion of the Mass of Holy Thursday.

complendam Missam, junior presbyterorum cardinalium portet Corpus Domini positum in pyxide ad locum præparatum, praecedentibus cum cruce & luminaribus, & papilione desuper.

This rubric provides for the processional transfer of the Host to a special place of reservation, the procession being provided with a cross, lights, and a canopy.

The recovery of the reserved Host for the *Missa Præsanctificatorum* on Good Friday is provided for in the same *ordo* as follows:[12]

Tunc junior presbyterorum cardinalium ferat adornatum capsidem cum Dominico Corpore hesterna die reservato; & sic subdiaconus cum papali cruce processionem præcedente, omnes discalceati sine cantu psallendo ad ecclesiam Sanctæ Crucis, quæ est Jerusalem, ubi statio fieri debet, ordinate tamen, procedant, quando dominus Papa est Laterani. Cum autem illuc pervenerint, ingrediuntur ecclesiam sine cantu, & prostrati in medio ecclesiæ diutius orent. Presbyter, qui portat Corpus Christi, in secretario ponat illud, dum dominus Papa præparat se.

This passage describes the papal procession conducting the reserved Host from St. John Lateran to Santa Croce in Gerusalemme, the papal station for the *Missa Præsanctificatorum*. The clergy are bare-footed, they proceed without chant, and at their destination prostrate themselves in prayer.

With the ceremonial of papal Rome we may profitably compare the use of France as prescribed in the eleventh century for Rouen by the archbishop, Jean d'Avranches. The reservation on Holy Thursday is arranged as follows:[13]

Ipsa die plures hostiæ consecrentur, quibus clerus et populus communicetur; et medietas hostiarum absque vino in crastino reservetur, unde iterum communicentur. Ipsæ vero hostiæ a sacerdote et ministris altaris indutis, cum processione, scilicet cum cereis et incenso, super quoddam altare honorifice deportentur, ubi cum nitidissimis linteaminibus optime recondantur. Ibi semper lumen usque ad ultimæ candelæ extinctionem in Matutinis ardeat.

It will be observed that in this case the procession sequesters the reserved Host upon a special altar, and that a light is kept burning before it until the next morning.

---

[12] Mabillon, II, 102.

[13] Jean d'Avranches, *Liber de Officiis Ecclesiasticis*, in Migne, *Pat. Lat.*, CXLVII, 50.

The bringing forth of the reserved Host for the *Missa Præsanctificatorum* is briefly ordered by Jean d'Avranches as follows:[14]

Post ministri crucis casulis induti afferant ad altare, cum vino non consecrato, reservatum Corpus Domini, ubi a sacerdote incensetur.

Only one other liturgical rubric need be cited here: for the papal reservation of Holy Thursday as ordered in the fifteenth Roman *Ordo*, of the fourteenth century:[15]

Postquam dominus Papa intrat ad sacrificandum, conficit duas hostias, unam pro se, & aliam pro die Veneris. . . . Percepto corpore & sanguine Domini nostri Jesu Christi cum calice & sine calamo, antequam abluat manus, ipsum calicem cum Corpore Domini nostri reservato, non illum calicem in quo celebravit, sed solum magnum de auro, sibi præsentet coopertum cum magna reverentia sacrista papalis cum sindone, cum lustris aureis. E sinistro brachio pendet unum caput, & in dextra manu portat calicem coopertum alio capite, & reverenter ponit prædictum calicem prope Papam circa medium altaris cum alia tobalea de sirico, cum qua cooperitur calix, in quo est Corpus Christi. Et nota, quod antequam abluat digitos dominus Papa, Corpus Christi cum reverentia magna infra prædictum calicem ponit, & super calicem corporalia illa; pars minor corporalium, & super corporale patenam, & super patenam caput illius tobaleæ de sindone. Statim quo facto, abluit digitos infra calicem cum quo celebravit, & bibit illud; & antequam abluat manus in magnis bacilibus Papae, ipse Papa vel episcopus cardinalis qui servit sibi in Missa, prædictum calicem cum Corpore Christi sic coopertum, & super humerum sinistrum pendet aliud caput illius tobaleæ, & tenens cum ambabus manibus calicem per medium portat ad armariolum, in quo conservatur usque in crastinum, antecedentibus luminaribus, cruce, & incenso processionaliter cum devotione. Quo reposito, genuflexus thurificat Corpus Christi; quo facto, revertitur ad altare; & sic lavat manus ut moris est.

For our present purpose the significance of this ceremonial lies not in the details of the procession but in the fact that the reserved Host is carried and kept in a chalice,[16] and that the chalice containing the Host is deposited in some sort of chest or tabernacle.

With these several examples of the authorized ceremonial before us, we may briefly observe several resemblances between the liturgical reservation from Holy Thursday to Good Friday

[14] Migne, *Pat. Lat.*, CXLVII, 52.

[15] Mabillon, II, 482–483.

[16] Compare the modern practice, expounded in *Decreta Authentica*, IV, 420–421.

and the extra-liturgical "burial,"—*Depositio*—*Elevatio*,—from Good Friday until Easter:

1) The chest, or tabernacle, in which the reserved Host is placed[17] has an exact parallel in the *sepulchrum* of the *Depositio* and *Elevatio*.

2) The placing of the reserved Host upon a special altar[18] has a parallel in several versions of the *Depositio* and *Elevatio* in which the *sepulchrum* is the altar itself,[19] or is closely attached to an altar.[20]

3) The light kept burning before the altar of the reservation[21] calls to mind the lights furnished for the *sepulchrum*.[22]

4) The depositing of the reserved Host in a chalice[23] is clearly a possible antecedent for the use of the chalice in numerous versions of the dramatic observances.[24]

Although the extant documents do not allow us to demonstrate that each of these uses connected with the reservation of Holy Thursday was established before the date of the earliest versions of the *Depositio* and *Elevatio*, in the tenth century,[25] the probability is that in these matters the extra-liturgical observances are antedated by the authorized ceremonial. In any case, this fundamental observation is sound: Whatever the ceremonial details of the reservation may have been in any particular locality or at any particular time, the traditional depositing of the reserved Host in a place of repose furnishes an ancient and conspicuous model for the invention of a *Depositio* and an *Elevatio;* and the special ceremonials of the reservation at subsequent periods may well have influenced the variety to be observed in the *Depositio* and *Elevatio* during the course of their long development.[26]

---

[17] See *Ordo Romanus XV*, cited above, p. 13.

[18] See passage from Jean d'Avranches, cited above, p. 12.

[19] See below, p. 74.

[20] See below, pp. 34, 35, 44, 55.

[21] See citation from Jean d'Avranches, above, p. 12.

[22] For example, see below, pp. 102, 119.

[23] See the citation from *Ordo Romanus XV*, above, p. 13.

[24] See below, pp. 97, 102, 104, 106.

[25] The evidence for this date is cited below, p. 73.

[26] Concerning the date of the more elaborate ceremonials of the Thursday reservation Father Herbert Thurston speaks as follows (*Lent and Holy Week*, p. 296): "The practice of bringing the second Host in state to the place prepared

But the aptness of the model can be still more soundly established through an appeal to another body of evidence: the traditional symbolism surrounding the reservation of the Host. It will be observed that none of the *ordines* cited above specifically suggests that the place in which the reserved Host is deposited is a *sepulchrum*, or that the act of reservation is a "burial." In view of the meaning of the day, this silence is to be expected, for obviously the idea of Christ's burial and the name *sepulchrum* are inappropriate to Holy Thursday, since this day commemorates not the death or burial of Christ, but rather the Last Supper and the Institution of the Eucharist. There are, however, ample evidences that the place of the Thursday reservation did come to be regarded as a *sepulchrum*, and the sources of this conception are not far to seek.

It appears that at all periods of liturgical history the receptacle for reserving the Eucharist,—whether for the sick or for other purposes,—was symbolized as a tomb. That is to say, the vessel or tabernacle enclosing the *Corpus Domini* was, not unnaturally, regarded as a *sepulchrum*. Thus in early times the *capsa* for containing the Host was often designed in the form of a "tower," the actual tomb of Christ in Jerusalem being conceived in this form. Hence in early Christian art the tabernacle took the name *turris*.[27] In a commentary upon the Gallican Mass, assigned to the sixth century, we read as follows:

> Corpus vero Domini ideo defertur in turribus, *quia monumentum Domini in similitudinem turris fuit scissum in petra*, et intus lectum ubi pausavit Corpus Dominicum, unde surrexit Rex gloriae in triumphum.[28]

If, then, the receptacle for the reserved *Corpus Domini* (*Sacramentum consecratum*) was, in its general use, interpreted as *sepulchrum*, there is abundant justification for the presence

for it, although alluded to as early as the time of Lanfranc, seems only to have become generally established towards the end of the fifteenth century." After the latter part of the thirteenth century the ceremonial both of the Thursday reservation and of the *Depositio* and *Elevatio* were probably influenced by the procession of Corpus Christi day. Upon this point see Thurston, p. 296–297.

[27] See Raible, p. 262; *Decreta Authentica*, IV, 419; Y. Hirn, *The Sacred Shrine*, London, 1912, pp. 159–161. In regard to tabernacles in general, see Corblet, I, 550-563.

[28] Quoted in *Decreta Authentica*, IV, 419, from Martène, *Thesaurus Novus Anecdotorum*, Vol. V, col. 94. Cf. Raible, p. 262.

of this conception in connection with the reservation of Holy Thursday.

But a further basis for this symbolizing is found in certain specific details in the ceremonial of Holy Thursday. We have already noticed that the reserved Host was sometimes placed in a closed chalice,[29] and also that it was sometimes deposited at a special altar.[30] Once more, then, we encounter the idea of *sepulchrum*, for both the chalice[31] and the altar[32] are abundantly symbolized as receptacles for burial.[33]

There is, then, ample reason for citing the reservation of the Host for the *Missa Præsanctificatorum* as being among the formative antecedents of the *Depositio* and *Elevatio;* and in our

---

[29] See *Ordo Romanus XV*, cited above, p. 13.

[30] See Jean d'Avranches, cited above, p. 12.

[31] See Corblet, II, 241, 295; *Decreta Authentica*, IV, 419–420. The symbolizing of the chalice as *sepulchrum* can be found as early as the ninth century (see *Decreta Authentica*, IV, 420); but how early the chalice was used for containing the Host reserved on Holy Thursday, the liturgiologist of the *Decreta* does not say. On the general subject see also Moroni, *Dizionario di Erudizione storico-ecclesiastica*, Vol. LXIV, p. 87.

[32] See Hirn, pp. 16–27; J. K. Bonnell, in *Publications of the Modern Language Association*, XXXI, pp. 664–712; K. Young, in *Publications of the Modern Language Association*, XXIX, pp. 42–46. Hirn makes clear that this symbolizing of the altar as *sepulchrum* dates from the earliest Christian centuries. See also *De Processionibus Ecclesiasticis Liber*, Paris, 1641, pp. 181–191.

[33] I wish to keep from the center of our present discussion the obscurities that often arise in connection with the modern practice of revering the place of the Thursday reservation as a "sepulchrum." This practice may have arisen in either of two ways: (1) through the persistent mediaeval symbolizing of the place of repose as a sepulchre; or (2) through later confusion with the burial of the Host in the *Depositio* of Good Friday. Probably both influences are present in the modern practice. In any case the modern veneration of the "sepulchre" on Holy Thursday should be sharply distinguished from the *Depositio* and *Elevatio* of our present study. Although this distinction is adequately maintained by excellent authorities (*Decreta Authentica*, IV, 419–421; Thurston, pp. 299–300; J. T. Micklethwaite, *The Ornaments of the Rubric* [*Alcuin Club Tracts*, No. I], London, 1897, pp. 52–53; A. W. Pugin, *Glossary of Ecclesiastical Ornament and Costume*, London, 1868, pp. 206–208), it is unknown to some who have discussed the church drama (See Heales, in *Archæologia*, XLII, 265–266, 268–269; Moroni, *Dizionario di Erudizione storico-ecclesiastica*, LXIV, 87–89; F. G. Lee, *Glossary of Liturgical and Ecclesiastical Terms*, London, 1877, p. 118; J. C. Cox and A. Harvey, *English Church Furniture*, London, 1907, p. 74).

examination of the various versions of these offices we shall encounter continued reminders of this influence.[34]

This is, perhaps, an appropriate point at which to introduce a bit of external evidence showing that the Host was actually employed for the *Depositio* and *Elevatio* as early as the tenth century. In a life of St. Udalricus, bishop of Augsburg (†973), ✓ which appears to have been written within some twenty years from the date of his death, we read the following concerning the liturgical observances of this ecclesiastic on Good Friday and Easter:[35]

Die autem Parasceve . . . mane diluculo psalterium explere festinavit, et sacro Dei mysterio perpetrato, *populoque sacro Christi corpore saginato, et consuetudinario more, quod remanserat, sepulto,* interum inter ecclesias ambulando, psalterium explevit decantando. . . . Desideratissimo atque sanctissimo Paschali die adveniente, *post primam intravit ecclesiam Sancti Ambrosii, ubi die Parasceve Corpus Christi superposito lapide collocavit,* ibique cum paucis clericis Missam de sancta Trinitate explevit. Expleta autem Missa . . . . *secum portato Christi Corpore* et Evangelio et cereis et incenso et cum congrua salutatione versuum a pueris decantata . . . perrexit ad ecclesiam sancti Ioannis Baptistae.

From this passage we learn that, according to a custom established at Augsburg before the year 973, after Communion at the close of the *Missa Præsanctificatorum* in the cathedral on Good Friday, the remains of the Sacrament were deposited in the church of St. Ambrosius in some sort of *sepulchrum* closed by a stone (*lapis*).[36] Apparently the *Corpus Domini* thus buried remained in the *sepulchrum* until Easter morning, and it is reasonable to infer that at that time occurred some sort of

---

[34] I may anticipate one such reminder. The *ordinaria* of several churches (see below, for example, pp. 40, 45, 114) explicitly provide that in the Mass of Holy Thursday *three* Hosts shall be consecrated: one for the Mass of the day, one for the *Missa Præsanctificatorum* of Good Friday, and one for "burial" in the *sepulchrum* of the *Depositio* and *Elevatio*. Nothing could more emphatically suggest the bond between the reservation of Thursday and the *Depositio* than the fact that the objects to be venerated in the two ceremonials are consecrated, side by side, in a single ritual.

[35] *Acta Sanctorum*, July, Vol. II, Paris and Rome, 1867, p. 103. Concerning matters of authorship and date see *id.*, p. 95. See also Martène, p. 367; *Decreta Authentica*, IV, 430.

[36] For the use of the *lapis* in the extant versions of the *Depositio* and *Elevatio* see, for example, below, pp. 93, 94.

Elevatio.[37] Concerning the church of Ambrosius we have no information, but we may assume that it was near the Cathedral, and that for the *Depositio* of Good Friday the *Corpus Domini* was carried thither in procession.[38]

If we are correct in our inference that the reservation of Holy Thursday influenced the formation and development of such a *Depositio* and *Elevatio* as are referred to by Udalricus, we may summarize this phenomenon briefly as follows. The laying away of a Host in a *sepulchrum* from Good Friday until Easter was in some sort an extra-liturgical imitation, or reduplication, of the liturgical reservation of the Host from Holy Thursday to Good Friday. Whereas the idea of *sepulchrum* and "burial," though inherent in the instruments used in the reservation of Holy Thursday, was essentially inappropriate to that day, this idea finds complete appropriateness and realization in the laying down and raising of the Host in the extra-liturgical *Depositio* and *Elevatio* of Good Friday and Easter.

II

For the sake of lucidity, I have hitherto ignored the circumstance that the Host was not the only object deposited in the extra-liturgical *sepulchrum*. In citing the Thursday–Friday reservation as an influence toward the formation of the *Depositio* and *Elevatio* I have offered no explanation of the fact that in a large proportion of the extant versions of these dramatic offices the burial included both a Host and a Cross,[1] and that a good many texts prescribe the burial of the Cross alone.[2] In this use of the Cross we readily discern a second fundamental influence upon the *Depositio* and *Elevatio*: namely, that of the liturgical *Adoratio Crucis* of Good Friday.[3]

The *Adoratio Crucis* is certainly one of the oldest of the liturgical observances of Holy Week. The following passage

---

[37] Possibly the *Elevatio* is implied in the words *secum portato Christi Corpore*.
[38] See *Acta Sanctorum*, *loc. cit.*, p. 104.
[1] See below, pp. 92–127.
[2] See below, pp. 72–91.
[3] See *Decreta Authentica*, IV, 432; Chambers, II, 17–18.

from the *Peregrinatio Etheriæ* describes it as it was witnessed at Jerusalem in the fourth century by a noble lady from Gaul:[4]

Et sic ponitur cathedra episcopo in Golgotha post Crucem, quae stat nunc; residet episcopus hic cathedra; ponitur ante eum mensa sublinteata; stant in giro mensa diacones; et affertur loculus argenteus deauratus in quo est lignum sanctum crucis; aperitur et profertur; ponitur in mensa quam lignum crucis quam titulus. Cum ergo positum fuerit in mensa, episcopus sedens de manibus suis summitates de ligno sancto premet; diacones autem qui in giro stant custodent. Hoc autem propterea sic custoditur, quia consuetudo est ut unus et unus omnis populus veniens, tam fideles quam cathecumini, acclinant se ad mensam, osculentur sanctum lignum, et pertranseant. Et quoniam, nescio quando, dicitur quidam fixisse morsum et furasset sancto ligno, ideo nunc a diaconibus qui in giro stant, sic custoditur, ne quis veniens audeat denuo sic facere. Ac sic ergo omnis populus transit, unus et unus, toti acclinantes se, primum de fronte, sic de occulis tangentes crucem et titulum et sic osculantes crucem pertranseunt; manum autem nemo mittit ad tangendum.

The essential of the ceremonial at Jerusalem is that while the bishop holds the wood of the Holy Cross firmly in his hands, the clergy and people make obeisance and kiss it. This adoration of the true cross in Jerusalem gave the impulse for the adoration of relics of the cross elsewhere, and ceremonials clearly modeled upon the practice of Jerusalem were introduced into the West in the seventh or eighth century.[5] Before examining the content of these western ceremonials, however, we may do well in surveying briefly the structure of the Mass of Good Friday, into which the *Adoratio* was incorporated.[6]

The Mass of Good Friday (*Missa Præsanctificatorum*) is found not in the usual liturgical position of the daily and festal Mass,—between Terce and Sext,—but between None and Vespers. The office begins abruptly with two *lectiones*, the first of which is followed by a tract and a prayer, and the second of which is followed by a tract alone. Then after the *Passio* (from St. John) and a series of special *Orationes*, occurs the *Adoratio Crucis*. The office closes with the fetching of the presanctified Host, and the *Communio fidelium*.[7] The office of

[4] Duchesne, p. 510. The history and bibliography of this document are given by Duchesne, pp. 490–492.

[5] See Thalhofer, I, 633; *Catholic Encyclopaedia*, VI, 643.

[6] The explanation that follows conforms both to the mediaeval *Ordines Romani* and to the modern *Missale Romanum*.

[7] The general nature of the *Missa Præsanctificatorum* is explained above, p. 10.

Vespers follows immediately. The succession of liturgical pieces may be shown in outline as follows:[8]

NONA
MISSA PRAESANCTIFICATORUM
  LECTIO I
    TRACTUS
    ORATIO
  LECTIO II
    TRACTUS
  PASSIO
  ORATIONES SOLEMNES
  ADORATIO CRUCIS
    [DEPOSITIO]
  COMMUNIO FIDELIUM
    [DEPOSITIO]
VESPERAE
    [DEPOSITIO]

With the general structure of the Mass of Good Friday now before us, we may center our attention upon the *Adoratio Crucis* as observed in Western Europe. An early text of this ceremonial is forthcoming from the famous *Concordia Regularis* of St. Athelwold:[9]

<ADORATIO CRUCIS>[10]

QUIBUS EXPLETIS PER ORDINEM, STATIM PREPARETUR CRUX ANTE ALTARE, INTERPOSITO SPATIO INTER IPSAM *et* ALTARE, SUSTENTATA HINC *et* INDE A DUOBUS DIACONIBUS. TUNC CANTENT:

Popule meus, <quid feci tibi?>

RESPONDENTES AUTEM DUO SUBDIACONI STANTES ANTE CRUCEM CANANT GRECE:

Agios o Theos, Agyos ychiros, Agios athanathos, eleison ymas.

ITEMQUE SCHOLA IDIPSUM LATINE:

Sanctus Deus.

DEFERATUR TUNC AB[11] IPSIS DIACONIBUS ANTE ALTARE, *et* EOS ACCOLITUS

---

[8] For purposes of subsequent reference, I insert in this outline an indication of the three liturgical positions in which the extra-liturgical *Depositio* may be found.

[9] British Museum, Cotton MS Tiberius A. III, fol. 18ᵛ–19ᵛ. The bibliography of this document is cited below, p. 73. The document represents the use of Winchester in the tenth century. I print from the manuscript, with a result differing in no essential way from the text of W. S. Logeman, in *Anglia*, Vol. XIII (1891), pp. 418–421.

[10] Cotton MS Tiberius A. III, fol. 18ᵛ–19ᵛ.

[11] ab] ad (MS).

CUM PULUILLO SEQUATUR SUPER QUEM SAN*C*T*A* CRUX PONATUR. ANTIPHONA*QUE* FINITA QUAM SCOLA RESPONDIT LATINE CANANT IBIDEM SICUT PRIUS:

Quia eduxi[12] uos p*er* desertum.

ITEM U*ER*O RESPONDEANT SUBDIACONI GRECE SICUT PRIUS:

Agios, UT SUPRA.

ITEMQ*UE* SCOLA LATINE UT PRIUS:

San*ctus* De*us*.

ITEMQ*UE* DIACONI LEUANTES CRUCEM CANANT SICUT PRIUS:

Quid ultra <debui facere tibi, et non feci?>

ITEM[13] SUBDIACONI SICUT PRIUS:

Agyos, UT SUPRA.

ITEMQ*UE* SCOLA LATINE:

San*ctus* De*us*, UT SUPRA.

POST HEC UERTENTES SE AD CLERUM, NUDATA CRUCE, DICANT ANTIPHONAM:

Ecce lignum crucis.

ALIA:

Crucem tuam adoramus.

ALIA:

Dum fabricator mundi. <fol. 19^{r}>

<P>ange lingua.

ILICO EA NUDATA, UENIAT ABBAS ANTE CRUCEM SAN*C*T*AM* AC TRIB*US* UICIBUS SE PROSTERNAT CUM OMNIBUS FRA*tr*IBUS DEXTERIORIS CHORI, SCILIC*et* SENIORIBUS AC IUNIORIBUS, *et* CUM MAGNO CORDIS SUSPIRIO vii^{m} POENITENTIE PSALMOS CUM ORATIONIBUS SAN*C*T*E* CRUCI COMPETENTIBUS DECANTANDO[14] PERORE*t*. IN PRIMA QUIDEM ORATIONE TRES PSALMOS PRIMOS CUM ORATIONE:

D*omi*ne Ih*esu* Xp*iste*, adoro te in cruce ascendentem. Deprecor te ut ipsa crux liber*et* me de diabolo percutiente.

D*omi*ne Ih*esu* Xp*iste*, adoro te ut ipsa uulneratum. Deprecor te ut ipsa uulnera remedium sint anime mee.

D*omi*ne Ih*esu* Xp*iste*, adoro te descendentem ad inferos, liberante*m* captiuos. Deprecor te ut non ibi me dimittas introire.

D*omi*ne Ih*esu* Xp*iste*, adoro te resurgentem ab inferis, ascendentem ad celos. Deprecor te miserere mei.

D*omi*ne Ih*esu* Xp*iste*, adoro te uenturu*m* iudicaturu*m*. Deprecor te ut in tuo aduentu non intres in iuditio cum me peccante, sed deprecor te ut ante dimittas quam iudices, qui uiuis *et* regnas.

IN SEC*UN*DA DUOS MEDIOS CUM SEQUENTE[15] ORATIONE:

D*omi*ne Ih*esu* Xp*iste* gloriosissime conditor mundi, qui cum sis splendor glorie coeternus patri *sancto*q*ue* sp*iritu*i ideo dignatus es carnem ex inmaculata uirgine sumere *et* gloriosas palmas tuas in crucis patibulo permisisti configere, ut claustra dissipares inferni *et* humanum genus liberares de morte, respice *et* miserere michi misero obpresso facinorum pondere multarumq*ue* nequitiarum labe polluto no<n> me digneris derelinquere,

[12] Quia eduxi] Qua edux (MS).

[13] Item] Ite (MS).

[14] Competentibus decantando] compenitentibus decantato (MS).

[15] medios cum sequente] medioximus sequentem (MS).

piissime pater, sed indulge quod impie gessi. Exaudi me prostratum coram adoranda gloriosissima cruce tua, ut merear<fol. 19v>tibi mundus adsistere *et* placere conspectui tuo. Qui cum patre.

<I>N TERTIA ULTIMOS DUOS CUM ORATIONE:

Deus omnipotens Ihesu Xpiste, qui tuas manus mundas propter nos in cruce posuisti *et* de tuo sancto sanguine nos redemisti, mitte in me sensum *et* intelligentiam[16] quomodo habeam ueram penitentiam *et* habeam bonam perseuerantiam omnibus diebus uite mee, Amen.

ET EAM HUMILITER DEOSCULANS SURGAT. DEHINC SINISTERIORIS CHORI[17] OMNES FRATRES EADEM MENTE DEUOTA PERAGANT. NAM SALUTATA AB ABBATE UEL OMNIBUS CRUCE, REDEAT IPSE ABBAS AD SEDEM SUAM USQUE DUM OMNIS CLERUS AC POPULUS HOC IDEM FACIAT.[18]

According to this *ordo* the *Adoratio* opens with the *Improperia*, or "Reproaches." Two deacons supporting the cross before the altar begin these reproaches of Christ (*Popule meus*), to each of which two subdeacons respond in Greek, and the choir, in Latin. After the first of these responses the Cross is laid upon a cushion. After the singing of the *Improperia* the Cross is uncovered, and three antiphons and the hymn *Pange lingua* are sung. Then the Abbot, along with half the choir, prostrates himself before the Cross and sings the seven penitential psalms, with appropriate prayers. The ceremony closes with the kissing of the Cross.

Although in its general content the *Adoratio* in St. Athelwold's *Concordia* is sufficiently representative, we shall do well in scrutinizing the ceremonial connected with this observance also in Rome itself. *Ordo I* speaks of it only very briefly, as follows:[19]

Post orationes præparatur crux ante altare, interposito spatio inter ipsam & altare, sustentata hinc inde a duobus acolythis, posito ante eam oratorio. Venit Pontifex, & adoratam deosculatur crucem; deinde presbyteri, diaconi, subdiaconi, & ceteri per ordinem; deinde populus. Pontifex vero sedet in sede, usque dum omnes salutent. . . . Pontifex vero sedet dum persalutet populus crucem. Nam salutante Pontifice vel populo crucem, canitur semper antiphona, *Ecce lignum crucis, in quo salus mundi pependit; venite adoremus.* Dicitur psalmus cxviii: id est, *Beati immaculati.* Qua salutata & reposita in loco suo, descendit Pontifex ante altare.

---

[16] intelligentiam] intellegentiam (MS).

[17] chori] choris (MS).

[18] Followed immediately by a version of the *Depositio*, as printed below, p. 73.

[19] Mabillon, II, 23.

The first of the Roman *ordines* really to outline the liturgical content of the *Adoratio* is *Ordo XIV*, which offers the following:[20]

Finitis orationibus, procedit Pontifex ad altare; & stans ad dextrum cornu altaris accipit Crucem a ministris sibi præparatam sindone munda coopertam; & discooperiens eam a summitate, elevatis manibus solus incipit antiphonam, *Ecce lignum crucis*, adjuvantibus eum in cantu qui assistunt ei. Cum autem *Venite adoremus* cantaverint, omnes prostrati reverenter adorent, & usque ad terram se inclinent; & repetitur antiphona, *Ecce lignum*, &c. a cantoribus in choro. Iterum Pontifex paululum procedens, & Crucem ad medietatem discooperiens, amplius elevatis manibus, exaltando vocem, eamdem antiphonam solus incipit, in cantando juvantibus eum qui circa ipsum sunt; & secundo a cantoribus antiphona repetitur. Et tertio procedit Pontifex ante altare, discooperiens Crucem totam, erectis sursum manibus altius incipit, *Ecce lignum crucis;* & tertio a cantoribus repetitur antiphona; & tertio dum cantatur *Venite adoremus*, adoratur ab omnibus. Tunc Pontifex cum chirothecis nondum extractis deponit manibus suis Crucem super stratum pallium & mundissima linteamina ad radicem altaris, & discalceatus tertio prostratus solus Crucem adorat; quo facto, revertitur ad sedem suam, & ibi recipit deposita calciamenta. . . . Postmodum omnis chorus ordinate adorent. Interim autem cantores cantent vicissim, *Agios*, repetentes, *Sanctus Deus, sanctus fortis*, &c.; antiphona<m>, *Popule meus, quia eduxi te de terra. Quid ultra debui facere*, cum toto improperio; & alias antiphonas, *Adoramus te Christe, Crucem tuam*, & *Salva nos Christe, salva;* & psalmus, *Deus misereatur*, & hymnus, *Pange*, & *Crux fidelis*. Finita adoratione Crucis, sacrista vel alius ad hoc deputatus deponit Crucem in suo loco super altare, & accendit luminaria in altare.

In its liturgical elements this *ordo* does not differ fundamentally from that furnished in St. Athelwold's *Concordia*. The variation between them in sequence and in details of content is not important. Although *Ordo XIV* does not mention the actual kissing of the Cross, we may assume that the prostration before the Cross includes this additional act also.

Another of the *Ordines Romani* may be cited here, not for indications as to the liturgical content of the *Adoratio* itself, but rather for a description of the ceremonial preceding and following. In *Ordo XII* we find these rubrics:[21]

Feria fexta in Parasceve, in aurora dominus Papa facit omnes capellanos coram sua præsentia evocari, & voce mediocri cantat psalterium; quo cantato, revertuntur capellani. Sexta vero hora dominus Papa cum omnibus cardinalibus intrat basilicam sancti Laurentii; & facta oratione, ibi accedit ad altare; &

[20] Mabillon, II, 368–369.

[21] Mabillon, II, 181–182, 183.

aperto altari extrahit inde capita apostolorum Petri & Pauli, & duas cruces.[22] Quæ omnia postquam dominus Papa cum cardinalibus osculatus fuerit, reponit ibidem; & accepta una cruce, & iterum sigillato altari, unus presbyterorum cardinalium Crucem accipit, & sic vadit usque ad ecclesiam Lateranensem, sine aliquo cantu & psalmis; factaque ibi oratione ascendit cathedram post altare. Tunc dominus Papa induit quadragesimalia indumenta, & excalceatur. Episcopi vero induunt pluvialia, presbyteri autem cardinales & diaconi atque subdiaconi induunt planetam. Et deinde juniori presbytero cardinali accepto Corpore Christi in capsella ante pectus suum hesterna die reservato, & alio prædictam Crucem accipiente, & subdiacono regionario cum populo suo præcedente, omnes discalceati cum domino Papa & primicerio, sine cantu psallendo psalterium pergunt ad Sanctam Crucem[23] . . . <Lectiones, Passio, Orationes> . . . Finitis orationibus, Pontifex procedit ad altare, & adorat Crucem cum aliis, sicut in Ordine continetur. Sciendum tamen, quod secundum antiquam consuetudinem, quidquid super Crucem offertur, Scholæ Crucis debet esse. Osculata vero Cruce a clero & populo, dominus Papa revertitur ad altare . . . <Communio et Vesperæ> . . . Et deinde revertitur ad palatium;[24] & intrans Basilicam Sancti Laurentii,[25] Crucem quam acceperat ab altari, reponit.

For our present purpose the significance of this ceremonial lies in the two processions, one preceding the *Missa Præsanctificatorum* and the other following Vespers. The papal station for Good Friday is the Basilica Sanctæ Crucis (Santa Croce in Gerusalemme). Before proceeding from the Lateran Palace to this church, however, the Pope enters the Capella Sancti Laurentii (Sancta Sanctorum),[26] adjoining the Palace, and taking a cross from a chest under the altar, proceeds with it to the Church of the Lateran. Thence the procession, bearing the cross from the Sancta Sanctorum and a reserved Host from the Church of the Lateran, moves out through the city to the Basilica Sanctæ Crucis. The Cross serves for the *Adoratio*

[22] Concerning these relics see H. Grisar, *Die römische Kapelle Sancta Sanctorum und ihr Schatz*, Freiburg, 1908, pp. 39–108.

[23] This is the Basilica Sanctæ Crucis, or Santa Croce in Gerusalemme.

[24] The Lateran Palace.

[25] The Basilica Sancti Laurentii, or Sancta Sanctorum is a private chapel at the Lateran, as is explained below.

[26] For a description and history of this chapel and its relics see Grisar, pp. 11–108; M. Armellini, *Le Chiese di Roma dal secolo IV al XIX*, Rome, 1891, pp. 108–112; H. Marucchi, *Éléments d'Archéologie chrétienne*, Vol. III (*Basiliques et Églises de Rome*), Paris and Rome, 1902, pp. 101–102; *Johannis Diaconi Liber de Ecclesia Lateranensi*, cap. xiv, in Mabillon, II, 572–573. This famous chapel of St. Laurence, or *Sancta Sanctorum*, was the private chapel of the Popes during the centuries of their residence at the Lateran.

Crucis,[27] and the Host, for the Communion of the *Missa Præsanctificatorum*. After Vespers have been sung at the Basilica Sanctæ Crucis, the Pope carries the Cross in procession back to the Sancta Sanctorum and restores it to its place under the altar.[28]

Although the details of this *ordo* are highly satisfying in their completeness, the relatively late date of *Ordo XII* (twelfth century) suggests the desirability of examining a similar text of the eighth century from Einsiedeln:[29]

Fer. vi, hora quasi viii, descendit domnus apostolicus de Lateranis in sanctum Johannem, verumtamen discalceatus tam ipse quam reliqui ministri sanctae ecclesiae, et veniunt ad altare. Et praecipit domnus apostolicus accendere lumen in ungiario, et accendit ex ipso lumen cui ipse iusserit duas faculas albas, quas portant duo clerici de cubiculo ante domnum. Et procedent de sancto Johanne psallendo *Beati immaculati*, archidiacono tenente sinistram manum domni apostolici, et ipso pontifice in dextera sua portante turibulum cum incenso et alio diacono post dorsum domni apostolici portante lignum pretiosae crucis in capsa de auro cum gemmis ornata. Crux vero ipsa de ligno pretioso desuper ex auro cum gemmis intus cavam habens confectionem ex balsamo satis bene olente. Et dum preveniunt ad Hierusalem[30] intrant ecclesiam, et ponit diaconus ipsam capsam ubi est crux super altare et sic aperit eam domnus apostolicus. Deinde prosternit se ante altare ad orationem: et postquam surgit osculatur eam et vadit et stat circa sedem. Et per eius iussionem osculantur episcopi, presbiteri, diaconi, subdiaconi super altare ipsam crucem. Deinde ponunt eam super arcellam ad rugas et ibi osculatur eam reliquus populus. Tamen feminae ibi non introeunt; sed postea portant eam oblati et alii subdiaconi et osculatur a feminis. Verumtamen ut a domno apostolico fuerit osculata, statim ascendit subdiaconus in ambonem et incipit legere lectionem Oseae prophetae. Post cuius descensum ascendit cantor et canit gr(aduale) *Domine audivi* cum versibus suis. Et iterum ascendit subdiaconus et legit aliam lectionem Deuteronomii; post quem cantor ascendens incipit tractatum *Qui habitat*. Quo completo vadit diaconus discalceatus cum evangelio, et cum eo duo subdiaconi, et legit passionem Domini secundum Johannem. Et cum completa fuerit, dicit domnus apostolicus orationem *Oremus pro ecclesia*

---

[27] Concerning the *Adoratio Crucis* at Santa Croce in Gerusalemme see Armellini, p. 800; Marucchi, p. 347.

[28] This procession back from Santa Croce to the Sancta Sanctorum is described by A. De Santi, *Il Mattino di Pasqua nella Storia liturgica*, Rome, 1917, p. 12. This monograph is a revision of an article published in *Civiltà Cattolica* (1907), Vol. II, p. 3–22.

[29] Printed from Einsiedeln MS 326 by G. B. De Rossi, *Inscriptiones Christiani Urbis Romae*, Vol. II, Rome, 1888, p. 34.

[30] This is the Basilica Sanctæ Crucis—the modern church Santa Croce in Gerusalemme.

sancta Dei, et dicit archidiaconus *Flectamus genua*, et postea dicit *Levate*, et reliqua omnia in ordine suo. Et ad finem tantum dicit *Dominus vobiscum* et respondent *Et cum spiritu tuo*. Et procedent iterum ad Lateranis psallendo *Beati immaculati*. Attamen apostolicus ibi non communicat nec diaconi; qui vero communicare voluerit communicat de capsis de sacrificio quod v feria servatum est. Et qui noluerit ibi communicare vadit per alias ecclesias Romae seu per titulos et communicat.

This document is particularly generous in its description of the Cross itself[31] and of the actual *Adoratio*. One notes, however, the absence of reference to the fetching of the Cross from the Sancta Sanctorum and to the subsequent depositing of it again in the altar of this Lateran chapel. Nevertheless, in view of the fact that the Cross employed is undoubtedly identical with that mentioned in *Ordo XII*, the processions from the Sancta Sanctorum and back again are inevitable. The ceremonials of the Einsiedeln document and of *Ordo XII* are essentially similar.[32]

From the information now before us we may make some estimate of the possible influence of the *Adoratio* upon the *Depositio*. At least three of the documents cited above[33] record established ceremonials earlier than the date of the first recorded examples of the *Depositio*;[34] and in these documents are several suggestions toward the dramatic office under consideration.[35] In the first place, since the *Adoratio* itself is a vivid commemoration of the Crucifixion, nothing could be more natural than that a vivid commemoration of the Burial should be invented as a sequel to the *Adoratio*. Any taking down of the Cross after the ceremony of the *Adoratio* must inevitably suggest a representation of the burial of the crucified Christ

[31] This description is mentioned by Grisar (p. 70), whose own complete and scientific description of the relic is found on pp. 62–82 of the monograph mentioned above.

[32] For our present study there is no significance in the altered *position* of the *Adoratio* in the Einsiedeln *ordo*—before the *lectiones* of the *Missa Præsanctificatorum* rather than *after* the *Orationes solemnes*.

[33] The *Peregrinatio Etheriae*, *Ordo Romanus I*, and Da Rossi's *Ordo* from Einsiedeln.

[34] We hear of the *Depositio* first in the latter half of the tenth century. See above, p. 14, and below, p. 73.

[35] I do not, of course, mean to suggest that versions of the *Adoratio* later than the tenth century could not have influenced versions of the *Depositio* of a later date.

Himself.[36] Moreover the carrying back of the Cross from the *Adoratio* in Santa Croce in Gerusalemme to the chest under the altar of the Sancta Sanctorum may fairly be regarded as a conscious ceremonial of burial. In view of the wide-spread symbolizing of the altar as a tomb,[37] this procession inevitably suggests a *cortège* to a grave.[38] Whatever may have been the early practice elsewhere, the conspicuous ceremonial of Rome alone was quite adequate for suggesting the invention of a commemoration of Christ's burial in the dramatic form of a *Depositio*.

But the intimacy of the relation between the Roman liturgical use and the extra-liturgical dramatic offices of the *sepulchrum* is further to be discerned in what the *Ordines Romani* offer for Easter morning in the way of sequel to the laying down of the Cross after the *Adoratio Crucis* of Good Friday. This sequel, which occurs in the Sancta Sanctorum immediately after Prime, before the Pope's departure for Mass at the Church of Santa Maria Maggiore, is described in *Ordo Romanus XII* as follows:[39]

In die Paschæ mane post Primam indutus albo pluviali Romanus Pontifex, cum diaconis cardinalibus indutis, cum subdiaconis ceterisque minoribus ordinibus, dalmaticis, & mitris, & tunicis indutis, & cappelanis suis, vadit ad basilicam sancti Laurentii. Presbyteri cardinales induunt se planetis, episcopi pluvialibus in loco, qui dicitur basilica sancti Gregorii; ubi post orationem

[36] It is only fair to observe that the Cross used in the papal *Adoratio* at Santa Croce in Gerusalemme bears no figure of the *Corpus* itself. See Grisar, pp. 62–82.

[37] See above, p. 16.

[38] De Santi considers this procession—as prescribed in the passage quoted above from Ordo XII—to be a deliberate symbolical representation of Christ's burial in a *sepulchrum*, as he shows in the following words (p. 12): "Questa riposizione non deve passare inosservata, perchè ci sembra l'unico accenno nelle consuetudini pontificie all' uso assai largamente sparso nelle altre Chiese di deporre solennemente la croce adorata nella funzione del venerdì santo in una specie de sepolcro che allestivasi a questo intento, conservandola quivi devotamente fino al momento della risurrezione nel mattino di Pasqua." De Santi seems to regard the Roman procession as a definite example of the *Depositio*. I have remarked above (p. 26) that although this procession is not explicitly prescribed in the earlier *Ordines Romani*, it was, from the circumstances, inevitable.

[39] Mabillon, II, 184–185. This ceremony is the special subject of consideration in the monograph of De Santi (see particularly pp. 11–16). See also Grisar, p. 43; Armellini, p. 111; Marucchi, pp. 67, 102.

induitur usque ad dalmaticam; & exsurgens ingreditur ad adorandum Salvatorem. Aperit imaginem, osculatur pedes Salvatoris, dicens alta voce tribus vicbus, *Surrexit Dominus de sepulcro;* & omnes ei respondent: *Qui pro nobis pependit in ligno, Alleluia.* Tunc acolythi ponunt crucem cepellæ super altare, & dominus Papa adorat eam. Post osculationem Salvatoris, cum omnibus aliis deinde redit ad sedem, & dat pacem archidiacono redeunti ab osculo pedum ejus imaginis, dicens, *Surrexit Dominus vere;* & ille respondet, *Et apparuit Simoni.* Secundus quoque diaconus osculatis pedibus Salvatoris, accedit ad pacem summi Pontificis & archidiaconi, & ponit se in filo; ceteri vero diaconi cardinales similiter faciunt. Deinde primicerius cum cantoribus eo modo ad pacem vadit, & in filo se dirigit. Prior quoque basilicæ cum diaconis similiter; postmodum subdiaconi regionarii cum acolythis & capellanis, & aliis palatinis ordinibus, eodem modo pacem faciunt. Interim schola canit, *Crucifixum in carne,* & *Ego sum alpha & omega.*

This ceremony consists primarily in the kissing of the feet of the famous painting of Christ known as the *Acheropoiita* ("Not made by the hand of man"),[40] a figure of life size painted upon a panel of wood against the wall behind the altar. It appears that at all periods the painting was protected by some sort of covering;[41] and the *ordo* before us implies such protection in the words *aperit imaginem,* which indicate the exposing of the feet of the figure in order that they may be kissed. After the triple singing of the versicle *Surrexit Dominus,* a cross is placed upon the altar for adoration. If this is the cross previously used in the *Adoratio,* it must have been taken up from the relic-chest under the altar.[42] The ceremony closes with the Kiss of Peace.

This papal observance on Easter morning reinforces the ceremonial of Good Friday in providing a model for the extra-liturgical *Depositio* and *Elevatio* that we are to consider. Just as the return of the Cross to the altar of the *Sancta Sanctorum* on Good Friday suggests the *Depositio,* so the observance at this same altar on Easter morning offers a parallel to the *Elevatio.* Although the kissing of the feet of the *Acheropoiita*

---

[40] The most adequate description of this relic known to me is that given by Grisar, pp. 39–54. See also Armellini, p. 111; Marucchi, p. 102.

[41] The earliest extant reference to the *Acheropoiita* is from the eighth century. A covering of silver was provided by Innocent III (1198–1216). The nature of the earlier coverings is obscure. See Grisar, p. 41.

[42] Whether or not this cross is the one used previously on Good Friday, it was almost certainly elevated from the relic-chest under the altar. The two important crosses kept in this chest are described by Grisar, pp. 58–97.

seems to establish no particular bond with the *Elevatio*, the adoring of the elevated cross and the giving of the *Pax* will be frequently paralleled in the dramatic texts to be considered.[43]

Since a knowledge of the liturgical uses of Rome must have been widely disseminated, we are amply justified in citing the papal ceremonies as possible sources for the *Depositio* and *Elevatio*. We have already observed that the Roman *Adoratio Crucis* antedates the earliest versions of the *Depositio*.[44] Although the papal ceremony of Easter morning cited above comes from documents later than the earliest manifestations of the *Elevatio*,[45] it is highly probable that this ceremony is much older than these particular documents; and in any case, even though this particular ceremony may not be among the ultimate origins of the *Elevatio*, it may well have influenced the dramatic office at some period of its career.

III

From a consideration of the origins of the *Depositio* and *Elevatio* I now pass to the examination of actual texts of these dramatic offices. For convenience, I shall divide the versions before me into three groups. Into the first group fall the versions in which the object "buried" is the Host, in the second group of versions this central object is the Cross, and in the versions of the third group are found both the Host and the Cross. In arranging the texts within each group I shall proceed, in general, from the simple to the more complex. Hence I am guided not so much by chronology of documents as by relative amplitude of liturgical content and of ceremonial. One scarcely need remark that the simpler, and often earlier, versions are sometimes preserved in documents later than those containing examples of a more complex development. I do not, however, insist that the order in which I present the several versions, and groups of versions, demonstrably repre-

[43] For example, see below, pp. 99–101, 103, 108, 124.

[44] See above, p. 26.

[45] *Ordo Romanus XII* from which I quote above is of the twelfth century, as is also *Ordo Romanus XI*, which also describes the papal ceremony under consideration.

sents the precise historical evolution. For such a demonstration the historical *data* are, as yet, insufficient. The following survey, then, attempts not so much to establish an historical sequence as to present an orderly exposition.

In the present section of this study I shall examine those versions of the *Depositio* and *Elevatio*[1] in which is buried the Host alone.

The simplest example in this group is the following *Elevatio* of the eleventh century from St. Gall:[2]

<ELEVATIO HOSTIÆ>[3]

SUBLATO IGITUR CORPORE D*omi*NI DE MONUMENTO INCIP*iat* CANTOR *Responsiorium:*

Angelus D*omi*ni descend*it*<de cœlo et accedens revolvit lapidem, et super eum sedit, et dixit mulieribus: Nolite timere; scio enim quia crucifixum queritis; jam surrexit, venite et videte locum ubi positus erat Dominus, alleluia. VERSUS: Angelus Domini locutus est mulieribus dicens: Quem queritis, an Ihesum queritis? Jam surrexit.>[4]

INTRANTIBUS AU*tem* IN CHORU*m* INCIP*iat* CANTOR ANTIPH*onam:*

Surrexit Xpictus et illuxit populo suo, quem redemit sanguine suo, a<ll>e<l>uia.

VERSUS:

Haec est alma dies in qua spoliatur auernus;
Resurrexit homo Deus, exultate redempti.
Te Deum Laudamus.[5]

This brief text prescribes merely the raising of the *Corpus Domini* from the *sepulchrum*, after which the procession from the place of burial proceeds to the choir during the singing of the reponsory *Angelus Domini*. As the procession enters the

[1] Throughout this study I shall consider the *Depositio* and *Elevatio* in conjunction, and, as far as possible, shall allow the two offices to elucidate each other. Unhappily, however, a good many of the documents happen to preserve only one of the two offices. It should, of course, be remembered that the absence of either of the offices from a manuscript does not prove its absence from the use of the church concerned.

[2] St. Gall, Stiftsbibliothek, MS 387, Breviarium Sangallense saec. xi, p. 55. The *Elevatio* from this manuscript was first published by the present writer in *Transactions of the Wisconsin Academy*, XVI, Part II, pp. 897–898. The manuscript contains neither *Depositio* nor *Visitatio Sepulchri*.

[3] St. Gall MS 387, p. 55. In the manuscript this text is immediately preceded by the responsory *Dum transisset*, the last responsory of Easter Matins.

[4] This responsory is commonly found as the first of Easter Matins. See Migne, *Pat. Lat.*, LXXVIII, 769.

[5] Followed immediately by the rubric *In Matutinis Laudibus*.

choir the antiphon *Surrexit Christus* is sung. The two hexameters *Haec est alma . . . redempti* are probably to be regarded as a trope of the *Te Deum Laudamus*.[6] It is to be observed, however, that these lines contain a suggestion of the theme of the Harrowing of Hell, a theme that forms a prominent part of some of the more highly developed versions of the *Elevatio*.[7]

Particularly noticeable is the liturgical position of this text: between the third reponsory and the *Te Deum* at the end of Easter Matins. This is the position commonly occupied by the *Visitatio Sepulchri*, the *Elevatio* being found, almost without exception, before the beginning of Matins. Since the present text of the *Elevatio* is a relatively early one, and since Durandus assures us that the *Te Deum* of Easter Matins is to be interpreted as marking the moment of the Resurrection,[8] it may be that the St. Gall version represents an early usage. If Durandus' symbolizing of the Easter *Te Deum* is authentic for the early Middle Ages, the *Elevatio* is most appropriately placed at this point in the liturgy. It is entirely possible that this is an early arrangement, and that the *Visitatio Sepulchri* took this position only after the *Elevatio* had relinquished it.[9]

The following is a simple version of the *Depositio* from the use of Constance:[10]

<DEPOSITIO HOSTIÆ>[11]

POST COMMUNIONEM LEGANTUR VESPERÆ SUB SILENTIO.

HIS OMNIBUS PERACTIS, PROCEDUNT CUM CORPORE DOMINI AD LOCUM UBI DEBET RECONDI, NIHIL CANTANTES; SED DUM VENITUR AD LOCUM, CANTOR IMPONIT ANTIPHONAM:

---

[6] See L. Gautier, *Les Tropes*, Paris, 1886, p. 170.

[7] See below, for example, pp. 90–91, 111–118.

[8] Treating the liturgical practices at the end of Easter Matins, Durandus (†1296) observes (*Rationale Divinorum Officiorum* Lyons, 1559, fol. 372^{v}): *Te Deum laudamus* exprimit horam qua resurrexit.

[9] See also the version from Gran, below, p. 123. I explain below (pp. 127–130) my belief that the *Visitatio Sepulchri* developed at the *sepulchrum* later than did the *Depositio* and *Elevatio*.

[10] *Agenda seu Obsequiale, Simul ac Benedictionale, iuxta ritum et normam Ecclesiae ac Episcopatus Constantiensis*, 1570, fol. xciiii^{v}–xcvi^{r}. I have found copies of this book in the Royal Library, Munich, in the British Museum, and in the library of Quarr Abbey, Isle of Wight. Lange (p. 7) cites a copy in the Stadtbibliothek, Zürich, and prints (p. 47) the *Visitatio Sepulchri* from it (fol. cxxi^{v}–cxxiii^{v}). The book contains no *Elevatio*.

[11] *Agenda . . . Episcopatus Constantiensis*, 1570, fol. xciiii^{v}–xcvi^{r}.

In pace in idipsum dormiam et <fol. xcv^{r}> requiescam.[12]

ALIA ANtiphona:

Caro mea requiescet in spe.[13]

IN REDITUm AD CHORUm CANITUR Responsorium:

Sepulto Domino, signatum est monumentum, voluentes lapidem ad ostium monumenti; <fol. xcv^{v}> ponentes milites qui custodirent eum. *Versus:* Ne forte veniant discupli eius *et* furentur eum *et* dicant plebi: Surrexit a mortuis. Ponen <fol. xcvi^{r}> tes milites.[14]

In this version of the *Depositio* the ceremonial is very simple. At the close of Vespers, during the singing of the antiphons *In pace in idipsum* and *Caro mea*, the Host is carried to the *locus* where it is to be hidden. For the laying down of the Host no rubrics are given. The processional for the return to the choir is the reponsory *Sepulto Domino*.

In the *Ordinarium* of the year 1580 for the use of Gran, in Hungary, we find definite provision made for the reservation on Holy Thursday of two Hosts for Good Friday: one for the *Missa Præsanctificatorum* and one for burial in the *sepulchrum*:[15]

<IN CŒNA DOMINI>[16]

ET PRO DIE CRASTINA CONSECRANTUR HOSTLÆ DUÆ: ALTERA QUAM SUMPTURUS EST EPICOPUS VEL SACERDOS OFFICIUM PERACTURUS, ALTERA QUÆ REPONETUR IN SEPULCHRUm.

After Vespers on Good Friday the *Depositio* was performed as follows:

<DEPOSITIO HOSTLÆ>[17]

DEMUM[18] PONTIFEX[19] VEL SACERDOS OFFICIANS, EXUTA CASULA, PORTANS IN

[12] First antiphon of Matins of Holy Saturday. See Migne, *Pat. Lat.*, LXXVIII, 767.

[13] Third antiphon of Matins of Holy Saturday. See *id.*, col. 768.

[14] Followed immediately by the rubric: Ordo in Vigilia Paschæ.

[15] *Ordinarium officii Divini secundum consuetudinem Metropolitanae Ecclesiae Strigoniensis*, Tirnaviæ, 1580, sig. H 7 recto. I use the copy in the British Museum. The *Depositio* from this book is now reprinted, I believe, for the first time. The *Elevatio* and *Visitatio* have been reprinted by Lange, in *Zeitschrift für deutsches Altertum*, XLI (1897), p. 81. The uses attached to the *sepulchrum* in Hungary are treated by J. Dankó, in *Oesterreichische Vierteljahresschrift für katholische Theologie*, 1872, pp. 103–136, 175–208. The *Depositio* and *Elevatio* are considered by Dankó on pp. 175–190 *passim*.

[16] *Ordinarium . . . Ecclesiae Strigoniensis*, Tirnaviæ, 1580, sig. H 7 recto.

[17] *Id.*, sig. I 4 recto.

[18] Preceded immediately by Vespers.

[19] Pontifex] Pontefex (Print).

MANIBUS ALTERAM HOSTIAM CONSECRATAM QUÆ PRO SEPULTURA HERI FUIT RESERUATA, IN PATENA SUPRA CALICEM COLLOCATAM, PALLA & LINTEOLO TECTAM, DESCENDIT CUM MINISTRIS VERSUS SEPULCHRUM, PRÆCEDENTIBUS CEROFERARIIS & TURRIBULO, QUOD SEMEL CIRCUMIT. DEINDE REPONIT IN ILLUD EANDEM HOSTIAM UNA CUM CALICE, CLAUDIT, OBSIGNAT, & PER CIRCUITUM INCENSAT, CHORO CANTANTE RESPONSORIA:

> Hierusalem, luge, <et exue te vestibus jucunditatis; induere cinere cum cilicio, quia in te est occisus Salvator Israel. VERSUS: Montes Gelboe, nec ros, nec pluvia super vos descendat. Quia.>[30]

ET:

> Sepulto Domino.

QUIBUS COMPLETIS CANTAT VERSUS: Adoramus te, Christe, ETC.; Omnis terra, ETC.; ET ORATIONEM: Deus, qui pro nobis. COMPLETORIUM HORA CONSUETA LEGITUR UT HERI.

The ceremonial is here described in some detail. In the procession to the *sepulchrum* the bishop carries the Host upon a paten placed over the mouth of a chalice, the whole being covered with cloths. Eventually the Host, paten, and chalice are placed in the *sepulchrum*, which is closed, sealed, and censed during the singing of the responsories *Jerusalem luge* and *Sepulto Domino*. The office closes with versicles and a prayer.

The related *Elevatio* is provided for in the accompanying rubric:

<ELEVATIO HOSTIÆ>[31]

IN FESTO GLORIOSISSIMÆ RESURRECTIONIS DOMINI NOSTRI JESU CHRISTI. PRIUSQ*uam* PULSETUR AD MATUTINUM, CLAUSIS IANUIS TEMPLI, SUCCUSTOS[32] APERIT SEPULCHRUM, & APERTUM RELINQUIT. CORPUS DOMINI, QUOD IN SEPULCHRO POSITUM FUIT, REPONIT IN MONSTRANTIA*m*, QUAM IN MENSA INDUMENTO ALTARIS DECENTER VESTITA ANTE OSTIUM SEPULCHRI SUPRA CORPORALE COLLOCAT, CUM DUABUS CANDELIS IN CANDELABRIS ARDENTIBUS. SICUT ENIM CERTUM EST CHRISTUM ANTEQUAM MULIERES & DISCIPULI AD SEPULCHRU*m* VENIRENT RESURREXISSE, ITA CONUENIT HANC CÆREMONIAM PERAGI PRIUSQ*uam* POPULUS IN TEMPLUM CONUENIAT.[33]

One or two of the details in the rubric deserve special notice. Not only are we told that this office is performed by the sacristan in secret before Matins; we are also given the reason for the secrecy. It appears that since Christ rose before the arrival

---

[30] Second responsory of Matins of Holy Saturday. See Migne, *Pat. Lat.*, LXXVIII, 768.

[31] *Ordinarium . . . Ecclesiae Strigoniensis*, Tirnaviæ, 1580, sig. I 8 recto.

[32] succustos] succostos (Print).

[33] Followed immediately by the rubric: Ad Matutinum, Inuitatorium.

of the Maries and the disciples at the tomb, the commemoration of the Resurrection should be made before the entrance of the people into the church.[24] It should be observed further that after being taken up, the Host is placed in a monstrance and put upon the *mensa* of the altar, before the *sepulchrum*. This arrangement suggests that the sepulchre is in this case the tabernacle behind the altar-table. For further evidence as to the disposition of the monstrance containing the Host we may scrutinize the related text of the *Visitatio:*

<VISITATIO SEPULCHRI>[25]

Ad Matutinum Inuitatorium & alia omnia ut in libro. Dum autem <sig. I 8 verso> lectiones cantantur, induuntur in sacrario Diaconus & Subdiaconus, pro hoc festo in tabula notati, vestibus albis, suo ordini conuenientibus. Disponuntur duo ad ferendum thus & turribulum; item duo alii ad portanda vexilla. Et finita ultima lectione, dum in organo incipitur responsorium: Dum transisset Sabbatum, descendit officians cum praedictis & aliis ministris processionaliter ad Sepulchrum, & illud semel circumit, statque ante mensam in qua est monstrantia posita. Ubi finito responsorio incensat primum; deinde sumit in manus monstrantiam, incipitque & chorus prosequitur Introitum: Resurrexi, sine versu. Qui dum a choro cantatur, portat & ponit Sacramentum ad altare Sanctæ Crucis. Et postquam Introitus fuerit finitus, duo pueri veniunt ad ostium Sepulchri, quorum unus cantat:

Quem quae<sig. K 1 recto>ris mulier, alleluia.

Alter vero respondet:

Iesum Nazarenum, alleluia.

Rursus primus:

Surrexit, non est hic, alleluia; ecce locus ubi posuerunt eum, alleluia.

Deinde accipiens in manus monstrantiam, Officians ibidem apud altare Sanctæ Crucis, vertit se ad populum, incipitque antiphonam:

Pax vobis, ego sum, alleluia,

---

[24] Another reason for excluding the general congregation from the *Elevatio* is cited by H. Alt (*Theater und Kirche*, Berlin, 1846, p. 348) from the Synod of Worms of the year 1316:

Quum a nostris antecessoribus ad nos usque pervenerit, ut in sacra nocte Dominicae Resurrectionis ad sustollendam Crucifixi imaginem de sepulcro, ubi in Parasceve locata fuerat, nimia virorum et mulierum numerositas certatim sese comprimendo, ecclesiam simul cum Canonicis et Vicariis introire nitantur, opinantes erronee: quod si viderent Crucifixi imaginem sustolli, evaderent hoc anno inevitabilem mortis horam. His itaque obviantes statuimus ut Resurrectionis Mysterium ante ingressum plebis in ecclesiam peragatur.

[25] *Ordinarium . . . Ecclesiae Strigoniensis*, Tirnaviæ, 1580, sig. I 8 recto—K1 recto.

QUAM CHORUS PROSEQUITUR. ET HOC FIT TER, VOCE SEMPER ALTIUS ELEUATA. QUIBUS PERACTIS, CANTATUR:

Te Deum laudamus,

AC REUERTITUR PROSESSIO AD CHORUM, & MONSTRANTIA COLLOCATUR IN ALTARI MAIORI SUPER CORPORALE, & IBI STAT USQ*ue* AD FINEM LAUDUM.[26]

From this text we learn that after the third responsory at the end of the Matins the choir sings the Introit *Resurrexi*[27] while the monstrance is carried away from the altar at which the *sepulchrum* is located, and placed upon the *Altare Sanctæ Crucis*. This procedure leaves the *sepulchrum* empty and ready for the usual observances of the *Visitatio Sepulchri*, which are duly performed. During the singing of the antiphon *Pax vobis* the officiating priest blesses the congregation with the monstrance. The *Te Deum* is then sung, and the monstrance is carried to the main altar, to stand until the end of Lauds.

Several details in the observance at Gran suggest influences from the reservation of Holy Thursday: (1) the reservation together of the Host for the *Missa Præsanctificatorum* and the Host for the *sepulchrum*;[28] (2) the use of an altar tabernacle as the *sepulchrum*;[29] and (3) the placing of the Host in a monstrance.[30]

A still more elaborate ceremonial and a more extensive use of the monstrance are to be observed in a relatively late document, a *Rituale* of the year 1686 from Salzburg. The *Depositio* in this book has been described as follows:[31]

---

[26] Followed immediately by the rubric: Ad Laudes.

[27] This use of the Introit *Resurrexi* is important in its bearing upon the relation of the *Visitatio* of Easter Matins to the *Quem quæritis* trope at the Introit of the Easter Mass. See *Publications of the Modern Language Association*, XXIX, 3.

[28] See above, p. 17.

[29] See above, p. 14.

[30] This use of the monstrance seems to reflect a relatively late practice connected with the Thursday reservation. See *Decreta Authentica*, IV, 433–439.

[31] Since the Salzburg *Rituale* of 1686 has not been accessible to me, I quote the description of the *Depositio* from *Decreta Authentica*, IV, 429–430. Apparently the *Decreta Authentica* does not undertake to print the *Depositio verbatim* throughout.

<DEPOSITIO HOSTIÆ>[33]

Feria VI in Parasceve, vel ante, scribit suprascriptum Rituale Salisburgense sub titulo: "Ordo ponendi SS. Corpus Domini in Sepulchrum," tempestive paratur locus vel cappella pro Sepulchro, velis et luminaribus, quantum fieri potest. Et facta a Celebrante in Missa Præsanctificatorum Communione, ardentibus adhuc facibus vel candelis in choro, pro reverentia Hostiae in calice relictae, Celebrans stans imponit incensum in duo thuribula absque benedictione, incensat ter venerabile Sacramentum genuflexus. Interim ordinatur lugubris Processio. Praecedit crux, quam immediate sequitur clerus more solito, luminaria ferens, ultimo loco Sacerdos, casula nigra indutus, calicem coopertum velo albo manibus gestans, cum Ministris sub baldachino seu umbella incedens, choro interim cantante Responsorium: *Recessit Pastor* (ex II Noct. Matut. Sabb. S.) thurificantibus continuo duobus thuriferariis vel uno saltem in minoribus ecclesiis, adhibito quoque malleo ligneo cymbali loco. Interim reverenter ponitur calix cum hostia in loco, corporali mundo strato. Sacerdos facta genuflexione ac deposito velo humerali, removet calicis velum, patenam et pallam; et repetita genuflexione sacram Hostiam e calice desumptam ponit in lunula et in ostensorio, quod densiore velo sericeo albi coloris obtegit. Facta genuflexione purificat digitos super calicem, sumit ablutionem et extergit os et calicem purificatorio. Repetita genuflexione descendit in planum et genuflexus in infimo gradu expectat, donec Diaconus ostensorium in throno collocaverit. Deinde imponit incensum in thuribulum et genuflexus ter incensat Sanctissimum. Interim cantatur Responsorium: *Tenebrae factae sunt* (ex II Noct. Matut. feriae VI in Parasc.). Quo finito dicit Sacerdos v. *Christus factus est pro nobis obediens* etc. et Orationem *Respice*.

Haec expositio SS. Sacramenti in ostensorio velato durat per totam diem Parasceves usque ad horam septimam serotinam, qua SS. Sacramentum ex ostensorio sumitur et cum lunula in custodia ponitur; tum silentio cum luminibus ad tabernaculum defertur, ubi particulae pro infirmis asservantur. Sabbato Sancto autem mane ante vel post Missam (consuetudo in hoc puncto valde differt) iterum sub silentio SS. Sacramentum in custodia ad SS. Sepulchrum defertur, in ostensorium velatum includitur et sub silentio exponitur, incensatione more solito adhibita.

Ad Sepulchrum, dicit Rituale laudatum, ut supra paratum, non minus quam ad hesternum altare, adhibendi sunt nocte ac die testes quidam et custodes; nec desse debent, qui secundum ritum antiquum psallant.

Of the location of the *sepulchrum*, in this case, we are told only that it is in a "place or chapel." After the Communion of the *Missa Præsanctificatorum* the celebrant places the Host in a chalice covered by a paten and a pall, and carries it in procession to the *sepulchrum*, the choir singing the responsory *Recessit pastor*. Here the Host is removed from the chalice,

[33] From *Decreta Authentica*, IV, 429–430, the description being based upon the *Rituale Salisburgense* of 1686.

deposited in a monstrance, placed *in throno*, and censed. Meanwhile the choir sing the responsory *Tenebræ factæ*, at the conclusion of which the celebrant says the verse *Christus factus* and a prayer. After the monstrance has stood exposed until seven in the evening, it is placed in a tabernacle apart. On Saturday morning the Host is returned to the *sepulchrum*, where it is censed and again exposed in the monstrance. During the exposition of Friday and Saturday guards sing psalms at the *sepulchrum*.

The *Elevatio* at Salzburg takes the following form:

<ELEVATIO HOSTIÆ>[33]

Nocte sancta Paschae, hora congrua, Sacerdos indutus alba, stola, et pluviali albi coloris et Ministri sacri cum debitis paramentis, praecedentibus thuriferariis cum incenso et thurbulis fumigantibus, sequentibus iuxta crucem duobus ceroferariis cum candelis accensis, choro et clero, singulis cum suis candelis, veniunt ordine ad Sepulchrum, pro deferendo processionaliter SS. Sacramento, ubi facta genuflexione utroque genu aliquantisper orant. Sacerdos surgens et stans imponit incensum in thuribulum absque benedictione. Tum genuflexus thurificat venerabile Sacramentum triplici ductu; Diaconus deinde illud e throno depromptum ponit super altare, corporali stratum, et velum ab ostensorio removet. Sacerdos velo albo oblongo circumdatus, accipit Sanctissimum reverenter et processionali ritu, praecedentibus clericis cum luminibus et ministris continuo thurificantibus, cymbalisque personantibus illud deportat ex Sepulchro per totam ecclesiam (vel etiam extra ecclesiam circa loca vicina, uti in Austria mos est) et tunc ad altare maius, interim choro inchoante, et in tono festivo (interposito etiam, ubi fieri potest, organo) cantante hymnum: Aurora coelum purpurat, etc.

Itaque Sacerdos, cum pervenerit ad altare maius et posuerit ibidem venerabile Sacramentum, facit profundam genuflexionem, stansque iterum imponit incensum absque benedictione, et Sanctissimum triplici ductu genuflexus incensat. Postea canitur a Ministris vel ipso Sacerdote, ipsis deficientibus v<ersum>: Surrexit Dominus de sepulchro, Alleluia. r<esponsio>: Qui pro nobis pependit in ligno, Alleluia. Oremus: Deus, qui hanc sacratissimam noctem etc. (ex Missa Sabb. S.).

Tunc genuflectunt Celebrans et Ministri in infimo altaris gradu et a choro cantatur Hymnus Tantum ergo et Genitori. Interim imponitur thus et incensatur Sanctissimum; tum cantantur versiculus et Oratio de SS. Sacramento. Et facta venerabili Sacramento profunda reverentia, Sacerdos accepto super humeros velo oblongo albo, quo in processione usus fuit, ad altare ascendit, SS. Sacramentum reverenter accipit,

[33] From the *Rituale Salisburgense* of 1686 as quoted in *Decreta Authentica*, IV, 439.

ET STANS, CUM EODEM, POPULO IN MODUM CRUCIS BENEDICIT, NIHIL DICENS, ILLUDQUE IN TABERNACULO, ABSQUE ULTERIORE INCENSATIONE, RECONDIT ET CUM SUIS AD SACRISTIAM VEL CHORUM REDIT. IN MAIORIBUS ECCLESIIS INCHOATUR MATUTINUM, IN CUIUS FINE HYMNUS Te Deum SOLEMNISSIME CANTATUR; IN MINORIBUS CANTARI POTERIT CANTIO PASCHALIS: Surrexit Christus hodie, AUT ALIA CONVENIENS.

According to this version the *Elevatio* begins, before Easter Matins, with a procession, in which the monstrance containing the Host is carried from the *sepulchrum* through the length of the church to the main altar while the choir sings the hymn *Aurora coelum purpurat.* While the monstrance rests upon the main altar, it is censed, and a versicle (*Surrexit*), a response (*Qui pro nobis*), and a prayer are uttered. Still further, the hymns *Tantum ergo* and *Genitori* are sung, and a versicle and prayer are said. The priest now raises the monstrance, blesses the congregation with it, and places it in a tabernacle.

Once more, the conspicuous use of the monstrance at Salzburg seems to reflect the influence of the reservation of Holy Thursday in one of its relatively modern practices.

In the first version of the *Elevatio* considered in the present section of this study[34] we observed at least a hint of the theme of the Harrowing of Hell. A more substantial reference to this theme is present in the *Elevatio* from the cathedral of Strassburg. Of this *Elevatio*, and of the related *Depositio*, we have several texts; and since these texts vary among themselves in interesting matters of detail, I shall first present the documents, in their chronological order.[35]

A manuscript of the thirteenth century preserves both the *Depositio* and *Elevatio* in the following simple forms:[36]

---

[34] See above, pp. 30–31.

[35] I omit from consideration the texts printed by G. Milchsack (*Die lateinischen Osterfeiern*, Wolfenbüttel, 1880, pp. 122–123) as coming from "Ordo Wirceburgensis c. a. 1490." Lange (*Die lateinischen Osterfeiern*, pp. 8, 48) affirms that the book from which Milchsack quotes is a Strassburg "Agende" of the year 1513.

[36] London, British Museum, Additional MS 23922, Liber Responsalis Argentinensis saec. xiii, fol. 37^r, 41^v. The *Visitatio Sepulchri* from this manuscript (fol. 41^v–42^v) is printed by Lange, pp. 49–50. The *Depositio* and *Elevatio* are, I believe, now printed for the first time.

<DEPOSITIO HOSTIÆ>[37]

Et communicant omnes cum silentio. Deinde dum uadunt cum cruce ad locum Sepulchri, cantetur *Responsorium:*

Sicut ouis ad<occisionem ductus est, et dum male tractaretur non aperuit os suum; traditus est ad mortem, ut vivificaret populum suum>.
Versus: In pace factus est<locus eius, et in Sion habitatio ejus>,[38]

cum antiphona:

Antiphona: In pace in idipsum.
Antiphona: Caro mea.

Et presbytero nectente fila, cantetur *Antiphona:*

Sepulto domino<signatum est monumentum, ponentes milites qui custodirent illud>.[39]

<ELEVATIO HOSTIÆ>[40]

Priusquam[41] detur signum ad Matutinum, Sacerdotes lauent manus suas, et facta confessione, vadant ad Sepulchrum cum *psalmo:*

Domine, quid<multiplicati sunt>,[42]

et Antiphona:

Ego dor<mivi et somnum cepi, et resurrexi, quoniam Dominus suscepit me, alleluia, alleluia.>[43]

Recedendo dicatur *Antiphona:*

Cum rex *gloriae.*[44]

A more ample description of the ceremonial of the Strassburg *Elevatio* is found in the following text given by Martène from a manuscript of the fourteenth century:

<ELEVATIO HOSTIÆ>[45]

Priusquam detur signum ad Matutinum, conveniant in capellam S. Andreæ canonici, sacerdotes, & alii, & sacerdos indutus superpelliceo & desuper cappa, adjunctis lateribus suis duobus sacerdotibus cappatis,

---

[37] British Museum, Add. MS 23922, fol. 37ʳ.

[38] Responsory for the third nocturn in Matins on Holy Saturday. See Migne, *Pat. Lat.*, LXXVIII, 768.

[39] Antiphon from Lauds of Holy Saturday. See Migne, *Pat. Lat.*, LXXVIII, 769. My text is followed immediately by the rubric: Ad Vesperas.

[40] British Museum, Add. MS 23922, fol. 41ᵛ. This *ordo* for the *Elevatio* is written by a contemporary hand in the left margin.

[41] Through cutting away of the page, the reading of the first five letters of this word is rendered uncertain.

[42] Psalm iii.

[43] Third antiphon of Easter Matins. See Migne, *Pat. Lat.*, LXXVIII, 769.

[44] The marginal entry ends thus abruptly.

[45] E. Martène, *Tractatus de Antiqua Ecclesiæ Disciplina*, Lyons, 1706, pp. 504–505, from "Argentoratensis ecclesiæ Ordinarium ex veteri codice anno 1364 manu exaratum." Martène does not give a *Depositio* from this manuscript.

PRÆCEDENTE HEBDOMADARIO CAPPATO, CUM INCENSU & MAGNIS CANDELIS CONTORSIS, & LOTIS MANIBUS INTROEANT SEPULCHRUM. QUO INGRESSO, FACIANT CONFESSIONEM DICENDO: Confiteor Deo. Misereatur vestri. DEINDE DICATUR PSALMUS:

Domine, quid multiplicati sunt,

CUM ANTIPHONA:

Ego dormivi,

SUB SILENTIO PRONUNCIATA. TUNC SACERDOS ACCIPIAT CORPUS CHRISTI DE PIXIDE, & LEVANS IN ALTUM OSTENDAT ILLUD POPULO CORAM SEPULCHRO. POST OSTENSIONEM & ADORATIONEM POPULI, REPONAT IN PYXIDEM, & SIC TOLLENTES INDE CORPUS DOMINI, RECEDUNT CUM ANTIPHONA:

Cum rex gloriae,

SUB SILENTIO PRONUNCIATA. SED INTERIM IN CHORO CANITUR PRÆDICTA ANTIPHONA CANORA VOCE A CLERO, DEMISSOQUE IBI SUDARIO USQUE POST MATUTINAS. CUM AUTEM PERVENERINT IN CHORUM CUM CORPORE DOMINI, SACERDOS STET IN ALTARI, ET OSTENDAT CLERO & POPULO CORPUS CHRISTI, LEVANDO IPSUM SICUT SOLET LEVARI IN MISSA. DEINDE REPONAT IN PYXIDEM CORPUS CHRISTI, & PORTET AD ALTARE S. LAURENTII, & IBIDEM SIMILITER OSTENDAT. DIMISSOQUE IBI SACRAMENTO REVERTATUR IN CHORUM, LOTIS IBI PRIUS QUATUOR SUMMITATIBUS DIGITORUM SUORUM IN CALICE; STATIMQUE COMPULSANTUR OMNIA SIGNA.[46]

We may complete our presentation of the Strassburg texts with the series from an *ordinarium* of the year 1590.[47] The reservation on Holy Thursday of a Host for the *sepulchrum* is prescribed as follows:

<IN CŒNA DOMINI>

TRES QUOQUE HOSTIAE CONSECRENTUR HODIE, UNA PRO PRAESENTI MISSA, ALTERA PRO OFFICIO CRASTINO, TERTIA PRO SEPULCHRO DOMINI. SANGUIS AUTEM PENITUS CONSUMATUR. DENIQUE PARUAE HOSTIAE CONSECRANDAE HODIE SUNT, ET RESERUANDAE IN SEQUENTEM DIEM, PRO COMMUNICANDIS.[48]

The *Depositio* and *Elevatio* from the same document are ordered as follows:

The *Visitatio* from it is reprinted from Martène (p. 505) by C. Lange, in *Jahresbericht über die Realschule erster Ordnung in Halberstadt* (Program No. 223), Halberstadt, 1881, pp. 11–12.

[46] Followed immediately by the rubric: Ad Matutinum.

[47] *Agenda Ecclesiae Argentinensis* . . . , Coloniæ, 1590. I quote from the copy in the Hofbibliothek, Munich. All the texts now printed, together with the *Visitatio Sepulchri*, have been published by the present writer in *Transactions of the Wisconsin Academy of Sciences, Arts, and Letters*, XVI, Part II, 911–914. Lange duly mentions (*Die lateinischen Osterfeiern*, pp. 8, 50) the *Visitatio Sepulchri* in the print of 1590.

[48] *Agenda Ecclesiae Argentinensis* . . . , Coloniæ, 1590, p. 214.

<DEPOSITIO HOSTIÆ>[49]

COMMUNIONE[50] PERACTA, PROCEDAT SACERDOS AD SEPULCHRUM, CUM CORPORE DOMINI REPOSITO IN CORPORALI, UEL IN CALICE, UEL IN SACRATA PYXIDE. PRAECEDANT ERGO MINISTRI CUM INCENSO, ET DUO PUERI, CUM CANDELIS CUM PROCESSIONE, USQUE AD LOCUM SEPULCHRI, UBI DEBET RECONDI CORPUS DOMINI, CANTANDO RESPONSORIUM:

Sicut ouis ad occisionem ductus est, et dum male tractaretur non aperuit os suu*m*. Traditus est ad mortem, ut vivificaret populum suu*m*. VER*sus*: In pace factus est locus eius, et in Sion habitatio eius.

AN*tiphona*:

Caro mea requiescet in spe.

SACERDOTE NECTENTE FILA, CANTETUR HOC AN*tiphon*A:

Sepulto Domino, signatum est monumentum, ponentes milites qui custo<p. 226>dierunt illud.

STATIM LEGANTUR VESPERAE IN EODE*m* LOCO.

<ELEVATIO HOSTIÆ>[51]

ORDO VISITANDI SEPULCHRUM IN DIE SANCTO PASCHAE.

SUMMO MANE ANTEQUAM PULSETUR AD MATUTINAS CONVENIAT CLERUS, ET QUI UOLUERINT INTRARE SEPULCHRUM LAUENT MANUS SUAS, ET UENIANT ANTE PRINCIPALE ALTARE UEL PROPE SEPULCHRUM, ET LEGANT SEPTEM PSALMOS POENITENTIALES.<p. 252>QUIBUS FINITIS, DICANT:

Kyrie eleison. Christe eleison. Kyrie eleison.

Pater noster. Et ne nos inducas in tentatione*m*.

PRECES:

Exurge, Domine, adiuua nos. Et redime nos propter nomen tuum. Exurge gloria mea. Exurge psalterium et cithara. Exurgam diluculo. Confitebor in populis, Domine. Domine, exaudi orationem meam. Et clamor meus ad te ueniat.

Dominus vobiscum.

Et cum spiritu tuo.

Oremus:

ORATIO:

Exaudi, quaesumus, Domine, supplicum preces, et confitentium tibi parce peccatis ut pariter indulgentiam tribuas benignus et pacem. Per Christum Dominum nostrum.

DEINDE DICANT:

Confiteor Deo Patri, *et* Misereatur, *et* Indulgent, *etc.*

FACTA CONFESSIONE, UADANT AD SEPULCHRUM DICENDO PS*almum*:

Domine, quid multiplicati.

SEQUETUR AN*tiphon*A, QUAM CANTENT SUB SILENTIO:

Ego dormivi et somnum cepi, et exurrexi, quoniam Dominus suscepit me, alleluia, alleluia. Euouae.

---

[49] *Id.*, pp. 225–226.

[50] The Communion at the *Missa Præsanctificatorum.*

[51] *Agenda Ecclesiae Argentinensis* . . . , Coloniæ, 1590, pp. 251–252.

ET TOLLENTES INDE CORPUS DOMINI REDEANT IN CHORUM, CANTANDO SUBMISSA UOCE ANtiphonam:

> Cum rex gloriae Christus infernum debellaturus intraret et chorus angelicus ante faciem eius portas principum tolli praeciperet, sanctorum populus, qui tenebatur in morte captiuus, uoce lachrymabili clamauerat: Aduenisti desiderabilis, quem expectabamus in tenebris, ut educeres hac nocte uinculatos de claustris. Te nostra uocabant suspiriis; te larga requirebant lamenta. Tu factus es spes desperatis, magna consolatio in tormentis, Alleluia.

QUAE CONSUETUDO UBI FUERIT, SERVANDA ERIT. ET STATIM CUM REDIERINT IN CHORUM, OSTENSO SACRAMENTO IN ALTARI SICUT FIT IN MISSA, DEINDE CANTENTUR MATUTINAE.

With these several texts before us we may now examine some of the details of the Strassburg use. In liturgical content the two texts of the *Depositio* are substantially identical, and both are found between Mass and Vespers. According to the longer rubrics of the text of 1590, the Host[52] is carried to the *sepulchrum* in a corporal, a chalice, or a pyx, and the procession is provided with incense and lights. After the laying down of the Host, the sealing of the *sepulchrum* appears to be accomplished by the tying of chords.

For the details of the *Elevatio* we may center our attention upon the text from the fourteenth century communicated by Martène, because of its full indications as to ceremonial. The office occupies the usual liturgical position, before Easter Matins, and it opens with a familiar procession. It appears that the *sepulchrum* provided is of unusual amplitude, for at least a part of those in the procession are able to enter it. Those who enter make confession[53] and recite the psalm *Domine, quid multiplicati sunt*, with its antiphon *Ego dormivi*. The priest then takes the Host from the pyx and exposes it for the adoration of the congregation gathered before the *sepulchrum*. Replacing the Host in the pyx, the priest carries it in procession to the choir during the singing of the antiphon *Cum rex gloriæ*,

---

[52] In the *Depositio* in Add. MS 23922 the words *uadunt cum Cruce ad locum Sepulchri* raise a difficulty. They seem to indicate that the object buried was not the Host but the Cross, whereas the other Strassburg documents mention only the Host. The *Crux* of the passage quoted may be merely a *processional* cross.

[53] The liturgical text for the confession is more fully indicated in the *Elevatio* from the print of 1590.

and eventually exposes it to the congregation, both at the main altar and at the altar of St. Laurence.

We cannot assert that the treatment of the theme of the Harrowing of Hell in this version is notably developed. The antiphon *Cum rex gloriæ* presents the theme in vivid form, but the possibilities of the theme in the way of dialogue are approached only in certain more highly developed versions to be examined in later divisions of the present study.[54]

Waiving for the present, then, a further consideration of the *Decensus*, we come to a group of texts which are notable especially from the fact that the versions of the *Elevatio* are found in close combination with versions of the *Visitatio*. This phenomenon is clearly approached in the use of the cathedral of Parma. From this church we have particularly full *ordines*, of the year 1417, describing all the ceremonials of the *sepulchrum*. In the first place, the reservation, on Holy Thursday, of a Host for the *Missa Præsanctificatorum* and of one for the *Depositio* is provided for as follows:

<IN COENA DOMINI>

Et redit clerus ad Episcopum, qui Missam perficiat, reservatis duabus Hostiis consecratis, quae, finita Missa, in sacrario reverenter includantur.[55]

The *Depositio* occurs immediately after Mass of Good Friday, according to the following *ordo:*

<DEPOSITIO HOSTIÆ>[56]

Finita dicta Missa, descendant Dominus Episcopus cum Canonicis et toto clero ad cappellam Sanctae Agathae, et Corpus Christi quod est ibi reconditum cum ea processione modo et forma et solemnitate quibus portatum fuit, inde devote accipiatur, et reportetur, et in Paradiso post altare maius reverenter recondatur, ut in sepulcro, ibi dimisso lumine copioso per totam noctem duraturo, clericis cantantibus responsorium:

Sepulto Domino,

---

[54] See especially pp. 90–91, 111–118.

[55] *Ordinarium Ecclesiae Parmensis e vetustioribus excerptum reformatum A. 1417*, edited by L. Barbieri, Parma, 1866, p. 134. The passage quoted is preceded immediately by an *ordo* for the reservation of the Chrism.

[56] Barbieri, pp. 140–141.

Et cetera. Quo finito, dicuntur Vesperæ[57] ante ostium Paradisi[58] a Domino Episcopo et clericis suis genuflexis, submissis vocibus; et ipsis finitis, denudatur altare.

From this text it appears that the Host to be "buried" has been reserved in a chapel of the cathedral, from which it is carried, in a procession of the bishop and clergy, to a structure called *Paradisus* situated behind the main altar. Here the Host is deposited during the singing of the responsory *Sepulto Domino*. Vespers are then said before the door of the *Paradisus*, and lights are kept burning during the night.

The ceremony of the *Elevatio* is known to us only through a reference in the following text of the *Visitatio Sepulchri*:[59]

<ELEVATIO HOSTIÆ ET VISITATIO SEPULCHRI>[60]

In Matutino Paschae, hora quasi nona noctis pulsetur Baionus[61] solemniter cum aliis; ornetur altare solemnius quam ornari possit, et omnia luminaria ecclesiae, ut in Nativitate, accendantur. Ante inchoationem Matutini duo Guardachorii[62] et duo Cantores cum pivialibus Sepulcrum Domini reverenter intrant cum thuribulis et incenso, cereis ante Sepulcri ostium duobus positis. Et incensantes Sepulcrum[63] quaerunt de Corpore Christi, quod ante hunc actum Sacrista pervigil inde abstulisse debuit, et in sacrario deputato reverenter recondidisse, et palpant linteamina munda, quibus id erat involutum. Quod non invenientes, revertuntur ad ostium Sepulcri, foris tamen non euntes, sed versus altare maius iuxta quod sint aliqui Clerici dicentes:

Quem quaeritis?

Qui Clerici respondentes dicant:

---

[57] Vesperæ] Vesperi (Barbieri).

[58] The editor provides the following foot-note: Questo particolare non lascia dubbio che l'edificio, chiamato *Paradisus*, fosse chiuso; e così appunto esser dovea, vi grazia del nome attribuitogli, da poi ch' esso tanto vale quanto *hortus conclusus* (v. Isid. *Orig.* xiv, III, 1, 3).

[59] From Barbieri this text has been published by A. D'Ancona, *Origini del Teatro Italiano*, Vol. I, Turin, 1891, pp. 30–31; and from D'Ancona, by Lange, p. 28.

[60] Barbieri, pp. 147–149.

[61] *Baionus* is the name of a large bell—*campana grossa*. See Barbieri, p. 10.

[62] This word is explained by the following passage (Barbieri, p. 66): In Guardachoratus officio quatuor sint clerici instituti, qui moribus sint et discretione approbati, et cantus perfectione eruditi . . . istorum quatuor Guardachoriorum officio . . . totus chorus ecclesiae sublevatur atque regitur, et regi debet.

[63] Sepulcrum] sepulcro (Barbieri).

Iesum Nazarenum.

QUIBUS PRIMI RESPONDEANT:

Non est hic; surrexit sicut dixit,

ET CETERA. POSTEA EGREDIUNTUR SEPULCRUM ISTI QUATUOR, PRAEVIIS DICTIS CEREIS, ET DICUNT VERSUS POPULUM ANTIPHONAM:

Surrexit Christus; iam non moritur.

QUA FINITA MAIOR ILLORUM QUATUOR AD EPISCOPUM ACCEDIT SINE LUMINE, ET EI DICIT PLANE:

Surrexit Dominus,

ET OSCULATUR EUM. ET EPISCOPUS DICIT:

Deo gratias.

QUI EPISCOPUS ALTA VOCE DEINDE DICIT:

Te deum laudamus,

ET INCENSAT ALTARE, DICTIS DUPLERIIS ARDENTIBUS; ET DUM DICITUR Te Deum laudamus, ILLE QUI NUNTIAVIT DOMINO EPISCOPO CHRISTUM RESURREXISSE, SIMILITER NUNTIET DOMINIS CANONICIS. FINITO Te Deum laudamus INCIPIT DOMINUS EPISCOPUS: Domine, labia mea aperies.[64]

Concerning the *Elevatio* itself we have here merely a brief rubric directing the sacristan to remove the Host from the *sepulchrum* well before the beginning of Matins, and to secrete it reverently in the sacristy. As a whole, then, the text before us describes not the *Elevatio*, but the *Visitatio Sepulchri*, which seems to have been transferred, along with the *Te Deum*, from its usual place at the end of the Matins to the place preceding Matins usually occupied by the *Elevatio*. This version of the *Visitatio* is noteworthy in that those approaching the *sepulchrum* (representing, but not necessarily *impersonating*, the Maries) actually enter the *sepulchrum* in search of the *Corpus Christi*, and touch the *linteamina*, before they are challenged by the familiar interrogation *Quem quaeritis*. This bit of action may show the influence of the *Elevatio*, as may also the kiss bestowed upon the bishop by one of those who take part in the dialogue.[65]

Conditions somewhat similar to those at Parma are found in connection with the cathedral of Soissons, the *ordinaria* of which provide, in the first place, for the consecration on Holy Thursday of three Hosts as follows:

<IN CŒNA DOMINI>

SCIENDUM AUTEM QUOD DIE ISTA TRES HOSTIE PROPONANTUR IN ALTARI: I[a] PRO PRESENTI MISSA; II[a] PRO CRASTINA; III[a] RESERVETUR USQUE AD DIEM

[64] With this versicle begins Matins.

[65] Concerning the *Pax* in certain versions of the *Elevatio* see below, pp. 65–67, 88, 89, 97, 109.

RESURRECTIONIS. QUE DEFERANTUR A DIACONO AD SACRARIUM IN UASCULO QUOD DEPENDET SUPER ALTARE, UT IBI RESERVENTUR, CEREO ANTE ACCENSO.[66]

It will be observed that the third Host is reserved, not for burial in the *sepulchrum* on Good Friday, but for some ceremonial, not yet specified, on Easter. The object placed in the *sepulchrum* on Good Friday is not the Host, but the Gospel-book, as we learn from the following rubric:

FINITO EVANGELIO SUBDIACONUS ACCIPIAT ILLUD ET QUASI IN OCCULTO SUB INFULA SUA VELUT IN SINU SUO DEFERAT AD SEPULCHRUM, CLERICULO CUM THURE PRECEDENTE; IMPOSITOQUE SUPER ALTARE QUOD EST IN SEPULCHRO, AMBO REUERTANTUR.[67]

The *ordo* of Good Friday provides in no way for a burial of a Host.

A special form of the *Elevatio* appears in the *ordo* for Easter Matins:[68]

<ELEVATIO HOSTIÆ ET VISITATIO SEPULCHRI>[69]

SUMMO DILUCULO PULSENTUR OMNIA SIGNA; DEIN BINA ET BINA. AD ULTIMUM UERO TUM SIMUL ITERUM PULSENTUR. PAUIMENTUM INTEREA TOTIUS PRESBYTERII ET CHORI EDERA ET ALIJS UIRIDIBUS FOLIJS STERNATUR. ECCLESIA PRETEREA, CEREIS ACCENSIS, A CAPITE USQUE AD PEDES PER CIRCUITUM UESTIATUR. ALTARE SACROSANCTUM AMPLIFICATO NUMERO CEREORUM LUMINE CIRCUMDETUR. NUMERUS UERO CEREORUM CIRCA ALTARE ET ANTE SIT LXXXXa, ET UNUS FUNICULUS INSUPER A CAPITE USQUE AD PEDES PRETENDATUR; IN QUO CIRCULUS QUIDAM FERREUS HABENS VII CEREOS SUPER OSTIUM SEPULCHRI IN ALTUM DEPENDEAT. CIRCULUS AUTEM ISTE QUI ET STELLA A NOBIS NUNCUPATUR, UERUM LUCIFERUM, QUI MANE RESURREXIT, DESIGNAT. ADHUC AUTEM X CEREI AD CRUCIFIXUM ACCENDANTUR. IN INITIO UERO OMNIUM ISTORUM CUNCTUS[70] CLERICUS DEFERAT CUM SUMMO HONORE AD SEPULCHRUM IN SUPERPELLICIO CORPUS DOMINICUM IN UASCULO A DIE CENE RESERUATUM, PONENS ILLUD SUPER ALTARE.

HIS PERACTIS, DUOBUS SACERDOTIBUS ANTIQUIORIBUS AC DUOBUS DIACONIS IN CHORO SEDENTIBUS CUM CAPIS DE PALLIO, PONTIFEX IN SEDE SUA CUM CAPA DE PALLIO MITRATUS STANS INCIPIT:

---

[66] *Rituale seu Mandatum insignis ecclesiae Suessionensis*, Soissons, 1856, pp. 68–69. The manuscript (saec. xii–xiii) is described on pp. vii–x.

[67] *Rituale . . . ecclesiae Suessionensis*, Soissons, 1856, p. 86.

[68] This *ordo* is printed by Martène (pp. 496–498) from a "Rituale vetus tempore Nivelonis II episcopi scriptum" (*i.e.*, 13th century). From Martène, Lange (p. 26) reprints, with very unfortunate omissions. Martène's text and that now reprinted from the edition of 1856 differ only in unimportant details.

[69] *Rituale . . . ecclesiae Suessionensis*, Soissons, 1856, pp. 108–110.

[70] cunctus] cunctos (*Rituale*).

Domine, labia mea aperies. Deus in adiutorium.

. . . . [71]

Quo[72] finito, cum Gloria, iterum incipiant ipsum Cantor et Succentor r<esponsorium>: Dum transisset.

Tunc eat processio ad Sepulchrum sic. Pueri primum ferentes tintinabula, alij cum uexillis. Dein candelabra, thuribula, cruces quatuor. Subdiaconus in albis hos sequatur. Duo presbyteri cum capis de pallio, ceteri quoque in ordine suo. Ad ultimum Episcopus cum baculo pastorali et mitra et capa de pallio, cum ipso uero capellanus. Et cum peruentum fuerit ad Sepulchrum, inueniantur ibi preparati duo Diacones albis simplicibus, capitibus amictis coopertis, niueis dalmaticis superindutj. Hij in similitudinem angelorum ad fenestram stantes Sepulchri, unus ad dexteram, alius ad sinistram, uoce humilima et capitibus inclinatis uersisque ad Sepulchrum:

Quem queritis in sepulchro, o Xpisticole?

Duo Presbyteri predicti cum capis de pallio in loco Mariarum:

Ihesum Nazarenum crucifixum, o Celicole,

Duo Diaconi angeli:

Non est hic; surrexit sicut predixerat; ite, nuntiate quia surrexit.

Presbyteri qui et Marie dicuntur uoce altiori respondeant:

Alleluya, resurrexit Dominus hodie, resurrexit leo fortis, Xpistus filius Dei; Deo gracias dicite eya.

Tunc Capellanus de Sepulchro ab intus in superpellicio stans porrigat Diaconis uasculum cum Corpore Dominico, et statim pulsentur tintinnabula et omnia signa ecclesie. Cantor autem incipiat:

Xpistus resurgens<ex mortuis iam non moritur; mors illi ultra non dominabitur, alleluia, alleluia.>[73]

Tunc extendat uelum quoddam super Corpus Dominicum a Subdiaconis quatuor; cerei quoque cum uexillis, thuribulis, et crucibus precedant. Presbyteri nempe predicti, acceptis thuribus, conducant illud semper incensantes, unus a dexteris et alius a sinistris, stella predicta semper duce. Quo deportato a Diaconis honorifice et super altare oblato, ferra circa altare claudatur; finitaque antiphona superiori, Xpistus resurgens, Episcopus in sede sua stans iussu Cantoris incipiat:

Te Deum laudamus.

Qui dum cantatur a choro, duo maiora signa tantummodo pulsentur. Interea vexille, cruces, cerei, thuribula cum tintinnabulis sonantibus ante altare morentur.

Finito Te Deum, iterum omnia signa pulsentur. Incensum quoque illud quod a Presbyteris Dominico Corpori offertur, ab ipsis Episcopo,

---

[71] Here I omit the usual liturgical routine of the Roman type of Easter Matins. See *Publications of the Modern Language Association*, Vol. XXIV (1909), p. 310, note 2.

[72] This refers to the third responsory of Matins.

[73] Antiphon at the *Communio* of the Mass of Wednesday in Easter Week. See Migne, *Pat. Lat.*, LXXVIII, 679.

CANTORI, ET SUCCENTORI, ET OMNIBUS PRESBYTERIS IN CHORO DEFERTUR. DEIN A CLERICULIS CETERIS DEPORTETUR.

The ceremonial here described begins early on Easter morning, before Matins. The choir is strewn with green branches, the altar and church are profusely lighted, a crown of seven candles is suspended over the door of the *sepulchrum*, and ten candles are lighted at the Crucifix.[74] Meanwhile the Host reserved from Holy Thursday is for the first time brought to the *sepulchrum* and placed upon the altar.[75] In so far as this act represents a *Depositio*, it is obviously inappropriate to Easter morning.

After the third responsory of Matins of the usual Roman type[76] occurs an office in which the *Elevatio* and *Visitatio* are combined. When the procession reaches the *sepulchrum*, two deacons in appropriate vestments, representing angels, utter the angelic challenge *Quem quaeritis*, and continue the familiar dialogue with two priests vested in copes. Then occurs the *Elevatio*. A chaplain,—apparently from within the *sepulchrum*,—hands to the deacons (*angeli*) the Host while the choir sings the antiphon *Christus resurgens*. After the Host has been deposited upon the main altar within the choir, and after the iron rail about the altar has been closed, the *Te Deum* is sung. During the singing of the *Te Deum* the bells are sounded, and the Host and altar are censed.[77]

---

[74] Possibly this crucifix is located at the door between choir and nave.

[75] As to the location of this altar with respect to the *sepulchrum*, I am uncertain. Since the *sepulchrum* seems to be capacious enough to allow the entrance of a *capellanus*, the structure may take the form of a chapel, with an altar within.

[76] See the note to the text above.

[77] For its information concerning the symbolic use of incense in Easter Matins I quote from the Soissons *Rituale* (pp. 110–111) a passage that immediately follows the text of the *Visitatio* printed above:

Notandum uero quod ad similitudinem trium Mariarum, incensum hodie ad Sepulchrum tantum defertur in initio lectionum sic: Incepto Euangelio, Decanus et Ebdomadarius exeant de Sacrario cum Capis de pallio, Clericulis precedentibus cum Thuribulis et igne; presententque se Episcopo in igne mittentes incensum, Episcopo dante benedictionem. Quo facto, eant simul ad altare. Episcopus autem accipiens Thuribulum, offerat incensum sacrosancto altari et Decanus cum illo. Interea Clericuli, elevatis Cereis suis, teneant illos ante altare. Quo facto, Episcopo in sede sua regresso, offerant incensum Decanus et Ebdomadarius. Postea cum Cereis eant ad Sepulchrum illud offerre,

In this version from Soissons we encounter for the first time an intimate combination of *Visitatio* and *Elevatio;* and we must observe at once that the combination is not entirely successful from the point of view of dramatic sequence. Nothing is clearer logically than that the *Elevatio* should *precede* the *Visitatio.* The *Quem quaeritis* dialogue, with its *Non est hic,* obviously implies an empty *sepulchrum.* In the present version, however, the implication is false, for the *Corpus Dominicum* is not removed from the sepulchre until *after* the delivery of dialogue mentioned.

In connection with this dialogue it is important to observe also that whatever of impersonation is present in the version before us attaches itself to the *Visitatio* element and not to the *Elevatio.* In the *Elevatio* is found no such rubric as that prescribing the impersonation of the angels at the supposedly empty tomb: *Duo Diacones albis simplicibus, capitibus amictis coopertis, niueis dalmaticis superinduti . . . . in similitudinem angelorum.*[78]

Similar to this version from Soissons, in some respects, is the following, from the cathedral of Laon:[79]

<ELEVATIO HOSTIÆ ET VISITATIO SEPULCHRI>[80]

In Pascha ad Matutinas due compane insimul pulsantur; sex cerei juxta magnum cereum ante altare ponuntur. Dum campane pulsantur, processio ante altare in hunc modum ordinata vadit ad Sepulchrum. Precedunt clericuli cum cereis, duo cum thuribulis, duo diaconi, alii duo cantaturi Dicant nunc, cantor, et succentor, omnes isti albis capis induti. Alii sequuntur in ordine, unusquisque cereum accensum deferens. Predicti vero diaconi ad ostium Sepulchri venientes incipiunt:

Ardens est <cor meum, desidero videre Dominum meum; quaero et non invenio ubi posuerunt eum, alleluia.>[81]

Clerico custode cum Capa de pallio acerram cum incenso perferente. Quo facto, reuersi in Chorum, Cantori et Succentori, ceterisque in ordine suo defertur. Processione presenti peracta, uicem secundam impleuimus, in fine Matutinarum, Tertiam exsoluemus. V. post *Te Deum*. Episcopus. *Surrexit Dominus uere.* Chorus. *Et apparuit Symoni. Alleluya.*

[78] See below, pp. 128–129.

[79] U. Chevalier, *Ordinaires de l'Église Cathédrale de Laon* (Bibliothèque Liturgique, VI), Paris, 1897, pp. 118–119, from Laon MS 215 of the period 1173–1249. From Laon we have no text of a *Depositio.*

[80] Chevalier, pp. 118–119.

[81] Antiphon of Easter season. See Migne, *Pat. Lat.*, LXXVIII, 775.

Clericulus in Sepulchro:

Quem queritis.

Diaconi:

Jhesum Nazarenum.

Clericulus:

Non est hic.

Quo finito Sacerdos alba casula vestitus, portans calicem cum Corpore Xpisti, egrediens de Sepulchro repperit ante ostium quatuor clericulos pallium super baculos tollentes; et illo protectus incedit ante processionem, precedentibus clericulis cum cereis, astantibus aliis duobus juxta ipsum cum thuribulis. Tunc diaconi predicti dicunt:

Surrexit Dominus vere, alleluia.

Post hec cantor et succentor incipiunt illam partem antiphone:

Cum rex glorie Xpistus.[82] Advenisti desiderabilis.

Et sic cantando procedunt omnes in medio ecclesie ante Crucifixum. Post antiphonam:

Christus resurgens<ex mortuis iam non moritur, mors illi ultra non dominabitur, quod enim vivit, vivit Deo, alleluia, alleluia>,

duo canonici cum capis versum:

Dicant nunc<Judæi quomodo milites custodientes sepulchrum perdiderunt regem ad lapidis positionem, quare non servabant petram justiciæ; aut sepultum reddant aut resurgentem adorent, nobiscum dicentes alleluia, alleluia.>

Post v<ersum>processio, cantando Quod enim vivit, vivit Deo, intrat chorum. Sacerdos calicem super altare deponit. Interim campane insimul pulsantur.[83]

This ceremonial occurs before Matins. The procession sets out from the main altar, and when it reaches the door of the *sepulchrum*, two deacons in the procession sing the antiphon *Ardens est*. A cleric within the *sepulchrum* now sings the interrogation *Quem quaeritis*, and continues the familiar dialogue with the two deacons of the procession. Then a priest issues from the sepulchre carrying a chalice containing the Host,[84] which is carried in procession to a place before the Crucifix,[85] appropriate persons meanwhile singing *Surrexit Dominus* and *Cum rex gloriæ*. At the Crucifix is sung the antiphon *Christus resurgens*, after which the priest places the chalice upon the main altar.

---

[82] Xpistus] Xpiste (Chevalier).

[83] Matins follows immediately.

[84] Such is a fair, but not an inevitable, interpretation of the rubric *portans calicem cum Corpore Christi*. See above, pp. 14, 16.

[85] Possibly this Crucifix is at the entrance to the choir from the nave.

It will be observed that in the combining of *Elevatio* and *Visitatio* this version is not essentially different from that of Soissons. Once more the *Visitatio* inappropriately precedes the *Elevatio*.

Another text of this office from Laon appears as follows:[86]

<ELEVATIO HOSTIÆ ET VISITATIO SEPULCHRI>[87]

IN DIE PASCHÆ AD MATUTINUM DUÆ MAGNÆ CAMPANÆ DE MIRACULIS INSIMUL PULSANTUR. PROCESSIO VADIT AD SEPULCRUM ORDINATA IN MODUM QUI SEQUITUR. PRIMO PRÆCEDIT CLERICULUS AQUAM BENEDICTAM DEFERENS; HUNC SEQUUNTUR DUO CLERICULI FERENTES INSIGNIA, DUO ALII CLERICULI FERENTES CEREOS, DUO ALII CLERICULI CAPPIS SERICIS INDUTI FERENTES DUAS CRUCES AUREAS; HOS SEQUUNTUR CLERICULI. DEINDE CANTOR & SUCCENTOR CAPPIS SERICIS INDUTI, PORTANTES BACULOS DEARGENTATOS IN MANIBUS. DEINDE DUO DIACONI SIMILITER CAPPIS SERICIS INDUTI, & QUATUOR SUBDIACONI CANONICI ALBIS TUNICIS INDUTI, PALLIUM SUPRA BRACHIUM TENENTES. HOS SEQUUNTUR ALII COMBINATI, UNUSQUISQUE CEREUM ACCENSUM DEFERENS. PRÆDICTI VERO DIACONI AD OSTIUM SEPULCRI VENIENTES INCIPIUNT:

Ardens est.

CLERICULUS STANS IN SEPULCRO RESPONDET:

Quem quaeritis?

DIACONI:

Jesum Nazarenum.

CLERICULUS:

Non est hic.

POSTEA CANTOR & SUCCENTOR INCIPIUNT:

Surrexit Dominus vere, alleluia.

DEINDE PROSAM:[88]

Victimæ paschali laudes.

ET SIC CANTANDO PROCEDUNT ANTE CRUCIFIXUM IN MEDIO ECCLESIÆ, SACERDOS ALBA CASULA VESTITUS, PORTANS CALICEM CUM CORPORE CHRISTI, EGREDIENS DE SEPULCRO REPERIT ANTE OSTIUM QUATUOR SUBDIACONOS, ALBIS TUNICIS INDUTOS, PALLIUM SUPER BACULUM TOLLENTES, & ILLO PROTECTUS INCEDIT IN FINE PROCESSIONIS, PRAECEDENTIBUS DUOBUS CLERICULIS CUM CEREIS, & ALIIS DUOBUS JUXTA IPSUM CUM THURIBULIS. DUM AUTEM PROCESSIO PERVENERIT IN MEDIO ECCLESIÆ CANTOR & SUCCENTOR INCIPIUNT R<ESPONSORIUM>:

Christus resurgens.

---

[86] Martène, pp. 478–479, from a "vetus ordinarium optimæ notæ, ante annos 400 scriptum." We may date this manuscript, then, about the year 1300. It may be observed that Martène's text does not differ substantially from the text indicated by the erasures and marginal entries in Laon MS 215 used by Chevalier. See Chevalier, p. 118. A mutilated reprint of Martène's text is given by Lange, p. 30.

[87] Martène, pp. 478–479.

[88] prosam] psal. (Martène).

Duo Diaconi cantant v<ersum>:
Dicant nunc.
Quo cantato processio intrat chorum cantando:
Quod enim vivit.
Sacerdos calicem super altare deponit. Interim campanæ simul pulsantur. Episcopus stans in cathedra mitra & cappa præparatus incipit: Domine, labia mea aperies.[89]

This text differs from the preceding one only in details, such as a more extended *ordo* for the procession to the *sepulchrum* and the substitution of the sequence *Victimæ paschali* for the antiphon *Cum rex gloriæ*.

For our knowledge of the ceremonial of the *sepulchrum* at Laon, however, we are not confined to these texts from the *ordinaria*. This cathedral was fortunate in having as dean, about the middle of the seventeenth century, Antoine Bellotte, a liturgiologist of the first order.[90] In his monumental volume *Ritus Ecclesiæ Laudunensis*[91] this author describes the dramatic office of Easter morning as follows:[92]

---

[89] With this formula Matins begins.

[90] He was dean from 1650–1662. See Chevalier, pp. vii–viii.

[91] Paris, 1652.

[92] Bellotte, pp. 215–217. The same author provides also (p. 819) a shorter description of this office as follows:

Vtrumque solet Ecclesia Laudunensis obire, dum summo mane paulo post medium noctis pulsantur in ea campanæ pro singulari festiuæ exultationis signaculo; & circa horam diluculi, conueniunt omnes in Ecclesiam candido apparatu, quibus statim cerei diuiduntur, quibuscum procedunt ad altare sepulcri, vbi fores occlusæ, & sanctissimum Corporis, & Sanguinis Dominici sacramentum in altari repositum, locum monumenti referunt. Et dum ibidem celebratur statio, Puer Choralis adheret altari agens personam Angeli sedentis in sepulchro, dicens: *Quem quæritis?* Respondentibus autem duobus Diaconis: *Iesum Nazarenum*, ipsemet Puer symphoniacus subjungit: *Non est hic.* Mox Cantor & Succentor cappis sericis & baculis choralibus accincti incipiunt: *Surrexit Dominus vere, etc.*, & statim præ lætitia in jubilum erumpentes intonant hymnum *Victimæ Paschali laudes immolant Christiani;* & sine mora aperiuntur fores sepulcri, e quibus Christus egreditur quippe conditus in sepulcro, cum sub mortis imperio captiuus ess<e> videretur, quasi præruptis inferni tepagulis, liber ad vitam rediit, iuxta illud quod ab Ecclesia canitur, *Hodie portas mortis & seras pariter Saluator noster disrupit.* Tandem procedunt omnes per circuitum, & mediam nauim Ecclesiæ ad Crucifixum cum cereis ardentibus in quibus lux est vitæ, & resurrectionis symbolum, de quo in Pentecostario Graecorum: *Prodeamus cum lampadibus obuiam Christo ex monumento prodeunti, tanquam sponso, & simul cum ordinibus Angelorum hac solemnitate lætantibus festum agamus.*

Inter antiquissimas Ecclesiæ Christianæ consuetudines annumeratur processio, quæ solemni ritu, quotannis celebratur in Dominica Resurrectionis ante Matutinum, quo tam salutaris mysterij gaudium, aliquo lætitiæ signo, fidelibus populis nuntietur. Hinc est, quod in Ecclesia Laudunensi summo mane pulsantur campanæ hora post mediam noctem secunda in signum festiuæ exultationis, priusquam detur signum Matutini. Quo tempore custos Sacrarij, vel alius Sacerdos ad hoc deputatus, superpellicio & stola paratus, accedit ad locum Pastophorij[illegible] præeuntibus duobus clericulis cum cereis ardentibus, & inde sanctissimum Sacramentum reuerenter & cum debitis genuflexionibus extrahit, vbi pridie fuerat ritu præscripto collocatum; ipsumque ambabus manibus tenens ob oculos eleuatum, defert super Altare Sepulchri, vndique cereorum sufficienti numero collustratum, vt locus lucidior appareat, & nox ipsa quasi dies illuminetur; nullusque Sæcularium illuc accedit, nec vllus alius præter Clericos qui dicti Sepulchri ritibus & ceremonijs inseruire debent, ac qui proinde fuerint chorali veste parati.

Hora vero quarta matutina conueniunt in Ecclesiam omnes de Clero, Episcopus, vel Decanus, aut Sacerdos Hebdomadarius in Sacrarium, cum ijs qui futuræ processioni debent inseruire. Canonici vero Chorum intrant, in albis, hoc est, superpelliceis, armilauzis parati, vbi stant in subsellijs, vsque ad initium præfate processionis. Celebrans & ministri parantur vestimentis albi coloris, ordini suo congruentibus; vbi Celebrans & duo ex senioribus Sacerdotibus Canonicis induunt planetam Subdiaconi vero pallium; seu baldachinum delaturi tunicas sine manipulis. Mox erogantur cerei singulis Canoncis & alijs de gremio Ecclesiæ per Custodes Laicos, tam in Choro, quam in Sacrario, dignioribus primo, subinde junioribus per ordinem, eodem ritu quo in festo, seu processione Purificationis Beate Mariæ, quos singuli deferre debent in honorem sanctissimi Sacramenti toto tempore processionis.

His vt supra dispositis, accenduntur prædicti cerei per ministros ecclesiæ, qui candelam accendunt primi cujusque ordinis ab vtraque parte Chori, vt cæteri deinde sibi mutuo candelas suas accendant; & dato signo procedendi, duo Diaconi pluuialibus induti procedunt de Sacrario in Chorum, cum alijs ministris, hoc ordine. Præcedunt duo Acolythi deferentes candelabra cum cereis accensis, tum duo Clericuli, qui Cruces aureas deferunt processionales. Has sequuntur duo prædicti Diaconi pluuialibus induti; deinde Præcentores cappis & baculis choralibus accincti; postremo quatuor Subdiaconi tunicis albi coloris induti, qui hastas pallij seu baldachini deferre debent, omnes ex ordine Canonicorum. A dextris & a sinistris eorum incedunt ab vtraque parte omnes de choro, primo Pueri chorales, deinde Mansionarij & Capellani; postea Canonici secundum ordinem antiquitatis vel dignitatis; ita tamen, vt discedentes a subselliis dexteræ partis, migrent in sinistram; & qui stant a sinistra transeant ad dexteram, suas quinque candelas ita deferentes propriis manibus, vt qui procedunt a dextris, dextra; qui vero a sinistris, sinistra deferant paululum ad extra inclinatas.

Probably the most significant aspect of this passage is the symbolizing of the opening of the *sepulchrum* as the Harrowing of Hell.

[illegible] The *pastophorium* is some sort of sacristy, which, as we learn below, is on the left side of the choir.

Proceditur autem per speciosam portam chori, recta per mediam nauim versus Sepulchrum, quo peruenientes qui deferunt baldachinum, seu pallium, consistunt ante ostium præfati Sepulchri, facie versa ad Altare, in quo existit sanctissimum Sacramentum, stantibus in eadem regione seu præcinctu Ecclesie, omnibus de choro vultibus ad inuicem conuersis dum Celebrans transit de Sacrario in Sepulchrum per aditum secretiorem, a duobus praedictis seniorbus Canonicis comitatus qui velum in modum gremialis ipsum deferunt, sequentibus eos duobus Thuriferariis, cum thuribulis igne tantum refertis. Quo cum perueniunt, Celebrans statim genuflectit in infimo gradu Altaris ante sanctissimum Sacramentum, cæteris post eum in plano genuflexis, vbi aliquantulum orant dum prædicti duo Diaconi, stantes ad ostium Sepulchri, cantant insimul, *Ardens est*. Quo decantato Clericulus juxta dictum Sepulchrum stans in abscondito, respondet eodem tono, *Quem quaeritis*. Tum duo supradicti Diaconi, iterum cantant *Iesum Nazarænum;* ad quos idem Clericulus dicit vt supra cantando, *Non est hic*. Mox Præcentores incipiunt, *Surrexit Dominus vere, alleluya*. Deinde sequitur immediate Prosa *Victimæ Paschali laudes*, quam prædicti Præcentores similiter incipiunt. Tunc Celebrans surgit, curatque incensum imponi in thuribulum; deinde genuflexus ad oram suppedanei, triplici ductu incensat sanctissimum Sacramentum cum debitis inclinationibus; & reddito thuribulo, accedit ad Altare, vbi iterata genuflexione sumit reuerenter sanctissimum Sacramentum, ambabus manibus tenens ante faciem eleuatum.

Sumpto vt supra sanctissimo Sacramento, Celebrans descendit in planum Sepulchri, & inde incipit procedere pallio feu baldachino protectus, præcedentibus eum prædictis duobus senioribus Canonicis prædictum velum hinc & inde ferentibus. Mox duo Thuriferarij cum thuribulis igne & incenso refertis, recessim incedentes, incensant continuo sanctissimum Sacramentum, ac eodem tempore incedunt omnes de Clero nudo capite, æquali passu, parem inter se mutuo seruantes distantiam, cauentes præcipue ne vltimi, plus justo distent a sanctissimo Sacramento. Proceditur autem circumcirca ecclesiam a prædicto loco Sepulchri vsque ad majorem porticum versus Occidentem, & ab eo per mediam nauim, in qua sistit processio per modum stationis ante Crucifixum, vbi Præcentores incipiunt responsorium *Christus resurgens;* cujus versum cantant duo prædicti Diaconi pluuialibus induti, cum quibus omnes de Choro genuflectunt sanctissimo Sacramento ad ipsum conuersi, ad hæc verba, aut *Resurgentem adorent nobiscum dicentes*.

Sub finem prædictæ stationis, dum repetitur a choro pars prædicti Responsorij, processio intrat Chorum, vbi omnes a subselliis iterum genuflexione adorant sanctissimum Sacramentum eo tempore quo transit per medium Chori. Et cum Celebrans ascendit gradus Altaris, sistunt qui baldachinum seu pallium deferunt, et statim illud a medio collocant a latere juxta Pastophorium a sinistra parte Presbyterij, donec officio completo remoueatur per custodem sacrarij. Thuriferarij vero peruenientes ad infimum gradum Altaris, secedunt paululum ab utraque parte, viam præbentes Celebranti, qua per medium eorum transire possit, et tunc cessant a thurificatione, ac ibidem in plano genuflexi, cum prædictis duobus senioribus canonicis in infimo gradu altaris genuflectentibus, sanctissimum Sacramentum adorant. Celebrans interim ascendit ad altare, vbi stans conuertit se statim ad Chorum sanctissimum Sacramentum tenens, vt prius, ante faciem eleuatum, omnesque simul cum eo benedicit, signum Crucis cum debita mora producens; attolit enim Sacramentum paulatim, vsque dum pars illa calicis quem ambabus manibus tenet respondeat oculis, ac eodem modo demittit infra pectus; deinde ad humerum sinistrum ducit, & ad dextrum reducit; iterumque ad pectus; et post breuem morulam versus cornu Euangelij conuertit se ad altare, nihil dicens, stantibus interim omnibus de Choro, qui a subsellijs suis summo silentio et profundissima inclinatione totius corporis sanctissimum Sacramentum adorant.

Circulo facto, Celebrans deponit SS. Sacramentum super altare conuertens imaginem Hostiæ ad Chorum, & facta genuflexione, descendit ad oram suppedanei, vbi genuflexus sumit thuribulum, in quod incensum curat imponi absque benedictione, quo triplici ductu incensat sanctissimum Sacramentum cum debitis inclinationibus; et reddito thuribulo, surgit omnibus etiam surgentibus; mox signans se in ore pollice dexteræ manus, relictis digitis extensis, alta voce Matutinum incipit dicens, *Domine labia mea aperies.*

Although Bellotte may have based this description upon the very text quoted above from an *ordinarium* of about the year 1200,[94] he adds, from authorities not specified, some information not available elsewhere. In the first place, he explains the presence of the Host in the *sepulchrum*. It appears that at two o'clock, before Matins, on Easter morning the Host is removed from the sacristy (*pastophorium*), in which it had been deposited on the preceding day, and is placed upon the brilliantly lighted altar of the *sepulchrum*. This act may be regarded as in some way a substitute for the *Depositio*,—a substitute similar to that employed in the cathedral of Soissons. Unlike the use of Soissons, however, the Laon ceremony separates the *Depositio* from the subsequent *Visitatio-Elevatio*, not by the singing of Matins, but only by a vacant interval of some hours. At Laon, in other words, the two ceremonials, the quasi-*Depositio* and the *Visitatio-Elevatio*, both occur *before* Matins. In liturgical content the dramatic office described by Bellotte is essentially similar to that reported by Martène. Bellotte, however, provides fuller ceremonial details for the procession and for the adoring and censing of the Host at the main altar.

Although the ceremonials of Laon are highly elaborated, their elaboration is brilliantly exceeded in the dramatic observances from the famous *Liber Sacerdotalis* printed in 1523 under

---

[94] See above, pp. 49–50; Chevalier, p. xii.

the editorship of Alberto Castellani.[95] The *Depositio* from this book takes the following form:

<DEPOSITIO HOSTIÆ>[96]

DE PROCESSIONES IN FERIA VI IN PARASCEUE AD PONENDUM CORPUS *Domini in* SEPULCHRO.

FERIA VI IN PARASCEUE POST OFFICIUM MISSE, VEL ETIAM POST PRANDIUM, ORDINATUR SOLENNIS SED LUGUBRIS PROCESSIO. PARATUR ENIM SACERDOS OMNIBUS PARAMENTIS ET PLUUIALI DESUPER CUM DIACONO ET SUBDIACONO *cum* DALMATICIS NIGRI COLORIS. PARANTUR ETIAM *qua*TUOR SACERDOTES, VEL DUO AD MINUS, INDUTI CAMISIIS NIGRIS *cum* AMICTU ET CINGULO EIUSDE*m* COLORIS; SI *habe*RI POSSUNT ALIOS, IN ALBIS PARANTUR ETIAM DUO ALII SACERDOTES, VEL UNUS TANTUM UBI PAUCI FUERINT SACERDOTES, *cum* AMICTU, ALBA, CINGULO, MANIPULO, ET STOLLA ET DUO THURIFERARII IN ALBIS. PREPARETUR ETIAM FERETRUM A *qua*TUOR PORTANDUM CUM SUPERIORI COOPERTURA IN MODUM SEMICIRCULI, ET COOPERIATUR ALIQUO PANNO NIGRO DE SERICO, SI HABERI POTERIT, IN QUO SACRAMENTUM DEPORTETUR. PARANTUR ETIAM LUMINARIA: SCILICET INTORTITIA ET CEREI AD<FOL. 263^v>ILLUMINANDUM CORPUS CHRISTI. ET CONGREGATO POPULO, SACERDOS ACCIPIT REUERENTER SACRAMENTUM DE ALTARI ET TENENS ILLUD IN MANIBUS VERSUS AD POPULUM, OMNIBUS ALIIS GENUFLEXIS, IPSE STANS INCIPIT *Responsorium:* Plange, CETERIS PROSEQUENTIBUS:

> Plange quasi virgo, plebs mea; ululate, pastores, in cinere et cilicio; quia venit dies Domini magna et amara valde. DUO CLERICI CANTENT VERSUM:[97] Accingite vos, sacerdotes, et plangite; ministri altaris aspergite vos cinere. Quia.[98]

COMPLETO *Responsorio cum versu* ET REPLICA, DUO SACERDOTES APPARATI CUM STOLLIS VT SUPRA STANTES ANTE SACRAMENTUM VERSIS VULTIBUS AD POPULUM CANTENT VERSUM: Popule me<us>, OMNIBUS ALIIS PRETER EUM QUI FACIT OFFICIUM GE<FOL. 264^r>NUFLEXIS ET *versis* VULTIBUS AD SACRAMENTUM:

---

[95] *Liber Sacerdotalis nuperrime ex libris Sancte Romane Ecclesie et quarumdem aliarum ecclesiarum et ex antiquis codicibus . . . collectus*, Venetiis, 1523. Concerning the several editions of this work and its liturgical history see R. Dörner, *Die Auferstehungsfeier am Charsamstag nach dem Sacerdotale Romanum*, in *Caecilien-Kalender*, Jahrgang X (1885), pp. 27–36. From an edition not precisely indicated, Dörner (pp. 32–35) reprints the *Elevatio-Visitatio*. He provides also (p. 32) a brief description of the *Depositio*. I reprint both texts from the edition of 1523. It should be observed that Castellani compiled this book from the uses of other localities than Rome, and that no edition of the work received complete papal approval (See Dörner, pp. 29–30). The texts here reprinted were communicated to me by my friend Dom G. M. Beyssac, of Quarr Abbey.

[96] *Liber Sacerdotalis*, 1523, fol. 263^r–269^v.

[97] versum] *printed twice*.

[98] Third responsory in Matins of Holy Saturday. See Migne, *Pat. Lat.*, LXXVIII, 768.

Popule meus, quid feci tibi, aut in quo contristaui te? responde mihi. quia eduxi te de terra Egypti, parasti crucem saluatori tuo.

Dicto versu predicto, chorus genuflexus vt supra cantet:

Sanctus Deus, sanctus fortis, sanctus et inmortalis, miserere nobis.

Hoc dicto, Sacerdos ponat Corpus D*omi*ni reuerenter in Feretro quod portabunt qu*a*tuor Sacerdotes predicti, vel duo vbi paucitas Sacerdotum est, in albis parati, capitibus amicto coopertis, et incepto *Responsorio:* Recessit pa<stor>, procedit processio isto ordine: Primo acoliti cum cereis accensis et cruce; postea Clerici, iunioribus *responsorio;* vltimo duo Sacerdotes parati qui cantauerunt: Popule meus. Post ipsos sequitur Feretrum cum Corpore D*omi*ni portatum a quatuor vel duobus, vt supra; et super Sacramentum baldachinum nigrum portetur ab aliquibus personis magis dignis. Ex latere sint duo acoliti cum turribulis, qui continuo Sacramentum incensabunt circum; circa sint luminaria et intortitia. Post Feretrum sequitur Sacerdos cum pluuiali et<fol. 264^v>Dyaconus et Subdiaconus; et vltimo seculares, maioribus precedentibus. Processione isto modo ordinata procedunt cum deuotione quousque dicta fuerit replica post *versum Responsorii*, quem *versum* dicent duo Clerici, et idem seruetur in aliis *Responsoriis* sequentibus. *Responsorium:*

Recessit pastor noster, fons aque viue ad cuius transitum sol obscuratus est; nam et ille captus est qui captiuum tenebat primum hominem. Hodie portas mortis et seras pariter saluator noster dirupit. *Versus:* Destruxit quidem claustra inferni et subuertit po<fol. 265^r>tentias dyaboli. Nam et.[99]

Finita replica post *versum*, firmetur processio, et omnes flectant genua, exceptis illis qui portant Feretrum et duobus Sacerdotibus qui cantauerunt Popule meus, qui stantes versis vultibus[100] ad populum omnibus aliis genuflexis ha<ben>tibus vultos suos ad Feretrum conuersos cantent *versum:* Quia eduxi; et hoc quidem seruetur in *omnibus* sequentibus stationibus. *Versus:*

Quia eduxi te per desertum quadraginta annis et manna cibaui te, et introduxi in terram satis optimam, parasti crucem saluatori tuo.

Chorus:

Sanctus Deus, vt supra.

Quo dicto, surgant omnes et incipiatur *Responsorium:* Ecce uidimus, et procedatur ad secundam stationem cantando *Responsorium* totum usq*ue* in finem cum *versu* et replica. Responsorium:

Ecce vidimus eum non habentem speciem neque decorem; aspectus <fol. 265^v> eius in eo non est; hic peccata nostra portauit, et pro nobis dolens; ipse autem vulneratus est propter iniquitates nostras, cuius liuore sanati sumus. *Versus:* Vere languores nostros ipse tulit, et dolores nostros ipse portauit. Cuius.

---

[99] Fourth responsory in Matins of Holy Saturday. See Migne, *Pat. Lat.*, LXXVIII, 768.

[100] vultibus] vulbentibus (Print).

OMNIBUS GENUFLEXIS DUO SACERDOTES STANTES VT PRIUS[101] DICANT VERSUM:

Quid vltra debui facere tibi, et non feci? Ego quidem plantaui te vineam meam spe<fol. 266r>ciosissimam; et tu facta es mihi nimis amara; aceto namque sitim meam potasti, et lancea perforasti latus saluatori tuo.

CHORUS:

Sanctus Deus, TOTUM DICITUR VT SUPRA.

SURGENTIBUS OMNIBUS INCIPIATUR *Responsorium:* Hierusalem, ET PROCEDATUR AD TERTIAM STATIONEM VT SUPRA.

Responsorium:

Hierusalem luge et exue te vestibus iocunditatis induere cinere et cilicio; quia in te occisus saluator Israel. *Versus:* Deduc quasi torrentem lachrymas per diem, et no<fol. 266v>cte non taceat pupilla oculi tui. Quia in.[102]

OMNIBUS UT PRIUS GENUFLEXIS, DUO SACERDOTES STANTES DICANT *Versum:*

Ego propter te flagellavi Egyptum cum omnibus primogenitis suis; et tu me flagellatum ad crucifigendum cum latronibus tradidisti.

CHORUS:

Sanctus Deus, VT SUPRA.

QUO DICTO OMNES SURGANT ET INCIPIATUR *Responsorium;* Calligauerunt, ET PROCEDAT PROCESSIO AD QUARTAM STATIONEM QUE FIAT CIRCA INGRESSUM ECCLESIE REDEUNDO ANTE SEPULCHRUM. RESPONSORIUM:

Calligauerunt oculi mei a fletu meo, quia elongatus est a<fol. 267r> me qui consolabatur me. Videte, omnes populi, si est dolor similis sicut dolor meus. *Versus:* O vos omnes qui transitis per viam, attendite et videte. Si est.[103]

OMNIBUS VT PRIUS GENUFLEXIS DUO SACERDOTES PREDICTI STANTES CANTENT *Versum* VT SUPRA:

Ego dedi tibi sceptrum regale, et tu meo capiti coronam spineam; ego te exaltaui magna virtute, et tu me suspendisti in patibulo crucis.

FINITO VERSU CHORUS CANTET:

Sanctus, TOTUM VT SUPRA: Sanctus Deus.

DICTO Miserere nobis, SACERDOS CUM REUERENTIA ACCIPIAT CORPUS *Domini* DE FERETRO ET ILLUD IN MANIBUS ELEUATUM TENEAT CONUERSUS AD POPULUM ET VERSIS RENIBUS<FOL. 267V>AD SEPULCHRUM. TUNC DUO CLERICI GENUFLEXI CANTENT VERSUM: Cum autem venissent, ET RELIQUOS INFRA NOTATOS:

Versus: Cum autem venissent ad locum ubi crucifigendus erat filius meus, statuerunt eum in medio omnis populi, et vestibus expoliatis, nudum dimiserunt corpus sanctissimum.

Versus: O dulcissime filie Syon, o dulcissime, videte dolorem meum. Inspicite nudum in medio omnis populi filium meum dulcissimum; vulneratus est in medio eorum.

---

[101] prius] primus (Print).

[102] Second responsory in Matins of Holy Saturday. See Migne, *Pat. Lat.*, LXXVIII, 768.

[103] Responsory in Matins of Good Friday. See Migne, *Pat. Lat.*, LXXVIII, 767.

1 V*ersus:* Cum vero venissent ad locum ubi sepeliendus erat filius meus, statuerunt eum in medio mulierum; et syndone inuoluentes sepultum dimiserunt corpus sanctissimum.

2 V*ersus:* O vos omnes qui transitis per viam, venite et videte si est dolor sicut meus; desolata sum nimis; non est qui consoletur me; salus mea infirmata est; vita occiditur et a me tollitur.

3 V*ersus:* O nimis triste spectaculum, o crudele supplitium impensum filio, o<fol. 268^{r}>felix rex tam indecenti morte coronatus, pontifices iniquitatis tantum ne in vestrum exardescitis Deum?

4 V*ersus:* Attendite vos, o populi et uniuerse plebes, dolorem maximum: morte turpissima mactauerunt filium meum. Vos optime sorores, flete vna mecum; de filio conqueramur.

5 V*ersus:* Cum vero deposuissent corpus Iesu de cruce, statuerunt illud in gremio matris sue, in medio mulierum amarissime flentium, mestissima matre filium nimis deplorante.<fol. 268^{v}>

Cantatis predictis V*er*sibus vel eorum parte, Sacerdos eleuatis manibus cum Corpore Christi in modum crucis benedicat populum et cum reuerentia illud ponat in Sepulchro, et ipsum claudat et sigillo suo signet. R*esponsorium:*

Sepulto Domino signatum est monumentum, voluentes lapidem ad hostium monumenti, ponentes milites qui custodirent illum.<Versus>: Ne forte veniant discipuli eius et furentur eum et dicant plebi: Surrexit a mortuis.

Finito R*esponsor*io predicto, duo Clerici dicant V*ersum:*

In pace factus est locus eius.

R*esponsio:*

Et in Syon habitatio eius.

Et Sacerdos, sine Dominus vobiscum vel Oremus, dicat absolute orationem:

Respice, quesumus, D*omi*ne, super hanc familiam tuam pro qua D*omi*nus noster Iesus Christus non dubitauit manibus tradi nocentium, et crucis subire tormentum.

Et non dicat Qui tecum, nec respondeatur Amen. Et sic terminetur processio.

Si processio debet fieri prolixior et in ea plures mansiones seu stationes fieri oporteat, finito R*esponsorio* Caligauerunt cum V*er*su et aliis que sequuntur, repetatur aliquod R*esponsorium* de predictis cum suo V*er*su et aliis que sequuntur, ita quod R*esponsorium*, Sepulto, vltimo loco reseruetur quando Corpus Domini ponitur in Sepulchro.<fol. 269^{r}>

Supra posita processio more Veneto fit infrascripto ordine. Paratis omnibus vt supra in precedenti processione, notatum est loco R*esponsorii*, Plange, incipitur a duobus Clericis genuflexis An*tiphon*a, Venite et ploremus, in cantu vt inferius notatum est. Postmodum totus chorus surgens dicat V*ersum*, Popule, vt supra. Quo finito illi duo Clerici qui cantauerunt Venite et plo<remus>, cantant V*ersum* Quia edu<xi>, et chorus repetit V*ersum* Popule. Item duo clerici dicant V*ersum* Ego propter te fla<gellaui>, et chorus repetit V*ersum* Popule. Et sic alternatim dicantur Improperia pro vt supra signatum est in Adoratione Crucis.

FO. 258. VEL IPSA IMPROPERIA CANTANTUR IN SEXTO TONO PSALMORUM. ET CUM IN DICTA PROCESSIONE FIERI DEBET ALIQUA STATIO SEU MANSIO, OMNES GENUFLECTANT ET ILLI DUO CANTENT AN*tiphonam* Venite et, VT SUPRA. QUA DICTA SURGANT OMNES ET SEQUANTUR PROCESSIONEM CANTANDO V*ersum* Popule, ET IMPROPERIA, VT SUPRA. CUM AUTEM PERUENERINT AD SEPULCHRUM FACIANT OMNIA VT SUPRA IN PRECEDENTI PROCESSIONE. <fol. 269^{v}>

Venite et ploremus ante Dominum, qui passus est pro nobis dicens.[104]

According to this *ordo* the *Depositio* is performed either after the *Missa Præsanctificatorum* or later, after dinner. The procession is made especially impressive through the use of a bier (*feretrum*) and a canopy (*baldachinum*). The ceremonial begins with the priest's taking the Host reverently from the altar at the singing of the responsory *Plange quasi virgo*. At the conclusion of the responsory two priests begin the Improperia (*Popule meus*),[105] to which the choir responds (*Sanctus Deus*). The priest places the Host on the bier, over which a canopy is held, and beside which are carried thuribles and lights. The procession to the *sepulchrum* is made in four stages, each stage having its processional responsory. At each station the two priests already mentioned sing a verse of the *Improperia*, to which the choir makes a response. The fourth station occurs before the *sepulchrum*, where, after a final verse of the *Improperia*, followed by the *Miserere*, the priest takes the Host from the bier and holds it aloft before the congregation while two clerics kneeling sing a series of *versus*. The priest now blesses the congregation with the Host and reverently places it in the *sepulchrum*. During the singing of the responsory *Sepulto Domino* he closes the *sepulchrum* and seals it. The office closes with a versicle, a response, and a prayer.

More significant than the splendor of this procession is the use of the *Improperia*, borrowed directly from the traditional *Adoratio Crucis* of the *Missa Præsanctificatorum*. The presence of this liturgical element is definitive proof of the influence of the *Adoratio* upon the *Depositio*.[106] Particularly noteworthy also is the use of the *feretrum* for bearing the *Corpus Christi* to

---

[104] The last word is written twice, with varying musical notation. It will be observed that this antiphon (*Uenite et . . . dicens*) is referred to above, on fol. 269^{r} of the print. The last word *dicens* is followed immediately by a rubric beginning: Sabbato Sancto.

[105] See above, pp. 20–29.

[106] See above, pp. 20–29.

the *sepulchrum*. It will be observed, however, that with all its careful construction and elaboration, this dramatic office contains no impersonation, and hence stops short of true drama.

No less striking in its content is the combined *Elevatio* and *Visitatio* from the same compilation of Castellani:

<ELEVATIO HOSTIÆ ET VISITATIO SEPULCHRI>[107]

DE PROCESSIONE IN NOCTE PASCHE ANTE MATUTI<NUM> AD SEPULCHRU*m* CHRIS*ti*.

DIE S*an*CTO RESURRECTIONIS CUM FUERIT PULSATUM AD MATUTI<NUM>, ANTEQ*uam* POPULUS INTRET ECCLESIAM, SACERDOS CUM CRUCE ET THURIBULO APPARATUS SUPERPELLICEO, STOLLA, ET PLUUIALI, PRECEDENTIBUS CEREIS ACCENSIS ET SEQUENTE TOTO CLERO CUM REUERENTIA, APERTO SEPULCHRO ACCIPIAT CORPUS DOMINI ET PORTET ILLUD IN LOCO SACRARII UBI SACROSANCTUM SACRAMENTUM SERUARI CONSUEUIT. ET INTERIM CHORUS CANTET SEQUENTES P*salmo*S VEL ALIQUEM EORUM:

Ps*almus:* Domine, quid multiplicati sunt qui tribulant me. . . . . et super populum tuum benedictio tua. Gloria patri et filio et spiritui sancto.[108]

Ps*almus:* Domine, probasti me et cognouisti me. Supra fo. 160.

Ps*almus:* Miserere mei, Deus, miserere mei, quoniam in te confidit anima mea. .<fol. 275^{v}>. . et super omnem terram gloria tua. Gloria patri et filio et spiritui sancto.[109]

FINITIS PSALMIS, SACERDOS, PRECEDENTIBUS CEREIS ET THURRIBULO, CORPUS DOMINI PORTET AD SANCTUARIUM SUUM, SEQUENTE CLERO ET CANTANTE R*esponsorium* Surrexit pastor; SEPULCHRUM PATENTER DIMITTATUR APERTUM. R*esponso*RIUM:

Surrexit pastor bonus qui animam suam postuit pro ouibus suis, et pro suo grege mori dignatus est, alleluia, alleluia, alleluia. V*ersus:* Surrexit Dominus de sepulchro, qui pro nobis pependit in ligno.<fol. 276^{r}> Et pro suo grege.[110]

TUNC SACERDOS FACIENS OFFICIUM STANS CUM SACERDOTIBUS IN CHORO DICIT V*ersum*:

Surrexit D*ominu*s vere, alleluia.

R*esponsio*:

Et apparuit Simoni, alleluia.

Oremus.

---

[107] *Liber Sacerdotalis*, 1523, fol. 275^{r}–278^{v}.

[108] Ps. iii. I omit the body of the psalm, giving only the beginning and ending.

[109] Ps. lvi. I omit the body of this psalm.

[110] Responsory for Matins of Thursday in Easter Week. See Migne, *Pat. Lat.*, LXXVIII, 773.

Oratio:

Omnipotens semipiterne Deus, qui hac sacratissima nocte cum potentia tue maiestatis resurgens portas inferni confregisti, et omnibus ibi detentis dexteram tue misericordie porrexisti, scilicet miserando diucius penis estuantis Gehenne cruciatis quos dudum ad ymaginem tuam creasti, quesumus nos indigni et vltima pars creature tue vt per gratiam tue miserationis ac per sancte resurrectionis tue amorem necnon omnium sanctarum animarum quas hac sacratissma nocte de penis inferni ad celestia regna perduxisti, simulque per omne mysterium quod in resurrectione tua celebrasti, nobis indignis ac fragilibus omnium peccatorum nostrorum indulgentiam largiri digneris atque iram et furorem et indignationem .tue vindicte a nobis repellas, et auxilium, consolationem, ac protectionem in omnibus peccatis, periculis, ac infirmitatibus animarum et corporum nobis concedas; et sicut corpus tue humanitatis, quod ad tempus pro nostra salute exuisti post triduum tue maiestatis potentia resuscitasti, ita corpora et corda nostra ab omnibus vicijs emundari et animas nostras in futura resurrectione beatorum spirituum cetibus facias aggregari. Qui cum patre et *cetera*.

In memoriam et laudem gloriose resurrectionis tue hymnum dicat tibi omnis creatura tua, Domine; et nos quamuis peccatores et dilinquentes hymnum dicimus et gratias agimus, venerandamque crucem tuam adoramus sanctamque resurrectionem tuam laudamus et glorificamus, quoniam per te redempti sumus; ideoque crucifixum Dominum laudamus, et sepultum propter nos magnificamus, resurgentemque a mortuis adoramus et petimus vt per te et sanctam resurrectionem tuam nos a morte animarum nostrarum resuscitare digneris. Qui cum patre.

Oratio:

Domine Iesu Christe, propter hoc gaudium quod tu cum sanctissima anima tua et corpore in tua sancta resurrectione <fol. 276v> voluisti habere cum omnibus fidelibus tuis iustis et peccatoribus viuentibus et mortuis miserere nobis, sicut vis et scis necessitates animarum et corporum; et da nobis spacium penitentie, et veram compunctionem, emendationem, omnium peccatorum nostrorum; et presta nobis, Iesu Christe, vt precium corporis et sanguinis tui cum quo nos in sancta cruce redemisti, percipiamus ad salutem animarum nostrarum in nouissima hora, et quod spiritalem unctionem spiritalis olei et salutaris cum omni affectu cordium et corporum percipiamus. Qui cum patre et spiritu sancto viuis ac regnas in vnitate, et *cetera*.

Orationibus finitis Sacerdos Corpus Domini reuerenter thurificet.

Dum predicte orationes dicuntur duo Diaconi parentur cum dalmaticis albis et in ecclesia remaneant. Sacerdos autem paratus vt supra cum toto clero exeat per portam ecclesie minorem, maiori porta clausa relicta, et veniant ad portam maiorem ecclesie cantando *Responsorium:* Dum transisset sabbatum; et cum illuc peruenerint, Sacerdos accedit ad portam clausam; clerus circumstat eum. Responsorium:

Dum transisset sabbatum Maria Magdalene, Maria Iacobi, et Salome emerunt aromata, ut venientes vngerent Iesum, alleluia, al <fol. 277r>

leluia. *Versus:* Et valde mane una sabbatorum veniunt ad monumentum, orto iam sole. Ut venientes. Gloria patri et filio et spiritui sancto, alle<luia>.

Et dum peruenerint ad fores ecclesie, completo *Responsorio* cum *versu* et replica, Plebanus vel Sacerdos paratus pulsat ad ostium manu vel cum cruce dicens sonora voce in tono lectionis:

Attollite portas principes vestras, et eleuamini porte eternales, et introibit rex glorie.

Et pro ista prima pulsatione illi deintus nihil respondent. Et facto modico interuallo, Sacerdos iterum vehementius pulsat ad ostium dicens voce altiori in tono lectionis:

Attollite portas prin<cipes>, et *cetera*.

Et illi deintus nihil respondent. Et tunc Sacerdos, modico interuallo facto, iterum in eodem tono sed altius quam secundo pulsans fortiter ostium ecclesie dicit:

Attollite portas pri*n*cipes, et *cetera*.

Tunc illi Dyaconi deintus statim cantando respondent:

Quem queritis in sepulchro, Christicole?

Et illi de foris respondent:

Iesum Nazarenum<fol. 277v>crucifixum, o Celicole.

Et iterum illi deintus respondeant:

Non est hic, surrexit sicut predixerat; ite, nuntiate quia surrexit a mortuis.

Hoc finito, qui deintus sunt aperiant portam ecclesiae, et omnes ingrediantur. Et iterum dicant qui deintus erant:

Venite et videte locum vbi positus erat Dominus, alleluia, alleluia.

Et cum fuerint portam ingressi, firment se omnes et diuidant per choros. Tunc Plebanus vadat ad Sepulchrum et ponat caput in fenestra Sepulchri; et postea conuersus ad populum dicat voce mediocri:

Surrexit Christus.

Chorus respondeat:

Deo gratias.

Quo dicto, Plebanus procedat aliquantulum versus populum, et exaltet vocem altius quam primum et dicat:

Surrexit Christus.

Chorus respondeat:

Deo gratias.

Iterum tertio Plebanus procedat versus populum aliquantulum, et exaltata voce adhuc altius quam se*cun*do fecerat et dicat: <fol. 278r>

Surrexit Christus.

Chorus respondeat:

Deo gratias.

Quo facto omnes procedant ad Sepulchrum et faciant choros hinc et inde. Tunc Plebanus vadit ad ostium Sepulchri et statim retrocedat versus chorum et det pacem primo Sacerdoti seu Clerico vel Domino terre, si ibi fuerit, et dicat voce submissa:

Surrexit Dominus.

ET ILLE RESPONDEAT:

Deo gratias.

DEINDE OMNES SIBI MUTUO DENT PACEM DICENTES:

Surrexit Dominus.

ET ILLE CUI PAX DATUR RESPONDEAT:

Deo gratias.

POSTMODUM VADANT OMNES AD ALTARE BEATE VIRGINIS PROCESSIONALITER, ET CORAM ALTARI GENUFLEXI SACERDOTE INCIPIENTE *antiphonam* Regina celi, EAM TOTAM CANTENT PRO GAUDIO RESURRECTIONIS FILII SUI DOMINI NOSTRI.

ANTIPHONA:

Regina celi letare, alleluia,
Quia quem meruisti portare, alleluia,
Resurrexit sicut dixit, alleluia.
Ora pro nobis Deum, alleluia. <fol. 278v>

V*ersus*:

Ora pro nobis, Sancta Dei Genitrix, alleluia.

R*esponsio*:

Ut digni efficiamur promissionibus Christi, alleluia.

Oremus:

ORATIO:

Deus, qui per unigeniti filii tui Domini N*ost*ri Iesu Christi resurrectionem familiam tuam letificare dignatus es, presta, quesumus, vt per eius venerabilem genitricem virginem Mariam perpetue capiamus gaudia vite. Per eundem Christum.

Oremus:

ORATIO:

Gratiam tuam, quesumus, Domine, mentibus nostris infunde, vt qui angelo nunciante Christi filii tui incarnationem cognouimus, per passionem eius et crucem ad resurrectionis gloriam perducamur. Per eundem Christum Dominum.

HIS FINITIS REUERTANTUR AD CHORUM ET CANTENT MATUTINAS.

This dramatic office occurs before Easter Matins, and the raising of the Host is accomplished before the arrival of the laymen.[111] During the singing of psalms by the choir, the priest opens the *sepulchrum* and takes up the *Corpus Domini*. Then while the choir sings the responsory *Surrexit pastor*, the priest carries the Host to the sacristy, where after a versicle, response, and prayer, it is given its final censing.

The clergy now proceed to a ceremony inspired by the theme of the Harrowing of Hell. While two deacons remain within the church, the priest and other clerics pass in procession to a position outside the closed central door, the processional

[111] One should note, however, the presence of the *populus* during the later parts of the office.

responsory being *Dum transisset.* The priest, or a *plebanus,* now strikes the door with his hand, or with a cross, saying *Attollite portas.* This is done three times. After each of the first two strikings follows an interval of silence. To the third challenge the two deacons within the church respond with the interrogation *Quem quæritis?* Now follows the usual dialogue of the *Visitatio Sepulchri,* at the conclusion of which the door of the church is opened. At the invitation of the two deacons (*Venite et videte*) the *plebanus* peers through the window of the *sepulchrum,* and then turning to the choir utters the *Surrexit Christus,* the choir responding *Deo gratias.* After this versicle and response have been repeated twice, and after the Kiss of Peace has been given, the whole congregation moves from the *sepulchrum* to the altar of the Blessed Virgin, where the office closes with an antiphon, a versicle and response, and prayers.

It may fairly be said that this version consists of three distinct parts: (1) the *Elevatio,* (2) a representation of the *Descensus ad inferos,* and (3) a *Visitatio Sepulchri.* These parts, however, do not occupy positions equally independent. Whereas the *Elevatio* may be said to stand by itself, the other two divisions are amalgamated in a somewhat conspicuous manner, and this amalgamation cannot be considered completely successful. Although the action of this part of the office is smooth, the incongruity of the themes is not surmounted. The *Quem quæritis* dialogue, implying the visit of the Maries to the empty tomb, is inappropriately used in a representation of the yielding of the gates of Hell.

Although in describing this ceremony I have used the word "representation," it should be observed that since the text presents no evidence of impersonation, we are dealing, once more, not with a true play, but with a dramatic office.

Finally one other detail in the version before us calls for comment: the *Pax,* or Kiss of Peace. It may be that this part of the ceremonial shows the influence of a certain practice prescribed as a prelude to Easter Matins by some of the oldest of the *Ordines Romani.* Thus in the *Ordo* of St. Amand, representing the liturgy of about the year 800, we read the following:[112]

[112] Duchesne, p. 471, from a manuscript of the ninth century.

In ipsa nocte sancta Resurrectionis, post gallorum cantu surgendum est. Et dum venerint ad ecclesiam et oraverint, osculant se invicem cum silentio. Deinde dicit *Deus in adjutorium meum*.[113]

In this case the celebration is very simple, consisting merely in the saying of prayers and in the Kiss of Peace. A similar observance is seen in the following from *Ordo Romanus I:*

In ipsa nocte post gallorum cantum, matutino irrumpente luce tenebras, surgentes in ecclesia veniunt, & mutua caritate se invicem osculantes dicunt: *Deus in adjutorium meum*.[114]

The same tradition is found outside Rome in such a passage as the following:[115]

In crastino su*mm*o diluculo ueniunt studiose om*nes* in eccl*es*iam & mutua pace inuice*m* se osculantes dicunt:

Surrex*it* Xp*istuc*.

Re*sponsio:*

Gaudeam*us* om*nes*.

Deinde:

D*omi*ne labia mea.[116]

It will be observed, however, that none of the observances just cited is explicitly associated with the *sepulchrum*. Such association is seen in the following:[117]

Dum classis pro officio nocturno pulsatur, duæ candelæ in Sepulcro ponantur, & ceroferarii mittantur ad Archiepiscopum, qui veniens indutus cappa serica alba ante Sepulcrum dicat:

Confiteor, &c.

Deinde intrans, facta oratione, Sepulcrum osculatur & altaria. Inde vero exiens Decanum osculetur. Postea intrans in chorum, ceroferariis præcedentibus, & stans inter Cantores in medio choro dicat:

Resurrexit Dominus,

& cantor respondeat:

Et apparuit Petro,

---

113 With the words *Deus in adjutorium meum* Matins begins.

114 Mabillon, II, 28. More extensive Roman ceremonials for early Easter morning, including the *Pax*, have been introduced above, pp. 27–29.

115 Udine, Biblioteca Arcivescovile, Graduale Ratisbonense saec. xi, fol. 1r. This manuscript of seventy-one folios has no shelf-mark in the Udine library. For the text now published I am indebted to my friend Dom G. M. Beyssac, of Quarr Abbey, Isle of Wight. To Dom Beyssac I am deeply grateful for many generous services in connection with the present study.

116 With these words begins Easter Matins.

117 Martène, p. 503, from an *Ordinarium Viennense*, of uncertain date.

& dat ei osculum pacis; similiter & alii Cantori. Alii Clerici ordinate idem faciunt ad Sepulcrum; & sic fiat quando Archiepiscopus agit officium, & quando ejus vicarius pro eo illud facit, hoc modo fiat. Primo Cantores induti cappis sericis albis, deinde vicarius Archiepiscopi accedentes ad Sepulcrum in introitu portæ genibus flexis Cantores stent, vicarius intret in Sepulcrum, & facta oratione, veniat ad portam, & dicat Cantoribus:

Resurrexit Dominus.

Cantores respondeant:

Et apparuit Petro.

Postea intrent omnes in Sepulcrum deosculando altaria. Deinde nocturnum officium incipitur.

It may be, then, that the use of the *Pax* in such observances as these is the source of the *Pax* in the *Elevatio-Visitatio* from the *Liber Sacerdotalis* of Castellani, and elsewhere.[118]

With the versions of Castellani we may appropriately associate those in use in the eighteenth century in the Church of St. Mark at Venice.[119] The characteristic elements seen in the texts of Castellani persist at Venice two centuries later. The *Depositio* of St. Mark's is prescribed as follows:

<DEPOSITIO HOSTIÆ>[120]

PROCESSIO AD SEPULCHRUM

POST PRANDIUM, HORA CONSUETA, IMMEDIATE POST PRÆDICATIONEM, FIT SANCTISSIMI SEPULCHRI CHRISTI PROCESSIO HOC MODO, VIDELICET. IN PRIMIS PRÆPARENTUR IN CANONICA SEXAGINTA INTORITIA ALBA A SEX MAGNIS SCHOLIS, DECEM PRO QUALIBET IPSARUM DISTRIBUENDA. QUIBUS ACCENSIS, DISCEDUNT PRIMO DECEM EX SCHOLASTICIS SCHOLÆ SANCTI THEODORI, CUM PRÆDICTIS INTORTITIIS ACCENSIS, & VENIENTES IN CHORUM VERSUS ALTARE MAJUS, VADUNT BINI & BINI PER MEDIAM CHORI PORTAM, QUÆ EST APUD SERENISSIMI PRINCIPIS SEDEM. ET SIC DEVOTE SUCCEDUNT ALII DECEM SCHOLÆ SANCTI ROCCHI. DEINDE ALII DECEM SCHOLÆ MISERICORDIÆ. POSTEA ALII DECEM SCHOLÆ SANCTI JOANNIS EUANGELISTÆ. DEINDE ALII DECEM SCHOLÆ CHARITATIS. POSTMODUM CLERUS SANCTI MARCI. POST QUEM SUCCEDUNT DUO CANTORES <p. 278> CHORI. DEINDE QUATUOR JUVENES PRESBYTERI CAMISIIS NIGRIS & STOLIS VIOLACEIS PECTORI TRANSVERSATIS INDUTI, QUATUOR CEREOS PARVOS

---

[118] See below, pp. 88, 89, 97, 109.

[119] *Officium Hebdomadæ Sanctæ secundum consuetudinem Ducalis Ecclesiæ Sancti Marci Venetiarum* . . . , Venice, 1736 (British Museum), pp. 277–282, 345–349. The *Elevatio* and *Visitatio* from this book have been reprinted by Lange, in *Zeitschrift für deutsches Alterthum*, XLI, 78–80. So far as I know, the *Depositio* has not previously been brought into relation with the drama.

[120] *Officium Hebdomadæ Sanctæ* . . . *Sancti Marci* . . . , Venice, 1736, pp. 277–282. The present text is preceded immediately by the rubric: Et sic Missa cum Vesperis terminetur.

accensos portantes. Postea quatuor Clerici dalmaticis nigris induti, thuribulum & navicellas cum incenso deferentes. Deinde quatuor Canonici cum dalmaticis velluti nigri, Feretrum cum Sanctissimo Christi Corpore deferentes. Postmodum duo alii juvenes Presbyteri camisiis nigris & stolis violaceis pectori transversatis induti, cereos majores accensos portantes. Et cum Sanctissimum Christi Corpus est super sacrarii portam, omnibus flectentibus genua, cantores canunt *Versum*:

Venite, & ploremus ante Dominum, qui passus est pro nobis, dicens:

Quo decantato omnes surgunt, & cantorum turba ad omnes pausas respondet *Versum:*

Popule meus, quid feci tibi? aut in quo contristavi te? responde mihi.

Versus:

Quia eduxi te per desertum quadraginta annis, & manna cibavi te, & inroduxi te in terram optimam.

Versus:

Aceto namque[121] sitim meam potasti, & lancea perforasti latus Salvatori tuo. <p. 279>

Postea exit e sacrario Reverendus Vicarius, seu qui facit Officium, cum pluviali & stola velluti nigri. Hunc sequuntur alii decem Scholastici Scholæ Sancti Marci. Deinde Scutiferi & Secretarii cereolos, quos apud portam chori in capsellis præparatos, & accensos ad hoc invenerint, deferentes. Postremo sequitur Serenissimus Princeps cum Illustrissimo Dominio. Et cum pervenerit subter porticum Palatii Clerus ordinate a quinque scholarum prædictarum scholasticis, partim a dextris & partim a sinistris comitetur. Sit autem subter Palatii porticum umbella nigra præparata cum sex Subcanonicis pluvialibus samiti nigri indutis, & ipsam umbellam delaturis. Cum pervenerit igitur Sanctissimi Corporis Christi Feretrum, ipsum subter umbellam magna cum reverentia recipiatur, & sic ad sanctam processionem devote procedatur, stantibus semper apud duas ultimas hastas umbellæ duobus ex honorabilibus Scholasticis Scholæ Sancti Marci. Post Feretrum sequitur Reverendus Vicarius, deinde Scutiferi, Secretarii, <p. 280> Magnus Cancellarius, & Serenissimus Princeps cum Illustrissimo Dominio. Cumque fit prima pausa ad Petram Banni, omnes flectant genua, & Cantores canent *Versum:*

Venite, <&>ploremus,

ut supra. Quo decantato, omnes surgunt. Et Cantorum turba respondente versum:

Popule meus,

ut supra, talis ordo per totam processionem servari debeat. Secunda pausa fit per mediam portam Ecclesiæ Sancti Marci, omnibus genua flectentibus &, ut supra, canendo. Tertia pausa fit per mediam portam Sancti Bassi, similiter flectendo genua & canendo, ut supra. Cum autem omnes scholæ in templum pervenerint, faciant chorum, prima apud portam majorem ecclesiæ, caeterisque taliter se disponentibus, ut ultima sit apud Sanctissimum Christi Sepulchrum collocata. Restitutisque ab

[121] namque] nanque (Print).

omnibus ad portam majorem ecclesiæ cereolis, Scutiferi & Secretarii ascendunt chorum per portam quæ ducit apud Serenissimi Principis sedem. Sed Clerus totus vadit contra Sanctissimum Christi Sepulchrum. Ad quod cum Sanctis<p. 281>simum Christi Corpus pervenerit, Serenissimus Princeps cum Illustrissimo Dominio sistit se. Reverendusque[122] Vicarius cum Tabernaculo in manibus stat super Sepulchri aram, & omnibus genua devote flectentibus, Cantores canunt *versum:*

> Cum autem venisset ad locum ubi crucifigendus erat filius meus, statuerunt eum in medio omnis populi, & vestibus expoliatis, nudum dimiserunt corpus sanctissimum.

Quo decantato, dictus Reverendus Vicarius cum Tabernaculo, more solito dat suam sanctam benedictionem. Deinde reverenter deposito Sanctissimo Christi Corpore in Sepulchro, Magnus Cancellarius recepto prius a Serenissimo Principe annulo, ipsum defert dicto Reverendo Vicario, qui ipsius Sepulchri ostium sigillat; quo sigillato Cantores canunt *versum:*

> Sepulto Domino, signatum est monumentum ad ostium monumenti: ponentes milites qui custodirent illud, ne forte veniant discipuli & furentur eum, & dicant plebi: Surrexit a mortuis.<p. 282>

Deinde omnes surgunt, & Serenissimus Princeps cum Illustrissimo Dominio chorum ascendit. Scholastici quoque redeunt in Canonicam ad extinquenda & restituenda intortitia. Clerus vero remanet ante Sepulchrum, & dicitur Completorium legendo, ut supra, cum reliquis. Et in fine oratio:

> Respice, quæsumus, Domine, fol. 175.

Quo finito omnes redeunt in chorum, & inchoatur Matutinum.

This office is performed *post prandium*, immediately before Compline. The most conspicuous part of the ceremonial is the elaborate procession into the church, and of this procession the most notable aspect is the use of the *Impropria* at the beginning and at three subsequent stations. Since the significance of this use of the *Impropria* has already been commented upon,[123] we need not emphasize it here. The actual placing of the Host in the *sépulchrum* is accomplished very simply, and the concluding *Sepulto Domino* allies the present version of the *Depositio* with the normal type.

The other ceremonials connected with the *sepulchrum* take the following form:

---

[122] Reverendusque] Reverendisque (Print).

[123] See above, p. 60.

<ELEVATIO HOSTIÆ ET VISITATIO SEPULCHRI>[134]

Dominica Resurrectionis Domini.

Summo mane, aperto prius a Sacrista Sepulchro & Sanctissimo Sacramento in suo loco debita reverentia collocato, Clerus noster hora competenti in sacrarium hodie conveniat, ac unusquisque Magistri Cæremoniarum cura suo fungatur officio. Et palla in primis aperta, ac thesauro super altare bene disposito, quatuor Acolyti ordinarii camisis mundis induti, cereos argenteos deferentes, e Sacrario moderate discedunt. Cruciferi autem dalamticis albis damascenis novis supra lineas tunicas induti, in medio eorum magnam Crucem argenteam deferunt. Hos sequitur Clericorum & Sacerdotum turba juniorum. Postea Subcanonici & Canonici gradatim solemnibus pluvialibus induti. Deinde Reverendus Vicarius vel Senior Canonicus pre<p. 346>tiosioribus cum Ministris indutus missalibus paramentis, cum tribus candelis accensis Sereniss. Principi, Procuratori, & Celebranti distribuendis. Postremo sequitur Cæremoniarum Magister una cum tribus Clericis, quorum alter deferat librum ordinarium, alter Orationale pro decenda Prima opportuno tempore ad Sepulchrum, tertius sit a negotiis ejusdem Magistri. Hujusmodi processio exit per portam Sancti Clementis & recta ad scalam majorem ad sinistram sub porticu contendit. Quæ firmatur sub porticu superiori palatii, & facto choro ex utraque parte, Celebrans una cum Ministris, comite Cærenoniarum Magistro, ascendens Scalam Ducalem, occurrit Sereniss. Principi e Scala Collegii descendenti, ubi prius facta debita reverentia, offert candelam accensam Suæ Serenitati, aliam Procuratori nostræ Ecclesiæ, qui hoc processionis itinere præcedit, de more, cæteros Oratores, & est prope Sereniss. Principem, sed in reditu locum petit suum. Tertiam candelam Celebrans sibi retinet. Quibus candelis oblatis, prædictus Clerus <p. 347> summa modestia descendens e scala majore Palatii, exit per portam auream, nisi pluat; tunc enim eodem ordine, quo venit, fieret introitus per portam Sancti Clementis, & iretur ad Sepulchrum per parvam Scalam Sancti Jacobi, prius amotis sedibus ob prædicationem ibidem præparatis. Et cum nostra Crux ingreditur plateam, campanæ pulsantur. Licet mane campana ducalis adventum Principis indicans, non pulsetur, neque a Celebrante de Dominica Resurrectione Sereniss. Princeps admoneatur. Cum pervenerit autem processio ad ecclesiam, omnes procedunt usque ad secundam januam majorem ecclesiæ, quæ clausa est, & omnes aliæ clausæ sint, præter duas parvas: scilicet quæ tendunt in canonicam & in Palatium ad Sanctum Clementem. Et facto choro inter duas illas januas majores sub porticu ecclesiæ, quo melius fieri potest, intrat etiam Sua Serenitas eo sub porticu cum Procuratore & Oratoribus. Canonicus Celebrans accedit ad januam clausam & pulsat ter cum annulo æneo pendente ex ipsa, tribus ictibus pro quali<p. 348>

---

[134] *Officium Hebdomadæ Sanctæ . . . Sancti Marci . . .*, Venice, 1736, pp. 345–349.

bet vice, ita ut sint novem ictus. Et Cantores interius cantant *versum:*

Quem quæritis in sepulchro, Christicolæ?

Et illi de foris extrinsecus cantantes respondeant:

Jesum Nazarenum crucifixum, o Cœlicolæ.

Et illi deintus dicant:

Non est hic, surrexit sicut prædixerat; ite, nuntiate quia surrexit, dicentes.

Quo facto iterum dicant qui deintus sunt:

Venite & videte locum ubi positus erat Dominus, alleluja, alleluja.

Cum autem dicunt: Venite & videte, panduntur fores ecclesiæ, & omnibus in eam ingredientibus procedit Clerus ordinate contra Sepulchrum. Ad quod cum Sereniss. Princeps pervenerit, firmat se, facie ad Sepulchrum versa. Tunc Celebrans ascendit ad Sepulchrum, & immisso capite, utrinque erigens se, versa facie ad Sereniss. Principem in porta Sepulchri cantat *versum:*

Surrexit Christus.

Et chorus respondeat:

Deo gratias.

Deinde in medio spatio chori idem decantat, aliquantulum extollens vocem, & chorus eo modo, quo supra, respondeat. Tertio canit apud Serenissimum Principem in debita distantia, semper exaltando <p. 349> vocem:

Surrexit Christus.

Responsio:

Deo gratias.

Et facta eadem per chorum responsione, accedens ad Sereniss. Principem, deosculatur eum & Procuratorem dicens:

Surrexit Christus.

Et illi respondeant:

Deo gratias.

Deinde Sacerdos deosculatur Diaconum & Subdiaconum, idem dicens; illi vero dant osculum sibi propinquioribus; et sic successive usque ad minimos Clericos qui adsunt, dicentes et respondentes, ut supra. Postea Sereniss. Princeps cum Senatu ascendit chorum. Clerus vero remanet ad Sepulchrum, præter Cantores qui suum ascendunt pulpitum ad canendam Missam, dicens Primam legendo.[126]

The observances outlined in this text occur on Easter morning immediately before Prime. The *Elevatio* proper is performed privately: that is, at an early hour a sacristan opens the sepulchre and removes the Host to an appropriate place. The simplicity of this observance is quite submerged in the ceremonial brilliance of the subsequent *Visitatio*. Since the *Visitatio*, however, is not our present concern, we need observe

[126] Followed immediately by the rubric: Ad Primam.

only that in general sequence and in the inclusion of the *Pax* the present version is similar to that of Castellani.

In view of the analyses already made of the actual texts of the *Depositio* and *Elevatio*, one need offer for the present division of this study only a very brief summary. The texts range in date from the eleventh century[128] to the eighteenth, they are distributed over Germany, France, Switzerland, Italy, and Hungary, and they show every possible degree of ceremonial elaboration. Particularly notable is the liturgical nature of their content. Although the *Depositio* and *Elevatio* are extra-liturgical in the sense of being deliberate additions to the authorized liturgical system, the actual utterances provided for these offices are well-known antiphons and responsories from the official liturgy itself. Most noteworthy of all, however, is the absence of dialogue and impersonation. An approach to dialogue, to be sure, is seen in connection with the theme of the *Descensus;* but in the *Depositio* and *Elevatio* proper, dialogue does not occur. None of the texts thus far examined shows unequivocal evidence that the clerics who serve in the dramatic offices undertake to impersonate characters connected with the events commemorated. In other words, none of the versions reviewed thus far can be considered true drama.

IV

We pass now to those versions of the *Depositio* and *Elevatio* in which the center of the ceremonial is not the Host but the Cross.

Since, as we have already observed,[1] the *Depositio* forms a natural sequel for the *Adoratio Crucis*, we may expect to find that a certain number of versions of the *Depositio Crucis* attach themselves to the *Adoratio* so directly as to form with the *Adoratio* a consecutive ceremonial. This is true of the earliest extant version of the *Depositio*, that preserved in the *Concordia*

[128] I refer to the *Elevatio* from St. Gall (above, p. 30). It should be remembered, however, that a *Depositio* of the type under consideration, and probably an *Elevatio*, are referred to in the tenth-century life of St. Udalricus (See above, p. 17).

[1] See above, p. 26.

Regularis of St. Athelwold. The *Adoratio Crucis* from this document, printed in full above,[2] is followed immediately by this version of the *Depositio*:[3]

<DEPOSITIO CRUCIS>[4]

NAM QUIA EA DIE DEPOSITIONEM CORPORIS SALUATORIS *Nostri* CELEBRAMUS, USUM QUORUNDAM RELIGIOSORUM IMITABILEM AD FIDE*m* INDOCTI UULGI AC NEOFITORU*m* CORROBORANDAM EQUIPARANDO SEQUI, SI ITA CUI UISUM FUERIT U*e*L SIBI TALITER PLACUERIT HOC MODO DECREUIMUS. SIT AUTEM IN UNA PARTE ALTARIS, QUA UACUUM FUERIT, QUEDAM ASSIMILATIO SEPULCHRI, UELAMENQ*ue* QUODDAM IN GYRO TENSUM QUOD DUM *Sancta* CRUX ADORATA FUERIT DEPONATUR HOC ORDINE. VENIANT DIACONI QUI PRIUS PORTAUERUNT EAM, *et* INUOLUANT EAM SINDONE IN LOCO UBI ADORATA EST. TUNC REPORTENT EAM CANENTES ANTIPHONAS:

In pace in idipsum. Habitabit,

ITEM:

Caro mea requiesc*et* in spe,

DONEC UENIANT AD LOCUM MONUMENTI,[5] DEPOSITAQ*ue* CRUCE, AC SI D*omi*NI N*ost*RI IH*es*U X*pist*I CORPORE SEPULTO, DICANT ANTIPH*onam*:

Sepulto D*omi*no, signatum est monumentu*m*, ponentes milites qui custodirent eum.

IN EODEM LOCO *Sanct*A CRUX CUM OM*n*I REUERENTIA CUSTODIAT*ur* USQ*ue* DOMINICE[6] NOCTEM RESURRECTIONIS. NOCTE UERO ORDINENTUR DUO FR*atr*ES AUT TRES AUT PLURES, SI TANTA FUERINT CONGREGATIO, QUI IBIDEM <FOL. 20^r> PSALMOS DECANTANDO EXCUBIAS FIDELES EXERCEANT.[7]

This text of the *Depositio* not only shows a direct attachment of this office to the *Adoratio*, but it also explains the didactic purpose of the dramatic ceremonial. The *Depositio* is

---

[2] See above, pp. 20–22.

[3] The *Depositio*, *Elevatio*, and *Visitatio* from the *Concordia Regularis* have been printed numerous times. An adequate bibliography of this monastic rule is given by Chambers, II, 306–307. I take my texts directly from Cotton MS Tiberius A. III., in the British Museum. This manuscript dates from the early eleventh century, and represents the use of Winchester in the latter part of the tenth century. I scarcely need say that I have made full use of W. S. Logemann's admirable texts from the same manuscript, in *Anglia*, XIII, 421–428. Except for my omission of the Anglo-Saxon glosses, my texts differ in no essential way from those of Logemann.

[4] Cotton MS Tiberius A. III., fol. 19^v–20^r. In the manuscript the first word *Nam* of the present text follows immediately the last word *faciat* of the *Adoratio Crucis* printed above, pp. 20–22.

[5] monumenti] monumento (MS).

[6] Dominice] dominica (MS).

[7] Followed immediately by the *ordo* for fetching the Host reserved for the *Missa Præsanctificatorum*.

designed for enforcing the intention of the *Adoratio*, and for strengthening the faith of the unlearned and of the neophytes. In a vacant part of the altar is prepared a likeness of the *sepulchrum*, with a veil stretched upon a ring. The deacons who have carried the Cross for the *Adoratio* wrap it in a cloth in the place of the adoration, and carry it to the *sepulchrum* singing the antiphons *In pace in idipsum* and *Caro mea*. The deacons now deposit the Cross in the *sepulchrum* as if it were the buried body of Christ, meanwhile singing the antiphon *Sepulto Domino*. Here the Cross is guarded until the night of the Resurrection. Two, three, or more brothers are appointed to keep faithful watch at the *sepulchrum* by night, singing psalms.

Our knowledge of the *Elevatio* is confined to the following sentence:[8]

<ELEVATIO CRUCIS>

Eiusdem tempore noctis antequam Matutinorum signa moueantur, sumant editui Crucem *et* ponant in loco sibi congruo.

In this brief rubric the sacristans of the church are charged with taking the Cross from the *sepulchrum* and putting it in an appropriate place,—this to be done before Matins on Easter morning.

The close relationship of the *Depositio* to the *Adoratio*, as seen in the *Concordia Regularis* of St. Athelwold, is further exemplified in the use of the cathedral of Rouen. The Rouen Gradual of the thirteenth century provides for the *Depositio* as follows:[9]

<DEPOSITIO CRUCIS>[10]

Quando Crux adorata fuerit a Clero *et* populo eleuet eam Sacerdos alte *et* incipiat Cantor hanc *Antiphonam:*

Super omnia ligna cedrorum, tu sola excelsior, in qua uita mundi pependit, in qua Xpistus triumphauit et mors mortem superauit in eternum.

Quo uiso Clerus et populus genuflectant et chorus finiat Antiphonam Qua cantata crux paruula in commemoratione sanguinis *et* aque deflenti.

---

[8] Cotton MS Tiberius A. III., fol. 21ʳ.

[9] Paris, Bibliothèque Nationale, MS latin 904, Graduale Rothomagense saec. xiii, fol. 92ᵛ-93ʳ. A photographic reproduction of this manuscript occupies the second volume of *Le Graduel de l'Église Cathédrale de Rouen au xiiiᵉ Siècle*, Rouen, 1907 edited by H. Loriquet, J. Pothier, and A. Collette. So far as I know, the *Depositio* from MS 904 is now printed for the first time. A bibliography of the Rouen manuscripts that contain liturgico-dramatic offices is given by the present writer in *Modern Philology*, Vol. VI (1908), pp. 224–227.

[10] Bibl. Nat. MS latin 904, fol. 92ᵛ–93ʳ.

DE LATere REDEMPTORIS AQua ET UINO LAUETur DE QUO comMEMORATIONEm SACRAM CLERus BIBAT et POPULus ET AD OPUS INFIRMORum RESERUETUR. QUO[11] Facto SACERDOTES et CLerici ACCIPIANT CRUCIFIXUM et PORTENT AD SEPULCHRUM preparatum CANTANTES HOC RESPONSORIUm:

Sicut ouis ad occisionem ductus est, et dum male tracta<fol. 93r>retur non aperuit os suum; traditus est ad mortem ut uiuificaret populum suum. *Versus:* In pace factus est locus eius et in Syon habitatio eius. *Repetendum:* Ut uiuificaret.

ET TUNC PONATur IN SEPULCRO, PEDIBus Uersis AD ORIENTEm ET COOPERIATur PALLIO, et InCENSANDO ILLUm DICAT ARCHIepiscopus UEL SACERDOS HANC ANTIPHOnam:

In pace in idipsum dormiam et requiescam.

QUA CANTATA CLAUDAT HOSTIUM SEPULCHRI.

RESPONSORIUm:

Sepulto domino signatum est monumentum, uoluentes lapidem ad hostium monumenti, ponentes milites qui custodirent illud. *Versus:* Ne forte ueniant discipuli eius et furentur eum et dicant plebi: Surrexit a mortuis. *Repetendum:* Voluentes.

HIS EXPLETIS MINISTRI CRUCIS CASULIS INDUTI AFFERANT AD ALTARE CUm UINO Non CONSECRATO RESERUATUm CORPUS DomiNI.[12]

The *Adoratio Crucis*, it will be observed, ends with the dramatic, and somewhat exceptional,[13] ceremonial of the washing of the Cross[14] with wine and water in commemoration of the Crucifixion. Then follows immediately the *Depositio* proper. After being carried to the *sepulchrum* during the singing of the responsory *Sicut ovis*, the Cross is laid in the *sepulchrum*, covered with a winding sheet, and censed. After the closing of the door of the *sepulchrum* is sung the responsory *Sepulto Domino.* Now follows immediately the Communion of the *Missa Præsanctificatorum*.

The same dramatic office, with somewhat different rubrics, is found in a Rouen *ordinarium* of the fourteenth century in the following form:[15]

---

[11] It may be said that the *Depositio*, in the strict sense, begins at this point.

[12] This rubric indicates the beginning of the Communion of the *Missa Præsanctificatorum*.

[13] See the *Depositio* from Barking below, p. 119.

[14] It is not clear that this *crux paruula* is the Cross used in the *Adoratio* or the one placed in the *sepulchrum*.

[15] Rouen, Bibliothèque de la Ville, MS 384 (*olim* Y. 110), Ordinarium Rothomagense saec. xiv, fol. 80r. So far as I know the *Depositio* from this manuscript is now printed for the first time. I assume that the same version of the *Depositio* is to be found in two other Rouen *ordinaria*, of the fifteenth century:

<DEPOSITIO CRUCIS>[16]

QUO[17] FINITO DEFERATUR CRUCIFIX*us* AD SEPULCHRU*m* A DUOB*us* *pres*BY*te*RIS REUESTI*tis* QUI CANTAU*eru*NT Popule meus. ARCHI*episcopus et* PLURES FRA*tr*ES CUM EIS CANT*antes* INCIP*iant* RE*sponsorium:*

Sicut ouis ad occis*ionem*. V*ersus:* In pace *factus* est.

QUO COLLO*c*ATO DICATUR AN*tiphona:*

In pace in idips*um* dor<miam>.

POSTEA ARCHI*episcopus* UEL SAC*er*DOS OSTIUM SEPULCRI CLAUDAT *et* DUO *pres*BY*te*RI C*um* EO *et* HUMILI UOCE INCIPIANT RE*sponsorium:*

Sepulto d*omi*no. V*ersus:* Ne forte ueniant. Ponentes.

QUO P*er*ACTO ARCHI*episcopus* UEL SAC*er*DOS LAUET MANUS SUAS, *et* C*um* MAGNA REU*er*ENTIA AD SACRATORIU*m* P*er*GAT.[18]

In liturgical content this text is identical with that printed above from the Rouen Graduale of the thirteenth century; and it cannot be urged that the differences in the rubrics are of substantial importance.

The extant service books of Rouen do not mention the *Elevatio*. That this office was introduced early into the Rouen use, however, is clear from the *Liber de Officiis Ecclesiasticis* of Jean d'Avranches, archbishop of Rouen in the eleventh century. This writer describes the *Depositio* and *Elevatio* as follows:

<DEPOSITIO CRUCIS>[19]

Quo<i.e. Adoratio Crucis>peracto, Crucifixus in commemoratione sanguinis et aquæ fluentis de latere Redemptoris vino et aqua lavetur, de quo post sacram Communionem chorus bibat et populus. Post responsorium *Sicut ovis ad occisionem*, cantando, ad<locum>aliquem deferant in modum Sepulcri compositum, ubi recondatur usque in diem Dominicum. Quo collocato, antiphona *In pace in idipsum*, et responsorium *Sepulto Domino* cantetur.

<ELEVATIO CRUCIS>[20]

Decima hora noctis pauci clerici induti veniant, et Crucifixum cum incenso et thymiamate levantes, antiphonamque *Surrexit Dominus de*

---

(1) Paris, Bibl. Nat., MS lat. 1213; and (2) Rouen, Bibl. de la Ville, MS 382 (*olim* Y. 108). On this point I happen not to have precise information at hand. For a bibliography of these manuscripts see *Modern Philology*, VI, 224.

[16] Rouen MS 384 (*olim* Y. 110), fol. 80r.

[17] This refers to the washing of the Cross at the end of the *Adoratio*.

[18] The Communion of the *Missa Præsanctificatorum* follows immediately.

[19] Migne, *Pat. Lat.*, CXLVII, 51–52. Substantially the same text is found in the anonymous twelfth century treatise in Montpellier MS H. 304, fol. 36v. In regard to this manuscript see *Modern Philology*, VI, 202–206.

[20] Migne, *Pat. Lat.*, CXLVII, 53. Substantially the same text is found in Montpellier MS H. 304, fol. 37v.

sepulcro<cantantes>, loco suo honorifice constituant. Post cúnctis campanis sonantibus, januas ecclesiæ aperiant, et Matutinas incipiant.

This brief *ordo* for the *Elevatio* provides merely that before Matins on Easter morning a few clerics open the *sepulchrum*, cense the Cross, and carry it to an appropriate place, singing the antiphon *Surrexit Dominus*.

The absence of the *Elevatio* from the Rouen service-books that contain the *Depositio* and *Visitatio* is unfortunate, but it does not prove definitely that during the thirteenth, fourteenth, and fifteenth centuries the *Elevatio* was obsolete.[21] It is, indeed, not easily conceivable that a use preserving the *Depositio* and *Visitatio* should suppress the intermediate office.[22]

The close attachment of *Depositio* to *Adoratio* which we have observed in the uses of Winchester and Rouen is further exemplified in a version of the fourteenth century from Durham:[23]

<DEPOSITIO CRUCIS>[24]

ET SCIENDUM *quod* DUM CRUX PORTATUR *et* REPORTATUR *per* ME<FOL. 177^{v}>DIUM CHORI, ADORARI DEBET AB OMNIBUS FLEXIS GENIBUS. CUM UERO PERUENERINT AD GRADUS PAUIMENTI, PROCEDANT DUO FRATRES CUM CANDELABRIS *et* TERTIUS CUM THURIBULO PRECENDENTES CRUCIS PORTATORES *et* EPISCOPUM UEL PRIOREM, QUI, CUM PORTATORIBUS CRUCIS, CRUCEM IN SEPULCRO COLLOCATURUS EST. FINITA *Antiphona* Super omnia, INCIPIAT CANTOR *Responsorium:*

Tenebre<factæ sunt dum crucifixissent Jesum Judæi, et circa horam nonam exclamavit Jesus voce magna: Deus, Deus, ut quid me dereliquisti? Tunc unus ex militibus lancea latus ejus perforavit, et inclinato capite

---

[21] The bibliography of these service-books is given in *Modern Philology*, VI, 224–225.

[22] A suppression of this sort is suggested by the editors of *Le Graduel de l'Église Cathédrale de Rouen au xiiie Siècle*, Vol. I, Rouen, 1907, p. 58.

[23] British Museum, MS Harl. 5289, Missale Dunelmense saec. xiv, fol. 177^{r}–177^{v}. The manuscript contains no *Elevatio* or *Visitatio*. So far as I know, the *Depositio* is now printed for the first time. Parts of this manuscript are printed in *Publications of the Surtees Society*, Vol. CVII (1902), pp. 172–191; but the *Depositio* is not included. With the *Depositio* now printed should be compared the sixteenth-century account of the *Depositio* and *Elevatio* found in *Surtees Society*, Vol. XV (1842), pp. 9–11 (reprinted by Chambers, II, 310–311), and in a new edition in *Surtees Society*, Vol. CVII (1903), pp. 11–13. With the Durham *Depositio* may be classed a version from Fécamp published by the present writer in *Transactions of the Wisconsin Academy of Sciences, Arts, and Letters*, XVI, Part II, 902.

[24] London, Brit. Mus., MS Harl. 5289, fol. 177^{r}–177^{v}.

emisit spiritum. *Versus:* Et velum templi scissum est a summo usque deorsum, et omnis terra tremuit. Tunc unus.>[25]

QUO DECANTATO, COLLOCETUR CRUX IN SEPULCRO, INCENSATO LOCO ANTE POSICIONEM *et* POST. DUM HEC AGUNTUR INCIPIAT CANTOR HAS *Antiphonas:*

Proprio filio suo non pepercit Deus, *pro* nobis omnibus tradidit illum.

Antiphona:

Caro mea requiescet in spe.

Antiphona:

Dominus tanquam ouis ad uictimam ductus est *et* non aperuit os suum.

Antiphona:

Oblatus est *quod* ipse uoluit, *et* peccata nostra ipse portabit.

Antiphona:

In pace in idipsum dormiam *et* requiescam.

DEINDE DUO UERTENTES UULTUM AD CONUENTUM CANANT HANC *Antiphonam:*

Ioseph ab Arimathia petiit corpus Ihesu *et* sepelliuit eum in sepulcro suo.

EAQUE PERCANTATA DESCENDAT IN REUESTIARIUM QUI OFFICIUM CELEBRAT.[26]

At the conclusion of the *Adoratio*, in this case, is sung the reponsory *Tenebræ*, after which the Cross is placed in the *sepulchrum*, and the place is censed. During the laying down of the Cross are sung a series of five antiphons. Then two clerics, turning toward the *conventus*, close the office with the singing of the antiphon *Joseph ab Arimathea*.

This immediate attachment of the *Depositio* to the *Adoratio* is, however, not general. Appropriate though the *Depositio Crucis* truly is as a direct sequel to the *Adoratio Crucis*, in most cases the extra-liturgical office is separated from the *Adoratio* by other liturgical elements. This is the situation in the following version from a thirteenth-century manuscript of Benedictine use:[27]

<DEPOSITIO CRUCIS ET ELEVATIO CRUCIS>[28]

SACERDOTES QUI AD ALTARE DOMINICUM MINISTRABANT, STATIM *post* MISSALE OFFICIUM CRUCEM QUAM FRATRES DEOSCULATI SUNT IN SEPULCHRO HOC ORDINE COLLOCANT.

---

[25] Fifth responsory in Matins of Good Friday. See Migne, *Pat. Lat.*, LXXVIII, 766–767.

[26] The Communion of the *Missa Præsanctificatorum* follows.

[27] Oxford, Bodleian Library, MS Canonici Liturg. 325 (19414), Ordinarium Benedictinum saec. xiii, fol. 78r. The manuscript is of German origin. See W. H. Frere, *Bibliotheca Musico-Liturgica*, Vol. I, London, 1901, p. 21. The *Depositio* and *Elevatio* are now published, I believe, for the first time. The *Visitatio* from this manuscript has been published by the present writer in *Publications of the Modern Language Association*, XXIV, 312.

[28] Bodleian, MS Canonici Liturg. 325, fol. 78r.

Duo ex ipsis ordine *priores* portant Cruc*em*, quos alii tres cum turibulis et candelabris *precedunt*, Sac*er*dote ebdoma*dario* *et* armario illos comitantib*us*, simulq*ue* cu*m* eis supp*ressa* uoce cantantib*us* *responsorium:*

Ecce quom*odo*.

Responsorium:

Recessit pastor noster, <fons aquæ vivæ, ad cujus transitum sol obscuratus est; nam et ille captus est, qui captivum tenebat primum hominem. Hodie portas mortis et seras pariter Salvator noster disrupit. Versus: Ante cujus conspectum mors fugit, ad cujus vocem mortui resurgunt, videntes autem eum portæ mortis confractæ sunt. Hodie.>

< Antiphona >:

Joseph ab *Arimathia*.

Antiphona:

Sepulto Domino <signatum est monumentum, ponentes milites qui custodirent illud.>[29]

Int*eri*m ponunt Cruc*em* sup*er* tapete stratu*m* in pauim*en*to; q*ui* op*er*ientes linteo *in*censant *et* apponunt cereu*m*, qui iugit*er* ardebit usq*ue* du*m* in nocte cu*m* aliis extinguat*ur*.

Ipsa v*ero* Crux a custodib*us* eccl*esi*e in paschali nocte inde auferenda e*st* ante*quam* pulsetur ad Noct*urnum*, relicto tam*en* linteo usq*ue* du*m* in ipsa nocte Sepulchru*m* a F*ratr*ib*us* uisitetur.[30]

The *Depositio* is performed immediately at the close of Mass, and the Cross employed appears to be that previously used in the *Adoratio*. The procession, with its musical pieces, is already familiar. The actual burial in the *sepulchrum* appears to be represented in a very simple manner. After being laid upon a carpet spread over the pavement, the Cross is merely covered with a cloth, censed, and provided with a lighted candle.[31] The *Elevatio* seems to have been performed before Easter Matins silently and secretly. No liturgical pieces are provided. The cloth is left for use in the later *Visitatio*.

At Moosburg, in Bavaria, the *Depositio Crucis* took place after Vespers, as we see from the following:[32]

[29] Antiphon of Lauds for Holy Saturday. See Migne, *Pat. Lat.*, LXXVIII, 769.

[30] Followed immediately by the following rubric: Communione peracta extinctis candelis percutitur tabula, ut fiat oratio uespertina.

[31] From the *Visitatio*, however, we learn that the *sepulchrum* was a contrivance of some definiteness and amplitude, for it could be entered. See *Pub. of Mod. Lang. Assoc.*, XXIV, 312.

[32] Munich, Hofbibliothek, Cod. lat. 23068, Breviarium Moosburgense saec. xiv, fol. 291v. The manuscript contains no *Elevatio*. The *Depositio* is now published for the first time. The *Visitatio* (fol. 295v) has not been printed; but it is described by N. C. Brooks, in *Zeitschrift für deutsches Altertum*, Vol. L (1908), p. 309.

<DEPOSITIO CRUCIS>[33]

DEINDE RECIPIATUR CRUX ET UOCE LENTA DICATUR RESPONSORIUM:

Ecce quomodo moritur.

Responsorium:

Sepulto Domino.

Responsorium:

Recessit pastor.

ASPERGATUR ET THURIFICETUR. SEQUITUR UERSUS:

In pace factus est locus eius.

ET SIC EST FINITUM.

From these meagre rubrics we learn little more than that after the laying down of the Cross the *sepulchrum* is sprinkled and censed.

More generous details are provided in the following *ordo* from Andechs:[34]

<DEPOSITIO CRUCIS>[35]

COMMUNIONE[36] EXPLETA, DICANTUR VESPERE SUBMISSA UOCE, PSALMI Confitebor CUM RELIQUIS. DEINDE SEQUITUR PSALMUS: Magnificat; QUO FINITO DICITUR UERSUS Proprio filio suo non.

SI UERO QUIS INTERFUERIT SEPULTURE, PERACTO OFFICIO SEPULTURE CRUCIFIXI, TUNC SUB SILENCIO CIRCA SEPULCHRUM LEGUNTUR VESPERE ET CLAUDUNTUR CUM UERSU In pace factus est locus eius, et in Syon habitacio eius.

DEINDE SEPULCHRO PREPARATO ET DECENTER ORNATO, SINT INPROMPTO TRIA THURIBULA CUM INCENSU, THURE, MIRRA, ET THIMIAMATE, ET QUATUOR CANDELE ARDENTES. ET PONTIFEX SIUE PRESPITER CUM ALIIS MINISTRIS ET SACERDOTIBUS PORTENT YMAGINEM CRUCIFIXI UERSUS SEPULCHRUM LUGUBRI UOCE CANTANTES RESPONSORIUM:

Ecce quomodo moritur iustus. *Versus:* In pace factus.

RESPONSORIO FINITO COLLOCETUR IN SEPULCHRO ET LINTHEAMINIBUS ET SUDARIO COOPERIATUR. DEINDE LAPIS SUPERPONATUR. QUO FACTO CLERUS INPONAT ISTA RESPONSORIA:

Sepulto Domino. *Versus:* Ne forte.

Responsorium:

Recessit pastor. *Versus:* Ante cuius.

---

[33] Munich, Hofbibliothek, Cod. lat. 23068, fol. 291ᵛ. The text printed above is preceded immediately by the *ordo* for Vespers.

[34] Munich, Hofbibliothek, Cod. lat. 24882, Breviarium Andecense saec. xv, fol. 269ᵛ. The *Depositio* is now printed for the first time. The manuscript contains no *Elevatio*. The *Visitatio* (fol. 274ʳ–275ʳ) is presented by Lange (pp. 99–101; cf. p. 13) by way of incomplete variants appended to another text.

[35] Munich, Cod. Lat. 24882, fol. 269ᵛ.

[36] The Communion of the *Missa Præsanctificatorum*. From the opening rubrics it appears that the *Depositio* is not obligatory. When the *Depositio* occurs, it occupies a position immediately after Mass and before Vespers.

QUIBUS FINITIS DICATUR *Versus:*
In pace factus est locus eius.
QUO UERSU OMNES SEQUENTES HORE CLAUDUNTUR.[37]

The *Depositio* is again designed for performance immediately before Vespers. During the singing of the responsory *Ecce quomodo* the *Imago Crucifixi*[38] is carried in procession to the *sepulchrum*. After the *Imago* has been laid down and covered with a linen cloth and sudary, the *sepulchrum* is closed by the placing of a stone.[39] The office is concluded by the singing of the responsories *Sepulto Domino* and *Recessit pastor* and of the versicle *In pace factus*.

In the present series of texts belong the *Depositio* and *Elevatio* from Raitenbuch, in Bavaria:[40]

<DEPOSITIO CRUCIS>[41]

ET POSTQUAM OMNES COMMUNICAUERINT, *et* SACERDOS PEREGERIT OFFICIUM,[42] UADAT CUM MINISTRIS *et* TOLLAT CRUCIFIXUM QUOD FUERAT ANTEA PRESENTATUM,

[37] The rubric *Ad Completorium* follows immediately.

[38] The term *Imago Crucifixi*, which we shall frequently encounter below, is far from clear. In most cases it probably indicates merely the Crucifix: that is, the cross with the *corpus* affixed. It may sometimes mean the *corpus* alone, detached from the cross, or even some sort of special representation of the Crucifixion—a painting or a carving. That the words *Imago Crucifixi* may indicate the *corpus* alone seems to be certain from the following passage in the *Custumarium* of Sarum (W. H. Frere, *The Use of Sarum*, Vol. I, Cambridge, 1898, p. 219): "Omnibus dominicis quadragesime, excepta prima dominica, deferatur una crux ante processionem lignea sine ymagine crucifixi." The sixteenth century "Rites of Durham" (*Surtees Society*, Vol. cvii, 1903) speaks of "a goodly large crucifix all of gold of the picture of our sauiour Christ nailed uppon the crosse" (p. 11), and of "another picture of our sauiour Christ, in whose breast they did enclose with great reuerence the most holy and blessed sacrament of the altar" (p. 12). We are told further that "in the north allye was a most faire roode or picture of our sauiour" (p. 18). From these passages one infers that the word "picture" of the Durham account refers merely to the ordinary crucifix (See *op. cit.*, p. 204).

[39] The use of the *lapis* here motivates, of course, the interrogation *Quis revolvet nobis ab hostio lapidem quem tegere sanctum cernimus sepulchrum?* at the beginning of the subsequent *Visitatio*. See Lange, p. 100.

[40] Munich, Hofbibliothek, Cod. lat. 12301, Breviarium Raitenbuchense anni 1431, fol. 88ʳ, 90ʳ. These texts are now printed for the first time. The *Visitatio* (fol. 90ᵛ) has not been published, but a description of it is given by N. C. Brooks, in *Zeitschrift für deutsches Altertum*, L, 299.

[41] Munich, Cod. lat. 12301, fol. 88ʳ.

[42] This rubric shows that the *Depositio* occurs immediately after the *Missa Præsanctificatorum* of Good Friday.

PRECEDENTE CANDELA EXTINCTA *et* CRUCE UELATA THURIBULO *et* ASPERSORIO. DEFERAT AD LOCUM SEPULCHRI CANTANDO LENTA UOCE *Responsorium:*

Recessit pastor bon*us*.

Responsorium:

An*te* cui*us*.

Responsorium:

In pace fac*tus* es*t*.

DEINDE LOCATUR CRUCIFIXUM IN SEPULCHRO. *Et* STANTES CITRA DICANT VESPERAS.

<ELEVATIO CRUCIS>[43]

IN SANCTA NOCTE AN*te* MATUTINUM SURGANT SACERDOTES *et* CLERICI, *et* INTRENT ECCLESIAM, NEC ETIAM LAYCOS INTRARE PERMITTANT. *Et* UADANT AD SEPULCHRUM CUM REUERENTIA, *et* DICANT PSALMUM: Dom*ine*, qu*id* multi*plicati et* PSALMUM: Miser*ere* mei, Deus, miser*ere* mei, *et* PSALMUM: Dom*ine*, *pro*basti me. DEINDE Kyri*e*, Pa*ter* nos*ter*. *Versus:* Exurge, Dom*ine*, adiuua nos. *Versus:* Dom*ine*, De*us* uirtutu*m* conu*erte*. *Versus:* Foderu*n*t ma*nus* meas. *Versus:* Dom*ine*, exaudi or*ationem*. ORATIO: Da nobis. DEINDE CRUX ASPERGATUR *et* THURIFICETUR. *Et* TOLLENTES CRUCEM CANTANT *Responsorium* SUBMISSA UOCE SCILICET:

Du*m* tra*n*sisse*t*.

Et DUM PERUENERINT AD LOCUM CRUCIFIXI DICATUR UERSUS:

In resur*re*ctio*ne* tua, X*piste*.

ORATIO:

De*us* qui hod*ierna* die *per* uni*genitum*.

IBIQUE LINTHEAMINA DIMITTUNT, *et* POST ECCLESIA APPERITUR, *et* PULSETUR AD MATUTINUM.

Since the *Depositio* calls for no special comment, we may confine our attention briefly to the *Elevatio*. This office is performed early Easter morning, before the laymen have been admitted to the church. At the *sepulchrum* three psalms are rendered, followed by the *Kyrie*, the *Pater Noster*, four versicles, and a prayer. After the sprinkling and censing of the Cross, it is raised, during the singing of the responsory *Dum transisset*, and carried in procession to its appropriate place, where the versicle *In resurrectione* and a prayer are said. The cloths are now removed from the Cross, and the doors of the church are opened for Matins.

In the present somewhat miscellaneous group we may include the following versions from Treves:[44]

---

[43] Munich, Cod. lat. 12301, fol. 90r.

[44] British Museum, Harleian MS 2958, Ordinarium Treverense saec. xiii, fol. 36r–37r. The *Depositio* and *Elevatio* are, I believe, now published for the first time. The *Visitatio* (fol. 37v) has been published by Lange (No. 105, pp. 10, 71–74).

<DEPOSITIO CRUCIS>[45]

His peractis exuat Sacerdos casulam et induatur cappa purpurea et ad requirendam Crucem descendatur hoc ordine. Precedat alicus indutus cappa cum aqua benedicta; sequantur duo acoliti in tunicis cum cereis, in medio eorum acolitus in cappa cum thuribulo; post hos Subdiaconus in subtili cum textu; duo alici induti tunicis a dextris et a sinistris eius cum crucibus sollempnibus; sequatur Dyaconus in dalmatica; deinde Sacerdos in cappa prout dictum est. Procedant sic ordinati ad Sanctam Agnetem. Ibi inueniri debet Crux ante altare uelata, quam teneant a dextris et a sinistris duo Subdiaconi induti casulis rubeis. Accedat Sacerdos, et leuato uelamine aspergat Crucem aqua benedicta. Post aspersionem reponatur uelamen super Crucem, et incipiat Cantor *responsorium:*

Iherusalem luge;

deinde *uersum:*

Plange quasi uirgo,

que cantentur uocibus submissis cum uersibus et repetitionibus, et procedat omnis processio suo ordine. Subdiaconi uero portantes Crucem uelatam immediate sequantur Sacerdotem. Cum peruenerint in criptam ante Sepulcrum, Sacerdos aspergat Sepulcrum aqua benedicta et thurificet. Deinde Crux ponatur in Sepulcrum et ueletur panno albo, et incipiat Cantor *responsorium:*

Ecce quomodo moritur iustus,

uoce submissa cum uersu et repetitione. Post modum claudatur Sepulcrum, et incipiat Cantor *responsorium:*

Sepulto Domino,

cum uersu et repetitione. Sacerdo<s> uero dicat versiculum:

In pace factus est locus eius.

Et <fol. 36v> respondeatur:

Et in Syon habitatio eius.

Quibus peractis egrediatur processio.[46]

<ELEVATIO CRUCIS>[47]

In die sancto Pasce mane ante pulsationem Matutini reuertatur processio ad Sepulcrum sicut processit ad sepeliendum. *Et* Sacerdos flexis genibus dicat orationes *et* aspergat aqua benedicta Crucem *et* thurificabit; *et* oblato uelamine dicat *uersum:*

Surrexit Dominus uere,

leuando Crucem. *Et* Cantor immediate incipiat *antiphonam:*

Xpistuc resurgens,

et uersum:

Dicant nunc,

---

[45] MS Harl. 2958, fol. 36r-36v. The present text is immediately preceded by this rubric: Deinde Sacerdos in altari Vesperas concludat.

[46] Followed immediately by the rubric: Sabbato Sancto ad Matutinum.

[47] MS Harl. 2958, fol. 37r.

CUM REPETITIONE. DEINDE EGREDIATUR PROCESSIO, RELICTO SUDARIO IN MONUMENTO, *et* PULSETUR AD MATUTINUM.

The most conspicuous aspect of this office is the location of the *sepulchrum:* in the crypt of the church. Neither the *Depositio*, after Vespers, nor the *Elevatio*, before Matins, includes any unusual ceremonial. Noteworthy, perhaps, is the fact that when the Cross is taken up from the *sepulchrum*, the *sudarium* is left behind, for use in the subsequent *Visitatio*.[48]

We may now consider a few texts that specifically provide for a bit of ceremonial reminiscent of the central act of the *Adoratio Crucis*,—the definite adoring of the Cross. This ceremonial detail is present in the *Depositio* from Clermont-Ferrand:[49]

<DEPOSITIO CRUCIS>

TUNC CRUX TOLLATUR ET DEPORTETUR IN SACRARIO, ET SEQUATUR AB OMNI CLERO CANTANDO:

Sepulto *Domino*.

IBIQUE DEPONATUR ET COOPERIATUR, ADORETUR, VENERETUR, INLUMINETUR; *et* IBI STET USQUE IN DIEM RESURRECTIONIS.[50]

In this simple office the Cross is borne, immediately after Vespers, to the sacristy. In the laying down of the Cross specific provision is made for an "adoration."

Similar reverence to the Cross is provided for in the use of the cathedral of Freising:[51]

<DEPOSITIO CRUCIS>[52]

QUANDO IMAGO CRUCIFIXI DEFERTUR AD SEPULCHRUM CANITUR *responsorium:*

Ecce qu*omodo* moritur iustus,

---

[48] See Lange, pp. 72–73.

[49] Clermont-Ferrand, Bibliothèque de la Ville, MS 63 (*olim* 58), Missale Claromontense saec. xiv, fol. 32v. This text is now printed for the first time. The manuscript contains no *Elevatio* or *Visitatio*.

[50] Followed immediately by the rubric: In Sabbato Sancto.

[51] *Breuiarium Frisingense, Pars Hyemalis*, Venice, 1516 (British Museum), fol. 194v, 196v–197r. These texts are now reprinted for the first time. The *Visitatio* (fol. 197v–198r) is reprinted by Lange, pp. 102–103. With the *Elevatio* may be compared the text from Indersdorf published by the present writer in *Transactions of the Wisconsin Academy of Sciences, Arts, and Letters*, XVI, Part II, 904–905.

[52] *Breuiarium Frisingense, Pars Hyemalis*, Venice, 1516, fol. 194v.

SUBMISSA VOCE. COLLOCATA IMAGINE AD SEPULCHRUM *responsorium:*

Sepulto Domino,

ET *responsorium:*

Recessit pastor,

UT INFRA SABBATO SEQ*u*ENTI. DEINDE *versus:*

In pace factus e*st* locus eius. Et habitatio eius in Sion.[53]

<ELEVATIO CRUCIS>[54]

IN NOCTE SA*n*CTA ANTE PULSUM MATUTI<NI>, CO*n*GREGATIS SACERDOTIB*us* CIRCA ALTARE SA*n*CTE CRUCIS, DECAN*us* CO*n*SUEUIT DICERE Confiteor, *et cetera.* RELIQ*ui* SUBIU*n*GUNT: Misereatur, *et cetera; et* REPETU*n*T Confiteor, <FOL. 197[r]> SICUT ANTE MISSA*m*.

DEI*n*DE REUERENTE*r* ACCEDU*n*T SEPULCHRU*m* ET IBIDEM DICU*n*T:

P*salmum*: Domine, q*ui*d multiplicati.

P*salmum:* Miserere mei, De*us*, misere*re*.

P*salmum:* Do*m*ine, p*r*obasti me, cu*m* Gl*or*ia.

Kiri<e eleyson>, Chri<ste eleyson>, Kiri<e eleyson>.

P*ater* no*ster*. Et ne<nos inducas in tentationem>.

V*ersus:* Exurge, D*om*ine, adiuua nos.

V*ersus:* Do*m*ine, exaudi ora*tio*ne*m* mea*m*.

Dominus vobiscum.

COLLECTA:

Da nobis, q*ue*sumu*s*, D*om*ine, auxiliu*m* gratie tue, ut paschalia gaudia que leta*n*tes exequimur perpetua virtute nos tueant*ur et* saluent. Per Christu*m*.

FINITA COLL*ecta*, THURIFICAT*ur et* ASPERGIT*ur* IMAGO CRUCIFIXI, DEFERTURQ*ue* AD ALTARE P*re*FATUM CANENTIBUS CLERICIS SUBMISSA VOCE *responsorium:*

Surrexit pastor bonus,

UT INFRA FERIA QUINTA. A*ntiphona:*

Christus resurgens,

UT INFRA IN V*esperis*. *Versus:*

Surrexit D*omin*u*s* vere, all*elu*ia. Et apparuit Petro, all*elu*ia.

COLLECTA:

Deus in hodierna,

UT IN MATUTI*no*. QUIB*us* PE*r*ACTIS MAIOR OSCULAT*ur* IMAGINEM ET DICIT:

Surrexit D*omin*us.

Gaudeamus o*m*nes.

SIMILITER *et* ALIJ FACIU*n*T.[55]

Although the Freising *Depositio* needs no comment, we may give at least passing notice to the *Elevatio*, performed before Easter Matins. After the *Confiteor* at the altar of the Holy Cross, the priests pass to the *sepulchrum*, where they say three

[53] Followed immediately by the rubric: Ad Ves<peras>.

[54] *Breuiarium Frisingense, Pars Hyemalis*, Venice, 1516, fol. 196[v]–197[r].

[55] Followed immediately by the rubric: Ad Matuti<num>.

psalms, the *Kyrie*, the *Pater Noster*, and another prayer. During the singing of the responsory *Surrexit pastor* the *Imago Crucifixi*, previously censed and sprinkled, is carried to the altar of the Holy Cross. Here are rendered an antiphon and a prayer. The office closes with the kissing of the *Imago Crucifixi* by each of the priests in turn, a ceremonial act suggestive of the *Adoratio*.

Relevant to the present stage of our survey are the following two texts from Prague:[56]

<DEPOSITIO CRUCIS>[57]

STATIM POST V*esperas* EUNT IN MEDIUM ECCLESIE *et* ACCEPTA CRUCE DEFERANT EA<M> IN LOCUM SOLE*m*NIBUS AULEIS ORNATUM CANTANTES R*esponsorium*:

Ecce quo*modo* morit*ur*,

CU*m* SUO V*ersu*, P*re*CEDENTIBUS CEREIS, CRUCIB*us*, AQ*ua* B*en*EDICTA, *et* INCENSO. ET REPOSITA IN LOCO CUM REUERENTIA A PRELATO ASPERGITUR *et* INCENSATUR, AC COOPERITUR SACRA PALLA, *et* DICITUR V*ersus*:

In pace factus est locus eius. Et in Sy<on habitatio ejus>.

REDEUNTES CA*n*TENT R*esponsorium*:

Sepulto Domino,

CUM V*ersu* ET REPETITIONE. LUMEN ARDENS REPONITUR AD SEPULCHRU*m* DOMINI, *et* LEGANT CANONICI A SENIORIBUS INCIPIENDO PSALTERIA VEL VICARII CANONICORUM SEDE*n*TES AD SEPULCRU*m* BINI ET BINI USQ*ue* AD VISITATIONE<M> SEPULCHRI MATUTINALE*m*.[58]

<ELEVATIO CRUCIS>[59]

IN SACRA NOCTE AN*te* MATUTIN*um* MAGNA CAMPANA[60] PULSAT*ur*, AD QUA*m* D*om*INI CANONICI *et* CLERICI CO*n*SURGANT *et* EANT AD SEPULCHRU*m* IN P*ro*CESSIONE P*re*CEDENTIB*us* CEREIS, VEXILL<IS>, INCE*n*SO, ET AQUA B*en*EDICTA. ET ACCEPTA CRUCE REDEU*n*TES CANTE*n*T AN*tiphonam*:

Cum rex glorie.

ET PONIT*ur* AN*te* MAIUS ALTARE, IBIQ*ue* A CLERO *et* POP*u*LO SALUTATA STATUIT*ur* *in* LOCU*m* SUU*m*.[61]

---

[56] *Breuiarium Horarum Canonicarum secundum veram rubricam Archiepiscopatus Pragensis*, Venice, 1517, fol. 199^{v}, 270^{v} (British Museum). The *Depositio* and *Elevatio* are now reprinted for the first time. The *Visitatio* (fol. 271^{r}–271^{v}), not yet reprinted, is identical with the *Visitatio* published by Lange (pp. 122–124) from a Prague "Brevier, 1572" (See Lange, p. 15, No. 194).

[57] *Breuiarium . . . Archiepiscopatus Pragensis*, Venice, 1517, fol. 199^{v}.

[58] Immediately followed by the rubric: Completo<rium> ut iero cantetur in choro.

[59] *Breuiarium . . . Archiepiscopatus Pragensis*, Venice, 1517, fol. 270^{v}.

[60] campana] campana*m* (Print).

[61] Followed immediately by the rubric: Ad Matu<tinum>.

In the case of the Prague *Depositio* we may confine our comment to the observation that a light is placed before the closed *sepulchrum*, and that here the canons, two by two, say the psalter continuously until Easter morning.[62] The notable aspects of the *Elevatio* are the adoration of the Cross at the main altar and the singing of the processional antiphon *Cum rex gloriæ*, the latter embodying the theme of the Harrowing of Hell.[63]

An additional consideration arises in connection with the following versions from Ranshofen:[64]

<DEPOSITIO CRUCIS>[65]

DEINde SEPULCHRO PREPARATO *et* DECENTER ORNATO, SINT IMPROMPTU TRIA THURIBULA *Cum* INCENSU ET THIMIAMATE, *et* IIII^{or} CANDELE ARDENTES. *Et* PONTIFEX SIUE PRESBYTER *Cum* ALIIS SACERDOTIBUS *et* MINISTRIS PORTENT YMAGINEM CRUCIFIXI UERSUS SEPULCRUM LUGUBRI UOCE CANTANTES *hoc* RESPON*sorium:*

Responsorium: Ecce quomodo moritur. *Versus:* In pace factus.

RESPONSORIO FINITO COLLOCETUR IN SEPULCHRO *et* LINTEAMINIBUS *et* SUDARIO COOPERIATUR. DEINde LAPIS SUPERPONATUR. QUO FACTO CLERUS IMPONAT RESPONSORIA ISTA:

Responsorium: Sepulto Domino. *Versus:* Ne forte.

Responsorium: Recessit pastor. *Versus:* Ante cuius.

QUIBUS FINITIS DICATUR UERSUS:

Versus: In pace factus.

POSTEA SEQUITUR VESPERA SUPPRESSA UOCE DICENDA.

<ELEVATIO CRUCIS>[66]

IN SANCTA NOCTE AD MATUTINAS CLAM SURGITUR, SINTQUE PARATA TRIA THURIBULA *Cum* THURE ET MIRRA *et* THIMIAMATE. ET DOMINUS PREPOSITUS *Cum* SENIORIBUS QUOS ASSUMERE UOLUERIT *Cum* MAGNA REUERENTIA ACCEDANT AD SEPULCRUM ET STANTES CANTANT:

. Domine, probasti.[67]

ET THURIFICENT YMAGINEM CRUCIFIXI, SUBLATAMQUE DE SEPULCHRO SECUM PORTANT IN CHORUM ANTE ALTARE PER UIAM CANTANDO HUMILI UOCE RESPON*sorium:*

---

[62] See above, p. 14.

[63] See above, p. 31.

[64] Munich, Hofbibliothek, Cod. lat. 12635, Ordinarium Ranshofenense saec. xiii, pp. 56, 59. The *Depositio* and *Elevatio* are now printed for the first time. The *Visitatio* (pp. 59–60), though described by N. C. Brooks (*Zeitschrift für deutsches Altertum*, L, 309), has not yet been published.

[65] Munich, Cod. lat. 12635, p. 56. This text is immediately preceded by the Communion of the *Missa Præsanctificatorum*.

[66] Munich, Cod. lat. 12635, p. 59.

[67] Ps. cxxxviii.

Surrexit pastor bonus<qui animam suam posuit pro ovibus suis, et pro suo grege mori dignatus est, alleluia, alleluia, alleluia>,[68]

CUM SUO UERSU:

Versus: Surrexit *Dominus*<de sepulcro, qui pro nobis pependit in ligno>.[69]

Antiphona:

Xp*istu*c resurgens.

QUIB*us* FINITIS STANTES AN*te* ALTARE *et* MUTUA CARITATE SE I*n*UICE*m* OSC*u*LANTES DICU*n*T *uersum:*

Surrex*it* D*ominus* u*ere*, *et* apparuit Symoni.

ET DICAT*ur* OR*at*IO DE RESURRECTIONE. DEIN*de* CO*m*PULSATIONE SIGNOR*um* FAC*t*A, CO*n*UE*n*IANT OM*n*ES AD MAT*utinum*.

In the use of Ranshofen the detail of special interest for the moment, is the Kiss of Peace administered at the end of the *Elevatio*. Since, however, the associations of the *Pax* have been considered in the preceding division of this study,[70] we need not re-examine the matter here, but may merely observe the same phenomenon in the fifteenth-century observances of Regensburg:[71]

<DEPOSITIO CRUCIS>[72]

POS*t*QUA*m* OM*n*ES CO*m*MUNICAUERI*n*T, UE*n*IA*n*T SAC*er*DOT*es* CU*m* MI*n*ISTRIS ALTA*r*IS *et* CETE*r*IS CANONICIS I*n*STANTIB*us* CU*m* MAGNA REUERE*n*TIA, P*r*ECEDE*n*TIB*us* DUAB*us* CRUCIB*us* UELAT*is* ET UNA CANDELA EXTINCTA *et* ASP*er*SORIO ET THURIBULO. ET TOLLA*n*T CRUCIFIXU*m* *quod* AN*te* FUIT P*r*ES*e*NTATU*m* ET DEFERA*n*T AD LOCU*m* SEPULCHRI *et* CA*n*TA*n*DO[73] LENTA UOCE R*es*PO*n*SORIU*m*:

Recessit pastor. *Versus:* Ante cui*us* *con*spectu*m*.

SEQ*ui*T*ur* R*es*PO*n*SORIU*m*:

Ecce quomod*o* morit*ur* iust*us*. *Versus:* In pace fact*us*.

TU*n*C LOCE*n*T CRUCIFIXU*m* I*n* SEPULCHRO. ET STA*n*TES CI*r*CA DICA*n*T VES*peras*.

---

[68] See Migne, *Pat. Lat.*, LXXVIII, 773.

[69] See *id.*

[70] See above, pp. 45, 65–67.

[71] Munich, Hofbibliothek, Cod. lat. 26947, Ordinarium Ratisbonense saec. xv, fol. 117v, 120v–121r. The *Depositio* and *Elevatio* are now published for the first time. The *Visitatio* has been published by N. C. Brooks, in *Zeitschrift für deutsches Altertum*, L, 298–299. With the *Depositio* and *Elevatio* from Regensburg and Ranshofen may be compared the versions from other churches published by the present writer in the following places: *Transactions of the Wisconsin Academy of Sciences, Arts, and Letters*, XVI, Part II, 899, 906–908; *Publications of the Modern Language Association*, XXIV, 313; *Pub. of the Mod. Lang. Assoc.*, XXV, 343, 351–354.

[72] Munich, Cod. lat. 26947, fol. 117v. The text is immediately preceded by the Communion of the *Missa Præsanctificatorum*.

[73] cantando] cantanda (MS).

<ELEVATIO CRUCIS>[74]

IN NOCTE ANte MATUTINAS SURGANT FRatres IN MONASTERIUM INTRANTES, NEC ALIQUEM LAYCORum INGREDI PERMITTUNT. TUNC UADUNT AD SEPULCHRUM CUm MAGNA REUERENCIA, ET FACIANT ORAtiones. DEINde CANTORES PSalmos:

Domine, quid multipli<fol. 121^r>cati.
Psalmus: Miserere mei, Deus, miserere.
Psalmus: Domine, probasti.
Kyrie.
Pater Noster.
Versus: Exurge, Domine, adiuua nos.
Versus: Domine, Deus uirtutum, conuerte nos.
Versus: Foderunt manus.
Versus: Domine, exaudi orationem.
Versus: Da nobis, Domine, auxilium.

DEINde CRUX ASPERGATUR et THURIFICETUR. DEINde TOLLANT CRUCEM et CANTANT RESponsorium:

Dum transisset Sabbatum, <Maria Magdalene et Maria Jacobi et Salome emerunt aromata, ut venientes ungerent Jesum, alleluia, alleluia. Versus: Et valde mane una Sabbatorum veniunt ad monumentum, orto jam sole. Ut venientes.>,

SUBMISSA UOCE. DUm PERUENERINT AD LOCUm CRUCIFIXI SACERDOS SUBIUNGAT UERSUm:

In resur<r>ectione tua, Xpiste.

SEQUITUR ORatio:

Deus, qui hodierna die.

IBIQUE LINTHEAMINA ET LUMINA DIMITTANTUR. POSTEA IUBENT IANUAS APERIRI ET MATUTINAS SONARE. POST HEC CLERUS MUTUA CARITATE SE INUICEM OSCULANTES DICANT UERSUm:

Surrexit Dominus.

ALII RESPONDEANT:

Guadeamus omnes.

DEINde AD MATutinas uersus: Domine, labia mea.

Hitherto in the present section of our study we have encountered only a slight suggestion of the theme of the Harrowing of Hell. Although we have observed the presence of the antiphon *Cum rex gloriæ*,[75] we have seen no evidence of a treatment of the theme dramatically. For a treatment of this kind we may resort to the use of St. Gall:[76]

---

[74] Munich, Cod. lat. 26947, fol. 120^v–121^r.

[75] See above, p. 87.

[76] St. Gall, Stiftsbibliothek, MS 448, Ordinarium Sangallense saec. xv, pp. 102, 105. The *Depositio*, *Elevatio*, and *Visitatio* from this manuscript have been previously published by the present writer in *Publications of the Modern Language Association*, XXIV, 319–324.

<DEPOSITIO CRUCIS>[77]

Antiphona[78] FINITA, OMNES ASCENDUNT CIRCA ALTARE ET DOMINUS ABBAS EXUENS CASULAM, STANTES ANTE CRUCEM AD DEXTRUM[79] CORNU ALTARIS CANTANTES *Responsorium:*

Ecce quomodo, SUBMISSA UOCE. *Versus:* In pace factus. Repeticio: Et erit.

POST ACCIPENTES CRUCEM DOMINUS ABBAS ET SENIORES PORTANTES AD SEPULCHRUM CANTANTES *Responsorium:*

Sicut ouis. *Versus:* In pace. Repeticio: Traditus.

INTERIM PONENT CRUCEM IN SEPULCHRO ET CLAUDUNT EUM, PONENTES ANTE SEPULCHRUM QUATUOR LUMINA IUGITER ARDENTIA, CANTANTES *Responsorium:*

Sepulto Domino. *Versus:* Ne forte. Repeticio: Ponentes mi<lites>.

DEINDE DOMINUS ABBAS DICAT *Versum:*

In pace factus est locus eius.

COLLECTA:

Respice, Domine.

ET ASPERGENS SEPULCRUM AQUA BENEDICTA, ET THURIFICETUR CUM INCENSU, ET MISSE SUNT.

<ELEVATIO CRUCIS>[80]

ORDO AD LEVANDUM CRUCEM SANCTAM IN SACRATISSIMA NOCTE PASCALI.

PARUM ANTE MATUTINAS DOMINUS ABBAS, PREPOSITUS DECANUS, CUSTOS, ET SENIORES AD HOC DEPUTATI SURGANT DILUCULO, ET INDUUNT SE ALBIS ET CAPPIS, PERGENTES CUM SUMMA REUERENCIA, CUM MINISTRIS PORTANTES AQUAM BENEDICTAM CUM INCENSU, ET CUM SILENCIO, AD SEPULCRUM. ET DOMINUS ABBAS CUM SUMMO HONORE TOTAQUE DEUITIONE FLEXIS GENIBUS DEPONAT SUDARIUM ET LINTEAMINA CUM QUIBUS SANCTA CRUX EST INUOLUTA, ET ASPERGENS AQUA BENEDICTA ET THURIFICETUR CUM INCENSU, ET CANTENT SUBMISSA UOCE:

Xpiste, salus rerum. *Versus:* Pollicitam, USQUE Surge, sepulte meus.

ET ELEUANTES CRUCEM DE SEPULCHRO CANTENT HOS *Uersus:*

Solue cathenatus.

Versus:

Redde tuam faciem.

QUIBUS FINITIS, CANTATUR *Antiphona:*

Cum rex glorie,

SUBMISSA UOCE, PORTANTES CRUCEM ANTE CHORUM IN MONASTERIO. *Antiphona* FINITA, CANTANT *Antiphonam:*

Attollite portas prin<cipes>,

TRIBUS UICIBUS, PULSANTES CONTRA IANUAM CUM PEDE CRUCIS IN SIGNUM REDEMPCIONIS ANIMARUM EX LIMBO. AD ISTUM PULSUM IANUA APERITUR. POSTEA PONATUR CRUX ANTE ALTARE BEATE VIRGINIS, PANNO SUPPOSITO AC LUMINE ACCENSO, UT A POPULIS ADORETUR. DEINDE DOMINUS ABBAS DICA<T> *Uersum:*

---

[77] St. Gall, MS 448, p. 102.

[78] The antiphon of the *Magnificat* at Vespers.

[79] dextrum] dextram (MS).

[80] St. Gall, MS 448, p. 105.

In resurrect*ione* tua, Xp*iste*.

Col*lecta*:

Presta, *quesumus*, omn*ipotens* De*us*.

Hys finitis, adorent Crucem osculando ac rigando lacrimis uulnera eius. Et tunc fiat compulsacio omnium campanarum, pulsantque tribus uicibus in signum resurrectionis. Post hoc pulsantur Matutine.

Confining our attention to the *Elevatio*, we note that this office occupies the usual position before Easter Matins. After reaching the *sepulchrum* in procession, the abbot removes the sudary and linen from the Cross, and sprinkles and censes it. These acts, together with the raising of the Cross aloft, are accompanied by the singing of liturgical verses. With the antiphon *Cum rex gloriæ* the Cross is conducted to the door of the choir. Here the antiphon *Attollite portas* is sung thrice, and the door is struck thrice with the shaft of the Cross, *in signum redempcionis animarum ex Limbo.* At the third striking the door is opened, and the Cross is placed before the altar of the Blessed Virgin for adoration by the congregation.

In brief summary we may observe that the versions of the *Depositio* and *Elevatio* reviewed in the present section of this study differ from those in the preceding section in nothing fundamental. The versions before us range in date from the tenth century to the sixteenth, and they come to us from England, France, Germany, and Switzerland. A clear majority of them, however, are of South German provenience. As we should expect, the burial and raising of the Cross bear conspicuous evidence of influence from the *Adoratio Crucis.* For their content these versions borrow traditional liturgical pieces from the *Graduale* and the *Liber Responsalis.* From the point of view of the history of the drama, however, the most important aspect of these versions is the prevailing absence of dialogue and the complete absence of unequivocal impersonation.

V

Now that we have examined the versions of the *Depositio* and *Elevatio* in which the Host and the Cross respectively are the centers of devotion, we must complete our survey by considering the versions in which are employed both the Host and the Cross, along with an inevitable extension of the ceremonial.

A simple *Depositio* of this type is at hand from the use of St. Adelph:[1]

<DEPOSITIO CRUCIS ET HOSTIÆ>[2]

POSTEA VADUNT CUM CANDELIS ARDENTIBUS ET INCENSU <FOL. 41v> AD LOCUM SEPULCHRI ET IMPONANT CRUCEM CUM EUCHARISTIA. IN EUNDO CANTETUR *Responsorium:*

Ecce quomodo moritur iustus, et nemo percipit corde; et viri iusti tolluntur, et nemo considerat; a facie iniquitatis oblatus est iustus, et erit in pace memoria eius. *Versus:* In pace factus est locus eius, et in Sion habitacio eius. Et erit.

Responsorium:

Recessit pastor noster, fons acque vive, ad cuius transitum sol obscuratus est, nam et ille captus est qui captiuum tenebat primum hominem, hodie portas mortis et seras pariter Saluator noster disrupit. *Versus:* Ante cuius conspectum mors fugit, ad cuius uocem mortui resurgunt, uidentes autem eum porte mortis confracte sunt. Ho<die>.

IMPOSITA AUTEM CRUCE, CANTENTUR HEE ANTIPHONAE. *Antiphona:*

In pace in idipsum dormiam et requiescam.

Antiphona:

Caro <fol. 42r> mea requiescet in spe.

SUDARIO SUPERPOSITO, CANTETUR *Responsorium:*

Sepulto Domino, signatum est monumentum, uoluentes lapidem ad hostium monumenti, ponentes milites qui custodirent eum. *Versus:* Ne forte veniant disciputi eius et furentur eum, et dicant plebi: Surrexit a mortuis. Ponentes.

SEQUUNTUR VESPERAE[3] SUB SILENTIO.

---

[1] Paris, Bibl. Nat., MS latin 9486, Ordinarium saec. xii, fol. 41r–42r. L. Delisle (*Inventaire des Manuscrits latins conservés à la Bibliothèque Nationale sous les Numéros 8823-18613*, Paris, 1863–1871, p. 35) mentions this document briefly as "Rituel de l'abb. de S. Adelphe." The manuscript contains no *Elevatio*. The *Visitatio* (fol. 60r–60v) has been published by N. C. Brooks in *Journal of English and Germanic Philology*, VIII, 466. Both the *Depositio* and the *Visitatio* are printed by the present writer in *Publications of the Modern Language Association*, XXV, 341–342, 351.

[2] Bibl. Nat., MS lat. 9486, fol. 41r–42r. The text printed here is immediately preceded by the following rubric: Tunc accedant omnes ad communionem—referring to the Communion of the *Missa Præsanctificatorum*.

[3] Vesperae] Vespera (MS).

This office occurs immediately after the *Missa Præsanctificatorum*. The Cross and the Host are carried to the *sepulchrum* in a single procession. For the laying down of the Host no special rubrics are given. The burial of the Cross evokes at least the ceremonial of wrapping it in a *sudarium*. The musical pieces accompanying the action are already familiar.

A similar version of the *Depositio*, with a fuller description of the ceremonial, is seen in the following from the use of Aquileia:[4]

<DEPOSITIO CRUCIS ET HOSTIÆ>[5]

Finito hymno[6] incipit officium diei, ut in Missali continetur. Oratione[7] vero expleta, *et* Sepulchro preparato *et* decenter ornato, assint inpromptu tria thuribula cum incenso thuris, mirrhe, *et* thimiamatis, *et* quatuor candele ardentes; *et* ministri cum Sacerdotibus portent Imaginem Crucifixi versus Sepulchrum, *et* Officians sequatur portans Sacramentum Eucharistie in sanctuario repositum. Chorus vero in tali processione lugubri voce cantet responsorium cum suo versu:

> Ecce quomodo moritur iustus, *et* nemo percipit corde; *et* viri iusti tolluntur, *et* nemo considerat; a facie iniquitatis oblatus est iu<p. 121>stus, et erit in pace memoria eius. <Versus>: In pace factus est locus eius, *et* in Syon habitatio eius. Et erit in pace.

Quo finito *et* dum ad Sepulchrum ventum sit, Officians locet Sacramentum in sanctuario repositum[8] ad locum in Sepulchro ad hoc paratum. Deinde Ministri, *et* Sacerdotes Imaginem Crucifixi collocent in Sepulchro, *et* cooperiant lintheaminibus *et* sudario, *et* supponant lapidem. Chorus cantet *responsorium* cum suo versu:

> Recessit pastor noster, fons aque viue, ad cuius transitum sol obscuratus est; nam *et* ille captus est qui captiuum tenebat primum hominem. Hodie portas mortis *et* seras pariter Saluator noster destruxit. <p. 122> *Versus:* Ante cuius conspectum mors fugit, ad cuius vocem mortui resurgunt; videntes autem eum porte mortis confracte sunt. Hodie portas.

Officians vero thurificet Imaginem Crucifixi sic in Sepulchrum positam, *et* aspergat aqua benedicta. Et postea clauditur Sepulchrum, *et* clauso apponunt sigilla Officiantes *et* Laici presidentes, *et* chorus cantet responsorium sequentem cum suo versu:

---

[4] *Agenda Diocesis Sanctae Ecclesiae Aquilegiensis*, Venice, 1575, pp. 120–123 (Paris, Bibl. Nat.). The *Depositio* is now reprinted for the first time. The *Visitatio* (pp. 115–117) has been published by Lange (No. 167, pp. 13, 105–106). The edition of 1575 contains (pp. 112–115) also an *Elevatio;* but the only copy of this edition accessible to me lacks the pages (pp. 113–114) containing the greater part of this office.

[5] *Agenda Diocesis Sanctae Ecclesiae Aquilegiensis*, Venice, 1575, pp. 120–123.

[6] The *Crux fidelis*, closing the *Adoratio Crucis*.

[7] The closing *Oratio* of the *Missa Præsanctificatorum*.

[8] repositum] reposito (*Agenda*).

Sepulto Domino, signatum est monumentum, voluentes lapidem ad hostium monumenti, ponentes milites qui custodirent illud. <VERSUS>: Ne forte veniant discipuli eius *et* furentur eum, *et* dicant plebi: Surrexit a mortuis. Ponentes.<p. 123>

QUO FINITO OFFICIANS DICAT VERSICULUM:

In pace factus est locus eius.

Et RESPONDENT MINISTRI *et* SACERDOTES:

Et habitatio eius in Syon.

TANDEM CIRCA SEPULCHRUM DICANTUR VESPERE SECUNDU*m* RUBRICA*m* BREUIARII. ET SUB Magnificat OFFICIANS *et* MINISTRI CUM TRIBUS THURIBULIS SEPULCHRUM THURIFICE*nt* *et* SACERDOS ACQUA BENEDICTA ASPERGAT. FINITIS AUTE*m* VESPERIS, SCHOLARES SECUNDU*m* MORE*m* PATRIE INCIPIUNT LEGERE PSALTERIU*m*.

The office here occurs immediately after the *Missa Præsanctificatorum*. In the procession to the *sepulchrum* the ministers of the Mass carry the *Imago Crucifixi*, and the officiant,[9] the Host.[10] The first deposits the Host in a part of the *sepulchrum* especially prepared for it. Then the ministers and priests, after laying down the *Imago Crucifixi*, cover it with cloths and the sudary,[11] and place over it a stone.[12] After censing and sprinkling the *Imago*, they seal the *sepulchrum*. The musical pieces accompanying the action require no comment. The most notable aspect of this version is the distinctness with which the Host and Cross are separated in their ceremonials.

In association with these two versions of the *Depositio* we may appropriately consider one or two relatively simple texts of the *Elevatio*. Such a text may be seen in the following from Harlem, in Holland:[13]

[9] I take this to be the priest who has officiated at the *Missa Præsanctificatorum*.

[10] I am not absolutely certain of the meaning of the phrase *in sanctuario repositum*, which occurs twice. The word *sanctuarium* may indicate the sacristy, or place of reservation, in which the special (third) Host was reserved from Holy Thursday; but the word may also indicate (see Du Cange) a *theca*, or box, for carrying the Host in the procession before us.

[11] In the *Visitatio* occurs (p. 117) the rubric *lintheamina et sudarium quibus Imago Domini erat inuoluta*, indicating that only the *Imago*, and not the Host, is covered in this way.

[12] The rubric may intend that the *lapis* for closing the door of the *sepulchrum* confines within the structure only the *Imago*, the Host being exposed upon a sepulchre—altar outside.

[13] Harlem, Bischöfliches Museum, MS 258, Graduale Harlemense (?) saec. xiii, fol. 44ᵛ. This text of the *Elevatio* has been previously printed by Lange

<ELEVATIO CRUCIS ET HOSTIÆ>[14]

ORDO *in* DIE RES*urrectionis*.

IN DIE DOMINICE RESURRECTIONIS ANTE MATUTINU*m* TEMPUS PRES*byteri* VISITENT SEPULCHRU*m* CU*m* THURIBULIS CA*n*TANDO R*esponsorium*:

Angelus D*omini*.[15]

EXTOLLANT *etiam* CRUCE*m* DE SEPULCH*ro* CU*m* EUCHARISTIA *et* IN ALIO LOCO PONA*n*T CU*m* REVERENTIA.

According to these meagre rubrics the *Elevatio* is found in the normal liturgical position, before Easter Matins, and provides merely a simple procession of priests who visit the *sepulchrum* and carry the Host and Cross thence to a place not specified. In its general simplicity, and in its use of the responsory *Angelus Domini*, the version before us resembles the *Elevatio* printed above from a manuscript of the eleventh century from St. Gall,[16] the latter text being found in a position before the *Te Deum* at the *end* of Easter Matins. The resemblance between the two versions suggests the possibility that at an early period the *Elevatio* normally occurred at the *end* of Matins, and that it was transferred to a place *before* Matins in order to make way, at the *Te Deum*, for a newly invented *Visitatio*.[17]

Another simple version of the *Elevatio* is found at Klosterneuberg in the following form:[18]

<ELEVATIO CRUCIS ET HOSTIÆ>[19]

IN SANCTA NOCTE ANTEQUAM SONENTUR MATUTINE, PRELATUS ALIQUIBUS SIBI ADIUNCTIS CORPUS DOMINICUM ET CRUCEM DE SEPULCHRO TOLLANT CUM

(No. 142, pp. 12, 93), along with the *Visitatio*. I print from a photograph of the manuscript page. Whether the manuscript contains a text of the *Depositio*, I do not know.

[14] Harlem, MS 258, fol. 44v.

[15] For the complete responsory see above, p. 30.

[16] See above, p. 30.

[17] See above, pp. 31, 72, and below, p. 123.

[18] H. Pfeiffer's article *Klosterneuburger Osterfeier und Osterspiel* (*Jahrbuch des Stiftes Klosterneuburg*, Vol. I, Vienna, 1908, pp. 1–56) supersedes all previous publication upon the Easter liturgical plays of Klosterneuburg, in Austria, and provides bibliography. Since I have not had access to the manuscripts of this monastery, I reprint the *Elevatio* as published by Pfeiffer (p. 16) from MS 629, fol. 102r–103r, of the fifteenth century. From this manuscript he prints (pp. 16–18) also the *Visitatio*. Although it appears (Pfeiffer, p. 20, note 2) that the Klosterneuburg manuscripts contain texts of the *Depositio*, he prints none of them.

[19] Klosterneuburg MS 629, fol. 102r–103r.

DEUOTIONE ET REUERENTIA, ADOLENTES ET ASPERGENTES EA, AC CANENTES SUB SILENCIO RESPONSORIUM:

Surrexit pastor bonus, qui posuit animam suam pro ovibus suis; et pro suo grege mori dignatus est, aeuia, <fol. 102v> aeuia, aeuia. <Versus>: Surrexit Dominus de sepulchro, qui pro nobis pependit in ligno. Et pro.

DEINDE HOS PSALMOS CANTENT:

Conserva me, Domine. <fol. 103r>

Domine, probasti me.

REQUIRE IN PARASCEVE.

VERSICULA:

Surrexit Dominus de sepulchro, alleluja. Qui pro nobis pependit in ligno, alleluja.

ORACIO:

Oremus: Deus qui hodierno die per unigenitum tuum eternitatis nobis aditum devicta morte reserasti, vota nostra, quae praeveniendo aspiras eciam adiuvando prosequere. Per eundem Dominum.

This office occurs before Matins. During the singing of the responsory *Surrexit pastor* the abbot, accompanied by other clerics, takes the Cross and Host from the *sepulchrum* and places them in some appropriate place. The observance concludes with the rendering of two psalms, a versicle, and a prayer.

We have already noticed a tendency to discriminate clearly between the Host and the Cross in the ceremonial.[20] This distinction is particularly evident in the following version of the *Elevatio* from Augsburg:[21]

<ELEVATIO CRUCIS ET HOSTIÆ>[22]

IN IP*s*A NOCTE, MATTUTINA LUCE APPROPINQUANTE, CUSTODES ECCL*esi*E CU*m* SACERDOTIBUS MATURI*us* AN*te* ALIOS SURGE*n*TES *con*UENIA*n*T IN ECCLESIA*m*. *Et* LOTIS MANIB*us*, CU*m* CEREIS DUOBUS *et* THURIBULIS *et* AQ*ua* B*e*N*e*DICTA REUERENTER, QUASI SECRETO, P*ro*CEDA*n*T AD LOCU*m* U*b*I CRUX *et* CORP*us* DO*m*I*n*I I*n* SEXTA FE*ri*A FUERA*n*T TUMULATA. ASP*er*SA AU*tem* *et* THURIFICATA CRUCE, MAIOR INT*er* SACERDOTES REUERENTISSIME TOLLAT CALICE*m* CU*m* CORPORE DO*m*I*n*I; CET*er*I U*er*O CRUCE*m* PORTENT. SINDONE QUA FUIT COOP*er*TA I*n* IPSO LOCO RELICTA, *et* LUMINIB*us*, NE LOC*us* DESPECTUS UIDEAT*ur*, P*re*CEDENTIB*us* CEREIS *et* I*n*CENSO PORTE*n*T ILLA*m* AD ALTARE UBI OFFICIU*m* E*st* P*er*AGENDU*m* SUBMISSA UOCE CA*n*TANTES R*esponsorium*:

Surrexit pastor bonus qui posuit a*nimam*,

---

[20] See the texts from St. Adelphe and Aquileia, above, pp. 92–94.

[21] Munich, Hofbibliothek, Cod. lat. 226, Rationale Officiorum Divinorum Augustanense saec. xi–xii, fol. 10r. The *Elevatio* is now published for the first time. The manuscript contains no *Depositio*. The *Visitatio* (fol. 10v–11r) is printed by Lange (No. 110, pp. 10, 82–83).

[22] Munich, Hofbibliothek, Cod. lat. 226, fol. 10r

CU*m* VERSU:

Surrexit D*ominus* de *sepulchro*.

SEQ*uitu*R OR*atio*:

Deus, q*ui* unig*enitum*.

ET COOP*er*IAT*ur* CRUX D*e* LINTEO MUNDO. CALIX AU*tem* CU*m* CORPORE D*omi*NI REPONAT*ur* I*n* P*r*INCIPALI ALTARE DONEC ALICUI DET*ur* AD *con*SUMENDU*m*. QUO FACTO REV*er*TANTUR I*n* CHORU*m* *et* OMN*es* MUTUA CARITATE SE[23] INVICE*m* OSCULENTUR. *Et* DICAT P*r*IOR:

Surrexit Xp*istus*.

RESPONDE*n*T:

Gaudeamu*s* omn*es*.

ET STATI*m* CO*m*PULSENTUR O*mni*A SIGNA SOLLE*m*NISSIME AD EXCITANDU*m* ET *con*UOCANDU*m*; *et* INT*er*VALLO MODICO FACTO, BINA *et* BINA SIGNA MOROSI*us* PULSENT*ur*; *et* I*n* FINE ILLOR*um* RURSUS *com*PULSET*ur*. ET I*m*PONAT SACERDOS TONALI VOCE:

D*omi*ne, labia mea ap*er*ies.

This office is performed privately before Easter Matins. After being sprinkled and censed, the Cross is taken up from the *sepulchrum* by the assistant clerics. Leaving behind the winding sheet, they carry the Cross to a special altar.[24] Here a prayer is said, and the Cross covered with a clean cloth. The chalice containing the Host[25] is taken up separately by the senior priest, and placed upon the main altar. The *ordo* provides that the Host shall be left upon the main altar until it is given to an appropriate person to be consumed. After these ceremonials the procession returns to the choir, where the *Pax* is given and a versicle and response delivered.

In the following versions from York the separation between Host and Cross is extreme:[26]

---

[23] se] si (MS).

[24] I infer that this is an altar connected with the *sepulchrum*. It may, however, be the *altare majus*.

[25] That the Host is carried *within* the chalice may fairly be inferred from the rubric *Calix autem cum Corpore Domini*. See above, p. 50. It may, however, be intended merely that the chalice *accompany* the Host. See below, p. 102.

[26] *Manuale et Processionale ad Usum insignis Ecclesiae Eboracensis*, in *Surtees Society*, Vol. LXIII, 1875, pp. 163–164, 170–174. This edition of the *Manuale* is based upon that of Wynkyn de Worde, London, 1509. The *Depositio*, but not the *Elevatio*, is found also in *Missale ad Usum insignis Ecclesiae Eboracensis*, in *Surtees Society*, Vol. LIX, 1874, pp. 106–107. The liturgical documents of York contain no *Visitatio*.

<DEPOSITIO CRUCIS>[27]

TANDEM ADORATA CRUCE BAJULANT EAM DUO PRESBYTERI ASCENDENTES PER PARTEM AQUILONAREM CHORI USQUE AD SEPULCHRUM, ET IBI SACERDOS INCIPIAT ANTIPHONA<M>:

Super omnia ligna cedrorum tu sola excelsior, in qua vita mundi pependit, in qua Christus triumphavit, et mors mortem superavit in æternum.

ANTIPHONA:

In pace in idipsum dormiam et requiescam.

ANTIPHONA:

Habitavit in tabernaculo tuo; requiescet in monte sancto tuo.

ANTIPHONA:

Caro mea requiescet in spe.

POSTEA EXSECUTOR OFFICII GENUFLECTENS PONAT CRUCEM IN SEPULCHRO, ET THURIFICET EAM, ET ERECTUS INCIPIAT, ET CHORUS FINIAT:

Sepulto Domino signatum est monumentum; ponentes milites qui custodirent illud.

<ELEVATIO CRUCIS ET HOSTIÆ>[28]

IN AURORA PULSATIS CAMPANIS AD CLASSICUM, CONGREGATO CLERO ET POPULO, FLEXIS GENIBUS DICITUR ORATIO DOMINICALIS; ET POSTEA SACERDOS THURIFICET SEPULCRUM, ET PROFERATUR SACRAMENTUM CUM IMAGINE CUM CORONA SPINEA. INCIPIATUR RESPONSORIUM: Christus regnat, QUOD CANTETUR CIRCA FONTEM, CEREIS PRÆCEDENTIBUS. RESPONSORIUM:

Christus resurgens ex mortuis jam non moritur; mors illi ultra non dominabitur. Quod enim vivit, vivit Deo, alleluja, alleluja. V<ERSUS>: Dicant nunc Judæi quomodo milites custodientes Sepulchrum perdiderunt regem ad lapidis positionem. Quare non servabant petram justitiæ? Aut sepultum reddant, aut resurgentem adorent nobiscum dicentes. Quod.

PSALMUS:

Te Deum laudamus . . . . non confundar in æternum.[29]

V<ERSUS>:

Resurrexit Dominus. Sicut dixit vobis.

ORATIO:

Præsta, quæsumus, omnipotens Deus, ut in resurrectione Domini nostri Jesu Christi cum omnibus sanctis percipiamus portionem. Qui tecum vivit et regnat Deus. Per omnia.

DEINDE OSCULETUR CUPPA IN QUA EST SACRAMENTUM, PRIMO A SACERDOTE, ET POSTEA A POPULO.

It will be observed that the York *Depositio* is attached directly to the *Adoratio Crucis*, and that the Host is not mentioned. That the Host was involved in the *sepulchrum* offices

---

[27] *Manuale . . . Ecclesiae Eboracensis*, in *Surtees Society*, LXIII, 163–164.

[28] *Id.*, pp. 170–174.

[29] In the Surtees text the *Te Deum* is given in full.

is clear, however, from the fact that the *Elevatio* mentions it particularly.[30]

Discrimination between the Cross and the Host is seen again in the use of the cathedral of Exeter.[31] The *Depositio* takes the following form:

<DEPOSITIO CRUCIS ET HOSTIÆ>[32]

DEINDE EXUAT SACERDOS CASULAM TANTUM, ET IN ALBA ASSISTENS ASSUMAT UNUM DE PRELATIS IN SUPPERELLICIO ET REPONAT CRUCEM PARITER CUM CORPORE DOMINICO IN SEPULCRO, INCIPIENS HOC RESPONSORIUM:

Estimatus sum.

CHORUS PROSEQUATUR: Cum descendentibus, ET CETERA. DEINDE INCENSATO SEPULCRO ET CLAUSO HOSTIO EIUSDEM, INCIPIAT IPSE SACERDOS *responsorium:*

Sepulto Domino.

CHORUS PROSEQUATUR: Signatum, ET CETERA. ITEM IDEM SACERDOS INCIPIAT ANTIPHONAM:

In pace in idipsum.

CHORUS: Dormiam.

IDEM SACERDOS INCIPIAT ANTIPHONAM:

In pace factus est.

CHORUS: Locus eius.

ITEM SACERDOS ANT*iphonam:*

Caro mea.

CHORUS: Requiescet in spe.

TUNC OMNES CUM DEUOCIONE GENUFLECTANT, ET ADORATA CRUCE, RECEDANT.[33]

This *ordo* provides that after Vespers, during the singing of the responsory *Aestimatus sum,* a priest, accompanied by one prelate, deposits in the *sepulchrum* both Cross and Host.[34] Then after the censing of the *sepulchrum* and the closing of the door, is sung the responsory *Sepulto Domino.* The office is concluded by the singing of three antiphons and an adoration of the Cross.[35]

[30] The York texts may serve as a reminder that the absence of Host or Cross from an isolated version of the *Depositio* or *Elevatio* does not definitely prove the absence from the *sepulchrum* offices of the object ignored in the rubrics.

[31] *Ordinale Exoniense,* edited from a manuscript of the fourteenth century by J. N. Dalton, in *Henry Bradshaw Society,* Vol. XXXVII, London, 1909. From Exeter no *Visitatio* is forthcoming.

[32] *Henry Bradshaw Society,* XXXVII, 321.

[33] Followed immediately by the rubric *In Vigilia Pasce.*

[34] The reservation of this Host on Holy Thursday is provided for in the following rubric (*Henry Bradshaw Soc.,* XXXVII, 318): Ponantur a diacono tres hostie ad sacramentandum, quarum due reseruantur in crastinum, una ad percipiendum a sacerdote, *reliqua ut reponatur cum cruce in sepulcro.*

[35] I am not clear as to what cross is the center of this concluding adoration. By this time the cross used in the *Depositio* is enclosed within the *sepulchrum.*

The *Elevatio* from Exeter is described in the following *ordo:*

<ELEVATIO CRUCIS ET HOSTIÆ>[38]

In aurora diei ante pulsacionem campanarum et ante eciam Matutinas conueniant Clerici omnes et laici ad ecclesiam, et accendantur omnia luminaria per ecclesiam. Episcopus et Decanus vel alie due digniores persone presentes in supperellicijs cum ceroferarijs et thuribularijs albis indutis ad Sepulcrum una cum toto choro circumstante accedant, et facta deuota genuflexione, incensatoque prius Sepulcro, cum magna ueneracione Corpus Dominicum accipientes priuatim super altare deponant. Item accipientes cum genuflexione Crucem de Sepulcro inchoent Episcopus et Decanus, si asint; sin autem, Decanus cum alia excellenciore persona, alta uoce hanc antiphonam:

Christus resurgens.

Cum qua antiphona eat processio choro canente totam antiphonam cum versu. Et tunc pulsentur omnes campane in classicum. Et sic cum magna ueneracione deportetur Crux solempniter inter eos super brachia, et thuribularijs et ceroferarijs precedentibus, per hostium australe presbiterij incedentes et circumeundo per medium chori regredientes, choro sequente habitu non mutato, scilicet in capis nigris, ad locum ubi prouisum fuerit, excellencioribus personis precedentibus. Finita antiphona cum suo versu a toto choro, dicat excellencior persona in ipsa stacione ante altare ad clerum conversus hunc *Versum:*

Surrexit Dominus de sepulcro;

R*esponsum:*

Qui pro nobis pependit in ligno, alleluya;

cum oracione:

Deus qui pro nobis.

Nec precedat nec subsequatur: Dominus vobiscum, set finiatur: Per Christum Dominum nostrum. Finita oracione, omnes cum gaudio genua flectant ibidem et ipsam Crucem adorent, in primis a dignioribus personis. Interim pulsetur ad Matutinas.

This office is celebrated before Matins on Easter morning in the presence of laymen and clergy. After the arrival at the *sepulchrum* of the Bishop, Dean, and two others in procession, and after the censing of the place, the Host is taken up separately and carried, without processional singing, to the altar. Then the Cross is raised and taken in procession into the choir, during the singing of the antiphon *Christus resurgens*. During the procession all the bells of the church are rung. In the choir are said a versicle and response, and a prayer. The office closes with an adoration of the Cross. The special reverence paid to the Cross in the *Elevatio*, along with the closing obser-

[38] *Henry Bradshaw Society*, XXXVII, 138–139.

vance of the *Depositio*, seems especially to indicate the influence of the *Adoratio Crucis*.

In the present part of our review belong the texts from the cathedral of Bayeux.[37] The *Depositio* is found as follows:

<DEPOSITIO CRUCIS ET HOSTIÆ>[38]

Deinde[39] exuat Pontifex casulam, et accipiens Crucem super altare jacentem, cum alio Sacerdote, incensato prius Sepulchro, ponat eam cum magna reverentia in ipso Sepulchro, suppositis pulvinari et mundis et albis lintheaminibus, astantibus duobus ceroferariis in supellitiis; et ponendo incipiat Cantor media voce *responsorium:*

> Estimatus sum<descendentibus in lacum; factus sum sicut homo sine adjutorio, inter mortuos liber. Versus: Et sicut vulnerati dormientes, projecti in monumentis, quorum non es memor amplius, et ipsi de manu tua repulsi sunt. Factus sum.>,

choro excipiente in eadem voce illud idem cum suo versu et regressu. Deinde accipiat Episcopus de manu Diaconi in pixide sindone cooperta Corpus Dominicum a die precedenti reservatum et reponat illud honorifice in ipso Sepulchro juxta Crucem. Ponat etiam ibidem Episcopus ex alia parte Crucis calicem [vacuum], patenam, [corporalia] sindone etiam involuta. Deinde claudens ipse Sepulchrum iterum incenset illud, et incipiat Cantor *responsorium:*

> Sepulto Domino,

voce qua primum, et similiter excipiatur a choro cum suo versu et regressu. Quibus cantatis incipiat ipse Pontifex anti*phonam:*

> In pace in idipsum.

Item incipiat [similiter] anti*phonam:*

> In pace factus est.

---

[37] I present the texts given by U. Chevalier, *Ordinaire et Coutumier de l'Église cathédrale de Bayeux* (*Bibliothèque Liturgique*, Vol. VIII, Paris, 1902), from Bayeux MS 121 of the thirteenth century. Martène prints the *Depositio* (p. 367) and *Elevatio* (p. 478) from "Bajocensis ecclesiæ ordinarium ante annos 400 quantum conjicere licet exaratum,"—a document that we may date about the year 1300. Except for a passage that I reprint in foot-note 40 below, Martène's *Depositio* does not differ substantially from the text given by Chevalier (pp. 133–134) from MS 121. Martène's *Elevatio* I reprint in a foot-note. From the Bayeux *Consuetudinarium*, contained in manuscripts of the thirteenth century, Chevalier gives brief *ordines* for the *Depositio* (pp. 388–389) and *Elevatio* (p. 390). Similar to this last text is the *Elevatio* printed by A. Gasté (*Les Drames liturgiques de la Cathédrale de Rouen*, Évreux, 1893, p. 63) from "indications que nous fournit Radulphe l'Angevin dans son *Cérémonial*, rédigé en 1269." The liturgical manuscripts of Bayeux do not contain the *Visitatio Sepulchri*.

[38] *Bibliothèque Liturgique*, VIII, 133–134. Cf. the *ordo* in the *Consuetudinarium*, *id.*, pp. 388–389.

[39] This text is immediately preceded by the *ordo* for Vespers.

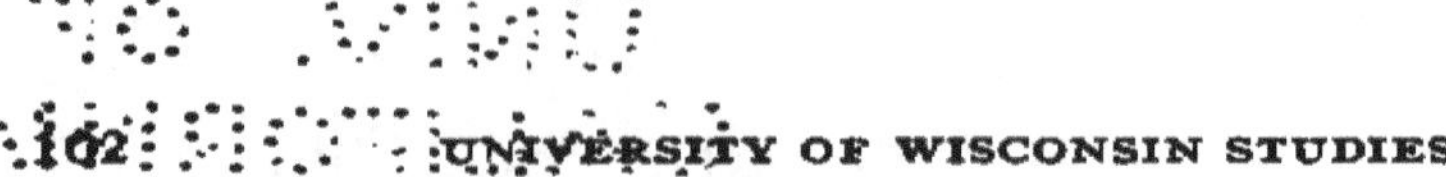

ULTIMO AUTEM INCIPIAT ANTI*phonam:*

Caro mea.

ET SIC COMPLEATUR DIEI ISTIUS OFFICIUM. NOTA VERO QUIA, QUAMDIU CORPUS DOMINICUM JACET IN SEPULCHRO, ARDENT CONTINUE DUO CEREI ANTE ILLUD SUPER TAPETUM IBIDEM PROTENTUM.

This office occurs after Vespers. The bishop, assisted by another priest, takes up the Cross lying on the altar, deposits it in the *sepulchrum*,[40] and places over it a cushion and clean white cloths. Meanwhile is sung the responsory *Aestimatus sum*. Then the bishop places beside the Cross a pyx containing the Host,[41] and on the opposite side of the Cross, an empty chalice and a paten. After the *sepulchrum* has been closed, are sung the responsory *Sepulto Domino* and three antiphons. It is to be observed that for the period during which the Host remains in the *sepulchrum* two lights are kept burning before the place.

The *Elevatio* at Bayeux is ordered as follows:[42]

---

[40] The location and furnishing of the *sepulchrum* are described briefly in the following rubric communicated by Martène (p. 367): Hodie paretur sepulcrum versus cornu altaris sinistrum, linteaminibus mundis et palliis pretiosis, et aliis sicut pretiosius fieri consuevit.

[41] That this Host is especially reserved from Thursday we learn from the *Consuetudinarium* of Bayeux, in which it is spoken of (*Bibliothèque Liturgique*, VIII, 389) as *Corpus Dominicum a die precedente reservatum*. See also Martène, p. 367.

[42] Since the *Elevatio* communicated by Martène (p. 478) differs considerably from the text of Bayeux MS 121 used by Chevalier, I reprint Martène's text entire:

Ante matutinas facta pulsatione & conglobato choro ante altare, cereis & thuribulis accensis, episcopus superpelliceo & stola indutus, facta oratione ante altare, stans ad cornu dextrum altaris, lavat manus, incensum benedicit, illudque ponit in thuribulo, & in medio altaris corporale explicat. Sacerdos similiter indutus. Deinde accedit ad sepulcrum ex utraque parte expansum, in quo pyxis cum reliquiis supradictis reservatur: quam flexis genibus incensat, eamque postea defert ad altare, & cum ea clero & populo in modum crucis benedicit more consueto, & supradictum corporale reponit & incensat, moxque ex ea sumptum Corpus Dominicum genibus flexis adorandum ostendit. Quo in pixide reposito, redit ad eumdem locum, unde calice cum patena & bursa sumptis, & ad altare delatis, ultimo vero crucem extollens, & ad altare conversus incipiat antiphonam *Christus resurgens* cum suo versu & regressu. Tunc omnes cum gaudio flexis genibus adorent crucem, cantantes eamdem antiphonam, quæ dum cantatur supra altare crucem deponit. Quo facto, stans episcopus dicat *versum Surrexit Dominus de sepulcro,* & orationem *Deus qui pro nobis Filium tuum.* Deinde cantatur antiphona *Regina cœli* cum suo versu & oratione.

<ELEVATIO CRUCIS ET HOSTIÆ>[43]

In die sancto Pasche fit festum duplex cum iiii^or capis de stallo altiori. Pulsatur etiam sicut in Natali Domini quasi per horam unam vel circa ante diem. Qua pulsatione finita, Clero ante altare conglobato, Episcopus, cereis et thuribulis accensis, accedat ad Sepulchrum. Quo incensato, Corpus Domini inde sumptum cum reverentia magna deponat super altare; deinde calicem, ultimo vero extollens ipse Crucem de Sepulchro incipiat anti*phonam:*

Xpistus resurgens.

Tunc omnes cum gaudio, flexis genibus, adorent Crucem, cantantes eandem antiphonam cum suo versu et regressu. Postea eadem Cruce posita ab ipso Episcopo super altare Beatorum Ravenni et Rasifi, dicat ipse Episcopus, stans ad idem altare *versum:*

Surrexit Dominus de sepulchro.

Et parvo Missali aperto super ipsum altare: scilicet, ad pedem Crucis, subjungat adhuc Episcopus: Oremus, et orationem etc. Dicat Episcopus *versum:*

Surrexit Dominus de sepulchro,

et orationem*:*

Deus qui pro nobis Filium,

in modum lectionis. Statim post Episcopus, capa serica, mitra, baculo, cerothecis, et anulo redimitus, incipit de stallo suo Matutinas modo communi.

According to this version the bishop proceeds in procession to the *sepulchrum*, censes the place, and, one at a time, carries the Host, the chalice, and the Cross to positions upon the altar. As he takes up the Cross he begins the antiphon *Christus resurgens.* The Cross is then adored, and subsequently taken to the altar of Saints Ravennus and Rasiphus, where two prayers and appropriate versicles are said. The *Elevatio* is followed immediately by Matins.[44]

---

quæ dum cantatur, episcopus iterum populo & clero cum pyxide benedicit eamque incensatam sacerdos in loco consueto reponit, deinde lavat manus ad idem cornu dextrum altaris, & dicit orationem *Deus qui per resurrectionem* . . . statim post episcopus cappa serica & mitra cum baculo, chirothecis, & annulo redimitus incipit matutinas.

[43] *Bibliothèque Liturgique,* VIII, 139. Cf. the *ordo* in the *Consuetudinarium, id.*, p. 390.

[44] In view of the especial reverence shown to the Cross in the *Elevatio* of Bayeux, I find this a convenient point at which to refer to a similar emphasis in versions from Caen, Dublin, and Sarum. Since these versions have already been brought into relation with the drama in recent publications, I do not reprint them in the present study. The *Elevatio* from the Church of St. Sépulcre, Caen,

We now proceed to a series of texts of especial interest through the fact that the versions of the *Elevatio* among them contain suggestions of the theme of the Harrowing of Hell.[45] From Eichstätt are available a text of the *Depositio* and two texts of the *Elevatio*:[46]

<DEPOSITIO CRUCIS ET HOSTIÆ>[47]

DEMUM[48] SACERDOS CUM PARTICULIS MINORIBUS RETENTIS *et* CALICE VACUO AC CRUCE QUAM PRIUS SUBDIACONI GESTABANT, PROCEDAT AD SEPULCHRUM *et* HEC IN SEPULCHRO HONORIFICE RECONDAT, CHORO SUBMISSA VOCE CANENTE RESPONSORIUM:

Recessit pastor noster,

ET RESPONSORIUM:

Ecce quo*modo* morit*ur* iustus.

ET IBIDEM VESPERE SUB SILENTIO.

<ELEVATIO HOSTIÆ>[49]

INCIPIT ORDO IN FESTO SANCTE PASCE. ITEM ANTE MATUTINUM ITUR AD SEPULCHRUM ET CANUNTUR ANTIPHONE SUBSCRIPTE. ET TRES DOMINI SIMUL CANTENT PREUIAM ANTIPHONAM:[50]

---

and the *Depositio*, *Elevatio*, and *Visitatio*, from the Church of St. John the Evangelist, Dublin, have been printed by the present writer in *Transactions of the Wisconsin Academy of Sciences, Arts, and Letters*, XVI, Part II, 901, 916–924. The *Depositio* and *Elevatio* of the Sarum use are fully presented by Chambers, II, 312–315.

[45] See above, pp. 31, 90–91.

[46] So far as I know, these texts are now published, or reprinted, for the first time. The *Depositio* is reprinted from *Missale secundum Chorum et Ritum Eiistetensis Ecclesie*, Nuremberg, 1517, fol. LXXXV^r (British Museum). This book contains no version of the *Elevatio* or *Visitatio*. The first text of the *Elevatio* published below is from Munich, Hofbibliothek, Cod. lat. 3918, Obsequiale Eystettense saec. xiv, fol. 75^r–75^v. The manuscript contains no text of the *Depositio*. The *Visitatio* (fol. 75^v–76^v) is mentioned by N. C. Brooks, in *Zeitschrift für deutsches Altertum*, L, 302, but is still unpublished. The second text of the *Elevatio* printed below is found in *Reverendissime in Christo patris D. Christophori pie memorie Episcopi Eistetensis iussu inchoatus est liber iste Obsequiorum Ecclesie absolutus vero electo iam Reverendissimo D. Mauritio ab Hutten: et Deus bene vertat*, 1539, fol. cxlviii^r–cl^r (British Museum). This book contains no *Depositio*. The *Visitatio* from it is printed by Lange (No. 106, pp. 10, 71–74).

[47] *Missale . . . Eiistensis Ecclesie*, Nurenberg, 1517, fol. LXXXV^r.

[48] Preceded immediately by the rubric: Et communicare volentes communicent.

[49] Munich, Cod. lat. 3918, fol. 75^r–75^v.

[50] antiphonam] antiphanam (MS).

Ad monumen*tum* venimus gementes; angelum Dom*ini* sedentem vidimus et dicent*em* quia surrexit Ih*esu*s.

Pr*i*mus eor*um* canit antiphonam[51] sequentem:

Surrexit Domin*us* de sepulchro qui p*ro* nobis pependit in ligno, alleluia.

Sec*un*dus eor*um* canit antiphonam: [51]

Surrexit Xp*istu*s et illuxit pop*u*lo suo, que*m* redemit sanguine suo, alleluia.

Tercius canit antiphonam:

Venit Maria nu*n*cians discipulis quia vidi Domin*um*, alleluia.

Deinde legantur or*ati*ones que in Parascave legebantur ante crucem flexis genibus sc*ilicet*:

Domine Ih*esu* Xp*ist*e gloriosissame conditor,

et cetera ut sup*ra* patescunt.[52] Finitis aut*em* or*ati*onibus portatur Corpus Xp*ist*i ad chorum sew ad locum suu*m* deputatum, et canitur an*tiphona* subscripta: <fol. 75^{v}>

Cum rex glorie Xp*istu*s infernu*m* debellaturus intraret, et chorus angelicus ante facie*m* eius portas[53] principum tolli p*re*ciperet, *s*a*n*ctor*um* populus qui tenebatur in morte captiu*us* uoce lacrimabili clamauerat: Advenisti desiderabilis quem exspectabam*us* in tenebris, ut educeres hac nocte uinculatos de claustris; te no*str*a vocabant suspiria, te larga requirebant lamenta; tu factus es spes desperatis magna consolacio in tormentis.[54]

<ELEVATIO CRUCIS ET HOSTIÆ>[55]

Ordo in festo sancto Pasche.

Item ante Matutinum itur ad Sepulchrum et canuntur ant*iphone* subscripte. Et tres Domini simul cantent primam ant*iphonam*:

Ad monumentu*m* venimus gementes; angelum Domini se<fol. cxlviii^{v}> dentem vidimus et dicentem quia surrexit Ihesus.

Primus eorum incipit:

Surrexit Dominus de sepulchro qui pro nobis pependit in ligno, alleluia. <fol. cxlix^{r}>

Secundus eorum incipit:

Surrexit Christus et illuxit populo suo quem redemit sanguine suo, alleluia.

Tertius eorum incipit:

Venit Maria nuncians di<fol. cxlix^{v}>scipulis quia vidi D*ominum*, alleluia.

Deinde legantur orationes que in Parasceue legeban*tur* Fol. cxi ante Crucem flexis genibus, sc*ilicet*:

Domine Ihesu Christe.

---

[51] antiphonam] antiphana*m* (MS).

[52] As to the reading *patescunt* I am uncertain.

[53] portas] portans (MS).

[54] Followed immediately by the rubric: Deinde Matutinum peragitur more suo.

[55] *Reverendissimi in Christo . . . Episcopi Eistetensis iussu . . . bene vertat*, 1539, fol. cxlviii^{r}–cl^{r}.

FINITIS ORATIONIBUS PORTAT CORPUS CHRISTI AD CHORUM SEU AD LOCUM SUUM DEPUTATUM ET CANITUR ANTHIPONA SUBSCRIPTA SUBMISSA VOCE;

> Cum rex glorie Christus infernum debellaturus intraret, et chorus angelicus ante faciem eius portas principum tolli preciperet, sanctorum populus qui tenebatur in morte captiuus<fol. cl[r]>voce lacrimabili clamauerat: Advenisti desiderabilis que*m* expectabamus in tenebris, vt educeres hac nocte vinculatos de claustris; te nostra vocabant suspiria, te larga requirebant lamenta; tu factus es spes desperatis, magna consolatio in tormentis, alleluia.

DEINDE FIT PULSUS CAMPANIS, ET MATUTINUM PERAGITUR MORE SUO.

The Eichstätt *Depositio* is unusual in its close attachment to the *Missa Præsanctificatorum*. Immediately after the Communion the Celebrant carries to the *sepulchrum* certain particles of the Host used in the Mass,[56] along with the empty chalice and the Cross. These objects he reverently lays down during the singing of two responsories.

It will be observed that the two texts of the *Elevatio* are substantially identical. At the *sepulchrum*, before Easter Matins, are rendered some four antiphons and a series of prayers. Then during the singing of the antiphon *Cum rex gloriæ* the *Corpus Christi* is carried to the choir, or to some other appropriate destination. The dramatic theme of the *Descensus* latent in this antiphon is in no wise developed. Noteworthy is the silence of the rubrics concerning the Cross.

Somewhat more highly elaborated than the versions from Eichstätt are those from Meissen. Of the *Depositio* from this church we possess the following two texts:[57]

---

[56] That no Host was reserved on Holy Thursday specifically for the *Depositio* appears from the following rubric in the *Missale* of 1517 (fol. lxxviii[r]): Duas hostias maiores, quarum unam ipse in hac Missa sumat, alteram uero in crastinum pro celebrante officium reseruet.

[57] One of these texts is found in *Benedictionale siue Agenda secundum ritum et consuetudinem Ingenue ecclesie Misnensis*, Meissen, 1512, fol. xxxvii[v]–xxxviii[r], reprinted in *Liturgische Bibliothek*, Vol. I (ed. A. Schönfelder), Paderborn, 1904, p. 14. A similar text from *Agenda Numburgense*, Nuremberg, 1502, fol. Lxxiiii, is reprinted *ibid.*, p. 69. The second text of the *Depositio* printed below is found in *Breuiarius denuo reuisus et emendatus Ceremonias Ritum canendi legendi ceterasque consuetudines in choro insignis et ingenue Misnensis Ecclesie obseruandas compendiose explicans*, Meissen, 1520, sig. F 3 recto (British Museum). I reprint also the *Elevatio* from this book (sig. F 4 verso). The *Visitatio* (sig. F 4 verso–F 5 recto) has been reprinted by Lange, in *Zeitschrift für deutsches Altertum*, XLI, 82–83.

<DEPOSITIO CRUCIS ET HOSTIÆ>[58]

DEINDE SACERDOS CONTINUET OFFICIUM MISSE SECUNDUM ORDINEM MISSALIS, ET VESPERIS FINITIS SACERDOS INDUTUS CAPPA CUM MAIORE QUI PRESENS FUERIT DEPORTET CRUCEM AD LOCUM SEPULCHRI CUM THURIBULIS ET CANDELIS SEQUENTE EOS CONUENTU CANTANTES SUBMISSA VOCE:

Ecce quomodo moritur iustus et nemo percipit corde; viri iusti tolluntur et nemo considerat; a facie iniquitatis sublatus est <fol. xxxviii> iustus. Et erit in pace memoria eius. In pace factus est locus eius, et in Syon habitacio eius.

QUO FINITO DICANTUR SEPTEM PSALMI. QUIBUS FINITIS RECEDANT A SEPULCHRO CANTANDO RESPONSORIUM:

Sepulto Domino signatum est monumentum, voluentes lapidem ad ostium monumenti, ponentes milites qui custodirent illud. Ne forte veniant discipuli eius et furentur eum et dicant plebi: Surrexit a mortuis.[59]

<DEPOSITIO CRUCIS ET HOSTIÆ>[60]

FINITIS VESPERIS, *omnes* PERSONE LUMINA ARDENTIA HABENTES IUUENES *et* SENES, PRECEDANTQ*ue* PHERETRUM SCOLARES, CHORALES, *et* CAPELLANI; POST HOS, QUI PHERETRUM PORTANT. MOX SEQUIT*ur* PHERETRU*m* OFFICIANS CU*m* SACRAME*n*TO; HU*n*C PRECEDIT DYACONUS ET SUBDYACONUS, UNUS TABULA*m* PERCUTIE*n*S. HINC SEQUU*n*TUR CANONICI, POST VICARII O*mn*ES CANTANTES:

Ecce quomodo morit*ur* iustus, *et cetera.*

FITQ*ue* PROCESSIO EX CHORO IN AMBITU*m* INTRANDO ECCLESIA*m*, CIRCU*m*GIRANDO PER CAPELLA*m* DUCU*m* USQ*ue* AD LOCU*m* UBI SEPULCHRU*m* PARATU*m* EST I*n* CAPELLA SIMONIS *et* IUDE. IBIQ*ue* PONAT*ur* CORPUS CU*m* PHERETRO ET SACRAMENTU*m* SUP*er* ALTARE IBIDEM. ET OFFICIANS AQUA BENEDICTA ASPERSO *et* THURIFICATO PHERETRO, INCIPIANT*ur* SEPTE*m* PSALMI MORE SOLITO. QUIBUS FINITIS DICITUR:

Christus factus est pro nobis obedie*n*s, *et cetera.*

ET OFFICIANS DICIT COLLECTA*m:*

Respice, q*uesumus*, D*omi*ne,

SINE Oremus *et* SINE CO*n*CLUSIONE. QUIBUS PERACTIS REDIT PROCESSIO AD CHORUM PER IANUAS DOMINORU*m* PREPOSITI *et* DECANI, CU*m* RESPONSORIO:

Sepulto D*omi*no.

ET TUNC CHORALES SINT STATIM PARATI AD LEGENDU*m* PSALTERIUM.[61]

This office[62] begins with a carefully arranged procession to the *sepulchrum* after Vespers. Especially noteworthy, for our present purpose, is the fact that the Crucifix is borne upon a

---

[58] *Benedictionale . . . Ecclesie Misnensis*, Meissen, 1512, fol. xxxvii^v–xxxviii^r.

[59] Followed immediately by the rubric *In Vigilia Pasce.*

[60] *Breuiarius . . . Misnensis Ecclesie . . .*, Meissen, 1520, sig. F 3 recto.

[61] Followed immediately by the rubric: Completorium.

[62] I refer to the fuller text, of 1520.

bier,[63] and that the Host is carried by the Officiant. The processional piece is the responsory *Ecce quomodo*. The Host and the bier bearing the Crucifix are placed upon the altar in the Chapel of Simon and Jude, where the *sepulchrum* is arranged. After the sprinkling and the censing of the *pheretrum*, the seven penitential psalms are said,[64] followed by a versicle and a collect. The procession returns to the choir with the singing of the responsory *Sepulto Domino*.

The *Elevatio* from Meissen is as follows:

<ELEVATIO CRUCIS ET HOSTIÆ>[65]

IN NOCTE PASCHE ANTE PULSUM MATUTINARum CIRCA HORAm UNDECIMAm AD LEVATIONEm CRUCIS FIAT CONUEnTUS IN CHORO, ET OMNES PERSONE ACCIPIUnT LUMINA ARDEnTIA IN MANUS. ET TRES CANONICI MAIORES CAPPIS RUBEIS SERICEIS INDUTI, SEQUENTE EOS CONUENTU, EXEUNT PROCESSIONALITER CHORUm PER IANUAS DomiNORUm PREPOSITI ET DECANI CUM VEXILLIS, THURIBULIS, ET CANDELIS AD SEPULCHRUm CUm SEPTEm PSALMIS QUI IN CHORO INCIPIUNTur SINE Gloria patri. QUIBUS DICTIS, DICITur Alleluia. ET TUnC PreDICTI MAIORES CANONICI THURIFICEnT CRUCEM ET LEUANT CANTAnDO SUBMISSA VOCE CUm CHORO:

Resurrexi.

DUO RECIPIUnT IMAGINEm RESURRECTIOnIS ET MAIOR SACRAMENTUm, ET OmnES REDEANT AD CHORUm. IMAGINE AD MEDIUm SUMMI ALTARIS LOCATA ET SACRAMENTO IN SUMMO ALTARI POSITO CANTETur ANtiphona:

Cum rex glorie, SUBMISSA VOCE.

QUA FINITA, DECANUS AUT PREPOSITUS DICAT VERsum:

In resurrectione tua, Christe, allelu*ia*,

CHORO RESPOnDENTE:

Celum *et* terra letentur, alle*luia*.

Co*llecta:*

Presta, q*uesmus*, *omnipotens* Deus, ut in resurrectione.

POSTEA CANONICI OSCULENTur IMAGINEm ET OFFERENT, ET DETUR PAX CIRCUMSTANTIBus. DATA PACE, QUILIBET DICAT ALTERI:

Surrexit Dominus vere, alle*luia*.

---

[63] The fact that the bier (*pheretrum*) supports the Crucifix is made clearer in the rubrics of the *Elevatio*, printed below. In the *Depositio* and *Elevatio* together the Crucifix seems to be designated by a variety of words: *corpus*, *crux*, *imago*. The Host is uniformly called *sacramentum*. The expression *Imago resurrectionis* puzzles me. It may indicate a special object, or it may—inappropriately, it would seem—refer to the Crucifix, or to the *Corpus* upon the Crucifix. See above, p. 81, note 38.

[64] The use of these psalms allies the *Depositio*, once more, to such forms of the *Adoratio* as that seen in St. Athelwold's *Concordio Regularis*. See above, pp. 20–22.

[65] *Breuiarius . . . Misnensis Ecclesie . . .*, Meissen, 1520, sig. F 4 verso.

ET ILLE RESPONDEAT:

Et apparuit Petro, all*eluia*.

TUNC CANTOR VEL UNUS DOMINORUM INCIPIAT ALTE:

Christ ist enstanden.

TUNC CAMPANATOR ACCEDAT *et* LUMINA ACCIPIAT, ET AD LOCA DESTINATA APPONAT; IBIQUE QUAMDIU DURENT, ARDEANT. HIIS PERACTIS PULSENTUR CAMPANE.[66]

This procession to the *sepulchrum*, before Matins, begins with the saying of seven psalms. After the censing of the Crucifix, it is taken up from the *sepulchrum* while the Introit *Resurrexi*[67] is being rendered. During the singing of the antiphon *Cum rex gloriæ* the *Imago Resurrectionis*[68] and the Host are carried separately to the choir and placed upon the altar. After a versicle and a response, a collect is said, the *Imago Resurrectionis* is kissed, and the *Pax* is administered. The office closes appropriately with the singing of the vernacular *Christ ist entstanden*.[69]

Although clearly belonging in the succession of texts now under examination, the following *Depositio* and *Elevatio* from Regensburg present unusual aspects:[70]

<DEPOSITIO CRUCIS ET HOSTIÆ>[71]

DICTIS VESPERIS SACERDOTES QUI INDUTI CASULIS AD ALTARE MINISTRABANT ACCIPIUNT CRUCEM UT EAM PRECEDENTIBUS EOS MINISTRIS CUM CEREIS *et* THURIBULO COLLOCENT IN SEPULCHRUM. *Post* HOS SEQUITUR DOMINUS ABBAS DEFERENS CORPUS DOMINICUM IN APERTO. HOS SEQUITUR CONUENTUS CANTANS *Responsorium:*

Ecce quomodo moritur, CUM *versu*.

Responsorium:

Recessit pastor, CUM *versu*.

---

[66] Followed immediately by Matins.

[67] See above, p. 35.

[68] The precise meaning of the term *Imago Resurrectionis* I do not know; nor am I certain as to the relation of the object signified to the *Imago Crucifixi*, discussed above. See p. 81.

[69] See Lange, pp. 99-129. *Erstanden* is, of course, the usual reading.

[70] Munich, Hofbibliothek, Cod. lat. 14183, Ordinarium Monasterii Sancti Emmeranni Ratisbonensis saec. xv, fol. 47^v–48^r, 50^v. The *Depositio* and *Elevatio* are now published for the first time. The important *Visitatio* from this manuscript has been published by N. C. Brooks, in *Zeitschrift für deutsches Altertum*, L, 300–302. It will be observed that the texts now printed differ substantially from those printed above (pp. 88–89) from the Regensburg *Ordinarium* in Munich MS 26947.

[71] Munich, Cod. lat. 14183, fol. 48^r–48^v.

Antiphona:

Ioseph ab Arimathia.

INTERIM DOMINUS ABBAS *et* SACERDOTES LOCAVERUNT CRUCEM *et* CORPUS DOMINI SUPER SEPULCHRUM, *et* IPSUM OPERIENTES LINTHEO INCENSANT, ET CANTANT *responsorium:*

Sepulto Domino.

FINITO *responsorio* DOMINUS ABBAS, DICTO *Pater Noster*, DICAT *versum:*

Tu autem, Domine, miserere mei.

ORATIO:

Deus, qui filium tuum unigenitum.

TUNC DOMINUS ABBAS CLAM <fol. 48v> SUB CASULAM ACCIPIT CORPUS DOMINI, *et* PRECEDENTIBUS EUM CEREIS PORTAT IPSUM IN SACRARIUM MORE SOLITO RESERVANDUM. DEINDE EXTRAHUNT SE MINISTRI *et* IPSI *et* CONUENTUS INDUUNT CALCEOS *et* PREPARANT SE AD REFECTIONEM. PULSATAQUE TABULA, UENIUNT AD REFECTORIUM.

<ELEVATIO CRUCIS>[72]

IN SANCTA NOCTE ANTE PULSATAS MATUTINAS, DOMINUS ABBAS *et* SENIORES VENIUNT AD SEPULCHRUM CUM CANDELIS *et* INCENSO *et* ASPERSORIO SUBMISSA VOCE DICENTES *psalmum:*

Domine, probasti me, TOTUM.

Sequitur Pater noster. Versus:

In resurrectione tua, *Xpiste*, alleluia.

Oratio:

Deus, qui hodierna die per unigenitum tuum eternitatis.

TUNC DOMINUS ABBAS THURIFICAT CRUCEM *et* ASPERGIT. TOLLENS CRUCEM SUPER HUMERUM SUUM CANTOR SUBMISSA UOCE INCIPIT:

Cum rex glorie.

QUO FINITO *sequitur:*

Alleluia, surrexit pastor bonus.

Et SIC CIRCUMEUNT TOTUM AMBITUM. ET INTRANTIBUS CHORUM DOMINUS ABBAS ASSIGNAT CRUCEM ECCLESIASTICO AD AMBONEM, QUI EAM CUM HONORE DEBITO LOCABIT AD LOCUM SUUM. POST HEC DATUR SIGNUM AD PULSANDAS MATUTINAS.

The *ordo* for the *Depositio* provides that after Vespers both the Cross and the Host be carried in the procession and placed upon the *sepulchrum*. The *sepulchrum* is now covered with a cloth[73] and censed. At the close of the office, after saying the *Pater Noster* and a collect, the abbot privately carries the Host from the *sepulchrum* to the sacristy, where it is reserved with accustomed reverence. In so far as the present study is con-

---

[72] *Id.*, fol. 50v.

[73] I construe the Latin to mean that both the *sepulchrum* and the objects upon it are thus covered.

cerned, this prompt removal of the Host from beside the Cross is unique.[74]

Since the Host has already been taken away from the place of burial, the *Elevatio*, before Easter Matins, is concerned with the Cross alone. The abbot and *seniores* go in procession to the *sepulchrum* rendering the psalm *Domine, probasti*. After saying the *Pater noster* and a collect, the abbot censes and sprinkles the Cross, and then carries it on its way toward the assigned place, the choir singing *Cum rex gloriæ*.

Although the group of texts that we have been examining contains several versions of the *Elevatio* in which appears the *Descensus* theme (*Cum rex gloriæ*), in none of these versions is the theme developed dramatically. We may appropriately pass, then, to the evidences that this development did occur. Such evidence appears, for example, in the following version of the *Elevatio* from the cathedral of Hereford:[75]

<ELEVATIO CRUCIS ET HOSTIÆ>[76]

Post mediam noctem ante Matutinas et ante campanarum pulsationem conueniant omnes clerici in capitulum; et ibi ordinata processione precedant ceroferarii et thuribularii cum Cruce, Episcopo et Decano in albis reuestitis, dictis Episcopo et Decano et omnibus aliis Canonicis cereos extinctos in manibus gestantibus, omnibusque luminaribus ecclesie preter Cereum Paschalem et preter cereum infra Sepulcrum extinctis; incipit Cantor antiphonam:

Cum Rex glorie,

submissa voce, ut magis lamentationem et suspiria representet quam cantum, et sic progrediantur ante Sepulcrum. Finita antiphona, Episcopus et Decanus accedant ad ostium Sepulchri; Episcopus humili voce antiphonam:

Elevamini,

fine tenus cantet. Chorus respondeat:

Quis est iste rex glorie? Dominus virtutum, ipse est rex glorie.

Episcopus vel executor officii paulo altius cantet antiphonam:

Elevamini, ut supra.

Chorus similiter:

Quis est iste rex glorie? Dominus fortis et potens, dominus potens in prelio.

---

[74] I mean unique, of course, in so far as explicitness of rubric is concerned. This practice may have been followed in other versions whose rubrics are laconic.

[75] *The Hereford Breviary* (*Henry Bradshaw Society*, Vol. XXVI, London, 1904, ed. by W. H. Frere and L. E. G. Brown), pp. 324–325, from the Rouen edition of 1505. This breviary contains no *Depositio* or *Visitatio*.

[76] *Henry Bradshaw Society*, Vol. XXVI, pp. 324–325.

EPISCOPUS TERCIO ALTIUS CANTET:

Elevamini, UT SUPRA.

CHORUS SIMILITER:

Quis est iste rex glorie? Dominus virtutum, UT SUPRA.

TUNC APERTO SEPULCHRO, EPYSCOPUS VEL EXECUTOR OFFICII INGREDIATUR SEPULCHRUM, ET ABLATO AMICTU CRUCEM ET SACRAMENTUM THURIFICET; INDE CEREUM QUEM TENET ACCENDAT A CEREO INFRA SEPULCHRUM, EX QUO OMNES ALII CEREI ACCENDANTUR. POSTEA EPYSCOPUS VEL EXECUTOR OFFICII ELEUANS CRUCEM ET SACRAMENTUM CONIUNCTIM DE SEPULCHRO INCIPIAT ANTIPHONAM:

Domine, abstraxisti,

ET FINE TENUS CANTET. CHORUS PSALMUM:

Exaltabo te, Domine,

PROSEQUATUR; ET IN FINE POST UNUMQUEMQUE VERSUM PSALMI FIAT REPETITIO ANTIPHONE, SCILICET: Domine, abstraxisti, QUOUSQUE SANCTA CRUX AB EPYSCOPO VEL EXECUTORE OFFICII SUPER ALTARE OFFERATUR, ET QUOUSQUE VEXILUM SANCTE CRUCIS APPOSITUM FUERIT; ET VEXILO APPOSITO EPYSCOPUS VEL EXECUTOR OFFICII INCIPIAT HUNC VERSUM:

Consurgit Christus tumulo,

CHORO PROSEQUENTE:

Victor redit de baratro.

DEINDE EPISCOPUS VEL EXECUTOR OFFICII:

Quesumus, auctor omnium,

CHORUS:

In hoc paschali gaudio.

EPYSCOPUS VEL EXECUTOR OFFICII:

Gloria tibi, Domine.

HIC OMNES GENUFLECTANT, ET PULSENTUR OMNIA SIGNA, CHORO PROSEQUENTE:

Qui surrexisti a mortuis.

TUNC EPYSCOPUS ALTA VOCE INCIPIAT ANTIPHONAM:

Surrexit Dominus de sepulchro qui pro nobis pependit in ligno, alleluya, alleluya, alleluya.

EPYSCOPUS VEL EXECUTOR OFFICII DICAT VERSICULUM:

Dicite in nationibus.

R*esponsio:*

Quia Dominus regnauit in ligno, alleluya.

ORATIO:

Deus, qui pro nobis . . . famulis tuis, ut resurrectionis eius gratiam consequamur.

QUE TERMINETUR SIC:

Per eundem Cristum Dominum nostrum.

CHORUS RESPONDEAT:

Amen.

NEC PRECEDAT NEC SEQUATUR Dominus vobiscum, NEC Benedicamus Domino. TUNC ACCENDANTUR DUO CEREI, ET PONANTUR A DEXTRIS ET A SINISTRIS CRUCIS; NON AMOUEANTUR USQUE AD PROCESSIONEM. SEPULCRUM VERO STET OSTIO APERTO VACUUM USQUE POST VESPERAS HAC DIE IN TESTIMONIUM RESURRECTIONIS. POSTEA REDEANT IN CAPITULUM EODEM ORDINE QUO VENERUNT. EPYSCOPUS VERO HAC DIE POST DEBITAM CAMPANARUM PULSATIONEM ASSUMPTIS PONTIFICIBUS ASCENDAT AD SEDEM SUUM, ET IBI INCIPIAT MATUTINAS HOC MODO.

The Hereford use provides that after midnight the whole *conventus* shall pass from the chapter-house to the *sepulchrum* in the church, the place being lighted only by the Easter candle and the candle at the door of the sepulchre. During the procession is sung lugubriously the familiar antiphon *Cum rex gloriæ.* At the door of the *sepulchrum* the bishop sings the antiphon *Elevamini,* to which the chorus responds *Quis est iste rex gloriæ?* This challenge and response are delivered three times, each time in a higher tone. The bishop now enters the *sepulchrum,* censes the Cross and Host, and from the sepulchre-candle lights his own candle and that in the hand of each cleric in the procession. He next takes up from the *sepulchrum* both Cross and Host, and proceeds with the Cross to the altar.[77] The raising of the Cross and Host is accompanied by the singing of the psalm *Exaltabo* and its antiphon *Domine abstraxisti.* After a banner (*vexillum*) has been attached to the Cross, appropriate persons deliver several versicles and responses, an antiphon, and a prayer; and leaving a light on either side of the Cross, the procession returns to the chapter-house. In commemoration of the Resurrection the door of the *sepulchrum* is left open throughout the day.

Although it will be readily admitted that in this version of the *Elevatio* the theme of the *Descensus* advances to the stage of dramatic dialogue, it will be observed both that the advance stops short of impersonation, and that it results in certain improprieties in detail. The use of the sepulchre itself as a *limbus* involves an obvious jostling of concepts, and the utterance of the choir, in that it includes both interrogation (*Quis est?*) and reply (*Dominus virtutum*), ignores dramatic consistency.

That improprieties of this sort were perceived and removed is clear from other versions of the *Elevatio,* such as that used at the cathedral of Bamberg. In the case of this church, however, we are fortunate in possessing the text not only of the *Elevatio,* but also of all the other offices and ceremonials associated with the *sepulchrum.*[78] The reservation of a par-

[77] The disposal of the Host is not elucidated.

[78] *Agenda Bambergensia* . . . , Ingolstadii, 1587 (Munich, Hofbibliothek), Part II, pp. 489–490, 522–527, 585–597, 597–604. The *Depositio* is now reprinted for the first time. The *Elevatio* and *Visitatio* have been reprinted

ticular Host for use at the sepulchre, for example, is provided for in the following rubric from Holy Thursday:

> Quoniam Ecclesia Catholica in die sancto Parasceves Corpus Christi consecrare non solet, idcirco Parochus sub sacro hodierno duas Hostias maiores consecret, quarum unam in Missa sumat, alteram vero in sequentem diem sumendam servet; eamque corporali involutam, peracto sacro, reverenter, praecedente lumine, et campanula tinniente, portet; atque recondat eo in loco, ubi aliae Hostiae consecratae asservari consueverunt. In Ecclesiis porro maioribus, Tertia quoque Hostia magna consecretur, quae postridie in Sepulchrum Domini posita, ibidem a populo Christiano usque ad tempus Dominicae resurrectionis adorari queat. Et haec quoque Hostia cum praedicta coniugatur et asservetur.[79]

In this rubric we are given the special information that the Host for the *Depositio* was of large size, and that it was to be exposed for general adoration from Friday until Easter.

The *Depositio* is ordered as follows:

<DEPOSITIO CRUCIS ET HOSTIÆ>[80]

POSTEA[81] REDEAT AD ALTARE, ET ACCIPIAT HOSTIAM MAGNAM CONSECRATAM, UNA CUM PARVA CRUCE, IBI RELICTAM, EAMQUE AD SEPULCHRUM PORTET, ITE-

---

by Lange in *Zeitschrift für deutsches Altertum*, Vol. XXIX (1885), pp. 247–251, and the *Visitatio* alone is reprinted again by Lange in *Die lateinischen Osterfeiern*, No. 141, pp. 12, 93–95. Because of their general resemblances to the texts from Bamberg, we may appropriately mention here the versions from Mainz, Wurzburg, and Augsburg. The *Depositio* and *Elevatio* from Mainz are published by the present writer in *Transactions of the Wisconsin Academy of Sciences, Arts, and Letters*, XVI, Part II, 914–915. The *Depositio* and *Elevatio* from Wurzburg are reprinted from a service-book of the year 1564 by G. Milchsack, *Die lateinischen Osterfeiern*, Wolfenbuettel, 1880, pp. 134–135. The *sepulchrum* offices of Augsburg are accessible in several prints. From *Obsequialis secundum diocesis Augustensis morem*, 1487, Milchsack (pp. 127–129) reprints the *Depositio*, *Elevatio*, and *Visitatio*. From *Ritus Ecclesiastici Augustensis Episcopatus*, Dilingæ, 1580, Milchsack (pp. 131–132) and Lange (No. 170, pp. 108–110) have reprinted the *Visitatio*. The *Elevatio* (pp. 582–593) has, I believe, not been reprinted. The *Depositio* referred to in a rubric (p. 517) may be supplied from *Missale . . . Augustensis Ecclesie*. Dilingæ, 1555, fol. 114v (British Museum), not yet reprinted. In *Obsequiale . . . secundum ecclesiam Augustensem*, [Augsburg, 1499] (British Museum) are found a *Depositio* (fol. xvr-xvv), an *Elevatio* (fol. xxxv-xxxiiv), and a *Visitatio* (fol. xxxiiv–xxxiiiiv), none of which has, I believe, been reprinted.

[79] *Agenda Bambergensia*, Ingolstadii, 1587, pp. 489–490.

[80] *Id.*, pp. 522–527.

[81] Preceded immediately by the Communion of the *Missa Praesanctificatorum*.

rum praecedente lumine, et sonante tabula. Sacerdotem immediate sequatur chorus cantans lugubri voce responsorium: <p. 523>

Ecce quomodo moritur iustus, et nemo percipit corde; viri iusti tolluntur, et nemo considerat; a facie iniquitatis sublatus est iu<p. 524>tus. Et erit in pace memoria eius.

Versus: In pace factus est locus eius, et in Syon habitatio eius. Et erit, etc.

Cum ad Sepulchrum pervenerit Sacerdos, Corpus Christi una cum Sancta Cruce reverenter deponat in Sepulchrum, factaque thurifactione, ac lustralis a<p. 525>quae aspersione, claudat, et sera diligenter muniat Sepulchrum, ne Christi Corpus, per impios aut haereticos vel Iudaeos inde auferri, vel alia queuis contaminatio fieri queat. Deinde sequens cantetur responsorium:

Sepulto Domino, signatum est monumentum, voluentes lapidem ad ostium monumenti. Ponentes mi<p. 526>lites qui custodirent illud. *Versus:* Ne forte veniant discipuli eius, et furentur eum, et dicant plebi: Surrexit a mortuis. Ponentes, etc. <p. 527>

Postea Sacerdos cum Ministris, vel choro flexis genibus, legat clara voce Vesperas, secundum ritum in Breviario descriptum. Curent postremo Parochi ut in honorem venerabilis Sacramenti sint et maneant continue ad Sepulchrum cerei ardentes; et Psalterium quoque per pueros vel alios lugubri lentaque voce legatur usque ad horam Resurrectionis. Sub divinis tamen lectio Psalmorum debet omitti.

This *ordo* provides that immediately after the *Missa Præsanctificatorum* the Host and a small cross (*parva crux*)[82] are carried in procession to the *sepulchrum*.[83] After both objects have been placed within the sepulchre, and have been censed and sprinkled, particular care is taken to lock the door against intrusion. The entire action is accompanied by familiar liturgical chants. Lights are kept at the *sepulchrum* until Easter, and during this period those who guard the place sing psalms.

The *Elevatio* contains an ample treatment of the theme of the *Descensus:*

---

[82] It appears that this cross is to be distinguished from the larger cross used in the *Adoratio* of Good Friday. See the text of the *Elevatio* below.

[83] Concerning the general arrangement of the *sepulchrum* we have the following rubric (*Agenda Bambergense*, p. 495): Alius quoque deligatur locus pro Sepulchro Domini erigendo, qui inter caetera contineat unam arcam, vel quid simile, quod claudi et obserari, atque in eo *venerabile Sacramentum* reponi, tutoque relinqui possit, usque ad tempus et horam Dominicae resurrectionis.

<ELEVATIO CRUCIS ET HOSTIÆ>[84]

ORDO CELEBRANDI COMMEMORATIONEM DOMINICAE RESURRECTIONIS IN SANCTA NOCTE.

ET HAEC QUOQUE DOMINICAE RESURRECTIONIS COMMEMORATIO CELEBRIORIBUS SERVIT ECCLESIIS. UNDE ALIARUM ECCLESIARUM, UT POTE MINORUM ET RURALIUM RECTORES ET PAROCHI, EX ORDINE HIC DESCRIPTO, ALIQUID SALTEM DESUMERE POSSUNT, QUOD PRO LOCI ET PERSONARUM ILLIC CONVENIENTIUM QUALITATE COMMODUM FORE IUDICAVERINT.

UBI IGITUR CORPUS DOMINI IN DIE PARASCEVES SEPULCHRO IMPOSITUM, INDE ELEVANDUM EST, SEQUENS SERVETUR MODUS. <P. 586> CIRCA HORAM NOCTIS HUIUS SACRAE UNDECIMA*m* POPULUS CHRISTIANUS AD SEPULCHRUM DOMINI CONVENIAT, SACERDOS VERO SUPERPELLICEO, STOLA, ET PLUUIALI, SEU CAPPA, UT VOCANT, CHORALI INDUTUS, E SACRARIO PRODEAT, VERSUSQUE SEPULCHRU*m* LENTO GRADU PERGAT, PRAECEDENTIBUS IPSUM DUOBUS CEROFERARIIS, UNOQ*ue* ET ALTERO CLERICO SIMILITER SUPERPELLICEATO SEQUENTE. AD SEPULCHRUM UBI PERVENERINT, IN GENUA PROCUMBANT, SICQUE CORAM VENERABILI SACRAME*n*TO SEQUENTES DUOS PSALMOS, FLEXIS GENIBUS, DEUOTE RECITENT:

Psalmus iii. Domine, quid multiplicati[85] . . <p. 587> super populum tuum benedictio tua. Gloria Patri et Filio et Spiritui Sancto. Sicut erat in principio, etc.

Psalmus cxxxviii. Domine, probasti[85] . . <p. 590> et deduc me in via aeterna. Gloria Patri et Filio et Spiritui Sancto. Sicut erat in principio, et nunc et semper, et in secula seculorum, Amen.

Kyrie eleison. Christe eleison. Kyrie eleison.

Pater noster, etc. Et ne nos inducas in tentationem. Sed libera, etc.

Versus: In resurrectione tua, Christe, alleluia.

Responsum: Coelum et terra laetentur, alleluia. <p. 591>

Oremus:

Gregem tuum, Pastor bone, placatus intende, et oves, quas pretioso sanguine redemisti, diabolica non sinas incursione lacerari. Qui cum Deo Patre in unitate Spiritus Sancti vivis ac regnas Deus, per omnia secula seculorum.

Responsum: Amen.

HIS DICTIS, APERIATUR SEPULCHRUM, FIATQUE THURIFICATIO ET AQUAE BENEDICTAE ASPERSIO SUPER VENERABILE SACRAMENTUM, ET PARVAM CRUCIFIXI IMAGINEM, QUAE UTRAQUE DEINDE SACERDOS REVERENTER IN MANUS CAPIAT, VERSUSQ*ue* AD POPULUM SEQUENTEM ANTIPHONAM TRIBUS VICIBUS, VOCE SEMPER ALTIUS ELEVATA, INCIPIAT, AC RELIQUUM CHORUS PROSEQUATUR:

Surrexit Dominus de sepulchro.

CHORUS:

Qui pro nobis pependit in ligno, alleluia.

POSTEA INSTITUATUR PROCESSIO, VEL PER COEMITERIUM, VEL (SI TUTUM NON VIDEBITUR) PER TEMPLI AMBITUM, HOC MODO: PRIMO PRAECEDANT DUO CERO-

---

[84] *Agenda Bambergense*, Ingolstadii, 1587, pp. 585–597.

[85] In the print these psalms are given in full.

ferarii praedicti, quos immediate sequantur duo Sacerdotes, vel Clerici, portantes eam Crucifixi Imaginem magnam, quam casula coopertam, in die Parasceves gestaverunt duo Sacerdotes. Deinde subsequatur Sacerdos cum venerabili Sacramento et Sancta Cruce, quae utraque paulo ante ex Sepulchro levavit; Chorus vero cantet antiphonam:

Cum rex gloriae Christus infernum debellaturus intraret, et chorus angelicus ante faciem eius portas principum tolli praeciperet, sanctorum populus, qui tenebatur in morte captivus, voce lacrymabili clamaverat: Advenisti desiderabilis quem expectabamus in tenebris, ut educeres hac nocte vinculatos de claustris; te nostra vocabant suspiria, te larga requirebant lamenta, tu factus es spes desperatis, magna consolatio in tormentis, alleluia.

Ubi ad primam vel proximam templi ianuam ventum fuerit, duo Sacerdotes praedicti cum stipite Cruci<p. 593>fixi tribus vicibus fortiter percitiant ianuam, huncque in modum inter percutiendum cantent:

Tollite portas principes vestras, et elevamini portae aeternales.

Chorus quod sequitur canit:

Et introibit Rex gloriae.

Sit deinde aliquis in templo (si tamen extra templum processio fit; si vero in templo instituatur processio, sit is extra templum) qui Diaboli personam simulans, per<p. 594>ro, malleo, aut cathena, fortiter quoque impingat in ianuam eandem, dicatque vel clamet alta voce:

Quis est iste Rex gloriae?

Mox chorus, vel eo deficiente, Sacerdos subiungat:

Dominus fortis et potens, Dominus potens in praelio.

Post haec chorus in incoepta, et paulo ante interrupta, antiphona: Cum Rex gloria, etc. canere pergat, totaque processio, ordine praedicto, versus secundam templi ianuam progrediatur, apud quam omnia fiant, uti apud primam. Et notandum quod haec utraque ianua manere debet clausa.<p. 595>Quando vero ad ultimam ianuam venerint, factis ibidem quoque iis quae circa primam indicauimus, aperiri debet illa. Per quod designatur, vel circumstanti populo ad oculum repraesentatur, quomodo Christus Dominus post passionem suo ad inferos descensu, eum inferni locum qui Patrum Lymbus dicitur aperuerit, vel quod alibi dicitur, portas aereas vel vectes ferreos confregerit, suosque captivos inde liberaverit. Deinde continuetur antiphona: Cum Rex gloriae, etc. usque ad finem, pergatque processio ad chorum templi. Sacerdos vero gradus altaris ascendat, ibique versus populum consistens, ac Christi Corpus adhuc in manibus tenens, cantet tribus vicibus, voce semper altius elevata: O vere digna hostia, etc., choro versum illum prosequente.<p. 596>

O vere digna hostia,
Chorus: Per quam fracta sunt tartara,
redempta plebs captivata,
redit ad vitae praemia.

Addatur deinceps eiusdem hymni ultimus versus, Sacerdote incipiente:

Gloria tibi, Domine. Chorus: Qui surrexisti a mortuis, cum Patre et Sancto Spiritu, in sempiterna secula, Amen.

SUB HOC ULTIMO VERSU, SACERDOS, FACTO SIGNO CRUCIS SUPER POPULUM CUM VENERABILI<P. 597>SACRAMENTO, PORTET ILLUD AD SUUM LOCUM IN QUO CONSERUARI SOLET; CHORUS VERO INCIPIAT:

Victimae paschali laudes, etc.

ET POST QUEMLIBET VERSUM, INSERAT UNUM TANTUM PASCHALEM GERMANICUM, QUEM POPULUS QUOQue CELEBRITER DECANTET; SITQUE PRIMUS:

Christ ist erstanden, etc.

HOS CANTUS INVENIES IN FINE HUIUS LIBRI. POST HAEC INCIPIANTUR MATUTINAE.

According to this version, a general congregation is allowed to gather at the *sepulchrum*, where they are joined by a procession of clerics from the sacristy. After the saying of two psalms, the *Gloria Patri*, the *Kyrie*, the *Pater Noster*, a versicle, and a prayer, the *sepulchrum* is opened and the Host and Cross are censed and sprinkled, and elevated into general view. Both the Host and Cross are then carried in procession through the cemetery outside the church, the chorus singing the antiphon *Cum rex gloriæ*. When the procession reaches the first door of the church, the two priests who carry the *Magna Crux*[86] strike the door three times with the shaft, singing *Tollite portas*. A person within the church, representing Satan, responds with the words *Quis est iste rex gloriæ?* The chorus in the procession outside replies *Dominus fortis*. Since this door remains closed, the procession passes on and repeats the dialogue at a second portal. When this door yields, the procession enters the church and advances to the choir. This ceremonial at the church-doors, the rubric tells us, specifically represents the Harrowing of Hell. Having entered the choir, the priest sings three times the verse *O vere digna Hostia*. After the Host has been put in its accustomed place,[87] the choir sings the sequence *Victimæ paschali*, the congregation responding to each sentence with a verse of the vernacular hymn *Christ ist erstanden*.

Our consideration of the representations of the Harrowing of Hell may appropriately conclude with an examination of the fifteenth century texts from the monastery of Barking, near London, for the *Elevatio* from this church shows a remarkable development of the theme of the *Descensus*. First, however,

[86] This *Magna Crux*—apparently from the *Adoratio* of Good Friday—is to be distinguished from the *parva crux* placed in the *sepulchrum*.

[87] This may be the tabernacle of the main altar.

we must glance at the following significant version of the *Depositio:*[88]

<DEPOSITIO CRUCIS>[89]

CUM AUTEM SANCTA CRUX FUERIT ADORATA, SACERDOTES DE LOCO PREDICTO CRUCEM ELEVANTES INCIPIANT *Antiphonam:*

Super omnia ligna,

et CHORO ILLO SUBSEQUENTE TOTAM CONCINANT. CANTRICE INCIPIENTE, DEFERANT CRUCEM AD MAGNUM ALTARE, IBIQUE IN SPECIE IOSEPH *et* NICHODEMI, DE LIGNO DEPONENTES YMAGINEM VULNERA CRUCIFIXI UINO ABLUANT *et* AQUA. DUM AUTEM HEC FIUNT, CONCINAT CONUENTUS *responsorium:*

Ecce quomodo moritur iustus,

SACERDOTE INCIPIENTE *et* CANTRICE RESPONDENTE *et* CONUENTU SUCCINENTE. *Post* VULNERUM ABLUCIONEM CUM CANDELABRIS *et* TURRIBULO DEFERANT ILLAM AD SEPULCRUM HAS[90] CANENTES *Antiphonas:*

In pace in idipsum.

Antiphona:

Habitabit.

Antiphona:

Caro mea.

CUMQUE IN PREDICTUM LOCUM TAPETUM PALLEO AURICULARI QUOQUE *et* LINTHEIS NITIDISSIMIS DECENTER ORNATUM ILLAM CUM REVERENCIA LOCAVERINT, CLAUDAT SACERDOS SEPULCRUM ET INCIPIAT *responsorium:*

Sepulto Domino.

Et TUNC ABBATISSA OFFERAT CEREUM, QUI IUGITER ARDEAT ANTE SEPULCRUM, NEC EXTINGUATUR DONEC YMAGO IN NOCTE PASCHE *post* MATUTINAS DE SEPULCRO CUM CEREIS *et* THURE *et* PROCESSIONE RESUMPTA, SUO REPONATUR IN LOCO.[91]

It will be observed that this office attaches itself directly to the *Adoratio Crucis;* indeed the *Depositio* may be regarded as a conclusion for it.[92] Especially noteworthy is the detaching of the *Ymago* (*Corpus*) from the Cross and the washing of the *vulnera Crucifixi.*[93] The rubric *in specie Ioseph et Nichodemi* may indicate that this action involves impersonation; but the

[88] Oxford, University College MS 169, Ordinarium Berkingense saec. xv in., p. 108. The *Depositio*, *Elevatio*, and *Visitatio* from this manuscript have all been published by the present writer in *Transactions of the Wisconsin Academy of Sciences, Arts, and Letters*, XVI, Part II, 926–931.

[89] University College MS 169, p. 108.

[90] has] hac (MS).

[91] Followed immediately by this rubric: Hiis itaque gestis, redeat Conuentus in chorum et Sacerdos in uestiarium.

[92] See above, p. 26.

[93] On the possible meanings of the word *Ymago* see above, p. 81. The washing of the *vulnera Crucifixi* has a parallel in the use of Rouen. See above, p. 75.

indication is not decisive. The text mentions the *Ymago* alone as the object placed in the sepulchrum; but from the *Elevatio* we infer that the burial included also the Host.

We may now consider the *Elevatio*, for which we have the following *ordo:*

<ELEVATIO CRUCIS ET HOSTIÆ>[94]

Nota quod secundum antiquam consuetudinem ecclesiasticam Resur<r>exio Dominica celebrata fuit ante Matutinas, et ante aliquam campane pulsacionem in die Pasche. Et quoniam populorum concursus temporibus illis videbatur deuocione frigessere, et torpor humanus maxime accrescens, venerabilis Domina Katerina de Suttone, tunc pastoralis cure gerens vicem, desiderans dictum torporem penitus exstirpare et fidelium deuocionem ad tam celeb<r>em celebracionem magis excitare, unanimi consororum consensu instituit ut statim post III. responsorium Matutinarum die Pasche fieret Dominice Resur<r>exionis celebracio, et hoc modo statuetur processio.

In primis eat Domina Abbatissa cum toto Conuentu et quibusdam Sacerdotibus et clericis capis indutis, quolibet Sacerdote et Clerico palmam et candelam extinctam manu deferente[95] intrent capellam Sancte Marie Magdalene, figurantes Animas sanctorum patrum ante<p. 120>adventum Xpisti ad inferos descendentes, et claudant sibi ostium dicte capelle. Deinde superveniens Sacerdos ebdomadarius ad dictam capellam appropians alba indutus et capa cum duobus diaconis, uno crucem deferente cum vexillo dominico desuper pendente, altero cum turribulo manu sua baiulante, et aliis Sacerdotibus et Clericis cum duobus pueris cereos deferentibus ad ostium dicte capelle incipiens ter hanc Antiphonam:

Tollite portas.

Qui quidem Sacerdos representabit personam Xpisti ad inferos descensuram et portas inferni dirupturam, et predicta antiphona unaquaque uice in altiori uoce incipiatur, quam Clerici tociens eandem repetant, et ad quamquam incepcionem pulset cum Cruce ad predictum ostium, figurans dirupcionem portarum inferni; et tercia pulsacione ostium aperiat. Deinde ingrediatur ille cum ministris suis. Interim incipiat quidam Sacerdos in capella existente Antiphonam:

A porta inferi,

quam subinferat Cantrix cum toto Conventu:

Erue, Domine, et cetera.

Deinde extrahet Sacerdos Ebdomadarius omnes essentes in capella predicta, et interim incipiat Sacerdos Antiphonam:

Domine abstraxisti,

et Cantrix subsequatur:

Ab inferis.

---

[94] University College MS 169, pp. 119–121.

[95] deferente] deferentem (MS).

TUNC OMNES EXEANT DE CAPELLA, ID EST, DE LIMBO PATRUM, *et* CANTENT SACERDOTES *et* CLERICI *Antiphonam:*

Cum REX GLORIE,

PROCESSIONALITER PER MEDIUM CHORI AD SEPULCRUM PORTANTES SINGULI PALMAM *et* CANDELAM, DESIGNANTES UICTORIAM DE HOSTE RECUPERATAM, SUBSEQUENTIBUS DOMINA ABBATISSA, PRIORISSA, *et* TOTO CONUENTU SICUT SUNT PRIORES.

Et CUM AD SEPULCRUM PERUENERINT, SACERDOS <P. 121> EBDOMADARIUS SEPULCRUM THURIFICET *et* INTRET SEPULCRUM INCIPIENDO *Versum:*

Consurgit.

DEINDE SUBSEQUATUR CANTRIX:

Xpistuc tumulo.[96]

Versus:

Omnis auctor.

Versus:

Gloria tibi, Domine.

Et INTERIM ASPORTABIT CORPUS DOMINICUM DE SEPULCRO INCIPIENDO *Antiphonam:*

Xpistus resurgens,

CORAM ALTARI, VERSO UULTU AD POPULUM, TENENDO CORPUS DOMINICUM IN MANIBUS SUIS INCLUSUM CRISTALLO. DEINDE SUBIUNGAT CANTRIX:

Ex mortuis.

Et CUM DICTA ANTIPHONA FACIANT PROCESSIONEM AD ALTARE SANCTE TRINITATIS CUM SOLENNI APPARATU, VIDELICET CUM TURRIBULIS *et* CEREIS. CONUENTUS SEQUATUR CANTANDO PREDICTAM *Antiphonam* CUM *versu:*

Dicant nunc,

et UERSICULO:[97]

Dicite in nacionibus.

ORATIO:

Deus qui pro nobis Filium tuum.

E HEC PROCESSIO FIGURATUR PER HOC QUO XPISTUC PROCEDIT POST RESUR<R>XIONEM IN GALILEAM, SEQUENTIBUS DISCIPULIS.[98]

From the generous rubrics in this text it appears that the present form of this office is due to the reform of Katherine of Sutton, Abbess of Barking from 1363 to 1376.[99] Although she recognizes the tradition of the *Elevatio* before Easter Matins, she undertakes to establish a special form of this office for observance *at the close of* Matins, directly before the usual *Visitatio.*

---

[96] tumulo] timulo (MS).

[97] uersiculo] *uersiculus* (MS).

[98] Immediately followed by a version of the *Visitatio Sepulchri.*

[99] See W. Dugdale, *Monasticon Anglicanum*, Vol. I, London, 1846, p. 437.

The *Elevatio* divides itself naturally into two parts: a representation of the *Descensus*, and a raising of the Host from the *sepulchrum*. The representation of the *Descensus* occurs neither at the *sepulchrum* nor at the church doors, but, very appropriately, at the chapel of St. Mary Magdalen. Behind the closed doors of this chapel are imprisoned all the members of the *conventus*, representing the spirits *in limbo Patrum*. After a triple challenge, *Tollite portas*, from a priest without, the door of the chapel is opened and the imprisoned spirits are allowed to depart in procession toward the *sepulchrum*. The full rubrics explaining this representation leave little doubt that impersonation is deliberately intended.

The subsequent raising of the Host from the *sepulchrum* includes no novelties in the way of action. The central observance is the adoration of the Host at the main altar. The concluding procession from this altar to the altar of Holy Trinity is interpreted for us as representing the journey of Christ into Galilee. The absence from this office of all mention of the *Ymago Crucifixi*, used in the *Depositio*, is somewhat puzzling.

As we approach the end of the present section of this study, we have still to consider certain versions of the *Depositio* and *Elevatio* which, by reason of one peculiarity or another, have thus far resisted classification, but which deserve at least brief notice. The following are fifteenth-century versions from Hungary:[100]

<DEPOSITIO CRUCIS ET HOSTIÆ>[101]

INTERIM[102] SUBCUSTOS EXPORTAT MONSTRANTIAM CUM SACRAMENTO PRO SEPULTURA AD ALTARE MAGNUM. HIS PERACTIS DESCENDAT CHORUS PROCESSIONALITER AD LOCUM UBI SEPULTURA ORDINATA[103] EST, EPISCOPO IPSOS CUM SACRAMENTO SEQUENTE, PRECEDENTIBUS QUATTUOR PRECEDENTIBUS SEU IUUENIBUS CUM BACULIS AURATIS CUM CANDELIS ACCENSIS. ET DOMINUS EPISCOPUS RECONDAT CRUCEM CUM SACRAMENTO REVERENTER THURIFICANDO

[100] Published by J. Dankó, *Vetus Hymnarium Ecclesiasticum Hungariae*, Budapest, 1893, pp. 535–538, from "Ordinarius Scepusiensis sive Strigoniensis saeculi decimi quinti e codice manuscripto Bibliothecae R. Universitatis Budapestinensis." With the *Depositio* should be compared the text from Gran printed above, pp. 32–33.

[101] Dankó, pp. 535–536.

[102] Immediately preceded by Vespers.

[103] sepultura ordinata] sepulturam ordinatam (Dankó).

ET ASPERGENDO AC SIGILLANDO SEPULCHRUM. INTERIM CHORUS CANTET *responsoria:*

Hierusalem luge.
Ecce vidimus.
Plange quasi virgo.
Recessit pastor bonus.

RECONDITO SACRAMENTO, CHORUS CANTET *responsorium:*

Sepulto Domino.

ET POSTEA DOMINUS EPISCOPUS DICAT VERSUM ET ORATIONEM UT IN MISSALI. TANDEM FACTA REVERENTIA RECEDAT.[104]

<ELEVATIO CRUCIS ET HOSTIÆ>[105]

ITEM IN MATUTINO POST ULTIMAM OMELIAM, DUM CHORALES INCIPIUNT AD RESPONSORIUM: Dum transisset, DEBENT PROCEDERE USQUE AD SEPULCHRUM; ET IBIDEM CHORALES VERSICULUM CUM Gloria Patri SOLLEMNISABUNT. IBIQUE MINISTRI STANTES CANDELIS ACCENSIS, THURE ET THURIBULO IBI EXISTENTIBUS, ET INTERIM UNUS LEUABIT SEPULCHRUM ET HOSTIAM ET DOMINUS PONTIFEX SIUE PLEBANUS PRECEDENTES SOLLEMNITER THURIFICABIT. DEIN CORPUS CUM PARVA CRUCE EXCIPIET, QUOD IMPOSITUM FUIT FERIA SEXTA MAJORIS EBDOMADE. ET EXCIPIT CUM VERSICULO ISTO:

Surrexit dominus de sepulchro, alleluia, qui pro nobis.

ET INTEREA CIRCA ALTARE BEATE VIRGINIS CALICEM CUM CORPORALIBUS PREPARANT. TUNC DOMINUS PONTIFEX SEU PLEBANUS ACCEDENS CORPUS XRISTI SUPER PATENAM TENENS IN MANU HONORIFICE ET AD MAXIMAM REUERENCIAM VERTAT SE TRIBUS VICIBUS AD POPULUM CUM CORPORE XRISTI CANTANDO:

Pax vobis, CUM SUO Alleluia.

CHORUS RESPONDET:

Nolite timere, alleluia.

DEINDE PROCESSIO CANENDO REDIBIT AD CHORUM SOLEMNISANDO:

Te Deum.

The notable circumstance connected with these texts is the unusual liturgical position of the *Elevatio:* before the *Te Deum* at the end of Easter Matins. As we have already conjectured,[106] this may have been the original location of the *Elevatio*, and the transference of this office to the beginning of Matins may have been made in order to provide a place for the *Visitatio*.

---

[104] Followed immediately by the rubric: In Completorio.

[105] Dankó, pp. 537–538.

[106] See above, pp. 31, 95.

Special considerations of a different sort arise in connection with the following versions from Diessen:[107]

<DEPOSITIO CRUCIS ET HOSTIÆ>[108]

HIS FINITIS DUO *Pres*BY*te*RI INDUTI ALBIS PO*r*TENT YMAGI*n*E*m* QU*e* SEPELIENDA E*st*, P*re*CEDENTE CO*n*UENTU CU*m* ACCENSI*s* CANDEL*is* ET THURI*bulo*; FACIA*n*T P*ro*CESSIO*nem* P*er* ECC*les*IA*m* C*ir*CU*m*EUNDO ET CANTANDO LUGUBRI VOCE *Responsorium*:

Ecce quo*modo* mori*tur*. *Versus*: In pace f*actus*.

POSTEA LOCENT YMAGINE*m* AD SEPULCHRU*m* CU*m* THURIFICA*tione et* ASP*er*SIONE. ET DICANT *Vesperas* IBIDE*m* P*r*IUATI*m*. *Psalmus*: Confitebor, CU*m* U*er*SICULO. SE*quitur* Magn*ificat*. A*ntiphona*: Cu*m* accepisset. *Psalmus*: Miser*ere* mei, CU*m* OR*atio*NE. <FOL. 20r> SE*quitur* RE*sponsorium*:

Sepulto D*omi*no. *Versus*: Ne forte ve*niant*.

ET SIC REDEA*n*T I*n* CHORU*m*. TU*n*C CO*m*PULSENT*ur* TABULE O*mnes*.

<ELEVATIO CRUCIS ET HOSTIÆ>[109]

IN SA*nc*T*A* NOCTE ANTE HOROLOGIU*m* DECANUS CU*m* SENIORIBU*s* TOLLANT YMAGINE*m* SALUATORIS, REPORTATO P*rius* SACRAME*n*TO, DE SEPULCHRO CU*m* PS*almo*:

D*omi*ne, *quid* multi*plicati*.

ET CANTA*nt* A*ntiphonam*:

Surrex*it* D*ominus*.

CU*m* INCENSO ET ASP*er*SORIO PORTENT YMAGINE*m* SUP*er* SUMMU*m* ALTARE, ET OSCULENT*ur* EA*m* CU*m* GAUDIO ET DEUOCIONE. TUNC CONPULSENTUR OMNIA SIGNA.

The specialty of the Diessen *Depositio* is its apparent assimilation of Vespers. After the Communion of the Mass, when the *Imago* has been placed in the *sepulchrum*, Vespers are immediately said in this place *privatim*. At the close of Vespers is sung the responsory *Sepulto Domino*. Since this responsory is commonly associated with the closing action of the *Depositio*, the present version of this office may be viewed as including Vespers within itself.

The *Elevatio* raises no particular question except through the obscurity surrounding the use of the Host. Although the

[107] Munich, Hofbibliothek, Cod. lat. 5545, Ordinarium Diessense saec. xv, fol. 19v–20v. The *Depositio* and *Elevatio* from this manuscript are now published for the first time. The *Visitatio* has been published by N. C. Brooks in *Zeitschrift für deutsches Altertum*, L, 305–306. It is possible that with these texts should be associated those cited above from Munich, Hofbibliothek, Cod. lat. 5546. See above, p. 88, note 71.

[108] Munich, Cod. Lat. 5545, fol. 19v–20r.

[109] *Id.*, fol. 20v.

Depositio does not mention it, the *Elevatio* indicates that the Host must have been included in the burial, and that it was secretly removed from the *sepulchrum* before the time of the *Elevatio*, early Easter morning (*reportato prius Sacramento*).

The last texts that we need consider are the following from Regensburg:[110]

<DEPOSITIO CRUCIS>[111]

EXPLETA AUTEM COMMUNIONE FIDELIUM, PARTICULAE CORPORIS CHRISTI, SI QUAE SUPERFUERINT, SERVENTUR ET PORTENTUR IN LOCUM HONESTUM.[112] QUIBUS OMNIBUS PERACTIS SACERDOS CUM MINISTRIS TOLLAT CRUCIFIXUM, QUOD REPRAESENTATUM FUERAT, ET DEFERANT AD SEPULCHRUM CANTANTES *Responsorium:*

Recessit pastor noster, VEL
Ecce quomodo moritur.

TUNC LOCENT CRUCIFIXUM IN SEPULCHRUM, ET FLEXIS GENIBUS LEGANT VESPERAS SUBMISSA VOCE. POSTREMO CANTETUR LENTA VOCE CUM VERSU RESPONSORIUM:

Sepulto Domino.

TUNC SACERDOS DICAT *Versum:*

In pace factus est,

ET ORATIONEM:

Respice.

ASPERGATUR ET THURIFICETUR.

<ELEVATIO CRUCIS ET HOSTIÆ>[113]

EPISCOPUS AUT PRAEPOSITUS AUT DECANUS SIVE SENIOR CANONICUS, INDUTUS STOLA, ANTE PULSUM MATUTINARUM, CONGREGATO CHORO, CUM PROCESSIONE ET DUOBUS LUMINIBUS, FORIS ECCLESIAE CLAUSIS, SECRETIUS TOLLAT SACRAMENTUM SEU CRUCIFIXUM; ET ANTEQUAM TOLLAT, DICANTUR PSALMI FLEXIS GENIBUS ET SINE Gloria Patri, videlicet:

Domine quid multiplicati sunt (Ps. 3),
Miserere mei Deus (Ps. 56),
Domine probasti me (Ps. 138).

SEQUITUR:

Kyrie eleison, Christe eleison, Kyrie eleison.
Pater noster. *Versus:* Et ne nos.
Versus: Exsurge Domine, adiuva, etc.
Versus: Foderunt manus meas, etc.
Versus: Domine exaudi, etc.

---

[110] In connection with these texts should be considered those from Munich Cod. Lat. 26947, printed above, pp. 88–89.

[111] *Decreta Authentica*, IV, 432, from *Obsequiale Ratisbonense*, 1491.

[112] The liturgiologist of the *Decreta Authentica* infers (p. 432) that the *locus honestus* is the *sepulchrum*.

[113] *Decreta Authentica*, IV, 440, from *Obsequiale Ratisbonense*, 1491.

ORATIO:

Da nobis, Domine, auxilium de tribulatione, qui dedisti pro nobis pretium magnum, et quos mors Filii tui D. N. I. C. redemit, eorum vita te digne glorficet. Per eumdem, etc.

FINITA COLLECTA ASPERGATUR ET THURIFICETUR CRUX, ET PORTETUR AD LOCUM SUUM, CUM *Responsorium:*

Cum transisset Sabbatum, etc.,

MEDIA VOCE CANTATUR. ET ANTEQUAM CRUX IN SUUM LOCUM REPONATUR, TANGATUR PORTA ECCLESIAE CUM CRUCE ET DICATUR *versus:*

Quis est iste Rex gloriae?

Responsum:

Dominus fortis et potens, Dominus potens in praelio.

FINITO RESPONSORIO EPISCOPUS VEL SACERDOS DICAT SUBMISSA VOCE *versus:*

In resurrectione tua, Christe, allel.

Responsum:

Coelum et terra laetentur, allel.

ORATIO:

Deus, qui hodierna die etc. (ex Offic. Dom. Resurr.)

SEQUITUR:

Versus: Surrexit Dominus vere, allel.

Responsum: Gaudeamus omnes, allel.

FINITIS HIS INCIPIATUR PULSUS MATUTINARUM, ET FINITO TERTIO RESPONSORIO REINCIPIATUR IDEM RESPONSORIUM:

Cum transisset, etc.

ET FIET PROCESSIO CUM TOTO CHORO AD SEPULCHRUM, IBIQUE PERFICIETUR RESPONSORIUM. QUO FINITO DUO PRESBYTERI STANTES ANTE SEPULCHRUM, ACCEPTIS (SIC!) OBUMBRALI LOCO SUDARII EXTENDENTESQUE ILLUD CANTENT ALTA VOCE TOTAM ANTIPHONAM:

Surrexit Dominus de Sepulchro, qui pro nobis pependit in ligno, alleluia.

ET CANTATA ANTIPHONA, EPISCOPUS, PRAEPOSITUS, VEL DECANUS AUT SENIOR CANONICUS INCIPIAT CANTICUM LAETITIAE:

Te Deum.

CUM QUO REDITUR AD CHORUM ET COMPLETUR MATUTINUM IBIDEM.

In its organic relation to Vespers, the *Depositio* of Regensburg resembles that of Diessen.

Perhaps the most notable feature of the *Elevatio* is the use of an abbreviated form of the *Descensus* dialogue *Quis est iste Rex gloriæ?* This brief dialogue is introduced *after* the taking up of the Cross, and the familiar command *Tollite portas* is omitted.

Brief mention should be made, finally, of the embryonic version of the *Visitatio*, at the close of Matins. Between the last responsory and the *Te Deum*, a procession visits the empty *sepulchrum*, where at the displaying of a veil representing the *sudarium*, is sung the antiphon *Surrexit Dominus*.

By way of summarizing this division of the subject one need only call attention to the considerable number of versions of the *Elevatio* in connection with which is developed the theme of the *Descensus*. This development involves not only a highly dramatic dialogue, but also, probably, a considerable measure of mimetic action. The *Elevatio* from Barking may intend something deliberate in the way of impersonation.

VI

The facts now at hand concerning the *Depositio* and *Elevatio*, along with our previous knowledge of the *Visitatio Sepulchri*, should enable us to draw certain final conclusions as to the probable inter-relations of these dramatic offices in the historical development. For a precise demonstration the data are, I think, insufficient; but for a statement of probabilities the facts now available are ample.

In view of the data surveyed in this study, the extra-liturgical *sepulchrum* can scarcely be regarded as an independent device invented exclusively for the purposes of the dramatic offices under consideration. From the earliest period of formal Christian worship the idea of burial seems to have attached itself to certain objects used in the authorized liturgy itself: especially the altar, the tabernacle, and the chalice. At one time or another during the early middle ages these objects were either associated with the grave through physical contact,—as in the case of the altar,[1]—or were interpreted as *sepulchra* through symbolism. When a dramatic impulse arose requiring a *mise en scène* for commemorations of the Burial and Resurrection,—apparently in the course of the tenth century,—the *sepulchrum* was already at hand for adoption. The dramatic offices, to be sure, gave added currency to the name "sepulchrum," and they eventually elaborated structures of their own; but they cannot be credited with the invention of the thing itself.

Concerning the general sequence of the dramatic developments at this *sepulchrum* we can, I think, be reasonably certain.

[1] See especially Hirn, pp. 19–30.

I infer that the *Depositio*, along with the complementary *Elevatio*, was the original development, and that the *Visitatio* attached itself to the *sepulchrum* later, as a sequel. In support of this inference I would cite first the difference between the *Depositio-Elevatio* and the *Visitatio* in liturgical content and tone. The former dramatic sequence is completely liturgical in content, devoid of original composition and of dialogue. The *Visitatio*, on the other hand, is essentially a free composition. Although the developed versions of it contain numerous liturgical pieces,[2] the invariable central element of the *Visitatio* is an independent literary production: the dialogued trope *Quem quæritis in sepulchro*.[3] I infer that if the *Visitatio* had preceded the *Depositio-Elevatio*, the later offices would, through natural imitation, have reflected something of the dialogue and freer composition of the *Visitatio*. That the *Visitatio* should not have conformed to the liturgical rigor of the *Depositio-Elevatio* is due, apparently, to the fact that the *Visitatio* brought to the *sepulchrum* an independent literary dialogue ready for dramatic use.

Another consideration leads me to the same general conclusion as to the priority of the *Depositio-Elevatio*. From the present study nothing is more apparent than that these offices, however *dramatic* their ceremonials, never in themselves developed true drama. That is to say, the performers never impersonated the characters concerned. However imitative or commemorative the acts may have been, the agents in the action never specifically assumed the personalities involved in the story inspiring the action.[4] In the *Visitatio Sepulchri*, on the other hand, impersonation is frequent. Of this fact one of the earliest extant versions of the *Visitatio*,—from St. Athel-

---

[2] See Lange, pp. 167–170, *et pass.*

[3] See, for example, *id.*, pp. 131–132; Chambers, II, 28; and above, p. 7.

[4] In making this statement I have in mind what we may call the normal forms of the *Depositio* and *Elevatio*, which are concerned with the laying down (or "burial") and the raising (or "resurrection") of the Cross or Host, or of both. The dramatic treatment of the Harrowing of Hell, added to certain versions of the *Elevatio*, does sometimes develop impersonation (See above, pp. 117–122); but the *Descensus* is not the central theme of either the *Depositio* or the *Elevatio*. In their central action, the *Depositio* and *Elevatio* do not develop impersonation.

wold's *Concordia Regularis*,—may serve as an illustration. Whereas in the pages above[5] we have found that the *Depositio* and *Elevatio* from this document involve no impersonation at all, the *Visitatio* prescribes it with insistent explicitness in such rubrics as the following:

> Dumque tertium percelebratur responsorium residui tres succedant, omnes quidem cappis induti turribula cum incensu manibus gestantes, ac pedetemptim ad similitudinem querentium quid ueniant ante locum Sepulchri. Aguntur enim hec ad imitationem Angeli sedentis in monumento atque mulierum cum aromatibus venientium ut ungerent corpus Jhesu.[6]

Now I assume that if the *Visitatio*, with impersonation of this sort, had preceded the *Depositio* and *Elevatio*, these latter offices would, in some measure, have imitated the *Visitatio* in this important aspect. The consistent absence of impersonation from the *Depositio* and *Elevatio* seems to me to indicate that they had attained their rigid liturgical character before the advent of the *Visitatio*.

I may, then, summarize my conception of the development as follows:

1) The authorized liturgy itself early developed the idea of *sepulchrum* in connection with such ritualistic objects as the altar, the tabernacle, and the chalice.

2) Availing themselves of this idea of burial, the extra-liturgical *Depositio* and *Elevatio* arose, in the course of the tenth century, under the influence especially of the reservation on Holy Thursday and of the *Adoratio Crucis* of Good Friday.[7] In many cases the *Depositio* allies itself to the authorized liturgy with especial intimacy.[8] I infer that the *Depositio* was invented first, and that the *Elevatio* arose as a necessary complement. The two offices are mutually complete,[9] and both are essentially liturgical in spirit and content.

3) During the early years of the tenth century was produced the trope *Quem quæritis in sepulchro* as an independent

---

[5] See pp. 73–74.

[6] Logemann, in *Anglia*, XIII, 427.

[7] See above, pp. 9–29.

[8] See above, for example, pp. 73, 76.

[9] "The *Depositio* and *Elevatio* mutually presuppose each other and, together, are complete" (Chambers, II, 25).

literary composition in the form of dialogue.[10] During the course of the tenth century this trope was very appropriately brought into association with the *sepulchrum*, and its dialogue became the basis of the dramatic *Visitatio Sepulchri*.[11] This office formed a fitting, but not an inevitable, sequel for the *Depositio-Elevatio*.

Many churches observed both the *Depositio-Elevatio* and the *Visitatio;* but since the former sequence is complete in itself, and since the *Visitatio* is quite capable of independent performance, a church could freely omit either the one or the other.[12]

---

[10] See *Publications of the Modern Language Association*, XXIX, 5–13. See above, p. 7.

[11] Some may wish to argue that *Depositio*, *Elevatio*, and *Visitatio* attached themselves to the *sepulchrum* simultaneously. As I have suggested above, these persons will have to account for the fact that even at an early period (represented by the *Concordia Regularis* of St. Athelwold) the *Visitatio* became true drama, whereas the *Depositio-Elevatio* never attained this development.

[12] Disregard of this simple fact sometimes leads to the investigator's confusion. The rarity of the *Visitatio* in England, for example, might seem puzzling in view of the large number of "Easter sepulchres" still to be seen throughout the country. These sepulchres, in general, were evidently designed not for the *Visitatio*, but for versions of the *Depositio-Elevatio*, such as those from Sarum, York, and Exeter. See above, for example, pp. 97–100.

UNIVERSITY OF WISCONSIN STUDIES
IN LANGUAGE AND LITERATURE
NUMBER 11

STUDIES

BY MEMBERS OF THE DEPARTMENT OF ENGLISH

Series Number 2

MADISON
1920

UNIVERSITY OF WISCONSIN STUDIES

[illegible] LANGUAGE AND LITERATURE NO. 11

[illegible] PRICE FIFTY CENTS

[illegible] at the University of Wisconsin at Madison, Wisconsin [illegible]

[illegible] postoffice at Madison, [illegible] Act of [illegible] for mailing at special [illegible] Act of October [illegible]

[illegible] September [illegible]

No. 1. British criticisms of American writings, 1783-1815, by William B. Cairns. [illegible] Fifty cents.

No. 2. Studies by members of the department of English. [illegible] One dollar.

No. 3. Classical studies in honor of Charles Forster Smith. [illegible] One dollar.

No. 4. [illegible] by Karl Young. 66p. Fifty cents.

No. 5. The position of the *Roode en Witte Roos* in the saga of King Richard III, by Oscar James Campbell. 170p. Fifty cents.

No. 6. Goethe's lyric poems in English translation prior to 1860, by Lucretia Van Tuyl Simmons. 204p. Fifty cents.

No. 7. Lucilius and Horace—a study in the classical theory of imitation, by George Converse Fiske. 524p. Two dollars fifty cents.

No. 8. The first quarto edition of Shakespeare's Hamlet, by Frank Gaylord Hubbard. 120p. Fifty cents.

No. 9. Traces of matriarchy in Germanic hero-lore, by Albert William Aron. 77 p. Fifty cents.

No. 10. The dramatic associations of the Easter sepulchre, by Karl Young. 130p. Fifty cents.

No. 11. Studies by members of the department of English, Series number 2. 144p. Fifty cents.

UNIVERSITY OF WISCONSIN STUDIES
IN LANGUAGE AND LITERATURE
NUMBER 11

STUDIES

BY MEMBERS OF THE DEPARTMENT OF ENGLISH

Series Number 2

MADISON
1920

CONTENTS

THE PLUNDERING OF THE HOARD IN *BEOWULF*

FRANK GAYLORD HUBBARD

Professor W. W. Lawrence, in an article entitled *The Dragon and his Lair in Beowulf*,[1] rejects the commonly accepted interpretation, which makes the plunderer of the hoard a slave (*þēow*), and proposes another rendering, in which the hoard is robbed by a thane, who has been driven from the court on account of a feud in which he is involved. Professor Lawrence gives the poor slave rather short shrift: "There is every reason, it seems to me, for banishing this fugitive slave forever from the pages of *Beowulf*."[2] "Is it not better to allow this fleeing thrall to take himself out of the epic completely?"[2] Perhaps he will have to go; perhaps (as suggested)[3] such a character was too lowly and contemptible, far beneath the notice of the Beowulf poet; still I must confess to a kindly feeling for the poor fellow, known to me for many years, and feel impelled to make a plea that he remain a little longer, or, if he must go, that he be allowed to depart as he went to the dragon's lair the second time, *hē ofer willan gīong*.

I

THE STRANGE MANNER OF BEOWULF'S DEATH

Before taking up the special question of the personality of the plunderer of the hoard, it will be well to consider the general tone and feeling of this part of the poem. It may well be entitled *The Strange Manner of Beowulf's Death*. In the

---

[1] *Publications of the Modern Language Association*, XXXIII, 547–583.
[2] P. 554; p. 557.
[3] P. 557. "The poet of *Beowulf* was not interested in slaves; they are never mentioned in the poem."

very beginning of the narrative (2208–11) we are told that Beowulf's reign was fortunate until the dragon began his devastation. This is followed by a brief account of the discovery of the hoard by the fugitive, the story of its hiding, the rousing of the dragon, and his devastation (in which we have, ll. 2309–11, a foreshadowing of the fatal ending). We are then told of Beowulf's great grief at this disaster, his thought that he must have greatly angered God to bring such a calamity upon his people:

brēost innam wēoll
þēostrum geþoncum, swā him geþȳwe ne wæs[4]

A few lines farther (2342–44), after an account of the preparation of the iron shield, it is intimated that this is all in vain, Beowulf is doomed to meet his death in the combat with the dragon:

Sceolde lǣn[5]-daga
æþeling ǣr-gōd ende gebīdan
worulde līfes.

He was over-confident in his determination to fight the dragon alone; he underestimated the prowess of the monster (2345–49). As he approaches the conflict, the impending doom casts its shadow:

þenden hǣlo ābēad heorð-genēatum,
gold-wine Gēata. Him wæs gēomor sefa,
wǣfre ond wæl-fūs, wyrd ungemete nēah.[6]

When the warriors go to look upon their fallen lord, the poet emphasizes the strange manner of his death:

þā wæs ende-dæg
gōdum gegongen, þæt se gūð-cyning,
Wedra þēoden, wundor-dēaðe swealt.[7]

---

[4] Ll. 2331–32.
[5] MS þend.
[6] Ll. 2418–20.
[7] Ll. 3035–37.

We find this note again in ll. 3062–68:

Wundur hwār þonne
eorl ellen-rōf ende gefēre
līf-gesceafta, þonne leng ne mæg
mon mid his māgum[8] medu-seld būan.
Swā wæs Bīowulfe, þā hē biorges weard
sōhte, searo-nīðas; selfa ne cūðe,
þurh hwæt his worulde gedāl weorðan sceolde.

These lines are followed by the account of the cursing of the hoard;[9] this curse, unknown both to the discoverer of the hoard and to Beowulf, has had its fateful effect, in spite of the fact that neither of them had disturbed the dragon nor attacked him primarily to rob him of the hoard. All this adds to the strangeness of Beowulf's death, truly a *wundor-dēaþ*.

In this connection it will be well to consider the manner in which the hoard was discovered, and the motives that prompted the combat with the dragon. Without discussing all the various forms of the story of a fight with a hoard-guarding dragon, it is sufficient for the present purpose to note that commonly the motive that prompts the hero is the winning of the treasure. Examples of this are the slaying of Fafnir, told in summary form in *Beowulf* 884–97, and the story of Frotho, in the Second Book of *Saxo Grammaticus*, which Sievers has discussed in connection with Beowulf's fight with the dragon.[10] This common motive is found also in *Beowulf*,[11] but it is noticeable that in the earlier part of the story the only motive is Beowulf's desire to put an end to the devastation that the dragon has brought upon his people.[12] As the story of the fight proceeds, however, the other motive becomes more and more prominent, until we have Beowulf, at the point of death, thanking God that he has won the treasure for his people.[13]

[8] MS *gum*.

[9] Ll. 3069–73.

[10] *Königl. sächs. Gesellsch. d. Wissensch. zu Leipzig, Phil.-Hist. Classe*, 47, 180–183.

[11] Ll. 2415, 2509, 2535–36, 2747–51, 2794–2801, 2842–43, 3084–86.

[12] Cf. ll. 2324–36.

[13] Ll. 2794–98.

Now the first motive, which is more in keeping with Beowulf's high character, has the effect of emphasizing the fact that he was not morally responsible for the tragic result, and it accords with the prominent motive in the account of the discovery of the hoard, namely, that the discoverer was prompted by no desire to win the hoard. The wretched fugitive, seeking shelter, comes by accident upon the entrance to the dragon's lair; he carries off the cup, not from a desire to possess the treasure, but in order that he may bring about a reconciliation that will put an end to his desolate condition.[14]

This hoard was cursed, like Fafnir's treasure, and we see the fateful working of the curse in the death of Beowulf; there is a likeness, too, in the fates of the hoards; one lies at the bottom of the Rhine, the other in *Bēowulf's Beorh,*

eldum swā unnyt swā hi[t ǣr]or wæs.

But in the *Bēowulf* (and this is the striking feature of the story) the treasure is not sought by gold-greedy men; the hero slays the dragon to protect his people; the dragon was roused by a poor wretch, who took but a single piece[15] for the purpose of bringing an end to his woeful condition. This insignificant man, by an act innocent of hostile intent to the dragon, set in motion the fateful train of circumstance that ended in the death of Beowulf.

II

The Plunderer of the Hoard was a Slave

I pass now to a consideration of the much disputed question of the plunderer's social status: Was he *þegn* or *þēow?* a thane or a slave? Lawrence gives a full discussion of the state of the manuscript at line 2223,

ac for þrēa-nēdlan þ::: nāt-hwylces,

which need not be repeated here.[16] His conclusion is: "No one can tell what the missing word in the MS was, but *þegn* is

[14] Cf. ll. 2221–31, 2280–85, 2408–9, 3074–75. Concerning the interpretation of ll. 3074–75, see pp. 17–19.

[15] See pp. 11–15.

[16] Pp. 553–555.

surely better than *þēow*. I think it will be clear, from an examination of the action, that we are not dealing with the escape of a slave, but with a feud in which a freeman was involved.''[17] Passing over, for the present, what seem to me to be weak points in the ''examination of the action,'' I shall set forth the evidence that appears to support the contention that the plunderer was a slave. Much of this evidence has been suggested by Bugge;[18] I shall try to state more explicitly what he has suggested and to adduce further evidence in support of his conclusion.

In the first place, the plunderer of the hoard, whatever his social status, was the most inconsiderable of men. He is first mentioned (l. 2215) as *niða nāt-hwylc;* in l. 2223 he is þ::: *nāt-hwylces hæleða bearna;* in ll . 2280–81 he is *ān mon;* he is *secg syn-bysig* (l. 2226), *earm-sceapen* (l. 2228); when he shows the way to the dragon's lair (ll. 2408–9),[19]

> hæft hyge-giomor sceolde hēan ðonon
> wong wisian. He ofer willan giong.

Now all this is language that fits a slave better than a thane, and it is in accord with the dominant motive of this part of the poem: the woe of the Geats had an insignificant beginning.

In the second place, the language in which his condition is described naturally (with meaning not forced) applies to a man in servile condition. In ll. 2223–24 it is said of him that ''for dire necessity he fled the blows of hate (hateful blows),''[20] *for þrēa-nēdlan....... hete-swengeas flēah.* Now it is true that the word *hete-swengeas* may be taken in an abstract or figurative meaning, ''hateful violence'' or ''hateful persecution,'' but it is just as natural to take it in a concrete meaning, ''scourging.'' That slaves were scourged in Anglo-Saxon times is plainly shown by the Anglo-Saxon laws.[21] The

[17] P. 554.

[18] *Zeitschrift für deutsche Philologie*, IV, 210. Paul and Braune, *Beiträge*, XII, 370–71, 374.

[19] Cf. Lawrence, p. 557.

[20] Cf. Lawrence, p. 555.

[21] See *Laws of Ine*, 48; 54, 2; *Laws of Æthelstan*, 19; *Ecgberti Poenitentiale*, II, 4. Cf. Bosworth-Toller, *Dictionary* s. v. *swingan, swinge, swingel.*

outcast took the cup stolen from the hoard to his lord (*man-dryhten*, l. 2281) and asked for a peace settlement, reconciliation, or pardon (*frioðu-wǣre bæd hlāford sīnne*, l. 2282);[22] this was granted (*bēne getīðad fēa-sceaftum men*, l. 2284). There is nothing in all this that does not naturally imply that the relation between the two men was that of master and slave, even though it be granted that it *may* imply that the relation was that of lord to thane.[23] In l. 2408 the word *hæft* is applied to the outcast.[24] This may be the past participle of *hæftan*, "bound, fettered;" in general, however, editors and translators have taken it as the noun *hæft*, and have translated it "captive." The word may have, however, the meaning "slave," as is plainly shown in the following passages:

> hweorfon þā hǣðenan hæftas fram þām hālgum cnihton
> *Daniel*, l. 267
>
> Gearwe stōdun
> hæftas hēarsume, þā þæs hālgan word
> lȳt oferlēordun *Guthlac*, 697.

Now, even without insisting that the word in this case (l. 2408) should be translated "slave," it is certainly reasonable to maintain that it implies here servile condition.

In the third place, all the words used to name the lord of the outcast are words that are used to name the master (owner) of a slave. I cite the following examples of such use: *man-dryhten* (l. 2281), *Laws of Wihtræd*, 9; 10 (*dryhten*); *hlāford* (l. 2283), *Laws of Ine*, 3; 74; *Laws of Cnut*, II, 45, 3; *frēa* (l. 2285), *Riddles* 44, 10; *āgend*[25] (l. 3075), *Laws of Hlothhære and Eadric*, 1; 3; *Laws of Wihtræd*, 27.

Concerning the word applied to the outcast in l. 2223, the first letter of which (þ) only can be read, Lawrence's statement may be accepted: "No one can tell what the missing word in the MS. was."[26] There is almost unanimous agree-

---

[22] For an example of freoðo-wǣr=reconciliation, pardon, see *Andreas* l. 1632, *Hī onfēngon ful-wihte and freoðu-wǣre*. Cf. Grein, *Glossar* s.v. *freoðo*.

[23] Cf. Lawrence p. 556.

[24] *hæft hyge-giomor sceolde hēan ðonon wong wisian.*

[25] Concerning this word, see p. 19; cf. Bugge, *Beiträge*, XII, 374.

[26] P. 554.

ment that it was either *þegn* or *þēow;* it *may* have been *þēow.* In l. 2219 there is applied to the outcast a word whose fourth letter is very indistinct in the MS; this is generally read by editors as *þēofes,* but Thorkelin in his edition of *Beowulf* (1815) reads the MS as *þēowès,*[27] and Wülker in his edition (1883)[28] reads the MS as *þēowes.* In connection with these disputed readings, it should be noted again that the word *hæft,* applied to the outcast in l. 2408, has the meaning "slave."[29]

From the material gathered together in the preceding paragraphs, I believe that it may be maintained with confidence that wherever the outcast is mentioned in the poem the language used indicates that he was a slave; that it does not indicate with any certainty that he was a thane; that Lawrence's rather summary ejection of the slave from the poem is not warranted by any reasonable interpretation of the text.[30]

III

The Plunderer Took from the Hoard only a Cup

In place of the commonly accepted version of the story, which makes the outcast a slave, who conciliates his master by a cup taken from the hoard, Lawrence proposes another version,[31] in which the outcast is a thane, who flees from the court to escape the violence of vengeance in a feud in which he has become involved.[32] He takes from the hoard not only the cup but other treasure. "By this means he had bought off the private vengeance of the injured man or his kinsman,"[33] his lord,

---

[27] In l. 2223 Thorkelin reads only þ.

[28] Grein-Wülker, *Bibliothek* I, 284.

[29] See above, p. 10.

[30] It is not to be denied, of course, that in some passages the language may apply as well to a thane as to a slave.

[31] Pp. 555–57.

[32] "The thief had committed some act which threatened to bring down violence upon his head." P. 555.

[33] Pp. 555–56. Cf. "It looks, as already noted, as though the feud were settled by rings plundered from the hoard .... while the mediator retained the cup." P. 556.

perhaps, acting as mediator. This "common procedure in early Germanic justice" Lawrence very aptly illustrates by reference to the story of Ecgtheow, *Beowulf,* 459–472.

Inasmuch as this proposed version of the outcast's story involves the question of the amount of treasure taken by him from the hoard, it may be worth while to examine the text with reference to that matter. The text of the narrative of the outcast's action in the dragon's lair is, unfortunately, in a very bad state, and subsequent references to it are not so specific as one might wish; nevertheless certain features of the narrative stand out very distinctly.

The outcast was very badly frightened, and saved his life by beating a hasty retreat, getting away so quickly that the dragon did not catch sight of him: *ðām gys*[*te gryre*]*-brōga stōd*[34] (2227); *se fǣr begeat* (2330); *he tō forð gestōp...... dracan heāfde nēah. Swā mæge unfæge ēaðe gedīgan wēan ond wrǣc-sīð* (2289–92); *hlǣw oft ymbehwearf ealne ūtan-weardne; nē ðǣr ǣnig mon on þǣre wēstenne* (2296–97). When the outcast directs Beowulf to the dragon's lair it is said of him, *Hē ofer willan giong;*[35] concerning this remark Lawrence well says, "Anyone who had once come to close quarters with the dragon had no taste for more of him."[36] Now, if the thief was as badly terrified as all this indicates, and if he beat such a hasty retreat, it is not at all probable that he tarried long enough to help himself generously to the treasure.

There is constant reference throughout the narrative to a precious cup that the outcast took. It is the most prominent feature; by means of it a reconciliation was effected, *mandryhtne bær fǣted wǣge, frioðo-wǣre bæd hlāford sīnne...... bēne getīðad fēa-sceaftum men* (2281–86); in one passage it is apparently considered as *fons et origo malorum, hǣfde* [*Bēowulf*] *þā gefrunen hwanan sīo fǣhð ārās, bealo-nīð biorna; him to bearme cwōm māðþum-fæt mǣre þurh ðæs meldan hond* (2403–5); it is mentioned in connection with the terror that

---

[34] Cf. Zupitza's note.

[35] L. 2409.

[36] P. 557.

came upon the thief, *þā hyne se fǣr begeat sinc-fæt* [*geseah*][37] (2230–31); in ll. 2280–82 there is a reference to the rousing of the dragon, in immediate connection with the cup, *oð ðæt hyne ān abealch mon on mōde; man-dryhtne bær fǣted wǣge;* it is the object for whose loss the dragon takes vengeance, *wolde se lāða*[38] *līge forgyldan drinc-fæt dȳre* (2305–6).

In the passage that tells of the reconciliation two expressions are used, *ðā was hord rāsod, onboren bēaga hord* (2283–84), that have been taken by some scholars to mean that the hoard was plundered and a quantity of rings carried off by the outcast. Lawrence translates, "So the hoard was plundered, a store of rings borne off."[39] It is in these lines apparently, that he finds expression of the idea that there was a feud which was settled by treasure taken by the outcast in addition to the cup.[40] As the position of these half lines, 2283[b] and 2384[a], in the context may be of some significance, I quote ll. 2278–86.

> Swā se ðēod-sceaða þrēo hund wintra
> hēold on hrūsan hord-ærna sum
> ēacen-cræftig, oð ðæt hyne ān ābealch
> mon on mōde; man-dryhtne bær
> fǣted wǣge, frioðo-wǣre bæd
> hlāford sinne. Þā wæs hord rāsod,
> onboren bēaga hord; bēne getīðad
> fēa-sceaftum men. Frēa scēawode
> fīra fyrn-geweorc forman sīðe.

The lines that follow tell of the rousing of the dragon and his vain pursuit of the thief. It is to be noticed that the lines quoted begin with a statement concerning the long time that the dragon had held the hoard undisturbed, and end with an expression on the same theme, "The lord looked upon the an-

---

[37] No word can be read here, but it was almost certainly a verb, of which *sinc-fæt* is the object.

[38] MS *fela ða*.

[39] P. 552.

[40] "It looks, as already noted, as though the feud were settled by rings plundered from the hoard, *onboren bēaga hord, bēne getīðad fēa-sceaftum men* (2284–5), while the mediator retained the cup, *him to bearme cwōm, māðþum-fæt mǣre* (2404–5)." P. 556.

cient work of men for the first time [since it had been hidden].''[41] The intervening lines tell, in summary form, the facts concerning the discovery; they do not seem intended to express additional facts concerning the discovery.

Inasmuch as the translation of the expressions in question turns upon the meaning given to the past participles *rāsod* and *onboren*, it is necessary to consider in some detail the use of these words in Anglo-Saxon.

The simple verb *rāsian* appears to have been rarely used; the only example recorded is in the passage under discussion. Of the compound *ārāsian* there are numerous examples, and it is from these that we must deduce the probable meaning of *rāsod*. Klæber (*Anglia*, 25, 315) connects *ārāsian* with *rīsan* ''seize, snatch away, carry off,''[42] examples of *ārāsian* in this meaning are given in Grein and Bosworth-Toller. But the word has other meanings. In *Genesis* 44, 16, *hæfð ārāsod* translates *invenit*;[43] in *Gregory's Dialogues*, 2, 14, *ārāsian* translates *explorare*;[44] in *Crist*, l. 1230, we have *ārāsade* (pp. n. pl.) ''detected, discovered, exposed.''[45] We may, then, with confidence translate, *ðā wæs hord rāsod*, ''then the hoard was discovered.''[46]

It is generally assumed by editors and commentators that the word *onberan* has the meaning (suggested by its derivation) ''carry off;'' but, on the basis of the recorded examples of its use, it would be difficult to establish that meaning; its general meaning seems to be, ''diminish, enfeeble, impair.''[47] Bugge (*Beiträge*, XII, 102) calls attention to the gloss *in-*

---

[41] Ll. 2285–86.

[42] Cf. Leo, *Angelsächsisches Glossar*, 327, 35.

[43] God hæfþ ārāsod ūre unrihtnessa, *Deus invenit nostras iniquitates.*

[44] þæt he sceolde gecunnian and ārāsian hwæþre se drihtnes wer hæfde wītedōmes gāst, *An vir Dei prophetiæ spiritum haberet explorare conatus est.* Grein, *Prosa*, Vol. 5, p. 130, ll. 28–30. Cf. also l. 13, *Hū hē ārāsode þā hiwunge Totillan þæs cyninges*, and p. 132, ll. 7–9 on hū mycelre hrædnysse hī wǣron ārāsode. See Thorpe, *Ælfric's Homilies* II, pp. 168, 472.

[45] þǣr hȳ ārāsade rēotað and beofiað fore frēan forhte.

[46] It is not to be denied, of course, that *rāsod* could here be translated "seized, carried off," if that meaning better suited the context.

[47] See Bosworth-Toller, Grein.

minutus, onboren (Wright-Wülker, 430, 12). He also notes that the phrase in *Beowulf* is parallel to *brēosthord onboren*, Guthlac, 917,[48] where *onboren* has the meaning "enfeebled."[49] We may, then, following Bugge's suggestion, translate *onboren bēaga hord*, "the hoard of treasures (precious objects[50]) was diminished."

We have established on a firm basis the translation "Then was the hoard discovered, the hoard of precious objects diminished;" we have shown that it is not necessary to translate, as Lawrence does, "So the hoard was plundered, a store of rings borne off," and that the translation *onboren*, "borne off," is doubtful. It has, further, been shown that in all other references to the thief's booty only a cup is mentioned. If, then, in the case of these lines (2283–84), whose translation is disputed, there has been established a translation that neither by direct statement or implication contains a reference to other objects than the cup, we are fully justified in the conclusion that the outcast took from the hoard only the cup.[51] The text, then, gives very little, if any, support to the theory that a feud was settled by rings taken from the hoard.

IV

The Curse Motive

It remains to consider two or three points in Professor Lawrence's discussion of passages in the poem (3047–57 and 3062–75) that refer to the curse and its effect. In this discussion much is made of "the reluctance of the poet not (*sic*) to allow full power to heathen charms,"[52] which (according to Lawrence) finds its chief expression in two pas-

---

[48] "Die verbindung *onboren—hord* wird durch Gu8 l. 917 *brēost-hord onboren* gestützt."

[49] Wæs þām bāncōfan æfter niht-glōme
nēah geþrungen, brēost-hord onboren.

For another example of the use of *onboren*, see *Beowulf*, 990.

[50] For *bēag*=precious object, see Klæber, *Mod. Phil.* 3, 462.

[51] Cf. Cosijn, *Beiträge*, VIII, 572, "*Was fehlte war bloss ein trinkgefäss.*"

[52] P. 563; cf. pp. 561–62.

sages, 3054–57 and 3074–75. It must be admitted that this reluctance may be inferred from the first of these passages (3054–57), which states that after the spell or charm had effectively protected the hoard for a thousand years, it came to pass, in God's providence, that a man opened it; but that the second passage (3074–75, called by Bugge *locus desperatus*) contains any expression of "the reluctance of the poet" etc. is very doubtful indeed.

I consider first ll. 3054–57

nefne God selfa,
sigora Sōð-cyning, sealde þām þe hē wolde
-he is manna gehyld- hord openian,
efne swā hwylcum manna, swā him gemet ðūhte.

Lawrence translates:[53]

unless God himself,
the true king of glories, should grant a favored man
-he is the protector of mankind- to open the hoard,
whatever man might seem to him meet for this.

The translation of l. 3055ᵇ, "should grant a favored man," is rather highly colored; the words *sealde þām ðe hē wolde* mean simply "should grant to whom he would." It is doubtful if the translation of l. 3057, colored in the same tone, is correct. In all recorded examples, the adjective *gemet* is used only in impersonal constructions; l. 3055 is exactly parallel to ll. 686–87, *on swā hwæþere hond........swā him gemet þince,* and 3055ᵇ is exactly parallel to *Genesis* 2895ᵇ, *swā him gemet þinceð*, and to *Boethius Metra* 29, 42, *swā him gemet þinceð*; in all four cases the expression is used concerning the Deity. We may be certain, then, that in the expression under discussion *gemet þūhte* is impersonal, and that l. 3055 is to be translated, "even to whatever man it should seem to him meet;" there is no basis at all for Lawrence's "whatever man might seem to him meet for this." Lines 3052ᵇ–57 state, in substance, that the hoard was so bound by a spell that no one could touch

[53] P. 561.

it, unless God, in his power and providence, should permit some man to open it. While they express the idea that the Christian God can break the heathen spell, so far as opening the hoard is concerned, they certainly carry no suggestion that a man of the right character could, in God's providence, open the hoard without incurring the peril of the curse.[54]

Inasmuch as Lawrence finds strong support for his views in ll. 3074–75 (for which he offers a new interpretation, confirming his interpretation of ll. 3054–57), it will be necessary to discuss this famous crux. For the purpose of ready reference I give the lines, with the preceding context.

Swā hit oð dōmes dæg diope benemdon
þēodnas mǣre, þā ðæt þǣr dydon,
þæt se secg wǣre synnum scildig,
hergum geheaðerod, hell-bendum fæst,
wommum gewītnad, sē ðone wong strude;[55]
næs hē gold-hwæte; gearwor hæfde
āgendes ēst ǣr gescēawod.

In l. 3074 Lawrence adopts the emendations *næfne* (MS *næs*) and *gold-hwæt* (MS *gold-hwæte*); in l. 3075 he capitalizes *āgendes,* making it refer to God; he translates, "unless he, rich in gold, had very zealously given heed in the past to the grace of the Lord." The emendation *næfne* seems to have been first suggested, but not adopted, by Sievers;[56] *gold-hwæt* has been adopted by some editors.

To the word *gold-hwæt* Lawrence gives the meaning "prosperous, rich in gold,"[57] and he objects to the rendering

[54] Cf. Lawrence, p. 563. "But piety, bringing the favor of the Lord, gives a man great practical advantages." "The Christian God was superior to spells, and the Christian hero was one who ought to be saved by the Christian God, on account of his piety."

[55] MS *strade;* cf. l. 3126, *hwā þæt hord strude.*

[56] *Beiträge* XII, 144, "Doch nehme ich anstoss *næs* in *næfne* zu ändern;" cf. Lawrence, p. 561, n. 14.

[57] P. 562, n. 15. "The meaning of the phrase *gold-hwæt* is difficult to render in modern English. It combines the significance of 'active, keen, bold' (See Chambers, Glossary, sub *hwæt*) with the idea of the possession of gold. Perhaps the word 'prosperous' might come near the meaning; I have rendered it here 'rich in gold' in order to keep the double significance of the phrase. It is quite in place as applying to the *secg* of 3071, who might plunder the hoard."

"greedy for gold," adopted by some editors, as reading "into the phrase a meaning which does not belong to it." As this is the only recorded example of the use of the word, we must look to the use and meaning of other compounds with *hwæt* to determine the meaning of *gold-hwæt*. The other compounds are *flyht-hwæt, fyrd-hwæt, sund-hwæt, dǣd-hwæt, dōm-hwæt, mōd-hwæt;* in all of these it is plain that the meaning of *hwæt* (as in the simple word *hwæt*) is "keen about, eager for, bent upon, active in;" they certainly give no support to the interpretation of *gold-hwæt,* as "rich in gold." To give to the word the meaning "greedy for gold" may be going too far, but it is going in the right direction.

Another weakness in the proposed translation lies in the rendering of the comparative *gearwor* by the superlative (absolute) "very zealously." Now it may be granted that, in some cases, such a substitution of superlative for comparative may be justified by the context, but in the case before us, where an emendation of the context is proposed (*næfne* for *næs*), it is a serious objection to the emendation, that it seems to require such a substitution.

I have called attention to these points of weakness in the proposed interpretation of these lines, because they are all connected with textual change and coloring of translation apparently necessary to bring this passage into accord with the proposed interpretation of ll. 3054–57. I have stated above[58] my objections to the proposed interpretation of the latter passage. I have shown that it has been found necessary to color the translation of both passages,[59] and to emend one of them, in order to bring them into accord, and to force them to the expression of the extraneous idea, that a man of the right character could, in God's providence, plunder the hoard without incurring the peril of the curse.

Against Lawrence's interpretation of ll. 3074–75 I wish to set another; it has, perhaps, little, if any, originality, as it follows Bugge[60] in some details, but it has, at least, the merit

[58] P. 16.

[59] Ll. 3054–57 and 3074–75.

[60] *Beiträge* XII, 370–1, 374–5. I do not accept Bugge's emendation, *Gæst be gold-fæte.*

of proposing no emendation of the text. The *hē* of l. 3074 refers to the outcast who disturbed the treasure, not to the hypothetical *secg* who should disturb it (*sē ðone wong strude*). The word *gold-hwæte* means "keen about, eager for gold."[61] The comparative *gearwor*, in connection with the negative in *næs* indicates that the first clause, *næs hē gold-hwæte*, expresses a rejected alternative, and the second an accepted (or approved) alternative. The noun *āgendes* refers to the lord or master of the outcast;[62] *ēst* has its ordinary meaning, "grace, favor," and refers to the grace that the outcast thought to obtain from his master by means of the cup taken from the hoard. The meaning of *gescēawod* has recently been discussed by Professor Samuel Moore;[63] he translates, "he had rather regarded the grace of the Lord," and quotes seven examples of the use of *(ge)scēawian* in the sense of "regard, pay respect to, give heed to." We need not hesitate, then, to adopt this meaning for the word in the passage under discussion. I would propose this translation. "He was not keen about (eager for) gold; he before had been the rather eagerly regardful of his master's favor." The outcast who disturbed the hoard did not do so because he was keen to possess the gold; it was rather that he had been eagerly intent upon gaining his master's grace.

As noted above, Lawrence associates these lines with ll. 3054–57; I would associate them with ll. 2221 ff.

> Nealles mid gewealdum wyrm-hord ābræc[64]
> sylfes willum, sē ðe him sāre gescēod;
> ac for þrēa-nēdlan þ[ēow] nāt-hwylces
> hæleða bearna hete-swengeas flēah,
> ærnes[64] þearfa, and ðǣr inne fealh[65]
> secg syn-bysig.

---

[61] For examples of the use of the adverb in place of the adjective with the verb "to be," see Moore, *Journal of English and Germanic Philology*, XVII, p. 215.

[62] For examples of *āgend*=the master of a slave, see p. 10. Cf. Rieger, *Zeitsch. f. d. Phil.*, III, 415, concerning the use of the word when it refers to Deity.

[63] *Journal of English and Germanic Philology*, XVII, pp. 214–15.

[64] MS *horda cræft*.

[65] See Zupitza's notes.

In both passages we have a disclaimer of evil intent, of malice aforethought towards the dragon and his hoard. In the later passage this suggestion of the innocence of the plunderer is associated with the curse; in the earlier, with the fateful effect of the plunderer's act. Both passages accord with the dominant motive, the strange manner of Beowulf's death.

SENTIMENTAL MORALITY IN WORDSWORTH'S NARRATIVE POETRY

Oscar James Campbell

I

Explanations of Wordsworth's purpose in writing his narrative poems about peasant life have been indistinct and inadequate. That these works of his were the expression of a direct moral purpose no one has doubted, and Wordsworth's express declaration of the mission of his poetry in his letter to Lady Beaumont[1] has always been tacitly applied to his narrative poems as much as to his poems of nature. Both were written "to console the afflicted; to add sunshine to daylight by making the happy happier; to teach the young and gracious of every age to see, to think and feel, and, therefore, to become more actively and securely virtuous."

Although usually it is only the poet's attitude toward nature that has been interpreted in the light of this lofty program, critics have often protested against the comparative neglect of his narrative poems as moral documents. Ruskin in *Modern Painters* says,[2] "Wordsworth's distinctive work was a war with pomp and pretence, and a display of the majesty of simple feelings and humble hearts, together with high reflective truth in his analysis of the courses of politics and the ways of men; without these, his love of nature would have been comparatively worthless." Mr. Paul Elmer More voices the same protest when he says, "Wordsworth has been

---

[1] May 21, 1807, in *Letters of the Wordsworth Family, 1787–1855.* (ed. Wm. Knight), I, 303. Wordsworth's continual insistence on the moral functions of a poet is too well-known to need recapitulation. Such statements as "Every great poet is a teacher;" "I wish either to be considered as a teacher or as nothing;" are common.

[2] Library Ed. London, 1903, III, p. 293.

much lauded as the high priest of Nature; whereas, in reality the important innovation introduced by him into English poetry is not the appreciation of Nature but his humanitarianism, his peculiarly sentimental mental attitude toward humble life.''[3]

In spite of such protests against the neglect of his narrative poems, the specific moral power which Wordsworth believed many of his *Lyrical Ballads* and such works as *Peter Bell* and some of the tales in *The Excursion* to possess, has not ordinarily been made clear. Wordsworth, it is commonly said, believed these poems to be of great ethical worth because he was a thorough-going democrat. He thought that the upper classes could learn specific lessons of conduct from contemplating the lowly peasant. The common man could teach the more complex civilized man, just because he devoted his life to the simple, primary, universal human experiences. For only in these essentials can any human being find real peace and happiness.

The attention of critics has been directed almost exclusively to this phase of Wordsworth's attitude toward the peasant. This is natural. The most memorable passages in the poet's preface to the *Lyrical Ballads* exalt the life of the peasant as a model for that of all men. ''Humble and rustic life was generally chosen because in that condition, the essential passions of the heart find a better soil in which they can attain maturity, are less under restraint and speak a plainer and more emphatic language,'' is the passage from the Preface most frequently quoted. It explains what qualities in the life of peasants he believed to be worthy of universal imitation,—the simplicity and intensity of their emotional life.

Comment on Wordsworth's narrative poems has usually been mere reiteration of the ideas contained in this sentence. John Churton Collins, for example, writes, ''The joy offered to us in the simple, primary affections and duties—and the extraordinary power with which, in case after case, he shows us this joy and renders it so as to make us share it, gives him this place mainly on the strength of the unique power

[3] Shelburn Essays, 1st Series, p. 208.

found in such poems as *Michael, The Fountain* and *The Solitary Reaper.*"[4] Mr. Paul Elmer More similarly calls attention to this democratic moral feeling which is expressed in his poems of peasant life. "Art is no longer the desire of select spirits to ennoble and make beautiful their lives, but an effort to teach and elevate the common man and to bring the proud into sympathy with the vulgar."[5] Professor Harper expresses a similar notion when he says that Wordsworth's sad tales show us "patience learned through suffering, humility through defeat, strength from striving, and many another virtue easily overlooked except by the eye of love."[6] It is scarcely necessary to accumulate critical comment of this nature; for Wordsworth's belief that the life of the peasant must be sympathetically comprehended by those seeking the durable satisfactions in life, has been generally understood.

Now and then, however, a voice has been raised in perplexity over Wordsworth's peasant stories. Many of them obviously can not perform the joyous democratic service expected of them. In certain of these tales neither joy nor hope is to be discovered. They are, on the contrary, tragedies of a peculiarly painful and hopeless sort. How are they to make the happy happier or to teach the young and gracious of every age to become more actively and securely virtuous?

Mr. A. C. Bradley suggests that these poems represent in a negative way Wordsworth's efforts to exalt Nature. "Wordsworth," he says, "yields here and there too much to a tendency to contrast the happiness, innocence and harmony of Nature with the unrest, misery and sin of man. How many of his most famous narratives deal with sad or painful subjects; even (as in *Ruth* or *The White Doe of Rylstone* or the story of Margaret in the *Excursion*) with subjects that are terribly sad or painful."[7] This fact is beyond question. It is probably not, however, as Mr. Bradley thinks, an indirect way of exalting Nature or an effort to

[4] *Posthumous Essays*, London, 1912, p. 101.
[5] Shelburn Essays, 1st Series, p. 209.
[6] *William Wordsworth*, II, p. 224.
[7] *English Poetry and German Philosophy in the Age of Wordsworth*, Manchester Univ. Press, 1909, p. 25.

show that although man's life is dark, in his celestial spirit there is a power that can win glory out of agony and even out of sin. It is rather the result of Wordsworth's complete adoption of the moral doctrines of 18th century humanitarian sentimentalism.

The essential tenet of this philosophy was that man could be stimulated to morality through awakening his compassion for undeserved suffering,—his pity for virtue in distress. Wordsworth, it will appear, did not at first give this familiar ethical principle an important place in his system of thought. Much of his first distinctive poetry was written while he was under the influence of the radical rationalism of William Godwin. A kind of humanitarianism, however, was consistent with Godwin's life of reason; and Wordsworth wrote a number of poems to display the sufferings of the humble among mankind under the weight of the irrational social institutions of property and war. The purpose of such poems was to awaken man's moral indignation by appealing to his sense of justice and to his cool understanding.

Later Wordsworth rejected Godwin's entire system as destructive of the most elemental and vital human qualities. About the same time he came under the influence of the philosophy of David Hartley as set forth in his *Observations on Man, his Frame, his Duty and his Expectations.* Hartley gave a central place in his moral system to compassion for undeserved human suffering. He regarded it as one of the principal incentives to a life of joyous virtue. Wordsworth found in this theory the highest philosophical sanction for the employment of one of his most characteristic mental qualities. Godwin's contempt for pity which was awakened by human misery served at this time only to commend the more urgently this doctrine of eighteenth century sentimentalism. Wordsworth, therefore, began to write a kind of poetry which he had not attempted before. He retained his interest in the common man, but he no longer presented his condition as one to invite the reforms of rational humanitarians. He made him the object of compassion by showing him enduring with fortitude undeserved suffering; he gave the reader authentic instances of the reformation of erring human beings by the sight of virtue in distress. In embodying these ideas in poetic tales he felt that he was not merely indulging his temperament, but softening human hearts into virtue by evoking the tender emotion of pity.

This, in brief, is the thesis which the writer will seek to establish in the following pages. It is offered as a key to the only satisfactory interpretation of a number of Wordsworth's poems.

II

Wordsworth at least once in his poetry explains his theory of sentimental morality with absolute directness and simplicity. In the first book of *The Excursion* the Wanderer stops in the midst of his narration of the story of Margaret to explain the significance which he wishes his listener to find in it. Why should he turn from the calm and comfort which he knows can be found in Nature to a distressing story of human sorrow?

> Why should we thus, with an untoward mind,
> And in the weakness of humanity,
> From natural wisdom turn our hearts away;
> To natural comfort shut our eyes and ears;
> And, feeding on disquiet, thus disturb
> The calm of Nature with our restless thoughts?[8]

This is exactly the question which Mr. Bradley answers by saying that this dallying with human sorrow is the poet's indirect way of exalting nature. Wordsworth, through the mouth of the Wanderer, it will be noted, makes a quite different explanation.

> "It were wantoness, and would demand
> Severe reproof, if we were men whose hearts
> Could hold vain dalliance with the misery
> Even of the dead; contented thence to draw
> A momentary pleasure, never marked
> By reason, barren of all future good;

[8] II, ll. 59 ff.

But we have known that there is often found
In mournful thoughts, and always might be found,
A power to virtue friendly.'"[9]

In this interesting passage Wordsworth, in the first place, explicitly denies that he tells the sad tale to luxuriate in sorrowful feeling. This form of sentimentalism was always abhorrent to him.[10] He clearly agreed with Coleridge in regarding this indulgence in the "softness of humanity" and in "sweet anxiety"[11] as a thinking disease.[12] He tells the story because he believes that the mournful thoughts that it produces will be a direct stimulus to virtue. A tale of distressing sorrow—such is his unequivocal statement—tends to make those who hear it morally better men.

This is one tenet of the familiar eighteenth century sentimentalism.[13] The history of this extensive literary movement need not be reviewed here. It will be enough to recall the philosophical beliefs upon which its central moral theory was founded and to indicate how the sentimental tale came to be regarded, by those who wrote it, as a very effective stimulus to virtue.

Belief in the innate goodness of human nature is the mainspring of sentimentalism. Man's benevolent and altruistic impulses are innate; his anti-social passions such as pride, envy, and malice, which are the instigators of vice, are acquired. If these fundamental and natural sympathies of

---

[9] Legouis says, (p. 395) that in these lines "The poet almost passes censure for having dwelt so long on a subject which can yield nothing but sorrow. In the midst of the narrative, the peddler who recounts it becomes ashamed of his tears and pauses abruptly to ask, 'Why should we thus, in an untoward mind' etc. Not without regret, not without a kind of remorse, does he yield to the entreaties of his listener and resume his story." This comment completely neglects the answer which the Wanderer very presently makes to his own question, one which justifies his telling of the tale.

[10] When Prof. Harper, *William Wordsworth*, II, p. 103 says, "No man, especially no poet, was ever less of a sentimentalist than Wordsworth," he is, of course, using sentimentalist in this sense of the word.

[11] These phrases appear in Steele's description of his own sensibility.

[12] *Anima Poetae*, p. 143.

[13] Bernbaum, Ernest, *The Drama of Sensibility*, Boston, 1915, p. 2. In the following résumé of the principles of the movement I am frequently indebted to this indispensable work.

man can be awakened and strengthened through pity for his fellow-men, the unsocial and derived evils of his nature will be driven out. He will be thus purged and reclaimed to his innate moral beauty.

Both comedy and tragedy were built upon the theory of encouraging man's naturally good impulses through the awakening of pity. Both forms appeared first in the drama. In sentimental comedy beginning with Colley Cibber's *Love's Last Shift*, played first in January 1696,[14] human beings essentially good at heart, after contending against distressful circumstances are reclaimed to themselves and to virtue. The consistently virtuous are rewarded by deserved happiness and those who have been perverted by the world are reformed by the sight of virtue in distress. At the close of Cibber's *The Lady's Last Stroke*, Lady Wronglove is bidden to lure her erring husband home with "soft affection". Therefore she weeps until Lord Wronglove exclaims, "Though perhaps my negligence of temper may have stood the frowns of love unmoved, yet I find no guard within that can support me against its tears." He thereupon swiftly repents and is reconciled with his wife. Then Sir Friendly Moral, who has brought the two together, remarks: "I knew you both had virtues." Pity for the distress of his virtuous wife has reformed him speedily and fundamentally.

In tragedy the same sort of innately virtuous persons are displayed overwhelmed by catastrophes for which they have no moral responsibility whatever. In this form of writing the reform of a character within the play could of necessity not be indicated. It was the spectator whose heart was to be washed into its natural state of virtue by having his compassion awakened for the undeserved suffering of the characters in the drama.

Both the comic and the tragic mode of this sentimental view of life were given literary form in the tale as it was developed by Steele in *The Tatler* and *The Spectator*. In both kinds of story the main situation presented was a picture of virtue

[14] Bernbaum, *op. cit.*, p. 1.

in distress. In the first sort of story this moving sight restored the villain to his native virtue and the catastrophe was avoided. In the tragic tale the catastrophe descended, and the reader was left with his pity actually aroused for the undeserved suffering he had witnessed. This pity was calculated to liberate and enfranchise his natural virtue.

The account given by Mistress Jenny Distaff of a noble lord's attempt to seduce her is a good example of Steele's tales of the first sort.[15] This virtuous girl at the tender age of sixteen falls in love with a nobleman. An evil woman Sempronia takes Jenny to the country and enables her lover to meet her at a seductive hour and a romantic spot. However, when the lord's immoral design becomes only too evident to Jenny, she falls upon her knees before him and says, "My lord, pity me, on my knees—on my knees in the cause of virtue. *Assume yourself* my lord, and do not attempt to vitiate a temple sacred to innocence, honour and religion"—and more to the same effect. The noble lord is effectually touched by this sight, "assumes himself",—that is becomes virtuous, so that Jenny sees her lover "astonished and reformed" by her behavior.

The History of Caelia[16] is an excellent example of the tragic sentimental tale. The charm and innocence of the heroine is at first abundantly established. "Her every look and motion spoke the peaceful, mild resigning, humble inhabitant that animated her beauteous body." Palamede becomes enamoured of her and she wins even his worldly-minded father by "a certain irresistible charm in her whole behavior." After her marriage, alas, she discovers that her husband is a bigamist. Then she can only lament her undeserved woe. "How bitter, heaven, how bitter is my portion! How much have I to say, but the infant which I bear about me stirs in agitation. I am, Palamede, to live in shame, and this creature to be heir to it. Farewell forever." Her only consolation is that "her sufferings are not the effect of any guilt or misconduct" and that she has "for her pro-

[15] *Tatler* 33, June 25, 1709.
[16] *Tatler* 198, July 15, 1710, written by Charles Johnson.

tection the influence of a Power which can give not only patience, but pleasure to *innocence in distress.*" Steele more than once makes clear his belief that "the contemplation of distresses of this sort softens the mind of man and makes the heart better."[17]

Fiction in the manner of Steele's pathetic tales appeared widely throughout the eighteenth century. There is little doubt, as Professor Bernbaum says,[18] that Richardson's "great edifices were built after smaller models of the sentimental tale and the sentimental drama." The tale of Caelia, summarized above, is remarkably close in its spirit and central idea to *Clarissa Harlowe;* and *Pamela* is analogous in plot and spirit to the tale of *Amanda,* which appears in *Spectator* 375. In Thomson's *Seasons,* tales of this nature first appeared in poetic form. The story in *Winter* of the swain lost in the snow is quite in Steele's manner and that of Celadon and Amelia, which appears in *Summer,* only a little less so.

To recount the subsequent history of these sorts of sentimental tales in English literature is not the purpose of this essay. The type existed in a distinct form in almost every kind of writing of the eighteenth century. It remains to discover first how far Wordsworth's belief that there existed in mournful thoughts "a power to virtue friendly" led him to fit his narrative poems into the well-worn moulds of the eighteenth century sentimental tale. Then it will be interesting to determine how this belief in the moral efficacy of tears seemed to Wordsworth thoroughly consistent with the philosophical views which are reflected in his most characteristic poems.

III

Among Wordsworth's poems there is at least one sentimental tale of the purely non-tragic sort,—that is a tale in which *a character in the poem* is reclaimed to himself and

[17] *Tatler* No. 82.
[18] *Op. cit.,* p. 165.

to virtue by the sight of undeserved human suffering. I refer to *Peter Bell.*

The traditional view of the author's purpose in writing this poem is quite different. It has been admirably phrased by Professor Harper as follows:

"The original *motif* was the same as that of the *Ancient Mariner.* A hard-hearted, wayward man is arrested and touched by nature. In the *Ancient Mariner,* nature unfolds her extraordinary powers; she shows a face of terror. In *Peter Bell* it is the 'blue and grey and tender green' of the mild night, it is a 'soft and fertile nook' a 'silent stream' that creeps into the soul." The ass, according to this view, is "the animal whose fidelity completes the conversion begun by the soft influences of 'moving waters at their priest-like task.' "[19] Legouis has almost the same idea of the poem. "It is," he writes, "an account of the conversion of a brutal and profligate churl, who is brought to a state of grace by the impressions made upon his sense, one fine evening, by a donkey and a landscape."[20]

A careful examination of the poem, however, will show the inadequacy of these explanations. Nature, whether by herself, or aided by the fidelity of the ass, had but little to do with Peter's conversion. The extraordinary fact about the reprobate at the beginning of the poem was that in spite of his out-of-door life, he had remained utterly impervious to the influences of Nature. For "two and thirty years or more" he had been "a wild and woodland rover", yet

> Nature could not find a way
> Into the heart of Peter Bell.

Michael's life alone on the heights had enobled him; Peter, though roving "among the vales and streams," had become debased.

> He was the wildest far of all;—
> He had a dozen wives.

---

[19] *William Wordsworth,* II, pp. 301–302.
[20] *Op. cit.,* p. 408.

The "hardness in his cheek" and "the hardness in his eye" were but indications of the hardness of his heart. His natural sensibility had become covered with an impenetrable casing from which the soft influences of Nature recoiled sharply.

Such a man is Peter Bell when he happens upon the soft spot where is the "blue and grey and tender green" to which Professor Harper refers. This natural loveliness has no effect on Peter. He sees only a solitary ass standing in the midst of it. His first impulse being theft, he shouts, "A prize!" When the beast refuses to allow himself to be stolen, Peter is aroused to brutal anger. The ass's mild reproachful looks, its three miserable groans, and its sharp, staring bones serve only to increase Peter's mad vexation at the beast's immobility. Finally, something uncanny in the "dry see-saw of his horrible bray" as it echoes among the rocks, stirs in Peter a vague fear. This feeling becomes a perfect access of horror when he catches sight of the dead man's face in the water, and finally he faints from sheer terror. No gentler force than sheer and primitive physical horror has served to penetrate the hard crust of Peter's nature.

After this experience, however, Peter Bell's emotions are somewhat more responsive to influences from man and nature. The ass begins to rouse faint stirrings of pity within him.[21] He mounts the beast, declaring

> "I'll do what he would have me do,
> In pity to this poor drowned man."

Then on his journey towards the dead man's cottage, Peter's heart is gradually prepared for the moral transformation which the sight of human suffering is to accomplish. The agents in his preparation are not delicate emanations from Nature; they are mostly resonant shocks to his senses.

The dolorous moan of the wood-boy searching for his lost

[21] It is the pathetic helplessness of the animal, a conventional route to the pity of a sentimentalist, and not his fidelity that seems first to stir Peter.

father leaves Peter "high in preparation" for his conversion. When he hears the rumbling of an explosion set off by miners underground, he is sure that the earth is about to yawn for him. The sound of drunken uproar from a tavern which he passes fills him with remorse. While in this state of mind, he makes the first step in his actual moral progress under the influence of sentimental tragedy evoked from his own past. He calls to mind the innocent highland girl who

> left her mother at sixteen,
> And followed Peter Bell.

When she learned of his evil courses, she died of a broken heart. At this moment the story recurs to his mind so vividly that he sees her in a vision and hears her crying as she cried

> The very moment that she died,
> "My mother! oh my mother!"

The contemplation of the undeserved suffering which he has brought upon this innocent girl has a powerful effect upon him. And when he fortuitously hears at this moment the voice of a fervent Methodist minister shouting "Repent, repent!"

> He melted into tears.
> . . . .
> Through all his iron frame was felt
> A gentle, a relaxing, power.

Through this series of percussions Peter's hardness has been relaxed until his mind is normally sensitive to influences of tenderness and pity. His true nature has been violently awakened. At that moment the sentimental tragedy of one of his victims, aided by the shock which the preacher's shouts gave him, melted him into tears. Then he feels the last recesses of his hardness relax; then he is ready for the transforming experience. This time he does not *remember*, he actually *witnesses*, the overwhelming grief of innocent human beings.

When Peter is carried to the door-yard of the dead man, his wretched wife, aroused by the cry of her little girl at sight of the ass, rushes out of the house to see,—not her husband, but Peter Bell. She falls in a half-swoon, but is raised by Peter while she weeps out her conviction that her husband is dead. The vagrant sees her "wring and wring her hands" and hears her lament:

> "He never will come home again—
> Is dead, for ever dead."
>
> Beside the woman Peter stands;
> His heart is opening more and more;
> A holy sense pervades his mind;
> He feels what he for human-kind
> Has never felt before.

But there are more tears for him to witness, more grief for him to behold. The man's little girl Rachael runs weeping loud for the neighbor; an infant makes a piteous cry in the house; the mother sighs that she has seven fatherless children.

> And now is Peter taught to feel
> That man's heart is a holy thing;
> And Nature, through a world of death,
> Breathes into him a second breath,
> More searching than the breath of spring.

This distress has roused Peter's sympathy and love for the woman, and his mind, for years in a trance, awakens. And when at last he beholds the little boy who has sought his father in the woods return, and at sight of the ass, in a fit of unfounded joy kiss the faithful beast a thousand times, his feelings of pity culminate.

> And Peter Bell, the ruffian wild,
> Sobs loud, he sobs even like a child,
> "Oh! God, I can endure no more!"

This is the undeniable sign that his reformation is complete. The sentimental belief in tears has been vindicated. We know that he has been softened into virtue, and we are not at all surprised that he

Forsook his crimes, renounced his folly,
And, after ten months' melancholy,
Became a good and honest man.

Peter Bell's case was an extreme one. His mind, therefore, needed to be brought by a series of violent shocks to a state nearly as sensitive as that of the normal man before the sentimental leaven could work. Then pity for undeserved suffering inevitably softened him into virtue by way of tears. The poem thus analyzed, proves to be not another piece of evidence for the beneficent influence of Nature upon wayward man, but cogent proof of the moral efficacy of tearful pity for undeserved human suffering.

IV

Although *Peter Bell* is the only one of Wordsworth's tales in which the sentimental reformation is circumstantially presented, the poet has written other tragic sentimental stories the influence of which for moral good upon those who hear them is definitely indicated. Such is the story of Margaret; its purpose is made explicit by the Wanderer. It is to be an agent of morality by awakening that compassion which arouses the innate virtue in the soul of man.

In its original form, as *The Ruined Cottage,* it was merely the story of a woman whose happy home was ruined by the plague of war. But it is generally agreed that as it appears in *The Excursion,* it carries new significance of some sort. This added meaning has commonly been thought to lie in the quiet courage with which Margaret endures her fate. In other words, it is supposed that she has been presented in such a way as to win admiration for one of the sturdiest and most necessary of human virtues. But it is hard to see how the wretched woman's actions after the loss of her husband can be considered essentially courageous or in any deep sense admirable. She seems to be unnerved and fairly possessed by her uncertainty and grief. She wanders disconsolately about the country-side; she neglects her infant; she allows her garden to become choked with weeds and to show first "the sleepy hand of negligence" and then actual decay. After her babe dies, "she lingers in unquiet widowhood nine tedious years, until she, too, dies in the ruins of her home." This woman, who allows all her natural duties to be swallowed up in grief, can hardly have been presented as a splendid example of the robust fortitude of the peasants. Her story is told for no such purpose, but, as the Wanderer carefully explains, to awaken moral impulses through its sheer piteousness.

The poet who hears the tale is moved as the narrator obviously desired:

> The old man ceased: he saw that I was moved;
> . . . .
> I turned aside in weakness, nor had power
> To thank him for the tale which he had told.
> I stood, and leaning o'er the garden wall
> Reviewed that woman's sufferings; and it seemed
> To comfort me while with a brother's love
> I blessed her in the impotence of grief.

This "impotence of grief" brought comfort to the listener, because in that feeling of softness he knew that his heart grew better and his aspiration to virtue more secure.

The Pastor's stories in the sixth and seventh books of *The Excursion* are told for the effect that they will have upon the Solitary. The purpose of the entire poem may be said to be the re-establishment of the misanthrope in the current of normal moral life. Professor Harper believes that the Pastor's sole method of reformation is the creation in the Solitary of a zest for life as it is. He says, "The mere recital of human stories, with no effort to point a moral, awakens in the Solitary a certain zest for things as they are."[22] Some of the stories are doubtless intended to restore his respect for men and a desire to share their virtues. But a careful examination of the discussion which provoked the Parson's narrative, will show that some of them, at least,

[22] *Op. cit.*, II, 222.

were intended to supply the misanthrope with a more positive moral principle than mere zest for living.

The Solitary and the two other principal characters come to a graveyard. The misanthrope presently expresses the belief that if he could read these graves as volumes, he would find them to be, without exception, tales of anguish and shame,—the *Spoon River Anthology* anticipated by a hundred years. The Pastor of the parish enters in the midst of this discussion and is asked by the Wanderer certain general questions concerning the value of human life. He replies that life, including virtue, cannot be appraised by pure reason. Its character, on the contrary, depends entirely upon the emotional point of view from which it is regarded.

This doctrine is hailed with "complacent animation" by the wise Wanderer, who approves the doctrine that "we see, then, as we feel." He then proceeds to make the following important pronouncement about the nature of morality.

> "Moral truth
> Is no mechanic structure, built by rule.
> .... but a thing
> Subject. you deem, to vital accidents;
> And, like the water-lily, lives and thrives,
> Whose root is fixed in stable earth, whose head
> Floats on the tossing waves."

But granted this be true, it still remains necessary to know how to gain the correct point of view. In other words, how is the necessary inward emotional principle, this soul of virtue, to be found. "How", asks the Wanderer,

> "shall man unite
> With self-forgetting tenderness of heart
> An earth-despising dignity of soul?
> Wise in that union, and without it blind!"

In his search for a principle which will consummate this union of sensibility and aspiration, he asks the Pastor to supply the necessary facts from life.

> "Give us, for our abstractions, solid facts."

Give us an account of the lives of the persons who lie in the churchyard and thus resolve our doubts. The Pastor's tales are told in answer to this request.

He presents his records, therefore, for two purposes. In the first place he will teach the Solitary

> "To prize the breath we share with human kind."

To accomplish this, he tells tales which prove that man has qualities of patience, fortitude, and endurance, which give him dignity and nobility in the eyes of those who really know him.[23] In the second place, the Pastor will reveal the essential moral emotion,—that principle which unites tenderness of heart with dignity of soul. To accomplish this he tells tales which arouse compassion for undeserved human misery. This pity, he makes clear, is the principle sought. After enumerating, in true sentimental fashion, those who lie buried in the churchyard[24] before him, the Pastor remarks that tribute of pity has been paid to each of them

> "As if Society were touched with kind concern
> And gentle Nature grieved that one should die."
> . . . .
> "And whence that tribute? Wherefore these regards?
> Not from the naked *Heart* alone of Man
> (Though claiming high distinction upon earth
> As the sole spring and fountain-head of tears,
> His own peculiar utterance for distress
> Or gladness) 'No,' the philosophic Priest
> Continued, ' 'tis not in the vital seat
> Of feeling to produce them, without aid
> From the pure soul, the soul sublime and pure.' "

Human compassion evoked by the death of such innocents as "the tottering little one" is not the product of tenderness

---

[23] *E. g.*, the tales told in the following lines (1) *Excursion* V, ll. 679ff; (2) VI, ll. 95–214; (3) VI, ll. 215–257; (4) VI, ll. 397–526. The purpose of these stories is made clear by such lines as

> "Stoop from your height, ye proud, and copy these."
> *Excursion* V, l. 737.

[24] *Excursion*, V, ll. 968 ff.

> "the tottering little one
> Taken from air and sunshine when the rose
> Of infancy first blooms upon his cheek."

alone, but also of the aspiring soul which "can upward look to Heaven." In other words, the birth of pity is proof of the union of tenderness of heart, and dignity of soul. It is the principle which the Wanderer has asked the Pastor to reveal. By arousing this compassion the Pastor can produce that fusion of spiritual faculties which signalizes the establishment of the highest moral equilibrium. Hence many of the stories are dedicated to this purpose. The first of these is the tragic tale of Ellen.[25]

In many respects this narrative follows closely the formula for sentimental tales of seduction established by Steele's *History of Caelia.* In the first place, our sympathies for the girl are made vividly awake. Her innocent and pathetic charm is insisted upon. Ellen, the daughter of a poor widow, is a paragon of beauty and simple virtue.

> Serious and thoughtful was her mind; and yet,
> By reconcilement exquisite and rare,
> The form, port, motions, of this Cottage-girl
> Were such as might have quickened and inspired
> A Titian's hand, addrest to picture forth
> Oread or Dryad glancing through the shade.

Trusting naturally, but alas! too easily, to the vows of her lover, she is seduced and then deserted by him. Her grief, though acute, is made patient and meek enough to arouse all our tender pensiveness. When her baby is born, she finds it

> A soothing comforter, although forlorn;
> Like a poor singing-bird from distant lands.

After four months she feels that she can no longer impose her support and that of her infant upon her mother. She therefore takes upon herself a foster-mother's office, and the parents of the child she nurses forbid her to visit her own baby. During Ellen's absence her child dies. She sees it only once during its illness, but we are given a picture of her at its burial gazing long into the unclosed coffin.

---

[25] *Excursion* VI, ll. 795–1064.

Weeping and looking, looking on and weeping,
Upon the last sweet slumber of her child,
Until at length her soul was satisfied.

Then it becomes her wont to visit her child's grave where she kneels "a rueful Magdalene," bewailing her loss and mourning her transgression. Thereafter she lives devoid of all interest in life, awaiting death with saint-like patience. At last she dies and is buried by the side of her infant. Thus are we brought back to the grave of the "tender lamb", the sight of which prompted this narrative.

This story is clearly told to awaken compassion. The narrative emphasis is such as to accentuate at every point the lovely innocence of the girl, her suffering, and her tears. When the story is finished, Wordsworth is at pains to make the reader realize the beneficent effect of this sentimental tale upon those who have heard it. The poet exclaims:

For me the emotion scarcely was less strong
Or less benign than that which I had felt
When . . . . .
. . . . . I heard
The story that retraced the slow decline
Of Margaret, sinking on the lonely heath
With the neglected house to which she clung.

The fates of Margaret and Ellen, similar in the appeal which the undeserved suffering of the innocent women makes to our pity, produce in the poet the same tenderness,—benign, because it is the soil from which moral impulses spring.

The other listeners were similarly affected, even the misanthrope:

I noted that the Solitary's cheek
Confessed the power of nature,—Pleased though sad,
More pleased than sad, the grey-haired Wandered sate;
Thanks to his pure imaginative soul,
Capacious and serene.

The innate goodness of the Solitary's nature, existing always beneath his crust of misanthropy, has been released by tears. The Wanderer, for his part, illustrates the truth that he imparted when telling the story of Margaret. By means of his compassion he rises above the immediate sadness produced by the tale to the serenity of moral aspiration.

No other tales of the Pastor have their sentimental moral character so clearly attested. Yet a number of the stories told in the seventh book of *The Excursion* have no other reason for existence than that carefully indicated for the story of Ellen. Of such a nature is the tale about the clergyman[26] who lived in a remote dwelling with his family for forty years without suffering from the death of a single member of his immediate circle. Then suddenly his house is swept by death as of a plague. Even "his little smiling grandchild" is taken and he is left alone, still cheerful and unsubdued in aspect but with

> his inward hoard
> Of unsunned griefs, too many and too keen,

until in one blest moment the sleep of death overcomes him. This story produced calm of mind and "tender sorrow for our mortal state," which the Wanderer, to be sure, relieves by drawing a trite moral of cheerfulness in affliction.

The Pastor then presently tells the story of the peasant parents[27] of seven lusty sons, to whom is born in their older age a daughter. She diffuses gladness throughout the family until she dies.

> Oh! dire stroke
> Of desolating anguish for them all!

The tale of Oswald follows.[28] He is a fine athlete and a noble patriot,—as brave as any who marched with righteous Joshua or Gideon. One morning he chases the reindeer and returning from that sport "weakened and relaxed," he plunges "into the chilling flood" to wash "the fleeces of his Father's flock." Convulsions seize him and he dies amid

[26] *Excursion* VII, ll. 38–290.
[27] *Ibid.*, ll. 632–694.
[28] *Ibid.*, ll. 695–890.

universal mourning. No moral is deduced from this tale; it is dedicated wholly to sentimental pity. The Solitary is properly touched and turns aside either from shame for his past misanthropy or to conceal

> Tender emotions spreading from the heart
> To his worn cheek.

These are perhaps the only stories of the Pastor which are devoted to his second and more ambitious object. They are designed not to bring the Solitary back into the current of life, but to show him that inward emotional principle which forms the animating soul of virtue. They prove that compassion for undeserved human distress converts human tenderness to moral aspiration.

V

In the sentimental poems hitherto discussed, the desired moral result has been made unmistakable. The regeneration of some witness of the sad events through his quickened compassion has been dramatically presented. Having received this clear indication of Wordsworth's belief in the tragic sentimental tale, the critic is justified in asserting that when such stories are told in simple form, that is, without the introduction of any reformed observer, they are intended to produce their effort upon the reader. He is to experience a moral awakening similar to that induced in *Peter Bell* and the *Solitary*.

Among Wordsworth's *Lyrical Ballads* there are many such tragic stories. Some of these are sentimental tales of seduction even more clearly in the eighteenth century tradition of such narratives than the story of Ellen discussed above. The approved method of such stories was first to establish almost extravagantly the charm and beauty of the girl. Her extraordinary innocence and trust make her betrayal and desertion both particularly easy and pathetic. After the birth of her child her undeserved suffering is displayed at length, usually through the medium of a long piteous lament.

Such a poem is *The Thorn.* It is a picture of the mad, despairing anguish of Martha Ray. The blithe and gay creature, abandoned by her false lover, Stephen Hill, on her wedding day, sits at the grave of her illegitimate child moaning,

> "Oh misery! oh misery!
> Oh woe is me! oh misery!"

Efforts to disinter the child in a search for evidence of murder against poor Martha are met by supernatural protests from Nature:

> But instantly the hill the moss,
> Before their eyes began to stir!
> And, for full fifty yards around,
> The grass—it shook upon the ground!

Nature will tolerate only pity for the abandoned girl. It joins with the poet in bidding us regard Martha Ray not as a criminal, but as a woman overwhelmed with suffering. The poem was written to invoke not justice but compassion.[29]

Her Eyes are Wild is almost exactly the same sort of poem, except that the abandoned girl seems to have been deserted after her marriage and not to have lost her child. The poem, however, like *The Thorn,* makes, through the mad lament, the same direct appeal to our pity. The *Lament of the Forsaken Indian Woman* presents another very similar tragic situation, and the form of the complaint makes the sentimental appeal the most direct and unavoidable.

---

[29] Wordsworth in the Fenwick note to the poem gives the following description of its inception: After observing a thorn-tree tossed in a storm, he asks himself, "Cannot I by some invention do as much to make this thorn permanently an impressive object as the storm has made it to my eyes at this moment?" In answering this question affirmatively he attaches to the tree a tragic sentimental tale. Critics have usually not recognized it as such. For example, Professor Harper says (I, 375) about *Martha Ray,* the *Mad Mother* and *Ruth:* "In the ruin of the faculties which once adapted these poor women to social life, they have preserved, he shows us, a healthful relation to Nature. Upon Nature they fall back for consolation when hopes of human life have failed." Ruth, to be sure, is made sane enough by Nature to realize that it is not to blame for her sorrow and to discourse upon the flute, but the spirit of the poem emphasizes not her fragmentary consolations, but her suffering. Martha Ray does not gain one scrap of consolation and leaves us with her cry "Oh misery, oh misery," ringing in our ears.

Ruth is another sentimental tale of a woman deserted by her lover. The girl from the first is a pathetic figure because, from the age of seven, she has been slighted by her step-mother. When she grows to maidenhood, a youth from Georgia's shore, like Othello irresistible because of his tales of adventure and romance, wins her love. Then Ruth

> did agree
> With him to sail across the sea,

but her lover was a wild fellow and deserted her. And

> Such pains she had,
> That she in half a year was mad,
> And in a prison housed.

After three seasons she flees the prison and lives as an innocent vagrant and beggar, and the reader is left with a moving picture of her wretchedness of both body and mind.

Vandracour and Julia is the tale of a youth compelled to abandon his low-born mistress at the command of his aristocratic father. Julia is sent to a convent and Vandracour takes their child to a retreat with one domestic servant. The baby dies, and the father lives on in morose imbecility. Thus Wordsworth follows the tale

> to its last recess
> Of suffering or of peace, I know not which.[20]

At least two of Wordsworth's poems, *Lucy Gray* and *There Was a Boy*[21] are stories written on the familiar sentimental formula of death snatching innocence from the midst of felicity. Lucy Gray

> The sweetest thing that ever grew
> Beside a human door,

---

[20] Professor Harper, I, 141, suggests that the situation in this poem reflects in some respects Wordsworth's own love affair with Annette, the mother of his natural child, Caroline. Doubtless the poet's grief and remorse over this experience made a tale of seduction or desertion seem the most effective vehicle for a sentimental moral message.

[21] To these might be added *George and Sarah Green*.

starts out in a snow storm, blither than "the mountain roe", to meet her mother. She becomes lost in the snow, steps off the bridge, and is gone. In *There Was a Boy,* the poet presents a child keenly sensitive to the natural beauty of the vale in which he lives. This boy dies and the pity of his early death causes the poet to stand a long half-hour

> Mute—looking at the grave in which he lies.

Two pseudo-ballads of Wordsworth, *Ellen Irwin* and *The Seven Sisters,* both founded on other works, are sentimental stories in which death overtakes an innocent girl at a moment when she is enjoying unusual felicity. Wordsworth's choice of this material to revamp is as strong proof of his sentimental bias as the composition of an original poem of the same sort would have been. *Ellen Irwin* is a version of *Helen of Kirkconnell,* a ballad appearing in *The Minstrelsy of the Scottish Border.*[32] The story is as follows: As Ellen sits caressing her accepted lover, Bruce, abandoned to innocent felicity, Gordon, her rejected lover, springs from a covert and jealously thrusts at Bruce with his javelin. Ellen interposes her body and is slain. Bruce immediately kills Gordon and after vainly seeking death in battle against the Moors, dies of a broken heart on Ellen's grave. The ballad is a lament of the lover; Wordsworth's poem gives much more prominence to the sad death of Ellen.

The Seven Sisters, founded on the German of Frederica Brun, is the story of the untimely death of the seven daughters of Lord Archibald Campbell. One day as the seven lovely girls, filled with boundless mutual love, "lie like fauns reposing," rapacious rovers break in upon them.

> Away the seven fair Campbells fly.

and rather than be subjected to the lust of their pursuers, they all plunge into a lake and drown.

The poems hitherto discussed in this chapter[33] seem to

[32] II, p. 217.

[33] To these might be added *Hart-Leap Well,* which seeks to arouse pity for a stricken animal.

have been written purely for a sentimental moral purpose. In none of them is any other sort of instruction to be discerned. There are other poems, however, in which another purpose is combined with the sentimental moral. *The Brothers* is in essence a story of undeserved suffering. A sailor comes back from the sea, where he has always felt himself an exile, to spend the rest of his life with his dearly loved brother. He learns from the village clergyman that the fellow has died. He has rolled over the edge of a precipice in his sleep and been killed. The last part of the poem describes the grief of the sailor, which drives him to resume his uncongenial life on the sea. *Michael,* too, is essentially a story of the undeserved affliction that comes upon the old peasant through the evil courses of his son. Wordsworth, himself, speaks with particular pride of the tears which this poem has drawn from its readers, as though these marks of pity were sure proof of its success.[34]

Wordsworth, however, gives a different account of his actual purpose in writing these poems. He says that they were both written to show "that men who do not wear fine clothes can feel deeply" and that they were designed to "excite profitable sympathies in many kind and good hearts" and may "enlarge our feelings of reverence for our species and our knowledge of human nature."[35] This democratic message did not require a tale of suffering for its vehicle. In this case, as in some of the stories in *The Excursion,* Wordsworth clearly shows that he believed those sympathies most profitable which stimulate, besides increased knowledge of human nature, compassion sympathetic to moral aspiration.[36]

---

[34] Cf. letter to Thomas Poole, April 9, 1901 quoted in Mrs. Margaret E. Sandford, *Thomas Poole and His Friends,* London, 1888, II, p. 54. "This poem has, I know, drawn tears from the eyes of more than one—persons well acquainted with the manners of the Statesmen, as they are called, of this country; and moreover, persons who never wept in reading verse before."

[35] Letter written in 1902 to Charles James Fox to accompany a copy of *The Lyrical Ballads.* (*Letters of the Wordsworth Family,* Knight Ed. I, p. 138.)

[36] *The White Doe of Rylstone* will doubtless seem to many to belong to this class of poems. But it seems to me clearly designed to show how one may triumph over grief. It never allows the mind to rest for a

Other poems were undoubtedly written, as Legouis has pointed out, to confute some of Godwin's ideas. *The Last of the Flock* may have been written as this critic suggests[37] to show that the feeling for property is not the evil offspring of human institutions, but a vigorous instinct.[38] Yet the story that he selects to illustrate this truth is a sentimental tale, surely not the only narrative form suitable for the author's purpose. The poem begins with a picture of

A healthy man, a man full-grown,

weeping in the public road, alone. He has in his arms the last of his flock of fifty sheep, all of which he has had to slaughter to feed his six children. He is lamenting, strangely enough, not the distress of his children, but the loss of his sheep. No adequate reason for this affliction is given in the poem:

"Six children, Sir, I had to feed;
Hard labour in a time of need!"

and therefore his "full fifty comely sheep" had to be slaughtered. Obviously the undeserved character of the

---

moment in mere compassion. The anguish of Emily at every moment suggests its own balm. The White Doe is the embodiment of the comfort that Wordsworth believed a person stricken with grief could find in the persistent gentle influences of Nature. We are shown through Emily's mastery of her fate how sorrow may lead the soul to a calm which for its impenetrability is a foretaste of the peace beyond death.

"The mighty sorrow hath been borne,
And she is thoroughly forlorn,
Her soul doth in itself stand fast,
Sustained by memory of the past,
And strength of Reason; held above
The infirmities of mortal love,
Undaunted, lofty, calm and stable,
And awfully impenetrable."

This poem, then, at least in moral intention, is much greater than Wordsworth's sentimental tragic tales.

[37] *The Early Life of William Wordsworth*, p. 310.

[38] Wordsworth says of *Michael* in the letter to Thos. Poole quoted above, that it is the picture of a man "agitated by two of the most powerful affections of the human heart—parental affection and the love of property—landed property."

peasant's suffering determines the emotional quality of the poem.[39]

In the *Old Cumberland Beggar,* according to Legouis,[40] the poet takes issue with Godwin's belief that charity is the evil consequence of a social order which ought to be regulated by Justice alone. Wordsworth shows that charity benefits both those who exercise it and its recipients. Such vagrants, apparently all noble and dignified, awaken in lofty meditative minds

> That first mild touch of sympathy and thought
> In which they found their kindred with a world
> Where want and sorrow are.[41]

The beggar's service is thus to prompt the villagers not only to tender offices in which there is moral exhilaration, but also to "pensive thoughts", whose power to virtue friendly the poet assumes to be obvious.

The meaning of many of the short narratives in Wordsworth's early collections has always been understood. Others of them, however, have clearly not illustrated the great truths which Wordsworth made it his business to inculcate. The significance of a few of these poems,[42] it is hoped, has been clarified by the above analysis. They too, it seems, had a considerable part to play in helping "the young and gracious of every age"—"to become more actively and securely virtuous."

VI

These poems, all vehicles of sentimental morality as the term has been defined, together form a considerable part of

---

[39] *Repentance* is, similarly, a poem written to illustrate the natural love of a peasant for property,—this time land. This poem is sentimental only in so far as the form of a lament makes it so.

[40] *Op. cit.*, p. 311.

[41] Contrast this with Godwin's characteristic utterance about charity, *Political Justice,* II, p. 335. "Observe the pauper fawning with abject vileness on his rich benefactor and speechless with sensations of gratitude for having received that which he ought to have claimed with an erect mien and with a consciousness that his claim was irresistible."

[42] *The Affliction of Margaret, The Sailor's Mother,* and *Maternal Grief* should be added to those already enumerated, as being pictures of mere innocent distress which we are invited to contemplate.

the work which Wordsworth produced between 1796 and 1804.[43] It is important, therefore, to discover how far this sentimentalism is consistent with the main philosophical views which Wordsworth held during these years. When Wordsworth abandoned his allegiance to the doctrines expounded in William Godwin's *Political Justice*, he adopted a system of thought utterly unlike this philosophy of rigid reason. His reaction against the whole tendency of this work was so strong that Godwin's acceptance of an idea became almost sufficient reason for Wordsworth's abhorring it.

In the rational system of *Political Justice*, however, there was room for one great principle of action, which at first sight seems closely akin to sentimentalism. I refer to humanitarianism. This feeling, Godwin believed, was inspired in no sense by pity, but through an appreciation of the principle of "moral equality", which established "the propriety of applying one unalterable rule of justice to every case that may arise."[44] This principle makes it just and reasonable that human beings "should contribute, so far as it lies in their power, to the pleasure and benefit of each other."[45]

Now Wordsworth, while under the influence of Godwin, wrote some poems illustrating this sort of reasoned humanitarianism. Of such a nature are *Lines Written in Early Spring*, *Lines Left on a Seat in a Yew Tree*, and *The Convict*.[46] Certain other poems such as *The Female Vagrant*[47] and *The Old Man Travelling* were written to advance the special form of humanitarianism which protested against the evils of war. All of these poems were devised to show

What man has made of man.

[43] The tales in the *Excursion*, Books VI and VII, are the only sentimental stories of any importance composed after this date.

[44] *Political Justice*, I, 99.

[45] *Ibid.*, I, 100.

[46] *The Convict*, it will be remembered, is a poetic version of Godwin's plea for a reformation of the penal laws.

[47] Of this poem Wordsworth himself says (Letter to Francis Wrangham Nov. 20, 1795) "Its object is partly to expose the vices of the penal law and the calamities of war as they affect individuals."

with his detestable system of property and its attendant evils.[48] They are all expressions of humanitarian zeal uncontaminated by sentimental notions. No one of them contains a hint of any sacredness in suffering or any moral good in the pity which it arouses.

The difference between his humanitarian and sentimental poems can be seen clearly in comparing *The Ruined Cottage* as it was written sometime before June 1797[49] with the revised form of 1801, which is incorporated into the first book of *The Excursion.* The earlier poem, though it lacks completely the horror and violence of *Guilt and Sorrow,* was clearly written to depict the spiritual evils caused by war. It contains none of the reflections and explanations of the Wanderer, which transform the tale, as I have indicated above, into a story designed to arouse feelings of compassion which are friendly to virtue.

Godwin, indeed, expressly denies that morality is, in any sense, dependent upon feeling. It is, on the contrary, entirely the offspring of understanding. Virtue he says "may be defined as a desire to promote the benefit of intelligent beings in general"—"If I desire the benefit of intelligent beings," he continues, "not from a clear and distinct perception of what it is in which their benefit consists, but from the unexamined lessons of education, *from the physical effect of sympathy* (italics are mine), or from any species of zeal unallied to and incommensurate with knowledge, can this desire be admitted for virtuous? Nothing seems more inconsistent with our ideas of virtue."[50] That Wordsworth conceived Godwin to regard mere pity for misery as worthy only of contempt, is evident from the words which he puts

---

[48] Cf. *Political Justice,* II, 334. "And here with grief it must be confessed, that, however great and extensive are the evils that are produced by monarchies and courts, by the imposture of priests and the iniquity of criminal laws, all these are imbecil (sic) and impotent compared with the evils that arise out of the established system of property."

Also (*Ibid.,* II, 346.) "It is clear then that war in every horrid form is the growth of unequal property."

[49] Cf. Legouis, *op. cit.,* 343, n. 1.

[50] *Political Justice,* I, 234.

into the mouth of Oswald, the Godwinian villain-hero of *The Borderers*. He says:

> A whipping to the moralists who preach
> That misery is a sacred thing; for me
> I know no cheaper engine to degrade a man
> Nor any half so sure.
> The wiles of woman
> And crafty age, seducing reason, first
> Made weakness a protection, and obscured
> The moral shapes of things.

Sympathy and pity have not, according to Oswald and Godwin, stimulated true virtue. They have obscured its true face and diverted man from the only path by which it can be achieved,—the one clearly marked out by human understanding.

Godwin's complete rejection of pity, even of sympathy, from his system may have led Wordsworth to give it an important place in his own, which was devised, in part, as a refutation of the principles of *Political Justice*.[51] Yet the negative character of Wordsworth's new system, the phase of it ably explained by Legouis, has, I believe, been over-emphasized. Its positive qualities are obviously more important. Of these not sympathy for human sorrow, but a deliberate and determined joy is the radiating center. This settled optimism, the poet believed, was the inevitable result of a true conception of the nature of the Universe. Therefore, to say that the chief end of poetry is to produce pleasure is not to attribute to it an unworthy aim. It is, on the contrary, to assign to it the highest degree of philosophic truth, because joy is "an acknowledgment of the beauty of the universe. It is homage paid to the naked dignity of man, to the grand elementary principle of pleasure, by which he knows and feels and lives and moves."[52]

---

[51] It is of no importance for the present inquiry whether Wordsworth's abandonment of Godwinism produced a severe moral crisis in his life (cf. Legouis, Chapter IV), or whether it was accomplished peacefully and naturally. (Cf. Harper I, pp. 290–291). The evidence clearly favors this latter view.

[52] Preface to the 2nd Edition of *The Lyrical Ballads*, *Works*, Knight's ed., IV, pp. 290–291.

It follows that no one can be an authentic poet who does not realize the central position of joy in the cosmos, for it is through "the deep power of joy" that "we see into the life of things." Coleridge, it will be remembered, gives poetic voice to this theory in his *Dejection: An Ode*. He there says that the "sweet and potent voice" which goes from the soul at the moment of poetic creation, or "the beauty-making power", is joy.

> Joy, virtuous William, joy that ne'er was given
> Save to the pure, and in their purest hour.
> Joy, William! is the spirit and the pow'r
> Which wedding Nature to us gives in dow'r.
> . . . .
> And thence flows all that charms or ear or sight,
> All melodies the echoes of that voice,
> All colours a suffusion from that light.[53]

Armed with this creative principle, this illumination from the soul, Wordsworth asserts that the ultimate truth of the world is revealed by immediate sensations, uninvolved with reason. Furthermore, he believes that he can trace the primary laws of human nature by examining the life of simple folk in whom "our elementary feelings co-exist in a state of greater simplicity." Life, if it is to be apprehended in its ultimate reality, must enter the mind of man in its simplest terms,—there to be transformed by the auxiliary light from the soul into the highest forms of wisdom.

This cursory review of the mode of thought which Wordsworth adopted after revolting from Godwinism, has been intended only to recall the essential position which creative joy henceforth held in the poet's artistic creed. How, it may be asked, can any belief in the moral value of sorrow and anguish, find place in such a system? This apparent inconsistency in Wordsworth's system can be partially reconciled, I believe, by reexamining the formative influence which the philosophy of David Hartley had upon him at this time.

---

[53] Cf. Knight's *Life of Wordsworth*, II, p. 86 for this, the earliest form of the poem.

Professor Arthur Beatty has recently shown[54] how much of Wordsworth's thought was based upon David Hartley's *Observations on Man, his Frame, his Duty and his Expectations.*[55] The main tenets of the associative philosophy explained in this work were the notion that all ideas are derived ultimately from sensations, which by the power of association are gradually transformed into simple ideas; then these simple ideas by means of association will run into the complexes of mature mental life, or what Hartley calls "intellectual ideas." From these various complexes come "pleasures and pains" or motives to conduct. These are, in an ascending scale the following: sensation, imagination, ambition, self-interest, sympathy, theopathy and moral sense.

Now these theories enable a man to turn back and retrace with mathematical surety the method by which his mind has been formed. Wordsworth, in performing this essential philosophical service for his own mind, wrote *The Prelude,* and was able in *Tintern Abbey* and the *Ode on the Intimations of Immortality* to connect in a causal relation, through reminiscence, the simple experiences of childhood with the complex ideas of maturity. In this way he retains for mature life, in transmuted form to be sure, the glory of childhood, and makes the child in a real psychological sense the father of the man. Retrospect, in other words, vitalized by Hartley's doctrine of constructive association, becomes a key with which to unlock the innermost secrets of personality.

Perhaps more constructive for Wordsworth's mind at this crisis was the relation of the grand elementary principle of pleasure which was to be henceforth the heart of Wordsworth's philosophy, to Hartley's system. Proving that the world is a system of benevolence, the philosopher's work culminated in joy. The last section of Hartley's volume is called *The Final Happiness of all Mankind in Some Distant*

---

[54] Arthur Beatty, *Wordsworth and Hartley, New York Nation,* Vol. XCVII, July 17, 1913, pp. 51 ff.

[55] This work was first published in 1751; Wordsworth read the three volume edition of 1791. It is possible that Coleridge first interested Wordsworth in this philosopher; he was so taken by his ideas, he called his son born in 1796, Hartley Coleridge.

Future State. There he shows, in the precise mathematical form of his work, the perfectibility and ultimate good and happiness of all men. Wordsworth, accepting the system, began his subsequent work in the joy to which this philosophy had triumphantly ascended.

This is not the place to develop the numerous points of similarity between Hartley's philosophy and Wordsworth's poetry. The point of present concern is to discover how the poet found in this system of benevolence and delight a sanction for his tragic tales. At the apex of Hartley's great structure of the pains and pleasures of our nature, or motives to action, are the passions of sympathy, theopathy, and moral sense. But the central place in the entire system from the point of view of human conduct is given to sympathy. One of the propositions in the chapter called *The Rule of Life* is as follows:[56] "The Pleasures of Sympathy improve those of Sensation, Imagination, Ambition and Self-Interest; and unite with those of Theopathy and the Moral Sense; they are self-consistent, and admit of an unlimited Extent; they may therefore be our primary Pursuit." Now it soon appears that compassion plays an important part in developing this essential sympathy or "benevolent affections." "Compassion is," we read, "in this imperfect probationary state, a most principal part of our benevolent affection." And under proposition *LXX*, a part of the book devoted to the deduction of practical rules for the conduct of men towards each other in society, we read:[57]

> The natural motives of good-will, compassion, etc., must have great regard paid to them, lest we contract a philosophical hardness of heart by endeavoring or pretending to act upon higher and more extensively beneficial views than vulgar minds, the softer sex, etc. Some persons carry this much too far on the other side, and encourage many public mischiefs, through a false misguided tenderness to criminals, persons in distress through present gross vices, etc.

In this interesting passage the philosopher issues direct warning against tenderness for deserved distress. It is ap-

[56] Part II, Chap. III, Section VI, Prop. LXVIII.

[57] Hartley, *op. cit.*, I, pp. 474–477, *passim.*

parently only the sympathy and tears for virtue in distress and for undeserved suffering in which he can see a moral virtue.

In an earlier part of the work where the pleasures and pains of sympathy are analyzed, Hartley devotes one section to an explanation of "the affection by which we grieve for the misery of others." There the importance of compassion in the moral system is clearly set forth:

Compassion is the uneasiness which a man feels at the misery of another . . . A compassionate temper being great matter of praise to those who are endued with it, *and the actions which flow from it being a duty incumbent on all,* (the italics are mine) men are led to practice these actions and to inculcate upon themselves the motives of compassion, by *attending to distress actually present* or described in history, real or fictitious. . . . The peculiar love and esteem which we bear to morally good characters make us *more sensibly touched with their miseries;*—In like manner the simplicity, the ignorance, the helplessness, and many innocent diverting follies of young children and of some brutes lead men to pity them in a peculiar manner.[88]

These passages are quoted not for the novelty of the ideas which they express, but because they show that the doctrines of sentimental morality were caught up into Hartley's system and given a central place there. Pity for undeserved human suffering is made the centre of a mathematically established moral system which culminates in joy.

Wordsworth in his Preface to the 2nd edition of the *Lyrical Ballads* is, himself, at pains to show that compassion introduces no real inconsistency into his system. "Wherever we sympathize with pain, it will be found that the sympathy is produced and carried on by subtle combinations with pleasure." Man is considered "as looking upon this complex scene of ideas and sensations and finding everywhere objects that immediately excite in him sympathies which from the necessities of his nature, are accompanied by an overbalance of enjoyment." This language sounds transcendental until we realize that the subtle combination with pleasure arises from

[88] Hartley, *op. cit.*, I, pp. 474–477, passim.

the impulses to noble action which lie at the heart of compassion.[59]

The precision with which Wordsworth fitted this sentimental doctrine of pity into his system of thought can be seen in those poems in which he clearly interprets the facts of his experience in accordance with the associative philosophy of Hartley. In *Tintern Abbey,* the poet, by connecting in a causal relation the reminiscences and experiences of childhood with the intellectual ideas of the adult mind, shows how "the pleasures of sense and those of imagination have generated the higher ones, particularly those of sympathy, theopathy and the moral sense."[60] In maturity Wordsworth, no longer looking on nature as in the hour of thoughtless youth when sensation furnished all his delight, finds there

1. The still sad music of humanity;
2. The presence that disturbs him with the joy of elevated thoughts;
3. The guide, the guardian of his heart, and soul of all his moral being.

In other words, the language of the sense and the imagination have generated, as Hartley's system explained, (1) that particular form of sympathy known as compassion, (2) theopathy, and (3) the moral sense.

In a similar way, the last three stanzas of the *Ode on the Intimations of Immortality* are devoted to an expression of

[59] In this connection the following verses from *The Recluse* assume a definite significance:

"If I oft
Must turn elsewhere—to travel near the tribes
And fellowships of men, and see ill sights
Of madding passions mutually inflamed;
Must hear Humanity in fields and groves
Pipe solitary anguish; or must hang
Brooding above the fierce confederate storm
Of sorrow, barricadoed evermore
Within the walls of cities—may these sounds
Have their authentic comment; that even these
Hearing, I be not downcast or forlorn."

The "authentic comment" is an explanation of the moral elevation which human sorrow gives to him who beholds it. This produces a subtle combination of pleasure that keeps the observer from being downcast.

[60] Hartley, II, p. 244.

joy over the truth derived from David Hartley,—that the experiences of childhood,—now become to Wordsworth's mind a rare blessedness,—are inevitably a part of the adult mind and so pronounce forever their benediction upon the life of man. Therefore man must not grieve at the loss of the first divine vividness of the senses; but find comfort first, in the fact of their persistence in the soul; second, in the sympathy; and third, theopathy which they have generated

We will grieve not, rather find
Strength in what remains behind,

1. In the primal sympathy which having
Been must always be;

2. In the soothing thoughts that spring
Out of human suffering;

3. In the faith that looks through death
In years that bring the philosophic mind.

In both of these poems compassion for human suffering is shown to be one of the principal sources of mature human satisfaction, one of the animating passions or motives to moral conduct. In the fourteenth book of *The Prelude,* a poem which is a special application of Hartley's theories of association, this passion is given an even more prominent place. There the supreme achievement of the busy associations of life is apparently the production of a sentimental tenderness and softness of heart, or an intense proneness to Hartley's essential sympathy.

And he whose soul hath risen
Up to the height of feeling intellect
Shall want no humbler tenderness; his heart
Be tender as a nursing mother's heart;
Of female softness shall his life be full,
Of humble cares and delicate desires,
Mild interests and gentlest sympathies.

I trust that the purpose of this brief analysis of Wordsworth's relation to Hartley will not be misunderstood. It is not intended to prove that the poet learned the moral value of the sentimental tragic tale from this philosopher. The literature of the 18th century was so thoroughly saturated with that belief that it would be folly to attempt to discover from what work the notion first came to Wordsworth.[61] The point of significance is that the poet found, in the moral system which he in large measure adopted, a central place given to compassion for undeserved human suffering. A type of literature to which Wordsworth may have been naturally attracted[62] was thus given the highest sanction. Without arousing feelings inconsistent with the grand elementary principle of joy or breaking with blessed primal sympathies existing between man and nature, such tales could inspire the loftiest morality. It is perhaps not too much to say that man gradually assumed the most important place in Wordsworth's world because of the central position which sympathy with man is given in Hartley's system.

We may then cease to wonder with the critics that so many of Wordsworth's tales of human beings are stories of deep distress and sorrow. A poet who believed that the importance of his poetry lay "in the quality and in the multiplicity of its moral relations," would feel it his solemn duty to arouse often that essential pity for undeserved suffering which was, to his mind, a mighty "power to virtue friendly."

---

[61] James Beattie, of whose work Wordsworth had intimate knowledge, in his discourse *On Poetry and Music* explains very clearly the sentimental moral theory. "By instruction," he says, "I do not here understand merely the communication of moral and physical truth. Whatever tends to raise those human affections that are favorable to truth and virtue—will always gratify and improve our moral and intellective powers and may properly enough be called instructive. All poetry, therefore, is entitled to this epithet, not only which imparts knowledge we had not before, but also which awakens our pity for the sufferings of our fellow creatures, promotes a taste for the beauties of Nature animate or inanimate" etc.

[62] We have numerous bits of evidence of the sensibility of both Wordsworth and his sister. Dorothy's journal records innumerable occasions when such things as a letter from Coleridge or a fine passage from Milton moved them both to tears.

THE SCANSION OF MIDDLE ENGLISH ALLITERATIVE VERSE

William Ellery Leonard

In one of the recent publications[1] of our University, I registered a long-time skepticism of the orthodox (two-accent) creed in Germanic versification, explaining what the four-accent theory really must mean, confessing my faith and setting down some reasons thereof. When I mailed my off-prints to a selected list of the judicious, I fully expected the humorous or impatient shrug, the neutral acknowledgment, or the unbroken silence. I was not disappointed, particularly in the silence. But quite to my surprise, a number of heartening letters came. Four or five old pupils of Sievers, or the Sievers' school, admitted they had long cherished misgivings in secret; others, too, now beginning to be troubled in spirit, vowed to investigate a little further for themselves. From Professor Otto Jespersen at Copenhagen—who had received the publication through the University and not through myself and whose comment could therefore not have the bias of mere personal good will— came a testimony as welcome as it was unexpected: "I am inclined to think you are right in all your main conclusions, though I say it with some diffidence, as I cannot pretend to be a specialist[2] in these matters. I have always had a kind of instinctive feeling against Sievers' metrical system, many parts of which appear to me as extremely artificial. Many verses belonging according to him to the same 'type' are so different in their

---

[1] *Beowulf and the Niebelungen Couplet*, *University of Wisconsin Studies in Language and Literature*, number 2.

[2] But Jespersen is the author of that profound and thorough metrical study, *Den psykologiske Grund til nogle metriske Faenomener*, published in *Oversigt over det kgl. danske Videnskabernes Selskabs Forhandlinger*, 1900, pp. 487 ff.

structure that the impression on the ear cannot possibly have been the same. Many of these difficulties seem to be obviated through a four stress reading, though in some cases it is not easy now to see which syllables to stress''. I'm quoting without permission, but I trust without offense. It is not that this open-mindedness toward the heterodox view—essentially, however, the primitive view, just as modern heterodoxy in Christianity is so largely a return to the primitive faith before Councils and Formulas and Authority—is witnessed by the countryman of Thorkelin and Grundtvig, the pioneer scholars in Germanic poetry; it is rather that Jespersen is a phonetician and a psychologist, a living master in the characteristics of Germanic speech as sound and as thinking, the *nature* of which speech is perhaps the outstanding argument for the four-accent delivery of old Germanic verse. Professor Jespersen's position is of course as such no proof: it is cited here simply as a reminder, for some American friends in the MLA, that anti-Sievers is perhaps not as negligible a heresy as they think; and that, if they mean to hand down their faith intact to the next generation, they may have to do more than chalk up the blackboard with the magic St. Andrew's crosses arranged ABCDE.

Perhaps ultimately, for the rehabilitation of Europe from war and diplomacy or for the redemption of mankind from thieving, thuggery, and peevishness, it doesn't much matter. But if our discipline as a phase of human culture matters, if old Germanic studies matter for those who have given to them nights and days of zeal and delight, then the metrical question is the question that matters most of all. The low-German authorship of the *Hildebrandslied,* the meaning of an Anglo-Saxon Riddle, the interpretation of the Dragon's Cave or the Finnsburg Episode, the Greenland provenience of one or another song of the *Edda* may be settled one way or another and is indeed worth settling right; but no one of these problems has the creative significance for the whole range of thought and imagination that belongs to the metrical problem. Creative significance: the term is not idle. The scholar lives in two different worlds, accordingly: the two accents *create* one, the four another. Which is right and real? The fight is not for a dry bone but for a living spirit; and concerns not one poem or one people, but the whole compass of Germanic life as it expressed itself in poetry, the one art in which it found adequate spiritual expression at all. The fight concerns a whole epoch in European culture, as individual and autochthonous as the epoch of the Greeks—dusky and delimited though it be in comparison with their radiant civilization. Any one who shakes his head with amusement, fails, it seems, to realize the function of form in man's eagernesses, passions, and dreams. Or would Vergil be Vergil if we read Vergil with the prose cadences of his prose-imitator Livy? It is only because the metrical question is vital, in the strictest etymological sense, that I ventured to raise it,—and to answer it as I could. For, in general, I have supinely left to others the problems of our discipline for any settlement in print. It is only because it is so vital that I'm now venturing on it again.

I

I want now to suggest some possible bearings of Middle English alliterative verse on the four-accent theory, presupposing the discussion of the previous paper. ME alliterative lines, whatever our theory, are, as we all know, the epigoni of the AS and the OG. The crescendo-decrescendo of the sentence cadences is lost; end-rhyme becomes more and more integral; the harmonious variation of types from first to second half-lines yields somewhat to a repetition of the type in the second half, especially where the half-lines are mated and *coupled* by rhyme; the old run-on style disappears and we have the end-stop style, with the long-line, rather than the half-line, as the unit, even when the long-line unit is not created by long-line rhyme. We note too—this review of familiar facts is brief enough to be pardoned, I hope—a number of departures from the older habits of alliterating, sometimes in the direction of less alliteration and of irregularity of recurrence, sometimes in the direction of over-alliteration and of alliterative refinements (runs on special combinations of letters aside from the *st, sp, sc* of the AS rules). With these differences of versification are associated differences of poetic style: the old parallelisms of phrase (and with them the kennings which contributed so much to their support) are lost; and the related phenomena of parallelism of sentences and ideas (repetitions of description, action, apothegm) are likewise lost. The differentiation from prose-speech, to which every thread in the texture of OG poetry contributed its due part, becomes less marked, or marked mainly in aural elements—in sound-combinations (initial or end rhyme), in stanza-complexes, and in the persistence of the old stress-system in the midst of greater speech-filling between stresses. But the differences reveal quite as much as they repudiate their OG ancestry; and it is generally conceded (with Luick's ingenious but unwarranted conjectures in the *Grundriss* on Layamon's verse as the one notable exception) that the theory which holds for existing AS verse holds for existing ME verse. So generally is it conceded, that in fact the argument for a two or four accent reading of ME alliterative verse has been generally based on one or the other theory for the AS.

This is in itself not an altogether illicit process. But it ought to be possible to come to some decision on the ME *as if the AS were not in existence*. ME alliterative verse is surely ample enough in quantity and clear enough in speech-form to reveal to Modern English readers its metrical purpose without recourse to a language and a poetry far more estranged. Most of it is indeed nearer to Modern English than to Anglo-Saxon,—some of it is essentially Modern English—and we have in our modern versification helps to its understanding of at least equal usefulness to those helps from the AS which for the present we arbitrarily reject. But when we have decided on our ME scansion *without* the AS, we can make all the inferences from ME we please *for* the AS. In other words, if ME alliterative verse is a four-accenter, we have additional proof for the AS and the OG as a four accenter.

One such study of a ME poem in the alliterative tradition there is: *Untersuchungen zur mittelenglischen Metrik*, by Professor K. D. Buelbring of Bonn.[3] After listing and discussing with bibliographical thoroughness the views of scholars to date, it subjects *The Avowynge of King Arther* to an almost meticulous analysis, citing other ME poems chiefly for illustration rather than for argument, and citing AS not at all. The opening stanza is representative:

He that made us on the mulde,
And fair fourmed the folde,
Atte his will, as he wold,
The see and the sande,
Giffe hom joy that will here
Of dugti men and of dere,
Of haldurs that before us were,
That lifd in this londe.
One was Arther the kinge,
With-owtun any letting;
With him was money lordinge,
Hardi of honde.
Wice and war, ofte thay were,
Bold undur banere,
And wigte weppuns wold were,
And stifly wold stond.[4]

Purely on internal evidence of syllables, stresses, alliterations, relations of end-verses to triplet-verses, etc., in sundry comparative tabulations, he comes to the conclusion that the end-verses were recited (let the fact of *recitation* not be forgotten) with three, the triplet-verses with four stresses (secondary, of course, intermingled with primary). "Kurz" —so ends his monograph on the 114th page—"die hier methodisch erschlossene Theorie ist den andern in jeder Hinsicht ueberlegen; fuer sie spricht alles, gegen sie nichts". Three readings of the monograph—no easy task for an im-

[3] Halle, 1913. *Sonderabdruck aus Studien zur englischen Philologie*, Heft L. Lorenz Morsbach gewidmet.

[4] From a manifolded MS copy in Buelbring's handwriting, made from the original, for use in his seminary. I have inserted punctuation and substituted Modern English letters for ME symbols (thorn, etc.), as regularly in ME citations throughout the paper.

petuous American—have convinced me. Fuer sie spricht alles; and it is one of life's little duties to the memory of an old teacher now dead (with whom youth in callow seminary days had too pertly contested) to make this public confession, while calling attention to a study less known than it deserves. His findings are of wide application: to Layamon, to the *Bestiary,* to the *King Horn* couplets, to the four-line rhymes at the end of the popular alliterative stanza-form of *Rauf Coilyear, The Awntyrs off Arthure, The Pistill of Susan,* etc.,—four-line rhymes which are exactly the same in metrics as any one of the four-line sections of the sixteen-line stanza above quoted, as

> Efter thame, baith fer and neir,
> Folkis following in feir,
> Thankand God with gude cheir
> Thair Lord was gane to toun.
> (*Coilyear,* l. 346 ff.)

They apply to the four-line rhymes at the end of the *Gawain and the Green Knight* stanzas, as

> He blenched agayn bilyve,
> And stifly start onstray,
> With alle the wo on lyve,
> To the wod he went away,
> (l. 1715 ff.)

lines of three stresses like the end-verses between the triplets of the *Avowynge.* But these same findings apply quite as cogently to the two halves of the ME alliterative long-line, showing the four-stress and the three-stress short rhymed lines as corresponding to, and obviously organically related to (as a derivative), a first half of four stresses, a second half of three—the scansion I accept for the ME long line.

This long-line is my main concern in this paper. Layamon is so near to the AS epic tradition—his very phrases, *e. g.,*

> mid sele than kinge
> spelles uncuthe
> domes waldend
> the eorl wes abolge,

being often like fragments of *Beowulf* merely a little mouthed—that any discussion too temptingly invites that reference to AS metrics I wish here to eliminate. I note simply that any collation of his rhymes plainly indicates the time-marking (stress) function of final secondary syllables. Besides a couplet like

and thu gif me swa muchel lond
to stonden a mire agere hond,
(M. and S. 401)[6]

where a final primary rhymes with a primary, we have a normal-secondary (= secondary in normal prose-speech) rhyming with a primary, as in

tha hit wes daeiliht
garu tha wes heore fiht;
(E. 182, 25)

and a primary rhyming with a verse-secondary (= a syllable, unstressed in prose-speech, taking stress in verse), as

this weoren tha faereste men
that avere her comen,
(M. and S. 13)

and other combinations of primary, normal-secondary, and verse-secondary that make inevitable a four-stress scansion (with secondary on the final syllables) of his so frequently recurring lines of the following type:

thurh thi lond heo aerneth
and haerieth and berneth,
(M. and S. 215)

and gunne to tellen
a feole cunne spellen,
(E. 184, 1)

for ich wat to iwisse
agan is al mi blisse.
(E. 182, 5)

[6] These few citations are from the handy selections in Emerson's *Reader* (by page and line) and Morris and Skeat's *Specimens* (by line), vol. I.

That makes a uniform four-stress scansion, I said, inevitable: unless one can digest comfortably the old idea that the son of Leovenath—on other grounds reputed a clever, clerkly fellow—in trying to manage the (hypothetical) two-accent theory, merely sometimes blundered into four accents through the influence of the four-accent couplets of his French master, Wace.[6] Something remains to be said on Layamon's verse, to judge from the bewildering sample-scansions in at least one recent ME Reader, and from the painstaking but futile statistics of the only extensive study that has been given to it;[7] yet this other interest—the long line—leads me away at once.

The alliterative long-line appears in stanzas of alternating rhymes, in unrhymed stanzas (with rhymed tail), and in long unrhymed poems (like *Piers Plowman*) that are without stanzaic division. *But it appears, too, sporadically in long poems of rhymed couplets,* though here it has never been formally listed under ME alliterative verse and I'm anticipating my argument by listing it now. I want to *communicate* the seven-accent (four plus three) character of all these lines to any one who has gone with me thus far and is persuaded to go farther, however disgruntled he be already. For, after all, the final appeal must be in the appeal of the lines themselves, as they affect our metrical consciousness. Even objective proofs, if we can't apply them in a metrically satisfactory reading aloud, leave us cold and unconvinced;[8] and even Buelbring, for all his objective analysis, makes a point of "gefaellige Verse" for his scansion and (only too justly) of "arge Ungeheuer von rhythmischen (oder vielmehr unrhythmischen) Gebilden" for the scansions of Luick, Schip-

[6] The untenability of this is the same for Layamon's English as for Otfried's German. Compare *Beowulf and the Niebelungen Couplet*, p. 141–2.

[7] *Studies in Layamon's Verse*, N. Y. U. dissertation, Sarah J. McNary, 1902.

[8] All reactions to my previous paper—favorable or unfavorable—ultimately deferred the problem to the ear: my correspondents all either liked or disliked the scansion—and there an end. My point is that if they will really *hear* (and really *speak*) the four-stress scansion, they will like it—and accept it.

per, *et al.* I frankly face this fact: the proofs we act upon (*i. e.*, apply in our reading of verse) are ultimately accepted not by our reason but by our ear,—by which, however, I do not mean that there are not still plenty of unused opportunities for the application of the reason to metrical science. And the devices for communicating that seven-accent character, the thoroughfares I hope to find to modern ears, may incidentally have some value as proofs for the modern reason, wedded as it is to pragmatic sanctions.

II

Let us first renew acquaintance with *The Tale of Gamelyn*,[9] written about 1350, famous as once accredited to Chaucer, and as a ME version of *As You Like It*, and in itself a well-conducted yarn in narrative movement and metrical manipulation. And let us take particularly to heart, as metrical students, its opening adjuration:

> Litheth, and lesteneth   and herkeneth aright.

The poem, like many another tale in alliterative rhymes, was obviously recited (at gatherings of the gentles): the call for attentive ears at the opening of each important new moment of the story—so often repeated that it becomes a veritable refrain—is something quite different from the dramatic devices of Chaucer, like

> Now wol I seye my tale, if ye wol here,

to remind us, while he is himself *writing*, that his pilgrims are supposed to be *speaking*. Thus one hearkeneth to its cadences aright most readily if it is read aloud, and from beginning to end. At least let a few lines be read aloud—for instance:

> Litheth, and lesteneth   and holdeth your tonge,
> And ye schul heere talkyng   of Gamelyn the yonge.
> Ther was ther bysiden   cryed a wrastlyng,

[9] Ed. Skeat, Clarendon Press.

And therfor ther was set vp a ram and a ryng;
And Gamelyn was in wille to wende thereto,
For to preuen his might what he cowthe do.
"Brother", seyde Gamelyn, "by seynt Richer,
Thou most lene me to-nyght a litel courser
That is freisch to the spores on for to ryde;
I most on an erande a litel her byside".
"By god!" seyde his brother, "of steedes in my stalle
Go and chese the the best and spare non of alle
Of steedes or of coursers that stonden hem bisyde;
And tel me, goode brother, whider thou wolt ryde".
(ll. 169–182)[18]

To put its scansion out of all doubt—for I want to reach the interested layman in ME and OG as well as the specialist—I have rendered it into Modern English. The movement is like this:

Heark ye, and listen ye and hold ye your tongue,
And ye shall hear a tale told of Gamelyn the young.
In the shire anear was cri-ed a wrestle-ing,
And for a prize was set up a ram and a ring.
And Gamelyn he devis-ed to wend him thereto
For to prove in true might what he'd learn'd to do.
"Brother", said this Gamelyn, "by sainted Rich-er
Thou must lend to me tonight, a little cours-er,
That's a fresh one to boot-spur, on for to ride;
I must on an errand a little here beside."
"By God", said his brother, "of steeds within my stall
Go and choose for thee the best and spare of none of all
Of stallions or of coursers that stand there side by side,
And tell me, good my brother, whither thou wilt ride".

The metrical system may be emphasized sufficiently for our purposes merely by quoting one or two more of the same cadences wrought out of different speech-material, and several cadences not represented above, all typical:

[18] Throughout this paper there is almost no explicit reference to the ME pronunciation of final *e* or of other syllables which were originally unstressed in prose, often unstressed in verse, and finally unpronounced in either prose or verse. But I have tried to take my examples where a *problematic* final *e*, etc., either does not occur or, if occurring, does not matter for our discussion.

Afterward cam his brother wálkŷnge tháre,
And séydè to Gámelŷn "is our mete yare?"

(89)

I am no worse gadelyng ne no worse wight,
But bórn òf a ládŷ and geten of a knight.

(107)

'Lórdès', he séydè 'for Cristes passioun,
Helpeth brynge Gamelyn oút of prísoún'.

(477)

A'fter thát ábbòt thán spák anóther,
"I wold thin heed were of though thou were my brother!"

(483)

(Note that *that*, as contrasted with *another*, takes the accent with legitimate narrative force.)

'Felaw', seyde the porter, 'stónd thére stílle,
And I wil wende to Gamelyn to wítèn his wílle'.
In wènte the pórtèr to Gamelyn anoon,
And seyde, "Sir, I warne you her ben come your foon."

(571)

(In went[e] the porter = "Póp, gòes the wéas-èl". Strictly these five syllables run with emphasis 4, 3, 1, 4, 2, *goes* being a stronger secondary than *-el*. This notation—Jespersen's—seems better than Kaluza's adopted in my earlier paper, for 0 really equals merely a *pause* not a syllable).

I cúrse nón óthèr but right mý-sélue;
They [=though] ye fette to yow fyue thánne yè be twélue!'

(651)

(This is not bad metre, but good dramatic emphasis in whole-hearted recitation.)

Gamelyn into the woode stálkède stille,
And Adam, the spenser, líkedè ful ýlle.

(617)

(Note the differing treatment of stress in the two weak preterits.)

Tho was Gámelỳn croúnèd   kýng of oútláwes,
And wálkèd a whílè   vnder woode-schawes.
(695)

Gámelyn toók him in his árm   and nó móre spák,
But thréw him óuer the bárrè   ànd his árm to-brák.
(851)

(But thréw hìm [pause] óv'r the bàrr[e] ?)

As they sete and eeten   and dronke wel and fyn,
Than séyde that oón to that óthèr,   ''thi's is Gámelýn''.
(681)

(Contrast the ample speech-material of this first half-line with the syncopated first half-line *Adam spenser* below, and note the three different metrical treatments of the last syllable of *Gamelyn*.)

This general movement is, I believe, not theoretically in dispute among scholars. It is familiar in many other ME poems, as Robert of Gloucester's and Robert of Brunne's. It is that of the *Niebelungen*[11] couplet, and essentially all that my previous paper remarked of that couplet (not stanza) holds of the *Gamelyn* couplet.

I'm not concerned with a formally complete analysis, or with any analysis beyond what prepares the reader to take in the more readily the comparisons and inferences to follow. The fourth stress of the first half-line is normally a secondary, after the manner of the *Niebelungen* couplet; but it is sometimes a primary, as in

Let we now this false *knight*   lyen in his care,
(615)

unless, as is quite possible, the gleeman lightened the stress on *knight* and increased the stress on *false* in accordance with the movement in a line like

Four and twenty yónge mèn   that beelden hem ful bolde,
(553)

---

[11] Several friends queried this spelling in my previous paper. It has no "esoteric significance"—it is simply the old-fashioned English spelling (found inconsistently in Taylor's *Medieval Mind*, etc.), which I had unconsciously adopted years ago—and haven't unlearned as I should.

which is like (except for the syllable *e* in *yonge*) the

"Four and twenty blackbirds"

of the nursery rhyme in the same old metre. There is clearly this shift of stress in a line like

For to colen thy blood as I dide myn, (540)

where *thy* robs *blood* of the primary stress, by the emphatic contrast with *I* and *myn*. Cases where a fourth stress fails altogether are extremely rare, if the lines are lilted properly, and point rather to the need of emending the text than of chiding the poet.[12] The line,

Chef Justice of al his fre forest (892)

becomes normal by simply changing the mid-line division:

Chef Justice of al his fre forest,

where we have two primaries plus two secondaries in the first half and in the second three primaries of the "three blind mice" sort, without speech-filling, as also in above examples or in

And I wil parte with the of *my free lond*. (402)

I need hardly note that omission of unstressed syllables between stresses (not only between primary and primary, but between primary and secondary) is an integral part of the metrical technique, and that stresses (secondaries) on syllables entirely unstressed in ME prose frequently occur, not only at the end of the first half, but in the body of either half, as in

Lithèth and lestenèth and holdèth your tonge

[12] Of course sometimes in ME alliterative verse this fourth stress is indubitably lacking; yet the typical movement is merely varied (rather than disturbed), if we supply its place by a longer musical rest than we instinctively supply after the fourth. But I anticipate.

of our sample, or in

> Had I now etèn and dronkèn aright.
>
> (421)

Considerable *flexibility* of language with reference not only to prose-speech, but to the speech-uses of his own verse, was his, even as it was every poet's of the good old days, even the scholarly Chaucer's. For instance,—though previous examples may suffice—in the verses

> Adam spenser me thinkth I faste to longe,
> Adam spenser now I byseche the,
> For the mochel loue my fader loued the......
>
> (398 ff.)

the *-er* of *spenser* is a secondary, even as it was a secondary normally in late ME prose-speech according to recessive accent of words from OF. (The solemn cadence *Adam spenser—take cup, drink up.*)[13] But in an adjacent verse (403) it is made a primary:

> Thanne seyde Adam that was the spenc-*er*,
> "I have served thy brother this sixtene yeer."

Or take the first verse of the couplet (a verse also in its syncopation significant for our subsequent comparisons):

> A'bbòt or prioùr mónk or chánóun,
> That Gamelyn ouertok, anon they yeeden doun:
>
> (509)

chanoun in prose was pronounced of course like *priour*, a primary plus a strong secondary; here *priour* retains the prose stress, but *chanoun* becomes primary plus primary.

But no disquisition of mine can take the place of an alert metrical ear in the service of an intimate philological experience with ME as a living tongue. And though Chaucer, too, makes an excited fellow swear *by Cristes passioun* to the same scansion of that good round oath, and though Chaucer, too, talked practically the same dialect and shared some of

---

[13] See my *op. cit.*, pp. 133–4.

the same speech-licenses in his verse, his metrics are founded on an entirely different system: the *Tale of Gamelyn* was never told either by Cook or by Yeoman. Chaucer cannot be in these matters our master dear, dear as he is in so many other matters. Again, the line of our couplet is not an Alexandrine nor a Septinarius, and the author of *Gamelyn* has handled it with more skill and conformity to type, I think, than Skeat in his *Introduction* allows. The movement is not theoretically in dispute; yet there is still need to hearken aright; for this line is the line to which the italics a few pages back referred: it is a long-line, sporadically alliterative and obviously of the alliterative, the Germanic, tradition *with the traditional mid-line division.* Or are such lines as the following mere accidents:

Tho that *w*ardeynes *w*ere   of that *w*rastelyng.
(279)

Other alliterative examples follow below, as the plot (against the established order) thickens.

We well know, we say, the scansion of the *Gamelyn* long-line (four plus three); we well know the scansion of the accepted alliterative long-line as in *Piers Plowman* (two plus two); we can distinguish them well enough. Let us see how well, after all. Can the gnostic distinguish herewith these five *Gamelyn* from these five *Piers Plowman*[14] long-lines, by any *metrical* clue:

1 For he *h*opede to God   for to *h*ave his deel
2 And pleyden with the *m*onkes   and *m*ade hem agast
3 And now *w*olde I *w*iten of the   what *w*ere the best
4 They ben ascaped *g*ood aventure   now *g*od hem amende
5 But I can *r*ymes of *R*obyn hood   and *R*andolf erle of Chestre
6 Tho that we *c*omen hider   it was a *c*old reed
7 If I shulde *d*eye by this *d*ay   me *l*iste nougte to *l*oke
8 And leet the wicket *st*onden   y-*st*eke ful *st*ille
9 He stumbled on the *thr*eschewolde   an *thr*ewe to the erthe
10 Whan alle the *g*estes were *g*oon   how Gamelyn was dight.

This last, which names its own author, is inserted for courtesy (G 344): as for the others, 3, 4, 5, 7, 9 are from *Piers Plow-*

[14] I use Skeat's small, one volume edition, Clarendon Press.

man (VI, 213; VI, 79; V, 402; V, 400; V, 357); 1, 2, 6, 8 are *Gamelyn* 635, 526, 531, 563. On any metrical theory, PP differs from *Gamelyn* in preserving far more fully and consistently the alliterative tradition, though (as to be noted above) a given *Gamelyn* line (as 10) may preserve it better than a given PP line (as 7), and a PP line may depart from it as far as any one of the *Gamelyn* lines that alliterates at all (as is not, however, indicated in these few examples). PP differs, too, from *Gamelyn* (as in fact from much unrhymed, no less than stanza-rhymed, alliterative verse) in the characteristically larger percentage of secondary syllables at the end of the second half-line. But, *metrically*, the present contention is that the PP line does not differ from the *Gamelyn* line.

Example 5 above, for instance, has, I believe, in PP the movement it has in the couplet I this minute make up:

> I am no courtly gleeman, nor a prince's jester,
> But I can rhymes of Robin Hood and Randolph, earl of Chester.
> (V, 402)

The line,

> There was laughyng and louryng and "let go the cuppe",
> (V, 344)

has in PP the movement it has in this made-up couplet:

> There was junketing o'midnight, a jump down and up!
> There was laughing and lowering and "let go the cup!"

These are just like *Gamelyn* couplets. The two lines in PP,

> For hunger hiderward hasteth hym faste,
> He shal awake with water wastoures to chaste,
> (VI, 323–4)

are a fortuitous rhymed couplet (if you'll permit Langland and me the bad rhyme of a ME short and long *a*) just like a *Gamelyn* couplet. How readily the two poems unite metrically may be felt with more immediate force if we combine a line of PP and a line of *Gamelyn* (at random, except as guided by a desire to have the combinations make sense so that the unity of metrical impression be as little disturbed as possible by lack of other unity):

> Gamelyn yede to the gate   and leet it up wyde; (G 311)
> A bolle and a bagge   he bare by his side. (PP V, 526)

> Alle lybbyng laboreres   that lyven with her hondes, (PP VII, 62)
> Thou schalt biseke hem alle   to bryng the out of bondes. (G 440)

> "Pieres," quod the prest tho,   "I can no pardoun finde, (PP VII, 112)
> And ben harde bystad   under woode-lynde". (G 676)

Except for the decisive word *Pieres* and the impeccable alliteration, if one were deciding between these last two lines, one would say the latter was more likely the rugged and ragged PP line than the former—"rugged and ragged", however, because the usual scansion is wrong.

The same sort of metrical jugglery is quite as easy between *Gamelyn* and the equally contemporaneous, though slightly more archaic, *William of Palerne*:[15]

> "Felaw", seyde the championn,   "Al-so mot I thrive, (G 227)
> For me non harm schal he have   never in his live![16] (WP 253)

> Anón às sche[17] hérdè   how it was bifalle, (G 685)
> Than studied sche stifly   as step-moderes wol alle.... (WP 130)

In both these couplets *Gamelyn* contributes the first line; and so one might say it contributes the movement too. But it will be noted that, in the last two couplets of the preceding exercise, PP lines preceded *Gamelyn* lines. So with the WP

[15] Citations of WP, *The Deluge*, and *The Destruction of Sodom* are from Morris and Skeat's *Specimens*, Vol. II.

[16] The above is particularly good, because the characteristic alliteration of WP is obscured.

[17] For *he* of the text, to give consistent sense to the cento-couplet.

lines below; it is quite indifferent to our metrical purpose which contributes the first:

I was bore here fast bi   by this wodes side;   (WP 240)
And tel me, goode brother,   whider thou wolt ryde.   (G 182)

And briddes ful bremely   on the bowes sing[e]   (WP 23)
To the maister outlawe   that tho was her king.   (G 683)

And sone as he it seiy[18]   sothe forto telle: (WP 34)
"Me ben comen tydynges   I may no lenger dwelle".
(G 692)

So we may make *Gamelyn* couplets by matching different lines of any poems in the accepted alliterative tradition. *William of Palerne* is still open before us; let us turn over the pages:

Ak nowthe ye that arn hendi   haldes ow stille,   (106)
To herknen after his houndes,   other horn schille.   (213)

That hade him sent tho sonde   swiche prey to finde,   (64)
And how that best therwe bale   was brougt out of kinde.
(107)

He was wigtliche a-wondered   and gan to wepe sore,   (310)
But themperour had god game   of that gomes lore.   (346)

Or from *The Destruction of Sodom*, these:

The grete god in his greme   bygynnes onlofte   (947)
That the thik thunder-thrast   thirled hem ofte.   (952)

Swe aboute sodamas   and hit sydes alle—   (956)
For it is brod and bothemles   and bitter as the galle.
(1022)

Or these from *The Deluge*:

For to ende alle at ones   and for ever twynne—   (402)
Al was wasted that ther wonyed   the worlde withinne.
(431)

[18] Musical rest for lacking fourth (secondary) stress (see p. 70), or preliminary secondary on *and*, with *seiy* a primary.

And he fonges to the flygt   and fannes on the wyndes; (457)
He croukes for comfort   when carayne he fyndes. (459)

And ho skyrmes under skwe   and skowtes aboute; (483)
Ledes logen in that lome   and loked ther-oute. (495)

On testing these comparisons (aloud!), as on testing all the others, if there be cases where the cadences tend to reveal to responsive ears differences from the norm with which we are making the comparisons, we must distinguish clearly between metrical differences that are variations and metrical differences that are cancellations of the norm—between differences that keep us still inside and differences that take us outside the seven-stress movement. Differences of the latter type are so few as to be negligible; of the former there are a number: WP, D, DS, for instance, in the cento-couplets above—in this respect representatively—tend to more frequent syncopation (and of one metrical variety) in the second half-line than *Gamelyn*—or, for that matter, than their acknowledged metrical brother, *Piers Plowman*, though the same syncopations are found sporadically in both.

PP, WP, D and DS are all unrhymed verse, whilst *Gamelyn* is rhymed; and rhyme technique is supposed to have introduced epochmaking changes in OG. May I not be producing similar changes,—as it were, artificially repeating a ME process that perhaps turned the two plus two alliterative line into a four plus three rhymed line? I give the objection a formal statement, merely to make a formal reply: there are probably more rhymed long-lines (stanzas) in the huge mass of ME verse in the accepted alliterative tradition than unrhymed, and they have never been distinguished, and cannot be distinguished, as metrically different. And, as we may compare later, these unrhymed alliterative lines above match with the *Gamelyn* lines precisely as the rhymed alliterative lines will be found below to match. Rhyme may have assisted in the original reduction of the second half-line from a four stresser to a three but it has nothing to do with the question before us now.

III

Yet all this is the manipulation of single lines; and one demands, in fairness, a chance to operate with consecutive passages. Let us return then to *Piers Plowman* and *Gamelyn*. Can one distinguish the following any better? The non-metrical ear-marks (and eye-marks) have been destroyed by tampering with dialect, with rhyme, with alliteration, and even with words that might betray by their meaning; but practically all syllabic, and absolutely all metrical values, have been preserved.

Question I. Identify *a* and *b*.

a) Gamelyn, quod this Adam, and put forth his hed,
"I knowe him as kyndely as clerke doth his bokes;
I have ben his folwer al this many dawes,
Bothe ysowen his sede, and sued his bestes".

b) "Adam", seyde Gamelyn, "We wiln nought don thus,
We wil lacchen lechours and lat the other go.
I wil unto the wise and with the Justice rede;
On gomes that ben gultif I wil ben ygolde.

Question II. Identify *a* and *b*.

a) "Adam", seide Gamelyn, "we wiln nought don so,
We wil slee the lechours and lat the other go.
I wil unto the wise and with the Justice speke;
On wights that ben gultif I wil ben awreke.

b) "Gamelyn", seide Adam, and put forth his hond,
"I knowe him as kyndely as clerke doth the lond;
I have ben his folwer al this many dawes,
Bothe ysowen his sede and dyk-ed his schawes".

I made no special search and have been guilty of no disingenuousness, in fact of no particular ingenuity. Example *a* is from the first page[19] I opened in Skeat's PP:

"Peter!" quod a plowman, and put forth his hed,
"I knowe him as kyndely as clerke doth his bokes....
I have ben his folwar al this fifty wintre;
Bothe ysowen his sede and sued his bestes".

[19] Page 62, Passus V, 544–5, 549–50, Students' one volume edition, Clarendon Press, 1900.

Example *b* is from the first page[20] I opened in Skeat's *Gamelyn*:

> "Adam," saye Gamelyn   "we wiln nought don so,
> We wil slee the giltyf   and lat the other go.
> I wil into the halle   and with the Justice speke;
> On hem that ben gultyf   I will ben awreke."

If I had hunted a bit I could have found passages better adapted to spare me any further comment as to the comparisons—passages where the *Gamelyn* author uses, as he so often does, a second half-line, *more* syncopated in speech than those just above, or where the PP author uses, as he so often does, a second half-line much *less* syncopated than those just above.[21] Of course a given *Gamelyn* passage characterized by second half-lines more syncopated than those of a given PP passage—even though such are a plenty—would create a false impression in the other direction. The shorter second-half would be no clue to either:

Question III. Identify *a* and *b*.

a) A little above the bely   the rigge-bone to-brak;
And set him in the feteres   ther he sat arst.
"Sitte ther, brother",   sayde Gardyner,
"For to colen thy blood   as I can min".

b) ....Gamelyn, we may
Bydde and biseche,   if it be thy wille,
That art our fader and our brother,   be merciable to us,
And have ruth on thise Abbotes,   that repente hem here sore
That evere they wrathed the in this toun,   in worde, thoughte. or deedes.

Question IV. Identify *a* and *b*.

a) A little above the bely   the rigge-bone to-barst;
And set him in the feteres   there he sat arst.
"Sitte ther, brother",   sayde Gamelyn,
"For to colen thy blod   as I can min."

[20] Page 31, l. 821 ff.

[21] Such second half-lines are to be found earlier in this paper, and others will be cited below.

b) Gamelyn, we may
Bydde and biseche, if be thy wille thus,
That art our fader and our brother, be merciable to us,
And have ruth on thise Abbotes, that repente hem here sore
That ever they wrathed the in this toun, in deedes,
worde, or lore.

Example *a* is—as my introductory comment implies—from *Gamelyn,* example *b* from PP. It will be observed how slight the alterations were:

a) A little above the girdel the rigge-bone to-barst;
And set him in the feteres ther he sat arst.
"Sitte ther, brother," sayde Gamelyn,
"For to colen thy blood as I dide min."[22] (537 ff.)

b) the sikerere we mowe
Bydde and beseche, if it be thi wille,
That art oure fader and oure brother, be merciable to us,
And have reuthe on thise Ribaudes that repente hem here
sore,
That evere thei wratthed the in this world, in worde,
thougte, or dedes.
(Passus V, 509 ff.)

And now these lines suggest another demur: though PP may not be distinguishable by *shorter* second half-lines, it is by *longer* first half-lines. So

Question V. Distinguish *a* and *b*.

a) His bretheren loved wel here fader and of him were afeered;
The eldest deserved his fadres curse, and had it at the last.

b) Sissoures and sompnoures,— suche men now were,—
Shireves of shires were shent if she nere.

These are from *Gamelyn* (7–8), with *afeerd* substituted for *agast,* and from PP (Passus III, 133–4), with *now were* substituted for *hir preiseth.* There is evidently as little help for identification by the character of either half-line as by the impression of the line as a whole. In the present experiment,

[22] The final *e,* if pronounced, gives this line a slightly different lilt from that of my variation, *as I can min.*

there are no metrical variations, even in narrowest limits, to furnish a clue to differences.

My purpose is not to enter into minute distinctions: that, poem for poem, PP (composed to be read) and Gamelyn verses (composed to be recited) will be found to differ in some nuances of *metrical* detail, creating some cumulative differences in the total *metrical* effect, is herewith once for all admitted. Moreover, the insistent alliterative technique of the one and the rhyme couplets of the other would alone tend to produce concomitant variations in metrics, like the concomitant variations of gait appearing in two varieties of pacers whom natural or artificial selection has differentiated, inside the one species, by diverse femurs and diverse knee-joints—though the analogy breaks down at least in one particular, since both varieties of horse go on *four* feet, while both varieties of verse go on *seven*. But the nuances of gait are less than, say, between Pope's and Leigh Hunt's five-stress line, the so-called iambic pentameter of the heroic couplet.

Let us attempt another similar, but more difficult, exercise. Let us weave together some random lines from *William of Palerne* and *Gamelyn*, into a consecutive narrative of the alliterative (unrhymed) tradition, striving only for as much clarity of action and characterization as we find in many a dull ME alliterative poem. We shall be in good Medieval company,—for the monks, too, made centos.

*E*rly on a mornyng   on the *e*ighte day
It bi*f*el in that *f*orest,   there *f*ast by-side,
We *f*ond the lord y*f*etered   *f*aste with-alle,
In *g*ode clothes of *g*old   a*g*rethed ful riche.
He was *w*igtliche a-*w*ondered   and gan to *w*epe sore:
''Now *w*ot i never in this *w*orld   of *w*hom y am come,
Ne what *d*estine me is *d*igt   but God *d*o his wille''.
He[33] smot the *w*yket with his foot   and brak a*w*ey the pyn,
And *c*ast awey the feteres   and *c*ome to me anoon,
And *s*eide, ''thou *s*wete *s*one,   seththe thou schalt hennes wende,
I have a *d*raught of good wyn—   *d*rynk er ye passe''.[34]

---

[33] Apparently "the lord"—if it was so easy to free himself, why the fuss?
[34] Was he fettered in the butlery of some greenwood tavern?

"Tho that we comen hider" [quod I], it was a cold reed:
He[25] *wolde* say afterward I *were* a traytour".

If in these thirteen lines the reader identifies lines 2, 4, 5, 6, 7, 10 as unaltered from WP (lines 1, 52, 310, 314, 315, 329) and the rest as unaltered from *Gamelyn* (except a *we* for *and*, lines 331, 602, 298, 454, 596, 531, 406), he does so because of characteristics of spelling, not because of characteristics of versification; for these WP lines (in an alliterative poem) —of course the point is that they are honestly representative lines—can be as little distinguished *in stresses* from these *Gamelyn* lines (in a long-line rhymed couplet poem)—equally representative lines except that they over-emphasize the alliteration in *Gamelyn* as a whole[26]—as these lines of the *Gamelyn* can be distinguished, *as to alliterative manner*, from these WP lines: the two sets of lines match in every particular which is significant in the ME alliterative versification, though only the *metrical* matching is the point of main concern.

I have amused myself with a number of other similar experiments, till I'm convinced one could ultimately play to the *Gamelyn* tune any typical long-line from any typical alliterative poem—for any line that doesn't go to that tune is, you see, *not* typical. This logical slip aside, such a quantity of accepted alliterative verses *can* be metrically matched with the *Gamelyn* verses, that one might do worse in his reasoning than to infer a probability that they *should* be so matched. It would be a choice then as to which, the accepted alliterative or the *Gamelyn*, furnishes the norm: the two plus two of the former, or the four plus three of the latter. But about the normal seven stresses of the latter there is no more doubt than about the six stresses of the *Iliad* or the five stresses of Cowper's blank verse translation of the *Iliad*—as little doubt (for some) as about the six

[25] Who?—the Sheriff of Nottingham?

[26] Of course, merely to minimize a non-metrical mark of differentiation and to repeat the reminder that *Gamelyn* is in the alliterative tradition, even if not uniformly alliterative.

stresses of a French Alexandrine. Thus, if the fact that they *can be made* to lilt to one tune (and this much will be granted me, I trust) is presumptive evidence that they really *are* one tune, then that tune must be the tune of *The Tale of Gamelyn* —ME alliterative verse must be, in short, a four plus three, a seven-stresser, as I've already insisted so eagerly and often.

IV

But just here is the rub, you say: *can be* is not presumptive evidence for *must be.* You may even embarrass my argument and my modesty by quoting my own words against me, italicized words too: in English "a line of verse has no independent existence";[27] and so the preceding illustrations show nothing more than the familiar plastic nature of English accentual speech. The performance is indeed what it was named a moment ago—"metrical jugglery", a pleasant game for a rainy day in mid-summer when one wearies of tinkering with the basement drainage; but scarcely to be taken seriously for a scientific monograph for reading between semesters in strenuous mid-winter. Yet the objection is to me as invalid as it is plausible. Aside from the fact that some of this "jugglery" was with consecutive passages and not single lines, I must reply that there are limits to the plasticity of speech, or any prose could be read as any metre; and that to affirm a line has no independent existence out of metrical context is not to affirm it may be forced into any metrical movement by any given metrical context.

Take two different verse-forms alike in rhymelessness and in number of stresses, say, hendecasyllabics and blank-verse, and take them both from one poet. Take from Tennyson:

> O you chorus of indolent reviewers
> Irresponsible, indolent reviewers,
> Look, I come to the test, a tiny poem
> All composed in a metre of Catullus,
> All in quantity careful of my motion,
> Like the skater on ice that hardly bears him,

---

[27] See my *op. cit.*, p. 118.

Lest I fall unawares before the people......
Hard, hard, hard it is only not to tumble,
So fantastical is the dainty metre ....
As some rare little rose, a piece of inmost
Horticultural art, or half coquette-like
Maiden, not to be greeted unbenignly.

Try forcing these by blank-verse context into a typical blank verse movement (say, that of *The Coming of Arthur*):

Be thou the King and we will work thy will,
Lest I fall unawares before the people.

Here by the stressing of *I* through the logical contrast prepared for in the stressed *thou*, and by the associated unstressing of *fall*, we have radically altered the metrical character of the line: this roughly illustrates rhythmical plasticity. But in the cento

Half-blinded at the coming of a light,
Hard, hard, hard it is, only not to tumble,

or

And Lancelot passed away among the flowers
(For then was latter April) and returned
Among the flowers, in May, with Guinevere—
Maiden, not to be greeted unbenignly,

the hendecasyllabics will not be altered from their native cadences: this illustrates a limit of placidity, though a rather nice limit. And to affirm that a line has no independent existence[28] is least of all to affirm that a goodly number of lines of one metrical texture in one metrical context can be forced in another metrical context to take on a metrical texture as crassly different as the two plus two is from the four plus seven.

This would be possible were the four plus seven rigidly dipodic with only a modicum of unstressed syllables between, —where the adaptation could be made by cancelling the

[28] This is, in any case, the statement of a general law: single lines there are which constitute exceptions (as far as mere stress, as distinct from pitch, tempo, etc., is concerned), but these are lines characterized by very elementary metrical structure.

metrical (time-marking) value of the regularly alternating secondary stresses. To illustrate. Here is a seven-accent monopodic couplet (monopodic, if read normally):

> The hills are green and green the dales, and children
> now may run
> In play till rings the curfew bell and sets the summer
> sun.

Here a seven-accent dipodic:

> Up the hill, across the hill, run, child, run—
> It's playtime till curfew and down goes the sun.

And here a four-accenter:

> The hills are green and the children run
> Till curfew rings at the set of sun.

We can combine

> The hills are green, and the children run—
> It's playtime till curfew and down goes the sun,

turning the dipodic seven-accenter into a four-accenter by destroying the secondary stresses in a changed metrical context. We cannot combine

> The hills are green, and the children run
> In play till rings the curfew bell and sets the summer sun

so that the second takes on the four of the first—the second remains a monopody of seven stresses. There are some regular dipodic lines in *Gamelyn,* as the first in our sample,

> Litheth and lesteneth and holdeth your tonge.

which can easily be made to read with four-stresses, like

> Harken and listen and bridle your tongue;

and old seven-stressers of this sort, in my opinion, contributed to the development of that four-stress "anapestic" verse of which my Modern English line here is one illustration and Gascoigne's famous couplet in *Certayne notes of Instruction* is another. But the verses as a whole are not built on a strictly dipodic (or a monopodic) pattern; they lilt along with primary and secondary stresses (and syllables or no syllables between stresses), like the verses of the *Niebelungenlied,* in permutations and combinations (some the same as the AS and OG types, but many new) incalculable except to the industry of a candidate for a degree in mathematics, though dipodic cadences (as distinct from regular dipodic lines) are characteristic. It would be possible, conversely, where the two plus two had a clearly defined tendency to regularly recurring heavy syllables between the stresses, to adapt the two plus two to a four plus three movement:

It's playtime till curfew and down goes the sun

of the last couplet cited is shiftable to the movement of

Up the hill, down the hill, run, child, run,

as above. But the accepted two plus two scansion of alliterative verse has no clearly defined tendency to regularity of recurrence of unstressed heavy syllables. If the two were as radically different as current theory assumes, certainly they could not be made by any jugglery to go alike: the jugglery is only possible because they are alike.

Were it admitted the particular lines cited from PP and WP are, for a fact, like the *Gamelyn* lines, one might yet declare them exceptional—as lines beginning to take on a seven-accent character through the influence of foreign (Latin) models or of the very seven-accenter typified by *Gamelyn.*[29] It would, then, be the objector's duty to point out in what ways they are exceptional, how they differ in speech-manipulation from the lines he reads as two plus two. It would also be his duty to explain how, in the very act of creating in a two plus two movement, a ME author (still

[29] Which has in turn, by hypothesis, developed its seven-accent character out of a two plus two Germanic line through foreign influence—and the Latin developed its through foreign influence, and that foreign influence its—*ad infinitum aut Adamum.*

a human being with psychic processes presumably like our own) would every now and then get so badly out of step through the embarrassing intrusion upon consciousness of a totally extraneous and different time and tune. Both the linguistic and the psychologic difficulty are noteworthy. Moreover, let him try himself the cento-game with PP or WP open beside *Gamelyn*. He should find, as I found, the lines may be metrically matched in nineteen cases out of twenty. I wish to be strictly honest—hence the admission of the twentieth case. Yet in justice to my position I should add that by "metrically matched" I mean a metrically easy and obvious matching, and that by twentieth case I really mean the fiftieth—and that the fiftieth itself, if not "obviously" matchable with a seven-stresser, is still less obviously matchable with a genuine four-stresser.

It may be that no lines from one poet can be interpolated into the lines of another, without a resulting organic disturbance (observed or unobserved), as Sievers in his seminary, in his table-talk, and in his published studies is set upon establishing: the *Lenz* complex may always be detachable from the *Goethe* complex in *Sesenheimerlieder;* and Sievers' wizardry may be—is, I think—the opening of entirely new chapters, not only in phonetics, versification, and text-criticism, but in the abysmal deeps of Personality and their subtle and unconscious manifestations in spoken or written speech. But this is another and profounder problem than ours, involving factors of another order—differences within what for our purposes are samenesses. For instance, Sievers' method is applicable to the putative three authors announced by Manly for *Piers Plowman*; it is irrelevant to our question of the seven accents of the putative three authors and the relation of these accents, as a generalized verse-form, to the *Gamelyn*. This is said to forestall the malicious.

V

It may be trifling with human nature to record my experiments with other types of poems of the accepted alliterative tradition. But I will risk an illustration or two. Here is a stanza (LIX) from *Rauf Coilyear.*[30]

Befoir mony worthie he dubbit him Knicht,
Dukis and digne Lordis in that deir hall:
"Schir, se for thy self, thow semis to be wicht,
Tak keip to this ordour, ane Knicht I the call;
To mak the manly man I mak the of micht.
Ilk yeir thre hundreth pund assigne the I sall;
And als the nixt vacant, be ressonabill richt,
That hapnis in France, quhair sa euer it fall,
Forfaltour or fre waird, that first cummis to hand,
I gif the heir heritabilly,
Sa that I heir, quhen I haue hy,
That thow be fundin reddy
With Birny and brand".

The seven stresses and the general movement are readily reproducible in Modern English:

Before full many worthies he dubb-ed him a Knight,
Dukes and daring Lordlings in that dear hall:
"See unto thyself, sir; thou seem'st a brave wight;
Have care to this order— a Knight I thee call;
To make thee a manly man I make thee of might.
Every year three hundred pound assign thee I shall;
And at the next vacance, by reasonable right,
That in France happeneth, wheresoever it fall,
Forfeiture or free ward, that first comes to hand,
I'll give thee the heritage,
So I hear, when war I wage,
Thou be ready to engage
With breast-plate and brand.

Old speech-habits, and with them some old-verse habits, have changed; some cadences have fallen out of mode, except as supported by more familiar cadences. We are used to fuller arses (Senkungen) than ME, though we have more omissions

---

[30] *Scottish Alliterative Poems*, ed. Armours, STS.

of unaccented elements than we realize—certainly more than our metrical Manuals realize. My own metrical modification is typified in the first line—a modification introduced·chiefly because, as the first line, it *is* unsupported. Note, incidentally, that by merely omitting an intermediate line—

Tak keip of this ordour, ane Knicht I the call;
Ilk yeir thre hundreth pund assigne the I sall—

we get again good *Gamelyn* couplets.

In a Modern English stanza, with its more allusive alliteration and its less allusive (irregular) "feet", the generic similarity is still obvious; and the genre itself perhaps more obvious to the unconverted than in the preceding reproduction from ME:

Yonder hides a woodthrush, singing in the May,
Yonder from my window, down amid the trees,
Where the bosky roadside bends along the bay,
And rush and reed is lolling landward with the breeze.
Now, whereof is she singing this old weird lay—
Heard by the blackbirds, and Indian tepees
In the sunny mornings of an earlier day,
Ere her haunts were pestered with thoughts like these:
What's the woodthrush singing with insistent throat?—
She sings: 'Leonard in your chair,
Meditating metrics there,
Come down here—take the air,
Come!—take your boat.''

That the long-lines of this graceful little lyric were intended by their author for seven (four plus three) stresses may be accepted without further discussion. But for any poem, ME as well, the question "how is it to be scanned" means how did the author *intend* it to be scanned; and familiarity with metrical intentions of one's own is at least no handicap in penetrating the metrical intentions of others.

Read now a metrically similar stanza (say LXXXII) of *Golagros and Gawane* from the same volume, without a Modern English version:

Lordingis and ladyis in the castell on loft,
Quhen thai saw thair liege lord laid on the landis,
Mony sweit thing of sware swownit full oft,

Wyis wourthit for wo to wringin thair handis.
Wes nowthir solace nor sang thair sorow to soft,
Ane sair stonay and stour at thair hartis standis.
On Criste cumly thay cry: "on croce as thou coft,
With thi blissit blude to bring us out of bandis,
Lat neuer our souerane his cause with schame to enchief!
Mary, farest of face,
Beseik thi sone in this cace,
Ane drop of his grete grace
He grant ws to geif!"

And now this:

Tho Gamelyn under the woode lokede aright;
He seyh there stonde lordes grete and stoute.
Sevene score of yonge men he saugh wel a-dight;
A'lle sátte atte mété compas aboute.
Ever stood Gamelyn even upright,
And seih the scherreve come with a grete route
(Was born of a lady and geten of a knight),
And bàd schítte the gáté and holde him withoute.
Than seyde Gamelyn the child that was ying:
"If I leete him goon
And we schulle ben at oon,
So Cristes curs have that oon—
Withoute lesyng!"

The alliteration (and the sense) may be a little obscure; for the thing is merely a patch-work of *Gamelyn* lines, unaltered except a *was* for a *but* (7), a *him* for a *the* (= thee, 10) without elision before *h*, and a *so* for an *and* (12)—long-lines 627, 808, 628, 629, 600, 108, 286, 389, 105; first half-lines 405, 156, 446; and the second half-line 659. But metrically it is not obscure; it is not like *Gamelyn* lines; it *is Gamelyn* lines—our seven-stressers. How does it differ from the ME thirteen-line stanzas above?—scanned by practically all Anglists in England and America and by most in Germany as two plus two!

Such cadences, as often observed, persist in nursery rhymes; but they have persisted, though unremarked by the Handbooks, in the literary tradition too. Indeed, the following four lines from *Love in the Valley*[31] are in the metrical man-

[31] Second version, stanza 5.

ner of the ME alliterative rhymed stanza (except for relative "regularity" of movement and relative irregularity in the position and length of the mid-line pause—in line three, as regularly in ME, after the fourth stress, in the others after the third, as only rarely in ME):

> Lovely are the curves of the white owl sweeping
> Wavy in the dusk lit by one large star.
> Lone on the fir-branch, his rattle note unvaried,
> Brooding o'er the gloom, spins the brown eve-jar.

A re-reading of Meredith's poem as a whole—whose music, even in the earlier version, was such delight to the great metrist Tennyson—will in fact do much to make manifest the ME versification under discussion.

But to keep a moment longer to our ME examples. Instructive are the verses of John Audelay,[32] "the penitent and righteous monk" of Haghmon[d] monastery, Shropshire, who composed his MS about 1426, ad honorem (as his colophon puts it) Domini nostri et ad exemplum aliorum. Ad exemplum, then, repunctuated (p. 16):

> Oure gentyl ser Jone, joy hym mot betyde!
> He is a mere mon of mony among cumpane;
> He con harpe, he con syng, his orglus ben herd ful wyd;
> He wyl noght spare his prese to spund his selare;
> Alas he ner a parsun or a vecory!
> Be Jhesu! he is a gentylmon and jolyle arayd;
> His gurdlis harneschit with silver, his baslard hongus bye,
> Apon his parte pautener uche mon ys apayd,
> both maiden and wyfe;
> I-fayth he shal noght fro us gon,
> Fore oure myrth hit were e-don—
> Fore he con glad us everychon:—
> y pray God hold his lyve.

Reproduced with metrical approximation:

> Our Sir John the gent-le, joy may him betide!
> He's a merry man of many among company;
> He can harp, he can sing, his "orgles" be heard full wide;

[32] Percy Society, vol. XIV. On Audelay see *Der Dichter John Audelay und sein Werk*, J. Ernst Wuelfing, *Anglia*, neue Folge, 6, p. 175–217.

He will never spare his purse   to spend his "salary";
If only he were a parson   or a "vicary"![58]
By Jesu! he's a gentleman   and jollily arrayed;
His girdles harnessed with silver   his dagger hangeth by—
Upon his party "pautener"   ev'ry man's "apaid,"
Both maiden and wife;
I' faith he shan't from us be gone,
For all our mirth it then were done—
For he can glad us every one:
I pray God hold his life.

These lines carry on the wholesome tradition of satire against clerical dandies and rascals; they might be Langland's of fifty years earlier, except that the flavor of their humor smacks more of Chaucer. But they carry on another tradition: it will be seen at once that they are the alliterative thirteen line stanza of *Coilyear,* etc., except for a different disposition of the rhymes of the second quatrain, and a second half-line (three stresses) in lieu of a long-line (seven stresses) for the ninth line; and except for a less insistent (but still well-defined) alliteration. But, approaching a little to our modern verse-habits, their seven-stress movement is a little easier for us to get. But these particular lines of Audelay's Middle English *can* still be read in the two plus two manner—as well, at least, as other accepted alliterative long-lines, rhymed or unrhymed. To what purpose, then, are they inserted here—after so many wearisome quotations? For an important comparison. Stanzas like the following can not possibly be read in the two plus two manner, even by metrical gymnasts; and still more could not possibly have been intended by the author to be so read, discounting his deafness and blindness and his metrical craftsmanship all you please.

Yif the prest unworthele   presume to syng his mas,
Serus, y say the sacrement   enpayrd hit may not be,
Bot hes owne deth and his dome   he ressayns [ressayus] alas!
Yif in his consians he knaw   that he be gulte;
Thagh he syng and say no [sic] mas,   the prest, unwothele [sic].

[58] A "Vicar", not a vicarage!

Both your maret and your mede   in heven ye schul have,
Fore God hath grauntyd of his grace   be his auctorete,
Be he never so synful   youre soulys may he save—
Have this in thoght;
The masse is of so hye degre,
Apayryd forsoth hit mai not be,
Ne no mon mend it may,
Theron doctours han sought.   (p. 44)

Suffice it to emphasize their metrical character by reproducing four lines:

Though he sing and say his mass,   the priest, unworthily,
Both your merit and your meed   in heaven ye shall have,
For God hath granted of his grace   by his authority,
Be he nev-er so sinful   your souls he yet may save.

These lines practically bring us round to our starting point. Stanzas in which such lines dominate the movement, while still being intermingled with the more syncopated lines (so that there can be no question of *two* distinct *metrical* forms for *different* stanzas of *one* distinct *stanzaic* form)—such stanzas are so numerous, so indisputable, I say, in their stress-intent, that I might have made them the basis of my presentation quite as well as the *Gamelyn* verses, except that initially I should have had to embarrass my case by attending to a metrical fact that has so often been misconstrued in accounts of ME, OHG, and MHG versification: the alternation of stress and non-stress is in the verses of Audelay more regular than in the *Gamelyn*, and is due presumably to his monkish practices in singing Latin verses,[34] and from his piety we can conjecture he sang them very often.[35]

And one final appeal. As between the two plus two scansion of the scholar's comfortable study and the outlawed

[34] See my *op. cit.*, p. 141–2.

[35] The reader will find in Wuelfing, *op. cit.*, p. 213, one of these stanzas of Audelay with the scansion marked. It happens to be a stanza I had previously carefully scanned myself, and I was naturally pleased to find our metrical reading identical; except that Wuelfing has omitted a stress (a misprint?) on the first word of the first line,

An a byrchyn bonke   ther boues arne bryght,

and has not attempted to differentiate on paper between primary and secondary stresses. He comments on the well-preserved character in the

four plus three, can there be any doubt as to which communicates the stirring qualities of this battle paean of Minot?[26]

Skottes out of Berwik   and of Abirdene,
At the Bannok burn   war ye to kene;
Thare slogh ye many sakles   als it was sene,
And now has King Edward   wroken it, I wene.
It es wroken, I wene,   wele wurth the while;
War yit with the Skottes,   for thai er ful of gile.

Whare er ye, Skottes   of Saint Johnes toune?
The boste of yowre baner   es betin all doune;
When ye bosting will bede,   Sir Edward es boune
For to kindel yow care   and crak yowre crowne.
He has crakked yowre croune,   wele worth the while;
Shame bityde the Skottes,   for thai er full of gile.

And isn't my metrical reproduction, after all, an impertinence:

Scotchmen out of Berwick,   Scots of Aberdeen,
At the burn Bannock,   ye were all too keen;
There slew ye many guiltless,   as was lately seen,
And now the King, our Edward,   hath venge-ed it, I ween.
It is veng-ed, I ween, O,   wel worth the while;
Ware ye of the Scotchmen,   for they are full of guile.

Where are ye, Scotchmen,   of Saint John's town?
The boast of your ban-ner   is beaten all down;
When ye boast-ing will bid, O,   Sir Edward is boun[d]
For to kind-le you care, O,   and crack.... your.... crown.
He has crack-ed your crown, O,   wel worth the while;
Shame betide the Scotchmen,   for they are full of guile.

The insistent lilt of each (variant) refrain should put the scansion out of doubt, though nothing else should. Or, if you say it is of course out of doubt—has with you never been in doubt—then, must come once more the damned itera-

whole poem of *die alte stabzeile.* Compare for late alliterative stanzas very similar in metrical details to Audelay's, where, too, the old form is used for religious matter, *Of Sayne John the Evaungelist*, poem XIV (19 stanzas) of William of Nassington (quondam advocati juris Eboraci), in *Religious Pieces.* Ed. George G. Perry, EETS.

[26] I quote but two of the six stanzas. See Emerson's *Middle English Reader*, revised edition, p. 160. The mid-line spacing is mine (as in other edited texts quoted in this section).

tion: "It differeth not from the rest." So the rest must be out of doubt, too.[36a]

VI

Such simple laboratory tests as those recorded in this paper—and the laboratory is a better analogy than the examination-room implied in section III—are, it seems to me, quite as clear proof of metrical identity as would be elaborate tabulations of speech-stresses, cadence-types, phrasal groups, etc. By which I don't mean, however, that such tabulations would be difficult in the making or superfluous for the proving. And for those still skeptical of my method as either trivial or unscientific or unsanctioned by academic tradition, I suggest (without bitterness or irony!), for example, a comprehensive tabulation comparing the speech-material of all second half-lines (902) from *Gamelyn*, or any other poem acknowledged to be scanned four plus three, with an equal number of second half-lines from any poem or poems supposed to be scanned two plus two. I jot down here a few of the possible types (with illustrations) from my own incomplete notes. The thorough investigator (whose harbinger I hope I am) will be able doubtless to collate many parallels still more correspondent in speech-details than some that follow.

1) Verbal identity.

Soth forto telle (G 691)
Sothe forto telle (WP 34, 303)

If one pronounces *sothe* as a dissyllable, the greater shortening is still in G,—contrary to expectations. Incidentally,

[36a] Once when I read this poem of Minot's aloud, a friend remarked (as others had remarked of my reading *Beowulf* aloud): "Why, that's Vachel Lindsay." "Yes," I replied: "but rather say, Vachel Lindsay's *that*." As he goes so sturdily up and down this new continent, banging out so resonantly his modern verses on Booth, the Chinese Laundryman, and the American negro—

"Then I saw the Congo, creeping through the black,
Cutting through the jungle with a golden track"—

this Illinois Gleeman is unwittingly reviving the ancestral metrics with something, I think, of the ancestral manner of delivery. My friend Lindsay may not thank me for this comparison: but I feel bound to thank him.

the phrase *sothely to say*, in various spellings, occurs and recurs in second half-lines of (supposed two plus two stress) unrhymed alliterative verse; and is to be compared with its occurrence in the (three-stress) end-verses of the *Avowynge* stanzas and of the tag-stanzas in poems associated with the *Avowynge* type (as in *Golagros and Gawane*, the *Pistell of Swete Susanne*)—the (four plus three) scansion of which has been settled by Buelbring, see p. 62.

2) Verbal similarity.

> withouten eny greeve (G 313)
> withoute ani faile (WP 316)

This type is perhaps not always distinguishable from

3) Similarities of syntactical groups, with its innumerable subdivisions (depending upon the analytic acumen, the patience, or the pedantry of the tabulator), for example,

a) Noun pair (here with possessives besides).

> his lond and his leede (G 71)
> thi menske and thi grace (WP 314)

b) Prepositional phrase pair.

> for hate and for ire (G 698)
> for kare and for drede (WP 288)
> in rigt and in skille (WP 336)

c) Prepositional phrase with noun-modifier.

> under woode-shawes (G 696)
> by this wodes side (WP 240)

(Note that each is a locative construction too.)

d) Prepositional phrase with noun-modifier corresponding to adjective modifier.

> agein the kinges pees (G 548)
> agene the hote sunne (WP 12)

e) Prepositional phrase with demonstrative and adjective.

> to that goode knight (G 729)
> of this semly childe (WP 298)

f) Adjective with dependent genitive.

the béste òf us alle (G 737)
thou gréttèst of alle (WP 312)

g) Dependent clauses (here discriminating subdivisions of subdivisions might be devised during many happy months).

tho I his rigge brak (G 712)
as yif it were hire owne (WP 99)

h) Infinitive groups (here also are infinite opportunities for the profession).

to hele his rigge-boon (G 614)
to listen ani more (WP 162)

i) Second halves of compound sentences (ditto).

and answerde nought (G 473)
and his criyinge stint (WP 61)

(Here the parallelism in the medial secondary stresses of the half-line should be noted too.)

Many second half-lines, of verbal or syntactical similarity, might be grouped, by another principle of division, under

4) Similarities of stock-phrases (*second* half-lines of course offer more temptation to padding).

as he wel couthe (G 164)
as he wel migt (WP 247)

I swere by Cristes ore (G 139)
on Godis holy name (WP 306)

as it mighte falle (G 16)
as that God wold (WP 215)

But whatever the classification, it is plain that phrasings like the above examples represent fairly fixed speech-material, not normally amenable to such radically different manipulation in discourse as required for these hypothetically radically different versifications. Aside from the two extremes,—exact identities among the groups, and a generalized collation like (g),—not only *similar* stock-phrases, but *similar* common syntactical groups acquire in any language *one generalized stress-mode*,[37] subject to the variations of pitch and tempo, but only under exceptional circumstances of emotional or logical emphasis subject to any such violation of the *generalized* cadence as is *consistently* demanded if these second half-lines of *Gamelyn* are three-stressers and these second half-lines of *William of Palerne* are two-stressers. The evidence in its full force would be cumulative, of course. Now and then one may remark in modern verse such speech-material treated in two different poems (or indeed within one poem) in two different metrical manners: one may remark the same in ME.[37a] It would be interesting to search Chaucer for parallels in Chaucer's accepted versification to *Gamelyn* second half-lines that depart from the accepted *Gamelyn* movement. They are there. The result would be one illustration of many of the differences between Chaucer's so-called French system of versification and the Old Germanic system; and of the subtle changes in English phrase and sentence cadences that this versification perhaps tended to create as well as to be created by. But it would be too fragmentary and casual to prove that *Gamelyn* was scanned like Chaucer, or Chaucer like *Gamelyn*, even were all other evidence in accord. Moreover, it could not depend upon that rigidly indicated structural delimitation which gives to such parallels in speech-material between *Gamelyn* and WP perhaps after all their greatest significance as indicating parallelism of metrics: the parallel speech-materials of the two latter are all in the same verse-position, all in the second half-line.

A last word: we know Chaucer's "French" system; we know the "Germanic" system of these many anonymous writers in the *Gamelyn–Niebelungen* couplets; the putative two plus two system of WP, PP, etc., has never been identified with anything of Chaucer's in four stresses, and it is admittedly Germanic too. Hence, we have as contemporaries

[37] Otherwise there'd be no learning to *speak* a foreign language.
[37a] See above, p. 71.

not only three systems of versification (three *systems*, not merely three metres), but the two Germanic representatives among these systems in some principles of speech and of metrics the two most widely separated. We have, for instance, in the *Gamelyn* type the crowding of stress upon stress with still one resultant, easily distinguishable *measure;* we have in Chaucer the alternation of stress and non-stress (his Germanic exceptions aside), with one distinguishable *measure;* and we have in WP or PP sometimes a crowding of stress upon stress, but more often huge irregular gulfs (gulps) between stresses, and only sporadically—a line here, a line there—anything that approaches *measure* at all. Crede quia absurdum.

VII

The only objection to the seven-accent reading that need give us pause is the contrary testimony of a well-known and respected contemporary, which indeed for some scholars is of itself decisive. In Chapter III of the *Revlis and Cavtelis of Scottis Poesie*[88] no less a personage than James I expounds as follows:

Let all zour verse be *Literall*, sa far as may be, quhatsumeuer kynde they be of, bot speciallie *Tumbling* verse for flyting. Be *Literall* I meane, that the maist pairt of zour lyne, sall rynne vpon a letter, as this tumbling lyne rynnis vpon F.

Fetching fude for to feid it fast furth of the Farie.

Ze man obserue that thir *Tumbling* verse flowis not on that fassoun, as vtheris dois. For all vtheris keipis the reule quhilk I gaue before. To wit, the first fute short the secound lang, and sa furth. Quhair as thir hes twa short and ane lang throuch all the lyne, quhen they keip ordour: albeit the maist pairt of thame be out of ordour, and keipis na kynde nor reule of *Flowing*, and for that cause are callit *Tumbling* verse: except the short lynis of aucht in the hinder end of the verse, the quhilk flowis as vther verses dois, as ze will find in the hinder end of this buke, quhair I gaue exemple of sindrie kyndis of versis.

---

[88] Arber's *English Reprints*, no. 8.

The customary summary method of disposing of these disconcerting paragraphs won't suffice. We read in Kaluza's *Englische Metrik*:[39]

Dass die aus dem Ende des 16. Jahrhunderts stammenden Aeusserungen Gascoignes und Koenig Jacobs I. fuer unsere Auffassung des Alliterationsverses des vierzehnten Jahrhunderts nicht weiter in Betracht kommen koennen, haben schon Trautmann (*Anglia* 18, 94f.) und Kuhnke (*Die alliterierende Langzeile in der mittelenglischen Romanze Sir Gawayn and the Green Knight*, Berlin 1900, S. 8ff.) zur Genuege auseinandergesetzt, und wenn Luick (*Anglia Beiblatt* 12, 35f.) trotzdem ueber diese "Zeugnisse des 16. Jahrhunderts nicht hinwegkommen" kann, so muesste er auch dem 'Zeugnis' Drydens (Vorwort zu den *Fables*) von der Mangelhaftigkeit des Chaucerschen Versbaues trotz der von uns inzwischen gewonnenen besseren Kenntnis Glauben schenken.

But Kaluza, keen thinker on metrics though he be, has himself unwittingly indicated later in the same volume[40] why this method won't suffice:

Die meisten der in § 156 erwaehnten in reimlosen Alliterationsversen oder in der dreizehnzeiligen Alliterationsstrophe abgefassten Dichtungen fallen wohl erst in unsere Periode, in das Ende des 14. oder in das 15. Jahrhundert; die beiden in der Percyhandschrift enthaltenen alliterierenden Gedichte *Death and Liffe* und *Scottish Feilde* (Schlacht auf dem Flodden Field 1513) und Dunbars *The Twa Marriit Wemen and the Wedo* gehoeren sogar erst in den Anfang des 16. Jahrhunderts. Der rhythmische Bau des Alliterationverses ist aber in diesen juengeren Gedichten genau derselbe wie in den aelteren; vgl. Adolf Schneider, *Die mittelenglische Stabzeile im 15. und 16. Jahrhundert (Bonner Beitr.* 12, 103–172).

Indeed, from Chapter VIII, the hinder end of this same Book of Cautions, Kaluza might have noted James' own sample alliterative stanza (cited as suited "for flyting, or Invectives"), explicitly named "Tumbling verse", in which the rhythmical structure is likewise "genau derselbe wie in den aelteren". No. It is plain there is something here that still needs disposing of.

But I must admit my own method of disposing of it will seem at first still more summary: I believe, as a good democrat,

[39] P. 185; see too Anmerkung, p. 30.
[40] P. 256.

that the royal expounder didn't know what he was talking about. I believe this literary protagonist of the Divine Right of Kings, this author of the *Demonology*, and of the *Counter-blast to Tobacco* was as ill a judge of poetic numbers as he was of politics, of witches, and of that blessed Indian weed without whose kindly assistance this monograph could scarcely be nearing completion.

In the first place, he makes two mistakes that all will at once recognize as mistakes. His *sample* of what "*Litteral*" means in a "tumbling lyne", shows how little he understood the principles of alliterative verse,—according to which, even in the over-ingenuities of later versifiers in the mode, "the maist pairt" did *not* run upon one letter in this mechanical and rhythmically meaningless fashion, but continued to follow, to a surprising degree, the traditional norm, as in the line below from *Scottish Field*[41] about "Henery, the Seaventh",

How he *m*oved in at *M*ilford, with *m*en but a fewe.

In general, their characteristic departures from tradition added but one more alliteration, sometimes in the first, sometimes in the second half-line: it was no part of their characteristic technique to hunt the letter after the simpering and mincing manner of the Euphuists or—the Stuart muse. Likewise, his distinction between the tumbling verse of the long-lines in the stanza, and "the short lynes of aucht in the hinder end of the verse, the quhilk flowis as uther verses dois" (a muddling use of "verse" both for a line and for a line-group) shows how little he understood the structural relations between the two major formal parts of an alliterative stanza. It would possibly be found that "the hinder part", the four short rhymed lines—perhaps, because they *are* short and run usually on three identical rhymes plus a tag-rhyme—do tend to greater metrical regularity, i. e., more uniformity of alternation of stress and non-stress "as uther verses dois",

[41] Quoted from that excellent study of Adolph Schneider's, *Die mittelenglische Stabzeile im 15. und 16. Jahrhundert. Bonner Beitraege*, 12. Schneider reads ME and Early MdE alliterative lines with seven stresses.

and as they dois in James' own example in Chapter VIII. I think this indeed probable for later alliterative verse. But even a very casual reading—a page here, a page there—shows they shared, as a *type*, from the earliest to the latest, the "tumbling" character of the long-lines, that precede them,—being, as we have perhaps seen, structurally related to the long lines as a rhymed triplet of first half-lines tailed by an end-verse of second half-line pattern—this even on a two plus two theory (Luick).

In the second place, his analysis of the two plus two scansion (though he says nothing about number of stresses, it may be assumed he has a four-stress scansion in mind), this "twa short and ane lang throuch all the lyne", is very questionable—even "quhen they keip ordour". Aside from that misuse of "long and short" as metrical terms in English, which has wrought confusion in metrical theory from Tudor times to our own, I may demur that it would be hard to collect from ME or Early MdE alliterative verse, or from James' sample stanza itself, enough cases of lines "flowing" with two unstressed plus a stressed syllable to justify making four regular "anapests" even the *theoretic* norm of the orthodox scansion. The most one could say would be that this scansion suggests now and then a tendency to "anapestic" movement.

Thus, with our witness already discredited as an ill-informed and inaccurate expositor of his own theory, we may with the more grace dare to discredit the theory itself of his Majesty—who, if he didn't start this metrical war, has by his despotic attitude and by his sundry atrocities contributed to render it so long and so bitter. I discredit his testimony as that of one who, like many who pin their faith to him, had no understanding of *secondary* stresses in metrics. That is really the whole story. From his own sample alliterative stanza take the first line,

In the hinder end of haruest upon Alhallow eue.

Here a secondary stress on *end, -est, al-* appears to have passed unnoticed in its *time-marking* function because less noticeable in its *stress* function. In line 6,

Some hotche and on a hemp stalk, hovand on a heicht,

the same is apparently true for *on, stalk, on*. Let the reader examine the whole stanza with this eventuality in mind. Yes, but James himself describes how the verses actually sounded, with a term, too, not of his own invention: "This kynde of verse . . . . callit Rouncefallis, or Tumbling verse". The description, however, fits the seven-accent scansion as well as the four: both, with reference to that rigidly monotonous monopodic "iambic" step of the early Tudor Renaissance verse, may be said to "tumble".[42]

This neglect of the time-marking function of secondary stresses—with a subsequent misinterpretation of the "flowing"—is a crime often committed by later and better metrists than James, and should make us more ready both to admit and to pardon that crime in him. I still recall with pain the confusion that once ruined an informal dinner-party of a dozen professors of English by my following up the recitation of this bit of Calverley's *Ode to Tobacco* with an exposition of its metrical niceties:

How they who use fusees
All grow by slow degrees
Brainless as chimpanzees,
Meagre as lizards;
Go mad and beat their wives;
Plunge (after shocking lives)
Razors and carving-knives
Into their gizzards.

The point made was that the triplet verses were of four, the intermediate of three stresses,[43] a definite secondary stress recurring with horrible solemnity immediately after the initial syllable (with its strong primary stress) of each line; and that the movement (consciously or unconsciously devised)

---

[42] But "tumbling verse", as a modern *terminus technicus*, belongs strictly to a (normally) four-stress line—Knittelvers in German—related to, but not identical with, the old alliterative line. It would take me away from the present enterprise to discuss it.

[43] Of course, not according to the metrical technique of the ME stanza in triplets and end-verses.

was to be distinguished from the three stress line with initial "dactyl" with which it was always identified,—*e. g.*, to be distinguished from a movement like this:

BROWNIES OR BEETLES?

Merrily all the day
Utterly lost in play
Under the bush and spray
Hidden from peepers,
Safe on their leafy shelves,
Scamper the ancient elves—
Called by our sapient selves
Wrigglers and creepers.

The distinction was pronounced "pedantic"; and the distinguisher left the chamber groggy and disconsolate and alone—save that one wiser colleague[44] and wisest Apollo and the Comic Muse were at his side. The same perversity seems to obsess some modern theorists when they analyze the French Alexandrine, illustrating, again, that contemporary testimony does not necessarily spell finality. Lewis in *The Foreign Sources of Modern English Versification*[45] quotes

C'est pour lui que l'on tremble; et c'est moi que l'on craint

as having its rhythmical parallel in

For the angel of Death spread his wings on the blast.

My Breton friend Dondo, in an unusually intelligent paper, *Vers Libre*,[46] scans

Je viens selon l'usage antique et solennel

with four stresses, by marking the four primary stresses and neglecting the secondary stresses on *-on* in the first half and on *sol-* in the second, which are surely there as Bernhard or Coquelin—or, I surmise, as Dondo himself—would read the

[44] Who happens to be a specialist in Modern English versification.
[45] *Yale Studies in English*, I, p. 66.
[46] PMLA, vol. XXXIV, no. 2, p. 195.

line; just as they are there in the second line of this couplet of Hugo's,[47]

> Carnage affreux! moment fatal! l'homme inquiet
> Sentit que la bataille entre ses mains pliait,

on *la* and *en-*, supporting the indisputable six primary stresses of the first line. The six-fold rhythmical complex of the French Alexandrine is as certain and as implicated with secondary stresses as is the sevenfold rhythmical complex of the ME long-line. But, as I have already involved myself in an academic unpleasantness with the Anglists and the Germanists, it is the part of discretion to leave my colleagues in the Romance languages to settle their own troubles.[48]

---

[47] *Les Châtiments, L'Expiation*, 99—100.

[48] The second verse of Hugo's couplet seems to represent the average numerical proportion of primary and secondary stresses in an Alexandrine. An examination of all the poems composed wholly or in part of Alexandrines in Passy-Rambeau's *Chrestomathie* where the *speech-stresses* are indicated by *caractères gras* shows an enormous preponderance of four, though three, five, and six occur. In English blank-verse the average proportion would be presumably three to two. But the four primaries (speech-stresses) as little eliminate the two secondaries (additional metrical stresses, often very delicately impressed, mere allusive hints of rhythm) in the Alexandrine, as the three primaries eliminate the two (though usually less allusively defined) secondaries of our own blank-verse. Most French Alexandrines can be read as four-stress verse; even as all can be read—by some modern Frenchmen are designedly read—practically as prose: but they are then not what *l'art poétique* long before Boileau and long after has meant by Alexandrines. But the English ear, particularly,—lacking the subtility of the French ear in catching secondary stresses, or brutally distorting them to totally un-French primaries,—is responsible for the English dislike of this beautiful measure (so delicately responsive both to intellectual and to emotional nuances) called by Byron

> That whetstone of the teeth—monotony in wire,—

a stupid remark, even in his specific application to the period of Boileau.

In reading Verhaeren's Alexandrines I have observed, however, that I tend to give even to secondary stresses an almost Germanic beat. Cf. the comment of Ludwig Lewisohn (in the study prefatory to his admirable translations, *The Poets of Modern France*, p. 31) on the poem, in *vers libre*,

> Je suis le fils de cette race:

"One feels in such verses almost the march and accent of Germanic versification". Is it in truth the *accent* of his Germanic temperament and blood? Or an intrusion of Lewisohn's and my Germanic speech—and verse-habits? But why, then, should they intrude in reading Verhaeren and not in reading Racine, Lamartine, Musset, or Rostand? A question which reminds us, again, how profoundly implicated with rhythmical form may be the individuation of man and his literary output.

THE SOURCES OF MILTON'S *HISTORY OF BRITAIN*[1]

HARRY GLICKSMAN

Milton's sources for his *History of Britain* were of two principal kinds. There were, first, those general compilations, written during or near his own time, in which the authorities for early English history were presented to him in an intermediate manner, and only after free handling by their interpreters. Secondly, there were those mediæval sources which, sometimes in a strict, and at other times in a more liberal sense may be called original.

Milton consulted works of the former class when he encountered a period for which a large number of separate authorities offered distinct contributions. He discovered, for example, that after the retirement of Agricola and until the fall of Rome, he would be obliged to piece together a structure of fact derived from a bewildering array of authors—among them Eutropius, Dion, Spartianus, Capitolinus, Eumenius, Zosimus, Ammianus Marcellinus, and Victor Aurelius.[2] With that prospect, he turned to the exhaustive *De Primordiis* of Usher,[3] published in 1639, which had, for several years before its appearance, been eagerly awaited by antiquarian

---

[1] *The History of Britain, That part especially now call'd England.* From the first Traditional Beginning, continu'd to the Norman Conquest. Collected out of the antientest and best Authours thereof by John Milton. London, Printed by J. M. for James Allestry, at the Rose and Crown in St Paul's Church-Yard, MDCLXX.

For helpful advice and suggestive material I acknowledge my indebtedness to Professor Albert S. Cook, of Yale University, under whose supervision I made a special study of the *History of Britain* during the academic year 1917–18.

[2] See pp. 219 ff. Throughout this article, a page citation is to be regarded, in the absence of other data, as a reference to Milton's *History of Britain* in Vol. V of the Bohn edition of the Prose Works.

[3] James Usher (or Ussher), Archbishop of Armagh (1581–1656). The work is known both as *Britannicarum Ecclesiarum Antiquitates* and as *De Britannicarum Ecclesiarum Primordiis*.

scholars. For its ecclesiastical data Milton had little regard, but mingled with these he would find material of a political character that could readily serve his ends. The treatise on the Roman occupation in Camden's *Britannia* was another valuable work; and in two instances Milton renders it plain, by marginal references, that only through Camden's conspectus has he found his way to the original sources.[4] For this period, also, he must have summoned the help of the painstaking Speed, who, with his abundant citations, doubtless recalled the days of the *Commonplace Book;* the elaborate description of British manners and customs in the Second Book, for instance, shows resemblance, in many features, to a chapter on the same subject in Speed's work.[5] The use of a conspectus is likewise indicated in the Third Book, especially for the period dealing with the Britons' resistance to the Teutonic invaders. Here one meets the names of Paulus Diaconus, Blondus, Sabellicus, Constantius, Sigonius, Widukind, and Sigebert,[6] each of whom makes a relatively insignificant contribution; and the direct marginal references to Usher's work[7] enhance the probability that it was employed as a *vade mecum.* It was largely to Usher, though in part also to Camden and Speed, that Milton seems to have owed his knowledge of the early British chronicler Nennius, whose *Historia,* which did not appear in print until 1691, he used freely.[8] The digests of modern writers were resorted to, moreover, for the legendary material, which Milton examined with sceptical scrutiny. He called Holinshed into service

[4] Pp. 227–9.

[5] Pp. 197–8; see also Speed, *History Great Brit.*, ed. 1627, pp. 166 ff.

[6] Pp. 241 ff.

[7] Pp. 245, 251, 256.

[8] The following letter from Usher to Sir Simonds D'Ewes is contained in Parr, *Life and Letters of James Usher* (p. 506).

Quo tempore & Ninium, (ità enim appello, & vetustissimi codicis authoritatem, & nominis ejusdem in Ninia, & Niniano expressa vestigia, secutus) cum variis MSS. à me nòn indiligentèr comparatum, tecum sum communicaturus; ut Exemplaria Cottoniana (quibus in hac ipsâ collatione ego sum usus) denuò consulete necesse nòn habeas. Nàm ad diplomata Anglo-Saxonica quod attinet: non in uno aliquo volumine simul collecta, sed per varios illius Bibliothecæ libros dispersa ea fuisse animadverti, de quibus in unum corpus compingendis, dabitur (ut spero) opportunus tecum

at an early point,[9] and there is clear evidence that he consulted Stow in recounting the adventures of Ebranc and Brutus.[10] It may be safely assumed, indeed, that Milton, throughout the work, bore in mind the plan and the treatment of Holinshed, of Stow, and of Speed, who were generously represented in the *Commonplace Book*.[11] To them, notably Speed, he could revert at any time to learn what sources were likely to provide the most reliable information, and the widest range of it, for a given period.

The foregoing suggests an important fact. Milton's employment of the works of modern compilers never enslaved him. He is always to be conceived as dividing his attention—or as instructing his readers and amanuenses to divide theirs—between the conspectus on the one hand, and the original authority on the other. He has Holinshed, Stow, and Speed at his elbow while he composes the First Book, but he knows that Geoffrey, for a half-historical and half-poetical purpose like that at hand, is the best of the mediæval chroniclers. He

---

coram consultandi locus; Interim ut egregiis tuis conatibus Deus adsit & benedicat, summis votis exoptat qui

Londini, xii Kal. Jul. Ex animo tuus est,
An M. D C. X L. *Ja. Armachanus.*

Cf. Nennius, ed. Stevenson, pp. xix–xx. On Usher's interest in early English history, see Adams, *Old English Scholarship*, p. 115.

[9] P. 167.

[10] Pp. 174–5; see also Stow, *Annales*, ed. 1631, p. 9.

[11] For a discussion of this topic, see Charles H. Firth, *Milton as an Historian, Proceedings of the British Academy for 1907–8.*

Fueter (*Geschichte der neueren Historiographie*, p. 166) implies that Firth's treatment is inadequate, since the latter compares Milton with only these three chroniclers. Fueter's criticism is unjust. Holinshed, Stow, and Speed were, as Firth shows, the modern English historians whom Milton had read with special attention; there is hence a special interest in comparing him with them.

On Milton's relatively sceptical and scientific attitude toward the legendary material, see Firth, pp. 233–6. Of special interest is his comment on the handling of the Arthurian story:

"Milton's treatment of the Arthurian legend is a still more interesting example of the progress of scepticism. The three chroniclers who were the standard historians of Milton's time all doubted the details of the legend, but believed that Arthur was a real king who gained genuine victories. 'Of this Arthur,' says Holinshed's *Chronicle*, 'many things are written beyond credit, for that there is no ancient author of authority that confirmeth the same; but surely as may be thought he was some worthy

consequently follows him page by page. When, in the Second Book, he takes up the *De Primordiis* of Usher, he does not limit himself to the scope of that history. Usher's scrupulous respect for ecclesiastical records would persuade Milton to pay him no more than a grudging heed. He therefore makes examination, on his own account, of Ammianus Marcellinus and Dion, of Zosimus and Orosius.[12] The employment of Usher's volume in the Third Book, in like manner, cannot preclude him from consulting Malmesbury, Huntingdon, Bede, and Gildas, with all of whom he has independent acquaintance, relying upon them, in fact, in other parts of his history.[13]

man, and by all likelihood a great enemy to the Saxons, by reason whereof the Welshmen, which are the very Britons indeed, have him in famous remembrance.' Then at great length he relates the legendary life and exploits of the hero (Holinshed, *Chronicles*, ed. 1587, bk. 1, pp. 90—3).

"Stow is briefer, but adopts much the same position. 'Of this Arthur there be many fabulous reports, but certain he was (saith William of Malmesbury) a prince more worthy to have advancement by true histories than false fables, being the only prop and upholder of his country.' He supports the truth of the story by identifying the sites of Mon Badonicus and the Castle of Camelot, and describing the remains found there (Stow, *Chronicle*, ed. 1631, pp. 53—5). The critical Speed quotes Malmesbury too, and condemns Geoffrey of Monmouth for discrediting the truth about Arthur by his toys and tales. 'Of his person,' he concludes, 'we make no doubt, though his acts have been written with too lavish a pen' (Speed, *History of Great Britain*, ed. 1632, p. 271).

"Milton is much more thoroughgoing. All that happened about that time is doubtful. 'The age whereof we now write hath had the ill hap more than any since the first fabulous times, to be surcharged with all the idle fancies of posterity.' He introduces Arthur by describing him as a British leader, 'more renowned in songs and romances than true stories.' With real insight he dismisses at once the mediæval fictions and examines the account of Nennius as the only evidence of any real value."

Firth's article, which contains an elaborate treatment of sources, discusses the relation of the *History* to certain additional fields of interest—to Milton's biography and personality, his thought and scholarship; to the literary and philosophical influences which operated upon the composition and content of the work; and to the political and ecclesiastical environment of Milton's age.

With respect to the sources, the present article, which includes some of Firth's material, aims to supplement his treatment by discussing (1) the comparative attention which Milton gave to his several authorities, and the relative degrees in which he employed modern compilations and original sources; (2) the extent to which he put himself in touch with the accessible authorities; (3) the relation of the *History* to Wheloc's Anglo-Saxon scholarship; (4) the use of chronological data; and, especially, (5) Milton's art as a translator from Latin into English.

[12] Pp. 223, 229, 233.

[13] Pp. 250 ff.

Milton's tendency, in a word, is not to put his trust in other men's research, nor to view the original sources through the medium of digests and synopses; it is rather to make these cumulative writings serve the ultimate authorities as supplements and aids. In this fashion he uses Higden's *Polychronicon,* Spelman's *Concilia,* and Calvisius' *Opus Chronologicum.*[14] His impatience with tradition and precedent is typical of his character. He aims, accordingly, to depend as little as possible on those intermediate and superfluous steps which intervene between himself and the original, and he ignores them wherever he reasonably can. There are, it is true, cases in which he is practically compelled to consult modern historical specialists, but here he manifests similar intolerance. He feels bound, for instance, to recognize in Camden the most authoritative English geographer of his age, and he consequently cites the *Britannia* whenever questions of topography arise.[15] But he takes pains to notify his readers that he finds it distasteful and beside the purpose "to wrinkle the smoothness of history with rugged names of places unknown, better harped at in Camden and other chorographers."[16] For occasional bits of Scottish history, or for points of contact between the English annals and the Scottish, he turns to Buchanan's *Rerum Scoticarum Historia,* but the fanciful accounts of that uncritical historian, whom he taxes with paraphrasing "the fables of his predecessor Boethius," invariably repel him.[17] It is curious, in the light of this unmitigated censure, that he distinguishes Buchanan with any mention whatever. The circumstance is probably to be explained by his conscientious and scholarly resolve to gather the accessible data, those both of higher and of lower merit, for his readers' individual inspection, and partly, it is feared, by the irrepressible desire to display his contempt for Scottish historical writing. Even more surprising is his use of the Dutch-Danish Pontanus, from whose *Rerum Dani-*

[14] Pp. 213, 259, 273, 308.

[15] *E. g.,* pp. 188, 255, 266, 274, 297, 319, 328, 362, 383.

[16] P. 299.

[17] Pp. 242, 261, 305, 331.

carum Historia he strives, with frail success, to develop a harmonious statement of the Scandinavian ravages.[18] There is here, also, a strong intimation that Milton, in spite of his stern judgment on the writer, regarded it as too radical and arbitrary to overlook him altogether. Though he "contributes nothing,"[19] it is the part of wisdom and sound scholarship to record that he has been searched.

Milton's usual practice, however, is to take his material from the early authorities. He attempts to discover the "ancientest author,"[20] and this done, he addresses himself to the task of determining in what manner his successors have supplemented or repudiated him. He shows his discrimination at the very outset. He knows that behind Geoffrey lie the fables of Nennius;[21] he is also aware that Geoffrey's account is presented, in substance, by the later Matthew of Westminster.[22] Yet in the version of Geoffrey, whom he declares to be "the principal author,"[23] he sees the most promising fund for the treatment of the centuries preceding Cæsar's invasion. Since he knows little or nothing of the more recent science of ethnology, since the terms Celtic, Gælic, and Cymric cannot signify to him what they do to subsequent scholars, he must rest content with the most intelligible and consistent exposition of the old fables and half-truths that he can find. Though he condemns Geoffrey for his simplicity,[24] there is the conviction that he, of all the earlier writers, will offer the best material. Varying the narrative with references to Cæsar, Mela, Nennius, Virunnius, Gildas, and Florus;[25] with borrowings, as indicated above, from modern English commentators; and with one quotation, by

---

[18] Pp. 301, 309, 317–8, 347.

[19] P. 347.

[20] See mention of Bede on p. 221.

[21] See p. 167.

[22] See Gross, *Sources and Lit. Eng. Hist.*, p. 362.

[23] P. 168.

[24] Pp. 220–1, 243.

[25] Pp. 165, 166, 167, 171, 179, 180. The reference to Florus seems traceable to Camden. Milton's passage reads (p. 180): "Thus much is more generally believed, that both this Brennus, and another famous captain, Britomarus, whom the epitomist Florus and others mention, were not Gauls, but Britains; the name of the first in that tongue signifying a

way of tribute, from the verses of his admired Spenser,[26] he clings to Geoffrey's story through the whole of the First Book. In no other part of the *History* does he employ a source so freely for the same number of consecutive pages.[27]

When Milton reaches the Second Book, he has his first opportunity to make known what he really believes about the use of historical authorities. He is now within grasp of authentic records; he pauses to reflect that "great acts and great eloquence have most commonly gone hand in hand";[28] and he forthwith devotes himself to what he calls the "transcription" of the Roman writers. The works of historians of the sixteenth and seventeenth centuries might have supplied him with a large proportion of the data affecting the period from Cæsar's first invasion to the end of Agricola's governorship; but the scruples of the true scholar direct him to ascertain whether "aught by diligence may be added or omitted, or by other disposing may be more explained or more expressed."[29] For Cæsar's British campaigns he follows the *De Bello Gallico* faithfully, though with ample regard for English idiom,[30] using Suetonius, Cicero, Valerius Maximus, Plutarch, Dion, Pliny, and Bede for only supplementary and confirmatory minutiæ.[31] Recognizing that the first century after Christ is known mainly through Dion's *Historia,* and through the *Annales* and the *Vita Agricolæ* of Tacitus,[32] he

king, and of the other a great Britain." Cf. *Britannia,* ed. Gough, I. lxxii–iii: "And some think they can easily prove king Brennus, so famous in Greek and Latin historians, to have been a Britan. Thus much I know, that this name is not yet worn out among the Britans, who call a king in their language *Brennin.* The name shews *Britomarus,* general among them mentioned by Florus and Appian, to have been a Britan, his name importing *Great Briton.*"

[26] P. 175. The verses are found in *F. Q.* 2. 10. 24.

[27] Specimens of Milton's translation of Geoffrey's text, with the Latin in parallel columns, are found below, pp. 125–9.

[28] P. 185.

[29] P. 186.

[30] See, for example, below, p. 130.

[31] Pp. 186, 188, 189, 192, 195, 196.

[32] The following is of interest as an illustration of Milton's close but idiomatic rendering of Tacitus:

Britannorum acies in speciem simul ac terrorem editioribus locis constiterat ita, ut primum agmen in æquo, ceteri per adclive iugum	The British powers on the hill side, as might best serve for show and terror, stood in their battalions; the first on even ground, the next

conexi velut insurgerent; media campi covinnarius eques strepitu ac discursu complebat. tum Agricola superante hostium multitudine veritus, ne in frontem simul et latera suorum pugnaretur, diductis ordinibus, quamquam porrectior acies futura erat et arcessendas plerique legiones admonebant, promptior in spem et firmus adversis, dimisso equo pedes ante vexilla constitit (*Vit. Agric.*, ed. Furneaux, pp. 142–3).

rising behind, as the hill ascended. The field between rung with the noise of horsemen and chariots ranging up and down. Agricola doubting to be overwinged, stretches out his front, though somewhat with the thinnest, insomuch that many advised to bring up the legions: yet he not altering, alights from his horse, and stands on foot before the ensigns (p. 217).

It is enlightening, also, to compare the close translation of Dion in Petrie's *Monumenta Historica Britannica (Ex Scriptoribus Græcis* etc., p. liv) with Milton's more independent, though accurate, rendering.

Plautius, therefore, had much difficulty in seeking them out; but when he did discover them, as they were not independent but subject to different kings, he overcame first Cataratacus, then Togodumnus, the sons of Cynobellinus, who was now dead. These taking to flight, he brought a part of the Boduni, who were under the dominion of the Catuellani, to terms of peace. Here leaving a garrison, he proceeded farther. But when they arrived at a certain river, which the barbarians supposed the Romans could not pass without a bridge, and in consequence had taken up their position carelessly on the opposite bank, he sends forward the Celti, who, even armed, were accustomed to swim with ease over the most rapid rivers; who, attacking them contrary to their expectation, wounded not the men indeed, but the horses which drew their chariots; which being thrown into confusion, they who rode therein were no longer secure. Next he sent over Flavius Vespasianus, who afterwards enjoyed the supreme rule, and his brother Sabinus as next in command; these also, having passed the river at a certain place, killed many of the barbarians by surprise. The rest, however, did not fly, but the following day again maintained the conflict nearly on equal terms, until Cneius Osidius Geta, though

Plautius, after much trouble to find them out, encountering first with Caractacus, then with Togodumnus, overthrew them; and receiving into conditions part of the Boduni, who then were subject to the Catuellani, and leaving there a garrison, went on toward a river: where the Britons not imagining that Plautius without a bridge could pass, lay on the further side careless and secure. But he sending first the Germans, whose custom was, armed as they were, to swim with ease the strongest current, commands them to strike especially at the horses, whereby the chariots, wherein consisted their chief art of fight, became unserviceable. To second them he sent Vespasian, who in his latter days obtained the empire, and Sabinus his brother; who unexpectedly assailing those who were least aware, did much execution. Yet not for this were the Britons dismayed; but reuniting the next day, fought with such courage, as made it hard to decide which way hung the victory: till Caius Sidius Geta, at point to have been taken, recovered himself so valiantly, as brought the day on his side; for which at Rome he received high honours (pp. 200–1).

assigns to those works the largest share of his attention, availing himself, however, of Orosius,[33] Suetonius, the *Historia* of Tacitus, Eutropius, and in one instance even of a Juvenalian satire, for the filling in and corroboration of his account.[34] After the recall of Agricola he turned for special guidance to the modern writers, in whose works he could find references to the *Historia Augusta,* Eumenius, Ammianus, Prosper Tiro, Zosimus, Procopius, and Socrates.[35] Arrived at the end of the Roman occupation, he must take leave of the Greek and Roman historians, and rely on the only original sources, with the exception of the *Anglo-Saxon Chronicle,* that are offered him—the chronicles of the monks. "Yet these guides," he comments resignedly, "where can be had no better, must be followed."[36] The language then ensuing augurs plainly what Milton's policy is to be. "In gross," he asserts, referring to the quality of the monkish sources, "it may be true enough; in circumstances[37] each man, as his judgment gives him, may reserve his faith, or bestow it." Since the details submitted by the monks need the narrowest scrutiny, their writings, Milton would argue, must be ex-

in imminent danger of being made prisoner, ultimately so completely defeated them, that he received triumphal honours, although he had not yet served the office of consul.

[33] Milton was sometimes constrained to adopt inaccurate references. Citing Paulus Orosius in support of the statement that "Cæsar in his first journey, entertained with a sharp fight, lost no small number of his foot, and by tempest nigh all of his horse" (pp. 196–7), he remarks that Orosius "took what he wrote from a history of Suetonius now lost." For Orosius' statement as to Cæsar's first journey, see Orosius, *Historiarum adversum Paganos Libri* vii, ed. Zangemeister, p. 377. That he believed he was following Suetonius in his account of Cæsar is made clear by a previous passage: "Hanc historiam Suetonius Tranquillus plenissime explicuit, cuius nos, conpetentes portiunculas decerpsimus" (*ibid.*, p. 369). Suetonius, in fact, furnishes no such data. The conclusion is that Orosius, using a contraction of Cæsar's *Commentaries,* mistook Cæsar for Suetonius. Milton was evidently misled by Orosius' error, inferring that the mysterious work of Suetonius had been lost. See Reifferscheid, *Remains of Suetonius,* p. 471.

[34] Pp. 196, 199, 207, 219.

[35] The ecclesiastical historian.

[36] P. 235.

[37] The first edition (1670) reads *circumstance.*

amined as a whole, and every one in comparison with every other. This theory is actually applied in the Third Book. Along with Gildas, the earliest of British historians, who furnishes him with much material, he considers Bede, who follows two centuries later, and their followers—Malmesbury, the imaginary Matthew of Westminster, Huntingdon, and Florence. With Usher's *De Primordiis* ready at hand, he is still sensible of the higher value of original authorities; and with these early sources before him, he is conscious that they must be treated as checks and balances upon each other.

In passing from the Teutonic conquest to the Christianization of England,[38] Milton encounters a monk whom, in spite of anti-monastic prejudice, he sincerely respects. The *Ecclesiastical History* of the Venerable Bede, with its strong flavor of "superstition and monastical affectation,"[39] is not, to be sure, the kind of work that Milton would select, had he the choice of his sources. Complaining in one breath that he is uncertain "whether Beda was wanting to his matter, or his matter to him,"[40] he acknowledges in the next that the absence of that author will, for the interval ending at the "Danish Invasion,"[41] be felt keenly. His attitude towards this standard history is, in practical effect, one of honest appreciation. In the presence of Bede, as in that of Cæsar and Tacitus, he realizes that he has come into contact with an ultimate source. Although he ignores most of the recitals of miraculous intervention, and the long accounts of ecclesiastical councils, he recognizes that he must delve in chapters full of such material, in order to construct a reliable version of the history of the Heptarchy for the seventh century and the first third of the eighth. The contributions of subsequent authorities, such as Malmesbury, Huntingdon, Florence, Matthew of Westminster, and the *Anglo-Saxon Chronicle*, are only incidental. But those and others like them are, after Bede's departure, the sources in which Milton

[38] Pp. 267 ff.
[39] P. 295.
[40] *Ibid.*
[41] *Ibid.*

must repose his faith. It is a dismal prospect he now sees. Some comfort he finds in the "style and judgment"[42] of Malmesbury, but apart from him he anticipates little except the irresponsible "conjectures and surmises" of the commentators on the "obscure and blockish chronicles." For the *Anglo-Saxon Chronicle,* though in large measure an original authority, offers only spasmodic help. Wheloc's imperfect Latin translation interfered somewhat with intelligent study of this valuable text;[43] there seems to have been the thought, besides, that even in its clearest passages it stood in constant need of interpretation. It is charged that the compilers are "ill-gifted with utterance,"[44] and, in one instance, that they "deliver their meaning with more than wonted infancy."[45] If he places little trust in the "chief fountain" of his story, as he terms the *Chronicle,*[46] he reposes

[42] P. 295.

[43] Abraham Wheloc's edition of Bede's *Ecclesiastical History* and the *Anglo-Saxon Chronicle* appeared in 1643. To those unfamiliar with Anglo-Saxon the printing of the *Chronicle* was an occasion of special importance; for by the side of the original text was a Latin translation. As to Wheloc, see Eleanor N. Adams, *Old English Scholarship in England from 1566–1800.*

It is clear that Milton, apparently unable to read or understand the Anglo-Saxon, relied upon the Latin. He charges the chronicler with running into "extravagant fancies and metaphors" in his version of the Battle of Brunanburh. Wheloc, indeed, confesses his helplessness before the task of translating the ballad account of the battle, and feels obliged to add the following marginal note for the year 938: "Idioma hic et ad annum 942 et 975 perantiquum et horridum lectoris candorem et diligentiam desiderat." Cf. *Sax. Chron.,* ed. Plummer, 1. CXXVIII. Wuelcker (*Cædmon und Milton, Angl.* 4.404) enlists Milton's disregard of the ballad to prove that he was not familiar with Anglo-Saxon.

The chronicler, wishing to name the place of Eadred's death, says simply: "On Frome" (*Sax. Chron.* 1. 112). Wheloc misinterpreted the phrase, translating it "in ætatis vigore" (*ibid.,* ed. Wheloc, p. 558). Milton, following Wheloc's Latin, says of Eadred that he sickened "in the flower of his youth" (p. 339). Wheloc was evidently misled by the Anglo-Saxon adjective *from (freom),* meaning "strong," "abundant," "virtuous."

Again, Wheloc writes "tum exercitus *Ite domum* vociferatur," in an attempt to render "þa se fyrdstemn for ham." See *Sax. Chron.* 1. 108; *ibid.* 2. CXXVIII, note 5; *ibid.,* ed. Wheloc, p. 553. Milton writes unsuspectingly: "Whereat the king's soldiers joyfully cried out to be dismissed home" (p. 330).

[44] P. 324.

[45] P. 318.

[46] *Ibid.*

even less in its interpreters, nearly all of them monks, of whom he contemptuously observes that they "gloss and comment at their pleasure."[47] Approaching his material in such a spirit, it is little wonder that, instead of casting his lot with any one writer, he searches among them all, convinced that the best is bad enough. To Simeon of Durham's *Historia Regum,* which became available in print at the appearance of Twysden's *Scriptores Decem* in 1652, and presented the annals in a reasonably clear and objective manner, he gives a certain preference.[48] It is evident, in the last analysis, however, that from Simeon he derives little more than a *prima facie* version. He borrows copiously from him, but only after weighing him with one or more of a number of others, with the *Chronicle,* Ethelwerd, Malmesbury, Florence, Huntingdon, Hoveden, Ingulf, and the *Flores* of the so-called Matthew of Westminster.[49]

---

[47] *Ibid.*

[48] Pp. 296 ff. Firth (p. 230) correctly assumes that Milton used this edition of Simeon, calling attention to the fact that that author is referred to not only in the last two Books, the Fifth and Sixth, but also towards the end of the Fourth (see references to Simeon beginning on p. 296). This circumstance sheds light upon a biographical passage in the *Second Defense* wherein Milton relates that he had hoped, after the establishment of the Commonwealth, to be released from engagements in the public behalf, and that he then turned his attention to continuing the *History,* which, he declares, was to be "from the earliest times to the present period" (Bohn 1. 261). "I had already finished four books," he adds, "when . . . . I was surprised by an invitation from the council of state, who desired my services in the office for foreign affairs." He refers to his appointment, in March 1649, as Secretary for Foreign Tongues. Since there is clear evidence of the use of Simeon in the Fourth Book, it is to be inferred that what Milton in 1649—and until 1654, the date of the publication of the *Second Defense*—regarded as the end of the Fourth Book, was a point at or about p. 296 of the Bohn text, where he is taking reflective leave of Bede's *Ecclesiastical History,* and is looking forward, with no little misgiving, to the authority of the later monks. About six years after, instead of beginning the Fifth Book at that point, he merely continued the Fourth, including in the latter the new material from Simeon which had become accessible during the interval.

[49] For the period of the Saxon Heptarchy, however, Milton's several authorities gave him only meagre satisfaction. "Such bickerings to recount, met often in these our writers, what more worth is it," he queries, "than to chronicle the wars of kites or crows, flocking and fighting in the air?" (p. 304).

Milton continues, indeed, during the remainder of the work, to exercise this caution. At the same time, he is not precluded from laying additional stress, wherever it is merited, on a given authority. For the reign of Alfred and the events immediately preceding it, he summons the aid of Asser; during the succeeding half-century[50] he avails himself largely of the *Chronicle*,[51] but never in entire disregard of its commentators; for whole portions of the reigns of Ethelred the Redeless, Cnut, Harold Harefoot, and Edward the Confessor, he borrows from the clearly arranged narrative of Simeon, showing, however, in his treatment of the Danish kings, that

---

Firth (p. 248) quotes this passage, citing Hume (*Hist. Eng.* 1. 25), who, referring to the figure of the kites and crows, declares it natural that the "great learning and vigorous imagination of Milton" could not contend with the task of bringing orderly arrangement out of the confused transactions and battles of the Saxon Heptarchy." Green remarks that Milton "scorned" as battles of the kites and crows the interesting and significant "struggles of Northumbrian, Mercian, and West Saxon kings to establish their supremacy over the general mass of Englishmen" (*Making of Eng.*, ed. 1882, p. 245). Plummer, citing Lappenberg, is disposed to connect the passage, "which for long did so much harm to the study of early English history," with the report, by the *Anglo-Saxon Chronicle*, of the murrain of the birds in 671 (*Sax. Chron.*, ed. Plummer, 2.29). See also Lappenberg, *A History of England under the Anglo-Saxon Kings*, ed. 1881 (*trans. Thorpe*), 1. 291–2.

[50] Pp. 327 ff.

[51] In illustration of a close use of the *Chronicle*, observe the following (the Latin is Wheloc's):

Tum perquam cito postea populus multus, cum de Cantio, tum de Suthregia, & East-Saxonia, tum de proximis urbibus collectus, Colecestriam quoq: adibat & obsidebat: tamque diu impugnabat, donec expugnabat: & populum illum totum occidebat: (quicquid autem intus erat, diripiebat;) hominibus exceptis, qui murum transilientes aufugerant: verum etiam postea, hac eadem æstate magnus exercitus East-anglorum, cum agros quidem tum portus incolentium se in auxilium conglomerarunt: arbitrati quoque posse suam ulcisci injuriam. Melodunum itaq; profecti; urbemque obsidentes, & impugnantes (*Sax. Chron.*, ed. Wheloc, p. 553).

Encouraged by this, the men of Kent, Surrey, and part of Essex, enterprise the siege of Colchester, nor gave over till they won it, sacking the town and putting to sword all the Danes therein, excepting some who escaped over the wall. To the succour of these a great number of Danes inhabiting ports and other towns in the East-Angles united their force: but coming too late, as in revenge beleaguered Maldon (p. 330).

he esteems the *Encomium Emmæ* a source to be reckoned with.[52] When occasion warrants the relating of personal anecdotes, or the recounting of picturesque and dramatic scenes, he acknowledges the skill of Malmesbury and Huntingdon, both excellent story-tellers, who furnish him with the gossip and the color necessary for such portions of his narrative as the adventures of Edgar,[53] the Battle of Brunan-

[52] Pp. 364 ff. On p. 368, for instance, under the year 1036, Simeon and the *Encomium Emmæ* are used collaterally (see Simeon 2. 158–9; *Enc. Emmæ, Scriptores Rerum Danicarum Medii Ævi* 2. 497–8). An example of Milton's more faithful use of Simeon follows:

Anno MXLII. Rex Anglorum Heardecanutus, dum in convivio, in quo Osgodus Clapa, magnæ vir potentiæ, filiam suam Githam Danico et præpotenti viro Tovio, Prudan cognomento, in loco qui dicitur Lamhithe, magna cum lætitia tradebat nuptui, lætus, sospes, et hilaris cum sponsa prædicta et quibusdam viris bibens staret, repente inter bibendum miserabili casu ad terram corruit, et sic mutus permanens VI. idus Junii feria iii. expiravit, et in Wintoniam delatus juxta patrem suum regem Canutum est tumulatus (Simeon 2. 162).

But Hardecnute the year following, at a feast wherein Osgod a great Danish lord gave his daughter in marriage at Lambeth to Prudon another potent Dane, in the midst of his mirth, sound and healthful to sight, while he was drinking fell down speechless, and so dying, was buried at Winchester beside his father (p. 371).

Observe, also, the following:

Ille vero fugæ præsidio celeriter arrepto, versus austrum cursum dirigens, brevi Sandicum ad portum est appulsus, et obsides qui de tota Anglia patri suo dati fuerant in terram exposuit, illorumque manibus truncatis, auribus amputatis, naribus præscissis abire permisit, et deinceps profectus est Danemarchiam, anno sequenti reversurus (Simeon 2. 147).

Canute in all haste sailing back to Sandwich, took the hostages given to his father from all parts of England, and with slit noses, ears cropped, and hands chopped off, setting them ashore, departed into Denmark (p. 357).

Writing of the persecution and killing of Archbishop Alfage, Milton says (p. 355): "One Thurn, a converted Dane, pitying him half dead, to put him out of pain, with a pious impiety, at one stroke of his axe on the head dispatched him." Firth (*Proc. Brit. Acad.* 1907–8, p. 246) seems to imply that the imaginative phrase, "with a pious impiety," is Milton's own. It was borrowed, however, from Florence's and Simeon's "impia motus pietate" (Florence of Worcester, ed. Thorpe, 1. 165; Simeon 2. 144).

[53] Pp. 342 ff.

burh,[54] Cnut's lesson to flatterers,[55] Harold's visit to Normandy,[56] and the battle of Hastings.[57] But at almost any juncture he is likely to consult the pages of Ethelwerd, or Ingulf, or Florence, or Hoveden. Eadmer, Brompton, Ælred's *Vita Edwardi,* the laws of Edward the Confessor, and Matthew Paris, receive smaller recognition.[58]

The eclectic habit of mind illustrated when Milton handles a period in which several sources compete has both good and bad phases. Its advantage is that the author is led to consult an authority up to the full measure of what it can profitably bestow. Milton can be depended upon, for instance, not to exclude Asser in favor of the *Chronicle,* or Bede in favor of Malmesbury. His judgment as to the comparative value of the sources before him is, generally speaking, that of a sound critic; and when he excerpts from one or another, his reader may feel assured that he has a sufficient reason. The vice in this eclectic temper is that it produces bewildering effects. In Milton's zealous endeavor to ascertain where his authorities are honest and accurate, and where they are deceptive and heedless, he too frequently forgets to construct a theory of his own. He seldom has difficulty in picking them apart; yet it rarely occurs to him to gather the fragments into orderly array. Though he shows every sign of knowing what the principal writers say about the reputed British birth of Constantine,[59] he expresses no settled opinion himself. In his closely crowded narrative of the wars and genealogies of the Heptarchy;[60] in his statement of the stories associated with Æthelstan;[61] in his discussion of Harold Harefoot's origin,[62] and of the relations between Edward the

[54] Pp. 334–5.
[55] Pp. 367–8. See below pp. 135–6.
[56] Pp. 384–5.
[57] Pp. 390 ff.
[58] Pp. 347, 358, 360, 365, 384, 388.
[59] P. 228.
[60] Pp. 301 ff.
[61] Pp. 332 ff.
[62] P. 368.

Confessor and Duke William;[63] and, in short, in many passages where the sources conflict, Milton leaves his reader with the sense that the subject has been abandoned prematurely.[64] The investigator, it is felt, has performed his labor; as artist and critical collator, however, he has been neglectful.

The objection that Milton is disposed to leave matters half-determined applies in far less degree to his chronology.[65] Contradictions in dates are not so likely to impede him as discrepancies in incidents. In spite of Huntingdon's assertion as to the time of the founding of the East-Saxon kingdom, he adheres to his own conclusion that it was not long after the origin of the East-Anglian;[66] even the authority of Tacitus cannot satisfy him that Caractacus resisted the Romans nine years, for a "truer computation" reveals that it was only seven.[67] Milton's chronology is, in large outline, confirmed by later historians.[68] There is some interest, however,

---

[63] Pp. 384–5.

[64] Cf. Stern, *Milton und seine Zeit*, bk. 4. 136: "Man sollte wünschen, dass die Kritik Milton's sich hie und da nicht bloss auf eine bequeme Negative beschränkt hätte . . . . Er überlässt es häufig dem Leser, sich selbst ein Urtheil zu bilden und begnügt sich, die verschiedenen einander widersprechenden Ueberlieferungen neben einander zu stellen."

[65] He disclaims any settled opinion as to the chronology of the legendary period. "Nor have I stood with others computing or collating years and chronologies," he asserts, "lest I should be vainly curious about the time and circumstance of things, whereof the substance is so much in doubt" (p. 184). Holinshed, on the other hand, says that "Brennus and Belinus began to reigne jointlie as kings in Britaine, in the yeare of the world 3574" (*Chronicles*, ed. 1807–8, 1. 452). Stow assigns the beginning of Locrine's reign to 1084 B.C. (*Annales*, ed. 1631, p. 9).

[66] P. 257.

[67] P. 204.

[68] There are, of course, some inaccuracies. In certain cases Milton erred in his copying. The date 629 (p. 280), for example, should be 628, as it appears in the source (see *Sax. Chron.*, ed. Wheloc, p. 514). See also *Sax. Chron.*, ed. Plummer, 1. 24, and cf. Hodgkin, *Hist. of Eng.*, p. 161. 855, which appears on p. 199 of the first edition, should obviously be 865 (the editor of the Bohn edition has substituted the correct date). Again, the date 953 (p. 339) should be 952, as it appears in Twysden's edition of Simeon, which Milton obviously used at this point (see Simeon 2. 952, and cf. *Sax. Chron.*, ed. Plummer, 2. 148 and Hodgkin, p. 342). The marginal note (see 1st ed., p. 235; Bohn, p. 341) indicating that the date 974 was derived from the *Chronicle* is wrong, for there is no entry for

that year in any MS. Milton perhaps inferred the date from Malmesbury's account of Edgar's ride on the Dee River (*Gesta Regum*, ed. Stubbs, 1. 165).

In other cases Milton was faithful to his source, but copied dates which have since been rejected. The date 681 (p. 289), for instance, which was derived from Wheloc, p. 517, is more probably 682 (see *Sax. Chron.*, ed. Plummer, 1. 38–9). As to the date 775 (p. 299), copied from Wheloc, p. 524, see *Sax. Chron.*, ed. Plummer, 1. 50–1; *ibid.* 2. 53–4; Hodgkin, p. 250. The date 837 (p. 310) should be 840 (see *Sax. Chron.*, ed. Plummer, 2. 76; on the subject of dislocation of dates in the *Chronicle* from 754 to 839, and especially as to this date, see Theopold, *Kritische Untersuchungen über die Quellen zur Angelsachsischen Geschichte*, p. 43; on the general topic, see *Sax. Chron.*, ed. Plummer, 2. ciii). The date 854 (p. 312), taken from Wheloc, p. 530, should be 855 (see *Sax. Chron.* 1. 66–7), and 907 (p. 327) should be 906 (see Lappenberg, *Hist. of Eng. under the Anglo-Saxon Kings*, ed. 1881 (trans. Thorpe), 2. 106; *Sax. Chron.* 1. 94–5). 938 (the date appears on p. 225 of the first edition, but is omitted in the Bohn edition) should be 937 (see *Sax. Chron.*, ed. Plummer, 1. 107; Hodgkin, p. 334).

Milton struggles to identify the battle of Cerdicesleah, in 527, with the fight at Mount Badon (see p. 260). For Cerdic, he argues, having abandoned his campaigns "on the continent," as well as his conquest of the Isle of Wight, must have been defeated by the Britons. There was a British victory at Badon, he adds, and that was surely the battle of Cerdicesleah. The weight of the evidence is, however, against Milton's theory. The date assigned by the *Anglo-Saxon Chronicle* to Cerdic's battle—527—is probably reliable, and the *Annales Cambriæ* give 516 as the year of Mount Badon, which Green and Guest would assign to 520 (see Green, *Making of Eng.*, pp. 88 ff.; Guest, *E. E. Sett.*, pp. 61–3).

A curious passage, showing Milton's extreme care, appears on p. 298. It is alleged that Cuthred died "two or three years before" 757, the date of Æthelbald's death. The words "or three," which are not found in the first edition, appear for the first time in the second edition (1677). The insertion, included among the *Errata* at the end of the first edition, and probably made during Milton's lifetime, was evidently intended to place Æthelbald's death at the correct distance from Cuthred's, in 754 (see p. 297). There is some uncertainty as to the date 757 (see *Sax. Chron.*, ed. Plummer, 2. 47). Milton himself, who found 757 (see marginal reference to sources on p. 176 of the 1st ed.) in Simeon of Durham (see Simeon 1. 41) and in the Continuation of Bede (see Bede, ed. Plummer, 1. 362), but 755 in the *Chronicle* (see *Sax. Chron.*, ed. Plummer, 1. 46 ff.; *ibid.*, ed. Wheloc, pp. 521 ff.), preferred 757.

For a typical chronological problem, see p. 245: ". . . . but sallying out, at length gave a stop to the insulting foe, with many seasonable defeats; led by some eminent person, as may be thought, who exhorted them not to trust in their own strength, but in divine assistance. And perhaps no other here is meant than the aforesaid deliverance by German, if computation would permit, which Gildas either not much regarded, or might mistake; but that he tarried so long here, the writers of his life assent not." There is little wonder that Milton became confused. Usher cites Bede and Vincentius to the point that Germanus returned to Britain shortly after his first visit (see Usher, *De Primordiis*,

in making a cursory survey of his sources. For the Roman period, to which the *Chronicle*, and the Brito-Latin and Anglo-Latin writers, could supply little in the aggregate, he consults in the main the modern treatises, notably those of Usher, Calvisius, and Stow. These works, with occasional glances at Matthew of Westminster[69] and Florence,[70] accompany him into the Third Book. Commencing with the Teutonic invasions, however, he follows the *Chronicle*, though with incidental reference to Florence, and in a measure to Bede.[71] In the Fourth Book, Bede and the *Chronicle* are employed together until the former is supplanted by Simeon. It is noteworthy, indeed, that from that point Simeon and the *Chronicle* furnish Milton with almost all his dates, continuing to do so until the meagreness of Wheloc's version compels him to lay the *Chronicle* aside.[72] After 1017, he uses Simeon almost exclusively. The neat and convenient manner in which the years were listed in the margins of Twysden's edition went far, no doubt, towards inducing Milton and his amanuenses to accept the *Historia Regum* as a chronological guide.[73]

Milton may accordingly be said to exercise a fairly keen critical faculty, both in the selecting of his authorities and in the comparative evaluation of them.[74] But he is at his

Elrington ed. of Wks., 5. 434), and in a later passage he quotes Constantius and others to the effect that he died a little after the second. Milton, however, found it necessary to adjust the British transactions of Germanus to the long period beginning in 429, the year of his arrival in Britain (see first edition, p. 104; the Bohn editor incorrectly says 426), and ending in 448 (see p. 247).

Cf. also p. 305: "In Northumberland, Eardulf the year following was driven out of his realm by Alfwold, who reigned two years in his room; after whom Eandred son of Eardulf thirty-three years; but I see not how this can stand with the sequel of story out of better authors."

[69] P. 244.

[70] P. 248.

[71] Pp. 255, 261, 262.

[72] Wheloc offers little after 975, the date of Edgar's death. Milton's last date from the *Chronicle* is 1017, the year of Cnut's accession.

[73] Milton used Simeon's *Historia Dunelmensis Ecclesiæ*, as well as the *Historia Regum*. Simeon's writings did not appear in a printed edition until 1652, when these histories were included in Roger Twysden's *Scriptores Decem*.

[74] An excellent illustration of the scrutiny with which Milton compared his sources occurs in the following passage on p. 378: "King Edward on

the other side made ready above sixty ships at Sandwich well stored with men and provisions." Simeon (*Historia Regum* 2. 165), who, with an incidental glance at John of Brompton, has been closely followed for the events of the year 1052, speaks of forty ships. Malmesbury, whose name appears directly at the side of this passage in the margin of the first edition, says (*Gesta Regum* 1. 243): "Contra quos, a regis parte, plusquam sexaginta naves in anchoris constiterunt." It is likely that the discovery of this slight variation prompted Milton to turn from the one narrative to the other.

See also p. 190: "Four days after the coming of Cæsar, those eighteen ships . . . . were by a sudden tempest scattered and driven back, some . . . . down into the west country; who finding there no safety either to land or to cast anchor, chose rather to commit themselves again to the troubled sea; and, as Orosius reports, were most of them cast away." Cæsar, whose *Commentaries* are used at this point, does not say that most of the ships were cast away. Hence this mention of Orosius' account (*Historiarum adversum Paganos Libri VII*, ed. Zangemeister, p. 378).

An interesting example of source-collation is the fixing of the boundaries of Old Saxony (see p. 248). Old Saxony, in the larger sense, extended from the Elbe to the Rhine (Speed, *Hist. Gr. Brit.*, ed. 1627, p. 286). Ethelwerd (see *Chronicorum Libri IV*, ed. Petrie, p. 501) adds that the Saxons stretched from the Rhine to Denmark. In connection with these data, Milton reads Usher's description of the narrower Old Saxony, or Holsatia, finding it bounded on the north by the Eider (Elrington ed. of Wks., 5. 447).

See also p. 284: ". . . . for Beda relates him [Kenwalk] ofttimes afflicted by his enemies, with great losses: and in six hundred and fifty-two, by the annals, fought a battle (civil war Ethelwerd calls it) at Bradanford by the river Afene—Camden names the place Bradford in Wiltshire, by the river Avon, and Cuthred his near kinsman, against whom he fought, but cites no authority." The reference to the Annals, as Milton calls the *Chronicle*, is based upon the following: "652. Her Cenwalh gefeaht æt Bradan forda be Afue." The mention of Ethelwerd is then prompted by the passage: "Post itaque quadriennium, ipse bellum gessit civile, in cognominato loco Bradanforda, juxta fluvium Afene" (Ethelwerd, ed. Petrie, p. 506).

The same care appears in a passage on p. 292: "Victred, loth to hazard all, for the rash act of a few, delivered up thirty of those that could be found accessory, or as others say, pacified Ina with a great sum of money." Cf. Malmesbury (*Gesta Regum*, ed. Stubbs, 1. 34): "Temptant regium animum muneribus, sollicitant promissis, nundinantur pacem triginta milibus auri mancis, ut pretio mollitus bellum solveret, metallo præstrictus receptui caneret."

Again, Wheloc's Latin is: "Hic Ethelbaldus castellum de Somertone obsidione cinxit" (*Sax. Chron.*, ed. Wheloc, p. 520). Ethelwerd says (ed. Petrie, p. 507): "Æthelbald rex in potestatem cepit villam regiam." Milton, translating both *castellum* and *villa*, writes (p. 296): "Ethelbald of Mercia besieged and took the castle or town of Somerton." Cf. p. 316 (passage beginning *the Danes, not daring*), where Milton translates *arx* (Asser, *De Rebus Gestis Ælfredi*, ed. Stevenson, p. 25) "town and castle"; p. 323 (passage beginning *and on the bank thereof*), where he translates *arcem* (*Sax. Chron.*, ed. Wheloc, p. 544) "a castle"; and p. 330 (passage

best in the literary methods he pursues when the source-texts are converted into a new fabric of his own. Here he is the artist, no less than the critic. In his use of the modern compilers, whom he consults either for general direction or for borrowings of minor consequence, there is no opportunity to give these methods free play, and little stimulus to exercise the imaginative and constructive faculties. It is when he sets out to translate the older writers—Cæsar, or Tacitus, or Bede, or Huntingdon—that both his literary scholarship and his literary art stand forth. Should any one desire to know how far freedom and fidelity may be conserved together in the translating of Latin texts, he can do no better than to compare passages in the *History of Britain* with their originals. Doing so, he discerns the fine quality of Milton's feeling for both Latin and English idiom, and the subtle adaptability with which he could bear both in mind at one time; his alert sense of the proper scope of condensation and amplification; and his intense interest in translation as an art. It is not word by word that he follows his sources, nor line by line; but with a certain flexible sympathy that catches the whole meaning of entire passages, suffusing them, in the process, with independent charm.[75] The boy who wrote Latin poems at Cambridge is reflected in the mature author of the *History of Britain*.

In order to illustrate Milton's rendering of the Latin texts, I have chosen a few specimens, which show both original and

beginning *whereupon the English, from towns and cities),* where he translates *burgum* (ed. Wheloc, p. 552) "town and castle."

For miscellaneous collations, see p. 189 (on Cæsar's landing in Britain); p. 219 (on the events succeeding Agricola's governorship); pp. 220–1 (on the historicity of King Lucius); p. 250 (on the aggressions of the Scots and Picts); p. 252 (on Guortimer's encounters with the Saxons); p. 256 (on King Nazaleod); p. 258 (a comparison of Gildas with the "Saxon relators"); p. 295 (a comparison of Bede with the *Chronicle);* p. 305 (on the period of Eanred's reign); p. 309 (on the extent of the slaughter at the Carr River); p. 334 (on the nomenclature of Brunanburh); p. 342 (on Edgar's dominion); p. 349 (on Æthelred's entertainment of Anlaf); p. 361 (on the alleged identity of "Sherastan" and "Scorastan"); p. 364 (on the manner of Eadric's death); p. 370 (on the place of Harold Harefoot's death); and p. 384 (on Tostig's revenge).

[75] In general, Milton's translations are also notable for their conciseness. Compare, for example, the two translations below. The original,

adaptation, and which I now submit. The following translation of Geoffrey reveals the ability of the translator to convert a story told in the ancient tongue into the "plain and lightsom brevity" with which he proposed to distinguish his version of the pre-Roman fables.[76]

Post illum Arthgallo frater ejus regio diademate insignitur, qui in omnibus suis actibus germano diversus extitit. Nobiles namque ubique laborabat deponere, et ignobiles exaltare, divitibus quibusque sua auferre, infinitos thesauros accumulans. Quod heroes regni diutius ferre recusantes, insurrexerunt in illum, et a solio regio deposuerunt. Erexerunt exinde Elidurum fratrem ejus, qui postea propter misericordiam, quam in fratrem fecit, Pius vocatus fuit: nam cum regnum emenso quin

Archigallo, the second brother, followed not his example; but depressed the ancient nobility; and, by peeling the wealthier sort, stuffed his treasury, and took the right way to be deposed.

Elidure, the next brother, surnamed the Pious, was set up in his place: a mind so noble, and so moderate, as almost is incredible to have been ever found. For, having held the sceptre five years, hunting one day in the forest of Calater, he chanced to meet his deposed brother, wandering in a

---

which is an extract from a purported letter of Queen Emma in the *Encomium Emmæ Reginæ* (see *Scriptores Rerum Danicarum Medii Ævi* 2. 497), reads: "Miror quid captetis consilii, dum sciatis, intermissionis vestræ dilatione, invasoris vestri imperii fieri cotidie soliditatem."

Holinshed *(Chronicles*, ed. 1807–8, 1. 734).

I marvell what you doo determine, sith you know by the delay of your ceassing to make some enterprise, the grounded force of the usurper of your kingdom is dailie made the stronger.

Milton (p. 369).

I admire what Counsel yee take, knowing that your delay, is a daily strengthning to the Reign of your Usurper.

It is pertinent here to quote Professor Wendell's apt comment on the Latinity of Milton's prose: "We might study in some detail the . . . fact that he [Milton] was among the last writers of English prose who, when moved to earnest expression, instinctively thought in Latin terms; and who therefore suffused what they supposed to be vernacular expression with such sustained and sonorous rhythm as would have animated their phrases if they had actually written Latin" (Barrett Wendell, *The Temper of the 17th Cent. in Eng. Lit.*, pp. 307–8).

[76] P. 165. Milton says *(ibid.)*: "I have therefore determined to bestow the telling over even of these reputed tales; be it for nothing else but in favour of our English poets and rhetoricians, who by their art will know how to use them judiciously." Wordsworth, having read this passage, wrote his *Artegal and Elidure* "as a token of affectionate respect for the memory of Milton." For Milton's version of the story, see p. 182.

quennio possedisset, forte in Calatherio nemore venans, obviavit fratri suo qui depositus fuerat. Ipse vero peragratis quibuscunque provincialibus regnis auxilium quæsiverat, ut amissum honorem recuperare quivisset, nec usquam invenerat: et cum supervenientem paupertatem diutius ferre non potuisset, reversus est in Britanniam, decem solummodo militibus sociatus. Petens ergo illos quos dudum habuerat amicos, prædictum nemus præteribat: quum Elidurus ipsius frater ipsum non speratum aspexit. Quo viso, cucurrit Elidurus, et amplexatus est illum, infinita oscula ingeminans. Et ut diu miseriam fratris deflevit, duxit illum secum in civitatem Alclud, et in thalamo suo occuluit.[77]	mean condition; who had been long in vain beyond the seas, importuning foreign aids to his restorement; and was now, in a poor habit, with only ten followers, privately returned to find subsistence among his secret friends. At the unexpected sight of him, Elidure himself also then but thinly accompanied, runs to him with open arms; and after many dear and sincere welcomings, conveys him to the city Alclud; there hides him in his own bedchamber.[78]

[77] Geoffrey, ed. San Marte, pp. 41–2.

[78] P. 182.

Milton frequently adorns his material with effective dramatic and rhetorical touches. Compare the following:

In his rebus circiter dies decem consumit, ne nocturnis quidem temporibus ad laborem militum intermissis (Cæsar, ed. Celsus (London, 1819), 1. 183).	. . . . . . and with a dreadful industry of ten days, not respiting the soldiers day or night, drew up all his ships . . . . . . (p. 193).
Further: Pugnare adversus suos propinquos et compatriotas pene omnes abhorrebant (Simeon of Durham, ed. Arnold, 2. 169).	. . . . . . and the soldiers on either side soon declared their resolution not to fight English against English (p. 379).
Further: Quod neque insequi cedentes possent, neque ab signis discedere auderent (Cæsar 1. 188).	. . . . . . for that the foot in heavy armour could not follow their cunning flight, and durst not by ancient discipline stir from their ensign . . . . . . (p. 194).
Further: Hoc anno de tota Anglia LXXII. millia et de Londonia XV. millia libræ exercitui Danorum sunt persolutæ (Simeon 2. 155. With collateral use of Henry of Huntingdon and Matthew of Westminster).	. . . . . . to maintain which, the next year he squeezed out of the English, though now his subjects, not his enemies, seventy-two, some say, eighty-two thousand pounds, besides fifteen thousand out of London (p. 364).

In Milton's rendering of Geoffrey's account of Lear and his daughters, special attention is called to the italicized passages.

Dato igitur fatis Bladud, erigitur Leir ejusdem filius in regem, qui sexaginta annis patriam viriliter rexit. Ædificavit autem super fluvium Soram civitatem, quæ Britannice Kærleir, Saxonice vero Leir-Cestre nuncupatur: Cui negata masculini sexus prole, natæ sunt tantummodo tres filiæ, vocatæ: Gonorilla, Regan, Cordeilla. Qui eas miro amore sed magis natu minimam, Cordeillam videlicet, diligebat. Cumque in senectutem vergere cœpisset, cogitavit regnum suum ipsis dividere: easque tali-

Hitherto, from father to son, the direct line hath run on: but Leir, who next reigned, had only three daughters, and no male issue: governed laudibly and built Cærlier, now Leicester, on the bank of Sora. But at last, falling through age, he determined to bestow his daughters, and so among them to divide his kingdom. Yet first, to try which of them loved him best, (a trial that might have made him, had he known as wisely how to try, as he seemed to know how much the trying behooved him,) he

---

Further:

Crebra hinc prælia (Tacitus, *Annales*, ed. Furneaux, 2. 263).

. . . . small frays and bickerings . . . . . . (p. 205).

Cf. also:

Et nox quidem gaudio prædaque læta victoribus (Tacitus, *Vita Agricolae*, ed. Furneaux, p. 148).

The Romans jocund of this victory, and the spoil they got, spent the night (p. 218).

Again (observe Milton's rhetorical independence):

Moris namque continui erat genti, sicut et nunc est, ut infirma esset ad retundenda hostium tela et fortis esset ad civilia bella et peccatorum onera sustinenda, infirma, inquam, ad exequenda pacis ac veritatis insignia et fortis ad scelera et mendacia (Gildas, *De Excidio et Conquestu Britanniæ*, ed. Mommsen. In *Monumenta Germaniæ Historica, Auct. Ant.* 13. 36).

And this quality their valour had, against a foreign enemy to be ever backward and heartless; to civil broils eager and prompt. In matters of government, and the search of truth, weak and shallow; in falsehood and wicked deeds, pregnant and industrious (p. 246).

Again:

Quibus omnibus ad velle peractis (Simeon 2. 145).

These things flowing to his wish . . . . . . (p. 356).

Again:

Vallum magnum . . . . . . imperavit (Asser, *De Rebus Gestis Ælfredi*, ed. Stevenson, p. 12).

He drew a trench of wonderous length (p. 302).

bus maritis copulare, qui easdem cum regno haberent. Sed ut sciret quæ illarum majore regni parte dignior esset, adivit singulas ut interrogaret, quæ ipsum magis diligeret. Interrogante ergo illo Gonorilla prius numina cœli testata est, patrem sibi plus cordi esse quam animam, quæ in corpore suo degebat: cui pater: "Quoniam senectutem meam vitæ tuæ præposuisti, te, charissima filia, maritabo juveni quemcunque elegeris cum tertia parte Britanniæ." .... *Deinde Regan, quæ secunda erat, exemplo sororis suæ benivolentiam patris allicere volens, jurejurando respondit:* se nullatenus conceptum exprimere aliter posse, nisi quod ipsum super omnes creaturas diligeret. Credulus ergo pater eadem dignitate, quam primogenitæ promiserat, cum alia tertia parte regni eam maritavit. *At Cordeilla ultima, cum intellexisset eum prædictarum adulationibus acquievisse: tentare illum cupiens aliter respondere perrexit:* "Est uspiam, mi pater, filia, quæ patrem suum plus quam patrem diligere præsumat? non reor equidem ullam esse, quæ hoc fateri audeat: nisi jocosis verbis veritatem celare nitatur. Nempe ego dilexi te semper ut patrem: nec adhuc a proposito meo divertor. Etsi a me magis extorquere insistis, audi certitudinem amoris, quem adversus te habeo: et interrogationibus tuis finem impone. Etenim quantum habes, tantum vales, tantumque te diligo." ....Porro pater ratus, eam ex abundantia cordis dixisse. vehementer indignans, quod responsurus erat manifestare non

resolves a simple resolution, to ask them solemnly in order; and which of them should profess largest, her to believe. Gonorill, the eldest, apprehending too well her father's weakness, makes answer, invoking Heaven, "That she loved him above her soul." "Therefore," quoth the old man, overjoyed. "since thou so honourest my declining age, to thee and the husband thou shalt choose, I give the third part of my realm." *So fair a speeding, for a few words soon uttered, was to Regan, the second, ample instruction what to say.* She, on the same demand, spares no protesting; and the gods must witness, that otherwise to express her thoughts she knew not, but that "She loved him above all creatures;" and so receives an equal reward with her sister. *But Cordeilla, the youngest, though hitherto best beloved, and now before her eyes the rich and present hire of a little easy soothing, the danger also, and the loss likely to betide plain dealing, yet moves not from the solid purpose of a sincere and virtuous answer:* "Father," saith she, "my love towards you is as my duty bids: what should a father seek, what can a child promise more? They, who pretend beyond this, flatter." When the old man, sorry to hear this, and wishing her to recall those words, persisted asking; with a loyal sadness at her father's infirmity, but something, on the sudden, harsh, and glancing rather at her sisters than speaking her own mind, "Two ways only," saith she, "I have to an-

distulit: "Quia in tantum senectutem patris tui sprevisti, ut vel eo amore, quo me sorores tuæ diligunt, dedignata es diligere, et ego te dedignabor, nec usquam in regno meo cum tuis sororibus partem habebis. ....Non dico tamen, cum filia mea sis, quin te externo alicui (si illum fortuna obtulerit) utcunque maritem. Illud autem affirmo, quod numquam eo honore quo sorores tuas te maritare laborabo. Quippe cum te hucusque plus quam ceteras dilexerim: tu vero me minus quam ceteræ diligas." ....Nec mora: consilio procerum regni dedit prædictas puellas duas duobus ducibus, Cornubiæ videlicet et Albaniæ cum medietate tantum insulæ: dum ipse viveret. Post obitum autem ejus totam monarchiam Britanniæ eisdem concessit habendam.[79]

swer what you require me: the former, your command is, I should recant; accept then this other which is left me; look how much you have, so much is your value, and so much I love you." "Then hear thou," quoth Leir, now all in passion, "what thy ingratitude hath gained thee: because thou hast not reverenced thy aged father equal to thy sisters, part in my kingdom, or what else is mine, reckon to have none." And, without delay, gives in marriage his other daughters, Gonorill to Maglaunus duke of Albania, Regan to Henninus duke of Cornwal; with them in present half his kingdom; the rest to follow at his death.[80]

[79] Geoffrey, pp. 24–6.

[80] Pp. 175–6.

Imaginative ardor obtains freer rein in the metrical rendering of the oracular verses delivered to the legendary Brutus by Diana. The source and the translation follow:

Brute, sub occasu solis trans Gallica regna,	Brutus, far to the west, in th' ocean wide,
Insula in Oceano est undique clausa mari:	Beyond the realm of Gaul, a land there lies,
Insula in Oceano est habitata Gygantibus olim,	Seagirt it lies, where giants dwelt of old,
Nunc deserta quidem: gentibus apta tuis.	Now void it fits thy people; thither bend
Hanc pete; namque tibi sedes erit illa perennis:	Thy course, there shalt thou find a lasting seat,
Hic fiet natis altera Troja tuis:	Where to thy sons another Troy shall rise;
Hic de prole tua reges nascentur: et ipsis	And kings be born of thee, whose dreaded might
Totius terræ subditus orbis erit (Geoffrey, p. 13).	Shall awe the world, and conquer nations bold (p. 171).

Of somewhat like interest is the translation of the Latin couplet disclosing the murder of Kenelm, and found by Milton in the *Flores Histori-*

In the ensuing, Milton blends his own characteristic fluency with Cæsar's plain directness.

At illi, intermisso spatio, imprudentibus nostris atque occupatis in munitione castrorum, subito se ex sylvis ejecerunt, impetuque in eos facto, qui erant in statione pro castris collocati, acriter pugnaverunt: duabusque missis subsidio cohortibus a Cæsare, atque his primis legionum duarum, cum hæ perexiguo intermisso loci spatio inter se, constitissent, novo genere pugnæ perterritis nostris, per medios audacissime perruperunt, seque inde incolumes receperunt.[31]

Here the British horse and charioteers....after some pause, while Cæsar, who thought the day's work had been done, was busied about the intrenching of his camp, march out again, give fierce assault to the very stations of his guards and sentries; and while the main cohorts of two legions, that were sent to the alarm, stood within a small distance of each other, terrified at the newness and boldness of their fight, charged back again through the midst, without the loss of a man.[32]

Milton frequently condenses, and with considerable discrimination. Compare the extracts below, with special reference to the italicized passages.

Ceterum animorum provinciæ prudens, simulque doctus per aliena experimenta parum profici armis, si iniuriæ sequerentur, causas bellorum statuit excidere. a se suisque orsus primum domum suam coërcuit, quod plerisque haud minus arduum est quam provinciam regere. *nihil per libertos servosque publicæ rei, non studiis privatis nec ex commendatione aut*

But by far not so famous was Agricola in bringing war to a speedy end, as in cutting off the causes from whence war arises. For he knowing that the end of war was not to make way for injuries in peace, began reformation from his own house; permitted not his attendants and followers to sway, or have to do at all in public affairs: lays on with equal-

arum of the imaginary Matthew of Westminster. The couplet reads (*Flor. Hist.* 1. 412):

In clenc sub spina jacet in convalle bovina,
Vertice privatus, Kenelmus rege creatus.

Milton's translation is (p. 206):

Low in the mead of kine under a thorn,
Of head bereft, lieth poor Kenelm kingborn.

For a more prosaic treatment, compare Speed, *Hist. Gr. Brit.*, ed. 1627, p. 322.

[31] Cæsar, ed. Celsus, 1. 187.

[32] P. 194.

precibus centurionem militesve asciire, sed optimum quemque fidissimum putare. omnia scire, non omnia exsequi. parvis peccatis veniam, magnis severitatem commodare; nec pœna semper, sed sæpius pœnitentia contentus esse; officiis et administrationibus potius non peccaturos præponere, quam damnare cum peccassent. frumenti et tributorum exactionem æqualitate munerum mollire, circumcisis quæ in quæstum reperta ipso tributo gravius tolerabantur. namque per ludibrium adsidere clausis horreis et emere ultro frumenta ac ludere pretio cogebantur. divortia itinerum et longinquitas regionum indicebatur, ut civitates proximis hibernis in remota et avia deferrent, donec quod omnibus in promptu erat paucis lucrosum fieret.

Hæc primo statim anno comprimendo egregiam famam paci circumdedit, quæ vel incuria vel intolerantia priorum haud minus quam bellum timebatur. sed ubi *æstas advenit, contracto exercitu multus in agmine, laudare modestiam, disiectos coërcere; loca castris ipse capere, æstuaria ac silvas ipse prætemptare; et nihil interim apud hostis quietum pati, quo minus subitis excursibus popularetur; atque ubi satis terruerat, parcendo rursus invitamenta pacis ostentare. quibus rebus multæ civitates, quæ in illum diem ex æquo egerant, datis obsidibus iram posuere, et præsidiis castellisque circumdatæ sunt tanta ratione curaque, ut nulla ante Britanniæ nova pars pariter illacessita transierit.*

Sequens hiems saluberrimis con-

ity the proportions of corn and tribute that were imposed; takes off exactions, and the fees of encroaching officers, heavier than the tribute itself. For the countries had been compelled before, to sit and wait the opening of public granaries, and both to sell and to buy their corn at what rate the publicans thought fit; the purveyors also commanding when they pleased to bring it in, not to the nearest, but still to the remotest places, either by the compounding of such as would be excused, or by causing a dearth, where none was, made a particular gain. These grievances and the like, he in the time of peace removing, brought peace into some credit; which before, since the Romans coming, had as ill a name as war. *The summer following, Titus then emperor, he so continually with inroads disquieted the enemy over all the isle, and after terror so allured them with his gentle demeanour, that many cities which till that time would not bend, gave hostages, admitted garrisons, and came in voluntarily.* The winter he spent all in worthy actions; teaching and promoting like a public father the institutes and customs of civil life. The inhabitants rude and scattered, and by that the proner to war, he so persuaded to build houses, temples, and seats of justice; and by praising the forward, quickening the slow, assisting all, turned the name of necessity into an emulation. He caused moreover the noblemen's sons to be bred up in liberal arts; and by preferring the

siliis absumpta. namque ut homines dispersi ac rudes eoque in bella faciles quieti et otio per voluptates adsuescerent, hortari privatim, adiuvare publice, ut templa fora domos extruerent, laudando promptos et castigando segnes: ita honoris æmulatio pro necessitate erat. iam vero principum filios liberalibus artibus erudire, et ingenia Britannorum studiis Gallorum anteferre, ut qui modo linguam Romanam abnuebant, eloquentiam concupiscerent. inde etiam habitus nostri honor et frequens toga. paulatimque discessum ad delenimenta vitiorum, porticus et balinea et conviviorum elegantiam. idque apud imperitos humanitas vocabatur, cum pars servitutis esset.[63]

wits of Britain before the studies of Gallia, brought them to affect the Latin eloquence, who before hated the language. Then were the Roman fashions imitated, and the gown; after a while the incitements also and materials of vice, and voluptuous life, proud buildings, baths, and the elegance of banqueting; which the foolisher sort called civility, but was indeed a secret art to prepare them for bondage.[64]

It is interesting to notice the graceful ease with which he weaves his own comment on Redwald's attitude towards religion into the straightforward account of the *Ecclesiastical History*.

Et quidem pater eius Redua'd iamdudum in Cantia sacramentis Christianæ fidei inbutus est, sed frustra; nam rediens domum ab uxore sua et quibusdam peruersis doctoribus seductus est, atque a sinceritate fidei deprauatus habuit posteriora peiora prioribus; ita ut in morem antiquorum Samaritanorum et Christo seruire uideretur et diis, quibus antea seruiebat; atque in eodem fano et altare haberet ad sacrificium Christi, et arulam ad uictimas dæmoniorum.[65]

He had formerly in Kent received baptism, but coming home, and persuaded by his wife, who still it seems was his chief counsellor to good or bad alike, relapsed into his old religion: yet not willing to forego his new, thought it not the worst way, lest perhaps he might err in either, for more assurance to keep them both; and in the same temple erected one altar to Christ, another to his idols.[66]

---

[63] Tacitus, *Vit. Agric.*, ed. Furneaux, pp. 113–8.
[64] Pp. 213–4.
[65] Bede, *Ecclesiastical History*, ed. Plummer, 1. 116.
[66] P. 276.

Milton displays considerable skill in the manipulation of parenthetical

Although the following passages show ruthless condensation, the translator contrives to express his feeling against mediæval asceticism.

Accepit autem rex Ecgfrid coniugem nomine Ædilthrydam, filiam Anna regis Orientalium Anglorum, cuius sepius mentionem fecimus, uiri bene religiosi, ac per omnia mente et opere egregii; quam et alter ante illum uir habuerat uxorem, princeps uidelicet Australium Gyruiorum uocabulo Tondberct. Sed illo post modicum temporis, ex quo eam accepit, defuncto, data est regi præfato; cuius consortio cum xii annis uteretur, perpetua tamen mansit uirginitatis integritate gloriosa; sicut mihimet sciscitanti, cum hoc, an ita esset, quibusdam uenisset in dubium, beatæ memoriæ Uilfrid episcopus referebat, dicens se testem integritatis eius esse certissimum; adeo ut Ecgfridus promiserit se ei terras ac pecunias multas esse donaturum, si reginæ posset persuadere eius uti conubio, quia sciebat illam nullum uirorum plus illo diligere. Nec diffidendum est nostra etiam ætate fieri potuisse, quod aeuo præcedente aliquoties factum fideles historiæ narrant; donante uno

Another adversity befel Ecfrid in his family, by means of Ethildrith his wife, king Anna's daughter, who having taken him for her husband, and professing to love him above all other men, persisted twelve years in the obstinate refusal of his bed, thereby thinking to live the purer life. So perversely then was chastity instructed against the apostle's rule. At length obtaining of him with much importunity her departure, she veiled herself a nun, then made abbess of Ely, died seven years after the pestilence; and might with better warrant have kept faithfully her undertaken wedlock, though now canonized St. Audrey of Ely.[88]

---

matter. Compare with its Latin source the text within the parentheses below.

Cognomento quidem coloniæ non insigne, sed copia negotiatorum et commeatuum maxime celebre (Tacitus, *Annales* 2. 431).

But Suetonius at these tidings not dismayed, through the midst of his enemy's country, marches to London (though not termed a colony, yet full of Roman inhabitants, and for the frequency of trade, and other commodities, a town even then of principal note) with purpose to have made there the seat of war (p. 209).

eodemque Domino, qui se nobiscum usque in finem sæculi manere pollicetur. Nam etiam signum diuini miraculi, quo eiusdem feminæ sepulta caro corrumpi non potuit, indicio est, quia uirili contactu incorrupta durauerit.

Quæ multum diu regem postulans, ut sæculi curas relinquere, atque in monasterio, tantum uero regi Christo seruire permitteretur; ubi uix aliquando inpetrauit, intrauit monasterium Aebbæ abbatissæ, quæ erat amita regis Ecgfridi, positum in loco, quem Coludi urbem nominant, accepto uelamine sanctimonialis habitus a præfato antistite Uilfrido. Post annum uero ipsa facta est abbatissa in regione, quæ uocatur Elge; ubi constructo monasterio uirginum Deo deuotarum perplurium mater uirgo, et exemplis uitæ cælestis esse cœpit et monitis. De qua ferunt, quia, ex quo monasterium petiit, numquam lineis, sed solum laneis uestimentis uti uoluerit; raroque in calidis balneis, præter imminentibus sollemniis maioribus, uerbi gratia paschæ, pentecostes, epifaniæ, lauari uoluerit; et tunc nouissima omnium, lotis prius suo suarumque ministrarum obsequio ceteris, quæ ibi essent, famulis Christi; raro præter maiora sollemnia, uel artiorem necessitatem, plus quam semel per diem manducauerit; semper, si non infirmitas grauior prohibuisset, ex tempore matutinæ synaxeos, usque ad ortum diei, in ecclesia precibus intenta persteterit. Sunt etiam, qui dicant, quia per prophetiæ spiritum, et pestilentiam, qua ipsa esset moritura, prædixerit, et numerum quoque eorum, qui de suo monasterio hac essent de mundo rapiendi, palam cunctis præsentibus intimauerit. Rapta est autem ad Dominum in medio suorum, post annos VII, ex quo abbatissæ gradum susceperat; et æque, ut ipsa iusserat, non alibi quam in medio eorum, iuxta ordinem, quo transierat, ligneo in locello sepulta.[57]

In the following passages one may observe Milton's treatment of episodic material found in Huntingdon and Malmesbury.

Tertium, quod cum maximo vigore imperii, sedile suum in littore maris, cum ascenderet, statui jussit. Dixit autem mari ascendenti "Tu meæ ditionis es; et terra in qua sedeo mea est: nec fuit qui impune meo resisteret imperio. Impero igitur tibi ne in terram meam ascendas, nec vestes nec membra dominatoris tui madefacere præsumas." Mare vero de more conscendens pedes regis et crura sine reverentia madefecit. Rex igitur resiliens ait: "Sciant omnes habitantes orbem, vanam et frivolam

He caused his royal seat to be set on the shore, while the tide was coming in; and with all the state that royalty could put into his countenance, said thus to the sea; "Thou, Sea, belongest to me, and the land whereon I sit is mine; nor hath any one unpunished resisted my commands: I charge thee come no further upon my land, neither presume to wet the feet of thy sovereign lord." But the sea, as before, came rolling on, and without reverence both wet and dashed him. Whereat the

[57] *Ecclesiastical History*, ed. Plummer, 1. 243–4.

[58] P. 291. In the passage immediately following the account of St. Audrey's death, the translator manages to include one of his characteristic attacks against Ireland (see also pp. 197, 223; also *Eikonoklastes* (Bohn 1. 407 ff.), *First Def.* (Bohn 1. 201), *Oberv. Art. P.* (Bohn 2. 181), and *Of. Ref.* (ed. Hale, pp. 57–8). Cf. source and translation:

Anno dominicæ incarnationis DCLXXXIIII. Ecgfrid rex Nordanhymbrorum, misso Hiberniam cum exercitu duce Bercto, uastauit misere gentem innoxiam, et nationi Anglorum semper amicissimam, ita ut ne ecclesiis quidem aut monasteriis manus parceret hostilis (*Eccl. Hist.*, ed. Plummer, 1. 266).

In the mean while Ecfrid had sent Bertus with power to subdue Ireland, a harmless nation, saith Beda, and ever friendly to the English; in both which they seem to have left a posterity much unlike them at this day; miserably wasted, without regard had to places hallowed or profane.

regum esse potentiam, nec regis quempiam nomine dignum præter Eum, cujus nutui cælum, terra, mare, legibus obediunt æternis.[89]

Denique in quodam convivio, ubi se plerumque fatuorum dicacitas liberius ostentat, fama est Kinnadium regem Scottorum ludibundum dixisse, mirum videri tam vili homuncioni tot provincias subjici; idque a quodam mimo sinistra aure acceptum, et Edgaro postmodum sollempni convitio in os objectum. At ille, re suis celata, Kinnadium, quasi magni mysterii consultandi gratia, accersiit, longeque in sylvam seducto, unum ex duobus, quos secum attulerat, ensibus tradidit; "Et nunc," inquit, "licebit vires tuas experiare cum soli simus. Jam enim faxo ut appareat quis alteri merito supponi debeat; tu quoque ne pedem referas quin mecum rem ventiles. Turpe est enim regem in convivio esse

king quickly rising wished all about him to behold and consider the weak and frivolous power of a king, and that none indeed deserved the name of king, but he whose eternal laws both heaven, earth, and sea obey.[90]

Kened king of Scots, then in the court of Edgar, sitting one day at table, was heard to say jestingly among his servants, he wondered how so many provinces could be held in subjection by such a little dapper man: his words were brought to the kings ear; he sends for Kened as about some private business, and in talk drawing him forth to a secret place, takes from under his garment two swords, which he had brought with him, gave one of them to Kened; and now, saith he, it shall be tried which ought to be the subject; for it is shameful for a king to boast at table, and shrink in fight. Kened much abashed fell presently at his feet, and besought him to pardon what he had simply spok-

[89] Huntingdon, *Historia Anglorum*, ed. Arnold, p. 189.

[90] Pp. 367–8. The prefatory note to Wordsworth's *A Fact, and an Imagination; or Canute and Alfred, on the Sea-Shore* declares that "one or two expressions are taken from Milton's History of England." The part of the poem so borrowed is apparently the following:

Deaf was the Sea;
Her waves rolled on, respecting his decree
Less than they heed a breath of wanton air.
—Then Canute, rising from the invaded throne,
Said to his servile Courtiers, —"Poor the reach,
The undisguised extent, of mortal sway!
He only is a King, and he alone
Deserves the name (this truth the billows preach)
Whose everlasting laws, sea, earth, and heaven, obey."

Milton, rather typically, adds his own comment on Cnut's lesson, remarking that the truth which the King intended to impress "needed no such laborious demonstration," and, further, that it was "so evident of itself . . . . . . that unless to shame his court-flatterers, who would not else be convinced, Canute needed not to have gone wetshod home."

dicaculum, nec esse in prælio promtulum. "Confusus ille, nec verbo mutire ausus, ad pedes domini regis procidit, simplicis joci veniam precatus et confestim consecutus.[31]

en, no way intended to his dishonour or disparagement; wherewith the king was satisfied.[32]

The following versions of Harold's death at Hastings show Milton's peculiar skill in selecting elements from two distinct sources, and in reducing them to a form wherein personal point of view transfigures the details supplied by the originals. The Latin accounts are those of Malmesbury and Simeon respectively.

Valuit hæc vicissitudo, modo illis, modo istis vincentibus, quantum Haroldi vita moram fecit; at ubi jactu sagittæ violato cerebro procubuit, fuga Anglorum perennis in nocte fuit.[33]

Ab hora tamen diei tertia usque noctis crepusculum suis adversariis restitit fortissime, et seipsum pugnando tam fortiter defendit et tam strenue, ut vix ab hostili interimi posset agmine. At postquam ex his et ex illis quamplurimi corruere, heu! ipsemet cecidit crepusculi tempore.[34]

Thus hung the victory wavering on either side from the third hour of day to evening; when Harold having maintained the fight with unspeakable courage and personal valour, shot into the head with an arrow, fell at length, and left his soldiers without heart longer to withstand the unwearied enemy.[35]

In the first edition (on p. 112), the names of Malmesbury, Huntingdon, Ethelwerd, Bede, and Nennius are noted opposite the passage which appears in the right-hand column below. The left-hand column contains passages from the

[31] Malmesbury, *Gesta Regum Anglorum*, ed. Stubbs, 1. 177.
[32] P. 342.
[33] Malmesbury, *Gesta Regum Anglorum*, ed. Stubbs, 2. 303.
[34] Simeon, *Historia Regum*, ed. Arnold, 2. 181.
[35] P. 391.

several sources.[96] The italicized passage in Milton's text illustrates his skill in weaving and assimilating material.

Quapropter, sicut hi quibus id muneris est lascivientes arboris ramos solent succidere, ut reliquorum, vitæ succo suo possit sufficere, sic incolæ aliquorum expulsione matrem allevant, ne tam numerosæ prolis pastu exhausta succumbat: sed, ut facti minuant invidiam, sorte ducunt eliminandos. Inde est quod illius terræ homines invenerint sibi ex necessitate virtutem, ut natali solo ejecti peregrinas sedes armis vendicent.[97]

Inierunt autem certamen contra Pictos et Scottos, qui jam venerunt usque ad Stanfordiam, quæ sita est in australi parte Lincolniæ, distans ab ea quadraginta miliariis.[98]

Et mox contra Scotos causa probationis mittuntur: tandem non morata juventus, pectora induunt armis, temptant quoque prælia peregrina: miscetur viro vir, ruit Germanus, ruit Scotus, ex utraque parte miserrima cædes: victores post Saxones existunt.[99]

Quod ubi domi nuntiatum est, simul et insulæ fertilitas, ac segnitia Brettonum; mittitur confestim illo classis prolixior, armatorum ferens manum fortiorem, quæ præmissæ adiuncta cohorti in-

The British Nennius writes, that these brethren were driven into exile out of Germany, and to Vortigern who reigned in much fear, one while of the Picts, then of the Romans and Ambrosius, came opportunely into the haven. For it was the custom in Old Saxony, when their numerous offspring overflowed the narrowness of their bounds, to send them out by lot into new dwellings wherever they found room, either vacant or to be forced. *But whether sought, or unsought, they dwelt not here long without employment.* For the Scots and Picts were now come down, some say, as far as Stamford, in Lincolnshire, whom perhaps not imagining to meet new opposition, the Saxons, though not till after a sharp encounter, put to flight: and that more than once; slaying in fight, as some Scotch writers affirm, their king Eugenius the son of Fergus. Hengist perceiving the island to be rich and fruitful, but her princes and other inhabitants given to vicious ease, sends word home, inviting others to a share of his good success. Who returning with seventeen ships, were grown up now to a

[96] For passages containing the material from Nennius, see Usher, *De Primordiis*, ed. 1687, pp. 207, 239. Cf. Nennius, *Historia Britonum*, ed. Stevenson, p. 24 (in *Collection of Monastic Chronicles*, published by *Eng. Hist. Soc.*). As to the manner in which Nennius may have been suggested to Milton at this point, see the marginal references in Bede, *Ecclesiastical History*, ed. Wheloc, pp. 58–9. As to the Scottish authority, cf. Buchanan, *History of Scotland*, trans. Aikman, 1. 227.

[97] Malmesbury, *Gesta Regum*, ed. Stubbs, 1. 8–9.

[98] Huntingdon, ed. Arnold, p. 38.

[99] Ethelwerd, ed. Petrie, p. 502.

uincibilem fecit exercitum. Susceperunt ergo, qui aduenerant, donantibus Britannis, locum habitationis inter eos, ea condicione, ut hi pro patriæ pace et salute contra aduersarios militarent, illi militantibus debita stipendia conferrent.[1]

sufficient army, and entertained without suspicion on these terms, that they "should bear the brunt of war against the Picts, receiving stipend, and some place to inhabit.'"[2]

When the *History of Britain* is compared with the works of other writers of English history belonging to Milton's age and to that immediately preceding it, one finds that the author has, in the large, been diligent and circumspect in choosing his authorities. There are numerous instances in which Holinshed and Speed consult modern digests totally ignored by him; but it cannot be urged that they have, on the whole, succeeded better than he in tracing their way to the ultimate springs. Bearing in mind the general availability, in the seventeenth century, of printed editions relating to the sources and literature of English history, Milton may be said to have put himself in touch with a considerable part of the entire field. If his work does not derive from the leading Welsh sources, the *Annales Cambriæ* and the *Brut y Tywysogion;* if it disregards Eddius' *Life of Wilfrith* and the valuable *Lestorie des Engles* of Geoffrey Gaimar; if, in the period of the Danish invasions, it might have been enriched through the *Heimskringla af Snorre Sturlasson,* it should not be forgotten that these writings were not accessible in print until after his time,[3] and that the eighteenth and nineteenth centuries did much towards introducing British and English material to historical scholars. In like manner, if his narrative of the Norman Conquest is uninfluenced by the stimulating pictures of the Bayeux Tapestry, it is to be recalled that this highly interesting piece of work was employed, throughout the seventeenth century, chiefly as a festal decora-

[1] Bede, *Eccl. Hist.*, ed. Plummer, 1. 31. See also Nennius, ed. Stevenson (in *Collection of Monastic Chronicles)*, p. 28.

[2] P. 250.

[3] See Gross, *Sources and Lit. Eng. Hist.*, pp. 237, 347, 107, 364, 255. See also Hodgkin, *Hist. Eng.*, Appendix I, where the authorities for pre-Conquest history are discussed.

tion for the nave of Bayeux Cathedral.[4] Yet some sources there were, overlooked or ignored by Milton, that he might have used. The contributions of the Norman William of Jumièges[5] and William of Poitiers,[6] bearing closely on the events of the Conquest and on Duke William's career, were included in Duchesne's *Historiæ Normannorum Scriptores*, published at Paris in 1619; yet he appears to owe no debt to these writers, who, along with other Norman and Anglo-Norman authorities, have been studied with eagerness by more recent historians. Nor can it be denied that he unjustly withholds recognition from the ecclesiastical writers and the theologians. Especially as to the former, his position is outspoken; he discerns no good purpose in reporting the "long bead-roll of archbishops, bishops, abbots, abbesses, and their doings, neither to religion profitable, nor to morality."[7] He resorts to the *Ecclesiastical History*, to be sure, but he picks his way gingerly, that he may avoid "bead-rolls" and the like. He manifests respect for Alcuin; yet instead of gaining a first-hand acquaintance, in accessible editions,[8] with the material furnished to English history by this "learned monk,"[9] as he calls him, he is content to know him through the pages of Malmesbury. It is certain that he had some familiarity with the early laws.[10] In Wheloc's volume of 1644, which added Lambarde's *Archaionomia* to Bede and the *Chronicle*,[11] he might have found them in Latin parallel texts. He makes no truly earnest attempt, however, to enlist their aid in reaching historical fact.[12] Milton's selection of his sources, in a word, is that of a judicious and conservative scholar who, though in no danger of missing the great high-

---

[4] Fowke, *The Bayeux Tapestry*, p. 3.

[5] Gross, p. 275.

[6] *Ibid.*, p. 286.

[7] P. 299.

[8] See Hardy, *Cat. of Materials*, 1. 688.

[9] P. 307.

[10] See *First Def.* (Bohn 1. 173).

[11] See Adams, *Old Eng. Scholarship*, p. 54. As to the volume of 1643, see supra, p. 115, note 43.

[12] Such passages as those on pp. 260–1, p. 249, and p. 358 are exceptional.

ways of research, is prevented by the difficulties of investigation, by the accumulation of other interests,[13] and by no small degree of personal and traditional prejudice, from searching out the narrow bypaths where rich yields are also to be found.

---

[13] Though Milton had originally proposed to bring the *History* down to his own time, he concluded it at the Norman Conquest. The composition of the text progressed intermittently during a period commencing about 1645 (but no earlier than 1643, the date of the publication of Wheloc's volume), and ending about 1660 (see Firth, pp. 229–30). Cf. Masson, *The Life of John Milton* etc., 6. 642–3. As to Wheloc's book, cf. Stern, *Milton und seine Zeit*, bk. 4. 134.

BIBLIOGRAPHY

Modern Editions of Milton's Sources

ALCUIN. *Epistolæ.* Ed. Dümmler. *Monumenta Germaniæ Historica, Epistolæ* 4. 1–493. Berlin. 1895.

ANGLO-SAXON CHRONICLE. Ed. Plummer and Earle. 2 vols. Oxford. 1892–9.

—— Trans. J. A. Giles. London. 1847.

ASSER. *De Rebus Gestis Ælfredi.* Ed. Stevenson. Oxford. 1904.

—— Trans. A. S. Cook. Boston. 1906.

BEDE. *Historia Ecclesiastica Gentis Anglorum.* Ed. Plummer. 2 vols. Oxford. 1896.

—— Trans. A. M. Sellar. London. 1907.

BUCHANAN, GEORGE. *The History of Scotland.* Trans. Aikman. 4 vols. Glasgow & Edinburgh. 1827.

CÆSAR, C. JULIUS. *Commentarii de Bello Gallico.* In Vol. I of *Opera Omnia.* Ed. Celsus. London. 1819.

CAMDEN, WILLIAM. *Britannia.* A Chorographical Description of England, Scotland, and Ireland. Trans. Richard Gough. 4 vols. London. 1806.

DION (CASSIUS DIO, OR DIO CASSIUS, COCCEIANUS). *Historiarum Romanarum Quæ Supersunt.* Ed. Boissevain. Berlin. 1895–1901.

EADMER. *Historia Novorum in Anglia.* Ed. Rule. Rolls Ser. London. 1884.

ENCOMIUM EMMÆ REGINÆ. *Scriptores Rerum Danicarum Medii Ævi* 2.472–502. Ed. Langebek. Copenhagen. 1773.

ETHELWERD. *Chronicorum Libri Quatuor.* Ed. Petrie. *Monumenta Historica Britannica,* pp. 499–521. London. 1848.

—— Trans. J. A. Giles. *In Six Old English Chronicles.* London. 1848.

EUTROPIUS. *Breviarium ab Urbe Condita cum Pauli Additamentis et Versionibus Græcis.* Ed. Droysen. In *Monumenta Germaniæ Historica, Auctores Antiquissimi,* Vol. II. Berlin. 1879.

FLORENCE OF WORCESTER. *Chronicon ex Chronicis.* Ed. Thorpe. 2 Vols. London. 1848–9.

GEOFFREY OF MONMOUTH. *Historia Regum Britanniæ.* Ed. San-Marte (A. Schulz). Halle. 1854.

—— Trans. J. A. Giles. In *Six Old English Chronicles.* London. 1848.

GILDAS. *De Excidio et Conquestu Britanniæ.* Ed. Mommsen. *Monumenta Germaniæ Historica, Auctores Antiquissimi* 13. 25–85. Berlin. 1898.

—— Trans. J. A. Giles. In *Six Old English Chronicles.* London. 1848.

HOLINSHED, RAPHAELL. *Chronicles of England, Scotland, and Ireland.* 6 vols. London. 1807–8.

HOVEDEN, ROGER OF. *Chronica.* Ed. Stubbs. Rolls Ser. 4 vols. London. 1868–71.

HUNTINGDON, HENRY OF. *Historia Anglorum.* Ed. Arnold. Rolls Ser. London. 1879.

INGULF. *Historia Croylandensis.* Trans. Riley. London and New York. 1893.

LIEBERMANN, F. (editor). *Die Gesetze der Angelsachsen.* 2 vols. (3 pts.). Halle. 1903–12.

MALMESBURY, WILLIAM OF. *De Gestis Regum Anglorum.* Ed. Stubbs. Rolls Ser. 2 vols. London. 1887–9.

—— Trans. J. A. Giles. London. 1847.

MATTHEW OF WESTMINSTER. (Imaginary author). *Flores Historiarum.* Ed. Luard. Rolls Ser. 3 vols. London. 1890.

NENNIUS. *Historia Brittonum.* Ed. Mommsen. *Monumenta Germaniæ Historica, Auctores Antiquissimi* 13. 111–222. Berlin. 1898.

—— ED. STEVENSON. (In *Collection of Monastic Chronicles. English Historical Society*). London. 1838.

—— Trans. J. A. Giles. In *Six Old English Chronicles.* London. 1848.

OROSIUS, PAULUS. *Historiarum adversum Paganos Libri VII*. Ed. Zangemeister. In *Corpus Scriptorum Ecclesiasticorum Latinorum*, Vol. V. Vienna. 1882.

PARIS, MATTHEW. *Chronica Majora*. Ed. Luard. Rolls Ser. 7 vols. London. 1872–83.

PETRIE, HENRY (editor). *Ex Scriptoribus Græcis atque Latinis Excerpta de Britannia*. In *Monumenta Historica Britannica*. London. 1848.

SIGONIUS, CAROLUS. *Historiarum de Occidentali Imperio Libri XX*. In *Opera Omnia*. 7 vols. Milan. 1732–7.

SIMEON OF DURHAM. *Historia Dunelmensis Ecclesiæ*. In Vol. I of *Opera Omnia*. Ed. Arnold. Rolls Ser. 2 vols. London. 1882–5.

—— *Historia Regum*. In Vol. II of *Opera Omnia*.

—— Trans. J. Stevenson: In Vol. III, pt. 2, *Church Historians of England*. London. 1855.

SPELMAN, HENRY. *Councils and Ecclesiastical Documents relating to Great Britain and Ireland*. Ed. Haddan and Stubbs. 3 vols. Oxford. 1869–78.

SUETONIUS (C. SUETONIUS TRANQUILLUS). *Opera Omnia*. Ed. Baumgarten-Crusius. London. 1826.

TACITUS, CORNELIUS. *Annalium ab Excessu Divi Augusti Libri*. Ed. Furneaux. 2 vols. Oxford. 1884–91.

—— *Vita Agricolæ*. Ed. Furneaux. Oxford. 1898.

—— *Historiarum Libri*. Ed. Fisher. Oxford. 1910.

USHER, JAMES. *Britannicarum Ecclesiarum Antiquitates* (*De Britannicarum Ecclesiarum Primordiis*). Vols. V and VI in Whole Works. Ed. Elrington. 17 vols. Dublin. 1864.

U.C. BERKELEY LIBRARIES
C008536908